T0219870

Lecture Notes in Computer Science 10707

Commenced Publication in 1973
Founding and Former Series Editors:
Gerhard Goos, Juris Hartmanis, and Jan van Leeuwen

More information about this series at http://www.springer.com/series/7410

Gregorio D'Agostino · Antonio Scala (Eds.)

Critical Information Infrastructures Security

12th International Conference, CRITIS 2017
Lucca, Italy, October 8–13, 2017
Revised Selected Papers

 Springer

Editors
Gregorio D'Agostino ⓘ
ENEA "Casaccia"
  and Network of Networks - Netonets
Rome, Italy

Antonio Scala ⓘ
CNR - Institute for Complex Systems (ISC)
Rome, Italy

ISSN 0302-9743   ISSN 1611-3349 (electronic)
Lecture Notes in Computer Science
ISBN 978-3-319-99842-8   ISBN 978-3-319-99843-5 (eBook)
https://doi.org/10.1007/978-3-319-99843-5

Library of Congress Control Number: 2018952640

LNCS Sublibrary: SL4 – Security and Cryptology

This Springer imprint is published by the registered company Springer Nature Switzerland AG
The registered company address is: Gewerbestrasse 11, 6330 Cham, Switzerland

Preface

This volume contains the papers presented at CRITIS 2017 – the 12th International Conference on Critical Information Infrastructures Security held during October 8–13, 2017, in Lucca.

CRITIS 2017 continued the tradition of presenting innovative research and exploring new challenges in the field of critical (information) infrastructures protection (C(I)IP) and fostering dialogue with stakeholders. CRITIS 2017 renewed efforts to bring together researchers and professionals from academia, industry, and governmental organizations working in the field of the security of critical (information) infrastructure systems.

As in previous years, distinguished invited speakers and special events complemented a program of original research contributions. According to the tradition, the conference invited the different research communities and disciplines involved in the C(I)IP space, and encouraged discussions and multi-disciplinary approaches to relevant C(I)IP problems.

This 2017 edition of CRITIS was hosted in Lucca, Italy, by the IMT School for Advanced Studies Lucca, an Italian public academic institution organized as a graduate school and research center that focuses on the analysis of economic, social, technological, and cultural systems.

Two satellite workshops on energy security and on water security took place on the closing days of the main conference.

Some specific innovations were introduced: beside the traditional sessions where original works and significant improvements were presented, specific sessions devoted to ongoing projects and operators took place. The "Projects Dissemination Session" provided an opportunity for the dissemination of ongoing project results both at the European and the Member States level for a total of 12 European and three Italian projects. The operators session in this edition was limited to the ICT sector and was led by TIM (the former Italian national telecommunication operator).

There were 63 papers submitted. Each submission was reviewed by at least two, and on average 2.8, Program Committee members. The committee decided to accept 21 full papers and four extended abstracts with a rejection rate of $\sim 67\%$ ($\sim 60\%$ accounting for the extended abstracts). Extended abstracts were selected among the 20 submissions accepted for poster presentation.

Each accepted full paper was allowed a 20-min slot for oral presentation. The program also included four keynote talks and one institutional talk; none of the invited speakers contributed with a non- reviewed proceedings paper.

As in previous editions, CRITIS 2017 awarded three prizes to the best contribution from young (<32 years) scientists. The winners were selected after a joint evaluation by both the audience and the academic committee of the Young CRITIS Award (YCA).

CRITIS 2017 received the endorsement of the Presidency of the Italian Council of Ministers ("patrocinio della Presidenza del Consiglio dei Ministri") UCE F 735/2017.

The conference was organized by NetONets, a nonprofit organization fostering the diffusion of interdisciplinary research, especially on complexity science and critical infrastructures.

The organizers are indebted to IMT Lucca for providing the location of the conference and for supporting the event in several different forms, among which were the lodgings provided in the beautiful medieval complex of S. Francesco. We also thank the IMT press office for their support.

We thank our communication chair, Alberto Tofani, for creating and maintaining the conference's website and registration services.

The conference organization benefited from the contributions of the program co-chairs, Cristina Alcaraz and Grigore Havarneanu, of the poster co-chair, Fabiana Zollo, of the Young CRITIS Award chairs, Bernhard M. Hämmerli and Marco Santarelli, and of the CRITIS Steering Committee chairs, Bernhard M. Hämmerli, Javier Lopez, and Stephen D. Wolthusen. We also thank the Program Committee and all the experts who participated in the reviewing process.

The event was mainly sponsored by TIM with the secondary involvement of the Kaspersky Lab; the YCA prize was supported by Res On Networks, an international institute for research and development based in London.

The submission and reviewing process was performed through the EasyChair platform.

November 2017   Gregorio D'Agostino
                                                                Antonio Scala

Organization

Program Committee

Cristina Alcaraz	UMA
Marc Antoni	International Union of Railways
Fabrizio Baiardi	Dipartimento di informatica, Università di Pisa
Robin Bloomfield	City, University of London, UK
Maria Cristina Brugnoli	CNIT
Arslan Brömme	GI Biometrics Special interest Group (BIOSIG)
Emiliano Casalicchio	Blekinge Institute of Technology, Sweden
Simona Cavallini	Fondazione Formit, Italy
Michal Choras	ITTI Ltd.
Kris Christmann	University of Huddersfield, UK
Gregorio D'Agostino	ENEA
Myriam Dunn	ETH Center for Security Studies Zurich, Switzerland
Mohamed Eid	commissariat à l'enrgie atomique et aux energies alternatives
Angelo Facchini	IMT
Adrian Gheorghe	Old Dominion University, USA
Dimitris Gritzalis	Athens University of Economics and Business, Greece
Stefanos Gritzalis	University of the Aegean, Greece
Bernhard Haemmerli	Lucerne University of Applied Sciences and Arts, Switzerland, and Acris GmbH
Chris Hankin	Imperial College London, UK
Grigore M. Havarneanu	International Union of Railways
Apiniti Jotisankasa	Kasetsart University, Bangkok
Sokratis Katsikas	Center for Cyber and Information Security, NTNU
Marieke Klaver	TNO
Panayiotis Kotzanikolaou	University of Piraeus, Greece
Rafal Kozik	UTP Bydgoszcz, Poland
Boban Krsic	DENIC eG
Elias Kyriakides	University of Cyprus, Cyprus
Javier Lopez	University of Malaga, Spain
Eric Luiijf	TNO
Jose Marti	The University of British Columbia, Canada
Richard Mcevoy	NTNU, Norway and HPE Ltd.
Maddalen Mendizabal	Tecnalia R&I
Iogor Nai Fovino	Joint Research Centre
Aristotelis Naniopoulos	Aristotle University of Thessaloniki, Greece
Hypatia Nassopoulos	EIVP
Eiji Okamoto	University of Tsukuba, Japan

Gabriele Oliva	University Campus Biomedico of Rome, Italy
Evangelos Ouzounis	ENISA
Stefano Panzieri	Roma Tre University, Italy
Alexander Paz-Cruz	University of Nevada, Las Vegas, USA
Reinhard Posch	UNC Charlotte
Erich Rome	Fraunhofer
Vittorio Rosato	ENEA
Brendan Ryan	University of Nottingham
Andre Samberg	TIEMS International Program Committee
Antonio Scala	IMT, CNR, Italy
Maria Paola Scaparra	The University of Kent, UK
Eric Schellekens	ARCADIS
Roberto Setola	University Campus Biomedico of Rome, Italy
George Stergiopoulos	Athens University of Economics and Business, Greece
Nils Kalstad Svendsen	Gjøvik University College, Norway
Dominique Sérafin	CEA
André Teixeira	Delft University of Technology, The Netherlands
Marianthi Theocharidou	European Commission, Joint Research Centre
Alberto Tofani	ENEA
William J. Tolone	UNC Charlotte
Simona Louise Voronca	Transelectrica - POLITEHNICA University Bucharest
René Willems	Eindhoven University of Technology
Stephen D. Wolthusen	Royal Holloway, University of London, UK and Norwegian University of Science and Technology, Norway
Christos Xenakis	University of Piraeus, Greece
Jianying Zhou	Singapore University of Technology and Design, Singapore
Enrico Zio	Politecnico di Milano, Italy
Fabiana Zollo	University of Venice Ca' Foscari, Italy
Urko Zurutuza	Mondragon University, Spain
Inga Žutautaitė	Lithuanian Energy Institute, Lithuania

Additional Reviewers

Kasse, Paraskevi
Lykou, Georgia
Lückerath, Daniel
Malatras, Apostolos
Mentzelioti, Despina
Mohammadi, Farnaz
Moulinos, Konstantinos
Virvilis, Nick
Xie, Jingquan

Contents

Resilience of Electrical Distribution Systems with Critical Load Prioritization

Zejun Yang and Jose R. Marti[(⊠)]

The University of British Columbia, Vancouver, BC V6T 1Z4, Canada
{zyang, jrms}@ece.ubc.ca

Abstract. In the highly interdependent environment of a large city, failures in the electrical distribution system can cause direct or indirect consequences to other critical infrastructures and to the Human Well-being Level (HWL) of the citizens. This paper discusses the electrical distribution system in terms of how topological reconfiguration, together with prioritized system recovery can maintain a high level of Human Well-being resilience during system failures. The Infrastructure Interdependencies Simulator (i2SIM) is used to prioritize load restoration and load shedding algorithms. To validate the proposed approach, spanning tree search algorithms, load shedding schemes and optimization methods are applied to find optimal restoration strategies on a standard IEEE 30-node system and on a 70-node distribution system with critical loads.

Keywords: Electrical distribution system restoration · i2SIM
Human Well-being Level · Smart city resilience · Load shedding
Spanning tree algorithms

1 Introduction

Society is strongly dependent on a resilient electricity supply to maintain its Human Well-being Level (HWL) [1]. Electricity supply interruptions lead to direct consequences for the HWL and will in general have an impact on other dependent critical infrastructures, such as water supply, emergency services, and information and communication technologies (ICT) [2]. For instance, in the Italian blackout of 2003, unexpected failures of a power station caused the simultaneous shutdown of the tele-communications and supervisory control and data acquisition (SCADA) network of the power system; the failures in the tele-communications system, in turn, caused further failures in the power supply network resulting in a large cascading event [3]. Another example of such interdependencies-related event happened in the same year in the USA [4]. In this event, smaller partial power system failures as well as computer and human mistakes led to cascading effects that ultimately resulted in a large magnitude event. These examples illustrate the need to consider critical infrastructure interdependencies when assessing the whole system resilience.

The Human Well-being Level - Distribution System Restoration (HWL-DSR) method proposed in this paper combines optimal topological reconfiguration with system recovery according to the criticality of the loads.

© Springer Nature Switzerland AG 2018
G. D'Agostino and A. Scala (Eds.): CRITIS 2017, LNCS 10707, pp. 1–12, 2018.
https://doi.org/10.1007/978-3-319-99843-5_1

A number of solutions including mixed integer non-linear programming [5, 6] and heuristic search [7] have been proposed for the reconfiguration problem. However, previous research [8–10] indicates that the Spanning Tree Search algorithm requires less computing time and fewer operations of the reconfiguration switches.

Resilience oriented critical loads' restoration has been proposed in [11, 12]. Generally, these approaches aim at measuring the adequacy of the electrical system to supply the demand of electricity after the contingency. Alternatively, critical infrastructure interdependencies for DSR have been considered and analyzed, for example, in [13–15]. The concept proposed here of Human Well-being Level (HWL) [1] considers both the power system's performance and performance of the other interdependent networks, simultaneously.

The paper makes the following contributions:

- The concept of resilience using the HWL-DSR is proposed. The Infrastructures Interdependencies Simulator (i2SIM) is used to establish the criticality of the loads' restoration sequence;
- A Shortest Path Tree Search and a Hybrid Load Shedding Scheme are proposed to minimize the number of switching operations while maximizing the HWL-DSR resilience;
- The importance of considering the interdependencies in DSR is illustrated by analyzing the results of two alternative optimization algorithms.

The remainder of this paper is organized as follows. Section 2 presents the problem formulation and implementation procedure. Graph search schemes are described in Sect. 3. Section 4 tests load shedding schemes and electrical constraints in the MATPOWER simulation environment. i2SIM is introduced in Sect. 5 to take into account the criticality of the loads. Section 6 presents simulation results using the standard IEEE 30-node distribution system and a 70-node 4-feeder system together with i2SIM. Conclusions and future work are presented in Sect. 7.

2 Problem Formulation

The resilience of the system of Critical Infrastructures (CI) considering the interdependencies among these CI can be measured in terms of the Human Well-being Table (HWT) [1]. The HWT is an example of the input-output HRT table concept [16] that relates an output resource or index value to a series of inputs. Table 1 shows an example of an HWT for some sample city. The output column y of the table gives the level of well-being, which in this simple example depends on the availability of electricity, water, services, and ICT. The least available resource determines the output level. To bring the level of well-being to 50%, we first need to restore services to 14 hr/day. Then restoring electricity to 22 hr/day, services to 18 hr/day, and ICT to 12 hr/day will bring the well-being level to 75%.

In mathematical terms, the HWL is defined as a function of N-nonlinear, independent eigenvectors, one for each human need, and its value is determined by the output level that corresponds to the least available input resource, as follows,

Table 1. Human Well-being Table.

Human Well-being Table (HWT)				
y_n(HWL) (%)	x_{n1} (electricity) (hr/day)	x_{n2} (water) (hr/day)	x_{n3}(service) (hr/day)	x_{n3}(ICT) (hr/day)
100	24	24	24	24
75	22	20	18	12
50	18	16	14	6
25	12	12	12	2
0	0	0	0	0

$$y_n = min(x_{n1}, x_{n2}, \ldots, x_{nmax}) \tag{1}$$

Resilience index (2) is a measure of for how long and by how much the HWL stays below the "normal" value (100% in Table 1) before the system is restored.

$$R = \frac{\sum_0^M y_n \Delta t_m}{t_M - t_0} \tag{2}$$

The better the restoration strategy, the less time the well-being level will stay below the normal level and the higher the R value will be.

In this paper, the electrical distribution network is assumed to be radial and a number of simultaneous faults are assumed (Fig. 1).

For the electrical service to be considered "available", the electrical constraints of operation need to be satisfied:

$$V_i^{min} < V_i < V_i^{min}, i \in I \tag{3}$$

$$\left| I_l^{min} \right| < |I_l| < \left| I_l^{max} \right|, l \in L \tag{4}$$

$$P_f^2 + Q_f^2 < (S_f^{max})^2, f \in F \tag{5}$$

R	Resilience of the HWL for the restoration strategy	N	Total number of independent eigenvectors (columns) of the HWL
y_n	Particular HWL value	m	m-th time step
t_0	Initial time when contingency occurs	n	n-th independent eigenvector (column) of the HWL
M	Total number of time steps	Δt	Time step for each restoration process
t_M	Time when restoration process completes	V_i	Voltage at node i
I_l	Current at line l	P_f	Active power injected into feeder m
Q_f	Reactive power injected into feeder m	S_f^{max}	Maximum capacity of feeder m
I	Set of all nodes	L	Set of all lines
F	Set of all feeders		

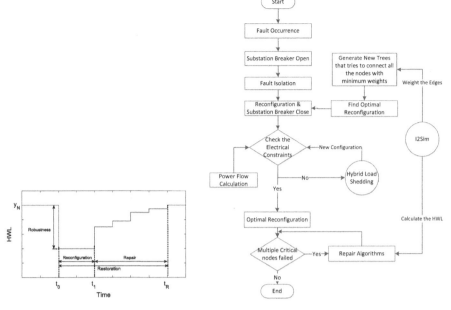

Fig. 1. Interdependent- infrastructures resilience index in terms of the Human Well-being Level

Fig. 2. Flow chart of proposed algorithm

In the paper, the following variables are defined:
The HWL-DSR algorithm follows these steps (Fig. 2):

1. Map the initial configuration of the distribution network into a graph G using an adjacency matrix;
2. The failure locations are isolated by the remotely controlled switches (RCS) and the status of the line switches is updated to G;
3. The optimal connection is found using a spanning tree search. The network switches are opened or closed accordingly;
4. Power flow calculations are performed to check the electrical constraints (3)–(5), using the MATPOWER toolbox in MATLAB;
5. If there are no electrical constraints violations, a candidate post-contingency reconfiguration is obtained; otherwise, a load shedding scheme is applied;
6. If the number of faults is larger than the number of repair crews, prioritization of repair is applied, according to i2SIM. After all faults are repaired, the HWL returns to the normal state.

To simplify the problem, the following assumptions are made:

1. A balanced three-phase network is considered; hence the system is represented by single-phase circuit;
2. Repairing time for per crew is constant for each fault removal;
3. Load demands are constant during restoration period;
4. Each branch and bus is equipped with a remotely controlled switch and optimal allocation of a limited number of switches is not considered in this paper.

3 Graph Search Schemes

Using graph theory, we can map each bus and each branch in the electrical distribution system into a vertex and an edge. The system can then be represented as a graph G (V, E) using a sparse adjacency matrix. The reconfiguration of the distribution system is essentially the reconnection of the graph G (V, E).

Distribution systems are normally operated in radial configurations [17], with the primary substation in the root node and all other nodes connected without loops. The resulting structures correspond to spanning trees in graph theory, containing all the vertices without any loops [18]. Compared with mixed integer non-linear programming and heuristic searches, the spanning tree search requires fewer switches' commutations and less computational time [9]. For a multi-feeder system, the tree graph can be viewed as a forest (a graph with more than one tree). If all the roots of the trees can be centralized and viewed as one main root, as in [9], then the multi-feeder system optimization problem can be reduced into a single feeder problem.

When a fault occurs, the circuit breaker at the primary substation of the faulted feeder will disconnect the supply to the feeder and all loads in the feeder will stop being supplied. If reclosing is unsuccessful, the substation breaker will stay open until the fault is isolated. With the substation breaker open, sectionalizing breakers along the feeder can be opened to isolate the faulted section. The substation breaker can then be reclosed and supply can be restored to the loads upstream from the faulted section towards the substation. If next the normally-open tie switches between feeders are closed, the downstream feeder load can be fed from a different primary substation. Spanning tree search schemes can be used to restore most of the load without violating electrical constraints. The distribution system is required to maintain a radial structure during the reconfiguration process.

Two different search schemes were tested in this work: (a) The Minimum Spanning Tree (MST) Search, and (b) The Shortest Path Problem.

The minimum spanning tree search aims at connecting all nodes in such a way as to achieve the least total weight in a connected graph, following Prim's algorithm [19]. Certain edges can be weighted so as to force the structure of the tree. For example, we can assign a higher weight to a line with normally open switches, which reduces the possibility of electrical and operational violations.

The shortest path problem aims at finding a path between two nodes (or vertices) in a graph such that the summation of the weights of its candidate path is minimized [20].

A Shortest Path Tree (SPT), rooted at a specific vertex, is a spanning tree T of G. This tree ensures that the path distance from root to any other vertex in T is the shortest. The original SPT is modified in our strategy according to the criticality of the vertices. The nodes connected to critical infrastructures, such as hospitals, water stations, ICT-network, etc., are defined as critical nodes. In contrast, those with low criticality, such as most of the residential, commercial and industrial loads, are pre-defined as non-critical nodes.

In this paper, instead of searching for all equally-weighted vertices in the shortest fashion, the SPT searches for the critical nodes at the beginning. This presents two advantages: it prevents the supply of the critical loads from being shed and, at the same time, it reduces the computational time.

4   Load Shedding Schemes

During faults, load shedding schemes are needed to maintain the electrical operating limits. There are typically two load shedding approaches: load curtailment and pruning.

Load Curtailment is characterized by the ability to alter the amount of electrical power consumed by a specific load bus [21]. This traditional approach seeks to optimize the power flow so that load and generation match precisely, and prevents electrical violations (3)–(5) as well as transient voltage stability conditions. If electrical violations occur at critical loads, non-critical loads should be curtailed. This paper adds a fast voltage stability index from [22] to determine the sequence of curtailment of non-critical loads. This strategy helps to preserve the critical loads and eliminate the unstable lines.

However, this approach requires extra network reconfiguration switches, with corresponding additional capital costs to install these breakers, and additional operations for each breaker, with a corresponding increase in breaker wear, malfunctioning, and deceased reliability [23].

We propose a hybrid load shedding scheme that combines load curtailment and pruning (Fig. 3). Pruning alone aims at isolating functional sections of the power system so that a contingency does not cascade [24] and avoids violations from reconfiguration. The required switching operations are comparatively lower than with the load curtailment approach. However, the disadvantage is that critical load preservation may not be guaranteed if there is not an adequate placement of the pruned buses.

In our proposed hybrid scheme, the system always tries to remove the leaf nodes first (nodes with degree one) until all remaining leaf nodes are critical nodes. Then load curtailment is performed. This results in reduced switching operations while preserving the critical loads.

5   The Infrastructure Interdependencies Simulator (i2SIM)

i2SIM [16] is a tool for modelling interdependencies among complex critical infrastructures. In this work, i2SIM is used to determine the sequence in which critical loads must be restored (if required) after the topological reconfiguration is achieved. Two different optimization methodologies are tested, a global optimization algorithm (GOA) and a greedy algorithm.

The GOA tries to maximize the resilience for the entire time line of the event, while the Greedy Algorithm chooses what appears to be the optimal immediate choice at every moment [25]. The computational complexity for GOA increases exponentially with the number of critical loads as well as with the number of vertices and edges in the graph. However, since there is a low possibility of there being a large number of unsupplied critical nodes [26], and this possibility is further reduced by load reconfiguration, it is possible to simplify the GOA algorithm as follows:

- Not all critical nodes are considered in the GOA;
- Multiple critical nodes with no faults between them are viewed as one group and these nodes are restored simultaneously;
- Critical nodes of the same type, or nodes within a certain area, can be categorized into one group.

6 Test Cases and Simulation Results

In this section, the proposed reconfiguration strategy is applied to two systems: (a) an IEEE 33-bus one-feeder system to validate the reconfiguration scheme, and (b) a 70-bus four-feeder system that illustrates the importance of infrastructure interdependencies in recovering the Human Wellness Level.

Multiple line faults and multiple critical nodes are generated for each test system. The computational tasks are performed on a personal computer with an Intel Core i5 Processor (2.66 GHz) and 8-GB of RAM.

6.1 Test System A—IEEE 33-Bus System

This test uses the IEEE 33-bus 12.66 kV radial distribution system, with 5 tie switches. The specific data, including active loads, reactive loads, branch impedances, etc. are identical with [27]. Two scenarios, with different fault locations and optimization methodologies, are studied:

Scenario (1) Validation of the Proposed Reconfiguration Scheme. The proposed reconfiguration scheme using the MST search, without a load shedding scheme and without i2SIM, is compared with case 3) of test system A of [13]. The results, using the methodology in this paper and the methodology of [13], present identical profiles, including loads, branches, fault locations (line 5–6, 8–9, 3–23, and 15–16), critical load locations (node 5, 11, 3, 15, 19, 21, 26, 28, and 29). The results are also almost identical regarding the total weighted and supplied active load after reconfiguration: 83.62% for our result and 83.42% for [13]'s, respectively. These results validate our basic reconfiguration scheme (Fig. 4).

Scenario (2) Validation of the Hybrid Load Shedding Scheme and the Spanning Tree Search Algorithm. In this scenario, in order to make the results more obvious, we assign the critical load busses (16, 17, 18, 29, 30, and 32) far away from the root

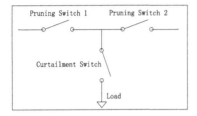

Fig. 3. Demonstration of hybrid load shedding

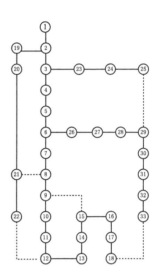

Fig. 4. Initial configuration of IEEE 33-Bus System

Table 2. Comparison of reconfiguration solutions

	Load curtailment with MST	Pruning with MST [9]	Hybrid load shedding with MST	Hybrid load shedding with SPT
Critical load preservation (%)	100	67.9	100	100
Shed load (kW)	3027.9	1975.1	3018.7	2920.2
Number of switch operations*	28	8	22	17
Minimum nodal voltage (pu)	0.9021	0.9024	0.9050	0.9099

*Every single tie, sectionalizing and curtailment switch operation accounts in the total number of switch operations

node, we set one failure location (line 2–3) close to the root node, and we include an extra line (line 16–17) between the critical nodes.

The results from Table 2 are based on four different reconfiguration methodologies. For the more severe scenario, the pruning scheme with MST cannot preserve the critical loads, although it has the lowest amount of shedded loads and switching operations. The rest of the three methodologies are capable of preserving the critical loads with almost the same amount of shedded loads. The hybrid load shedding with SPT has the best performance in terms of the least number of switching operations, and will be the strategy adopted for improving the Human Wellness Level.

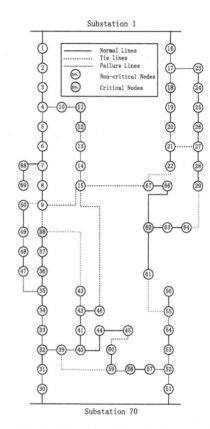

Fig. 6. 70-node radial distribution of Scenario (3)

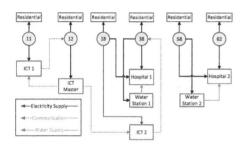

Fig. 5. Scenario (4) i2SIM interdependencies

6.2 Test System B - 70-Node System

This system is an 11-kV radial distribution system with two substations, 4 feeders, 70 nodes, and 78 branches (including 11 normally open tie switches) [28], as shown in Fig. 6. In this case, we assume there are 6 critical nodes (12, 18, 27, 38, 58, and 62) and that a severe natural disaster causes 30 failure locations on different lines selected randomly. We consider two cases: (a) Without i2SIM (Scenario 3), and (b) With i2SIM (Scenario 4). The scenario without i2SIM corresponds to the "standard" reconfiguration strategies. The result is that not all critical loads get reconnected, that is, no tie switches can help the restoration of some of the critical loads. The scenario with i2SIM includes 6 critical interdependent nodes, including 2 hospitals, 2 water stations, 2 ICT agents, 1 ICT master agent, and 6 residential loads. With respect to Table 1, y_n represents the availability of each infrastructure. This system is shown in Fig. 5.

Two optimization methodologies (Global and Greedy) are tested.

In the GOA methodology, the electricity supply is set as the only input (binary) to i2SIM, i.e. the status of each supply node is 1 or 0, and a binary number can be used for the node status. For example, given five critical nodes 01000 indicates that the second critical node has service "on".

Each binary status of the node supplying electricity is transferred into a decimal number before implementing the shortest path algorithm to find the global optimal operation sequences. The simplified scheme is as described in Sect. 4, that is, the adjacent critical nodes (11, 12) are regarded as one variable. Figure 7 gives the repair sequence (2–3–4–5–1) for each failure location to prioritize the post-contingency response when emergency crews are limited.

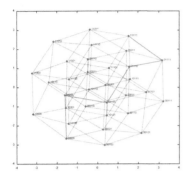

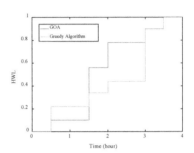

Fig. 7. Results of simplified critical-node repairing sequence from i2SIM based on GOA

Fig. 8. HWL results for GOA and greedy algorithm

For comparison, a greedy algorithm was also implemented to find the local optimal solution. The outputs from the HWL in i2SIM are shown in Fig. 8 throughout the recovery process. The global optimized repair sequence with i2SIM has the highest overall resilience index, which validates our proposed strategy (Fig. 8).

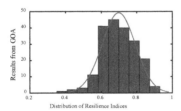

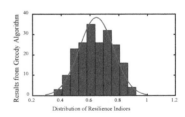

Fig. 9. Results of objective R from two optimization algorithms

Randomly Distributed Failure Locations. To test the effect of the fault location on the optimization results, the failure locations are randomly selected for 200 different cases. The Gaussian distribution results of the resilience objective R are shown in Fig. 9. The mean values for the GOA and Greedy Algorithms are 0.7211 and 0.6439, respectively. This result validates that for the interdependent DSR, the GOA enhances the resilience of the HWL better than the greedy algorithm.

7 Conclusion and Future Work

The proposed strategy for Human Well-being Level based Distribution System Restoration (HWL-DSR) combines a shortest path tree search algorithm and a priority-load load-shedding scheme, scheduled by i2SIM, to find an optimal distribution reconfiguration and restoration sequence that maximizes the availability of the most critical loads without electrical system violations. By using the HWL table, the proposed solution maximizes the Human Well-being resilience. The proposed framework can be applied both for long term planning and for optimal fast response during extreme contingencies.

The study cases assume radiality of the distribution system network, which is the most common scheme in current electrical distribution systems (DS). As technology improves, smart DS of the future will incorporate islanded sub-regions and mesh schemes. Further work is needed to extend this work for more complex interdependent schemes.

The paper assumes that the load demand and the generation are constant during the restoration period. A more accurate scenario will have to consider the variability of the load during the daily cycle, as well as the effect of the intermittence of the renewable energy sources (e.g., wind and solar).

In current electrical distribution systems, not all load nodes are equipped with remotely-controlled disconnect switches, and many of these switches have to be operated manually. This brings about the additional dimension of optimizing the repair crew transportation time needed to open or close the disconnect switches.

References

1. Martí, J.R., Ghahremani, E., Martí, A.: The GDW index: an extension of the GDP index to include human well-being. Eur. CIIP Newsl. **10**(2), 23–26 (2016)
2. Hokstad, P.: Risk and Interdependencies in Critical Infrastructures A Guideline for Analysis, pp. 67–79. Springer, London (2012). https://doi.org/10.1007/978-1-4471-4661-2
3. Veremyeva, A., Sorokin, A., Boginski, V., Pasiliao, E.L.: Minimum vertex cover problem for coupled interdependent networks with cascading failures. Eur. J. Oper. Res. **232**(3), 499–511 (2014)
4. Rahnamay-Naeini, M., Hayat, M.M.: Cascading failures in interdependent infrastructures: an interdependent Markov-chain approach. IEEE Trans. Smart Grid **7**(4), 1997–2006 (2016)
5. Khushalani, S., Solanki, J.M., Schulz, N.N.: Optimized restoration of unbalanced distribution systems. IEEE Trans. Power Syst. **22**(2), 624–630 (2007)
6. Romero, R., Franco, J.F., Leão, F.B., Rider, M.J., de Souza, E.S.: A new mathematical model for the restoration problem in balanced radial distribution systems. IEEE Trans. Power Syst. **31**(2), 1259–1268 (2016)
7. Liu, C.-C., Lee, S.-J., Venkata, S.S.: An expert system operational aid for restoration and loss reduction of distribution systems. IEEE Trans. Power Syst. **3**(2), 619–626 (1988)
8. D'Agostino, F., Silvestro, F., Schneider, K.P., Liu, C.-C., Xu, Y., Ton, D.T.: Reliability assessment of distribution systems incorporating feeder restoration actions. In: Power Systems Computation Conference (PSCC), Genoa, pp. 1–7 (2016)

9. Li, J., Ma, X.Y., Liu, C.C., Schneider, K.P.: Distribution system restoration with microgrids using spanning tree search. IEEE Trans. Power Syst. **29**(6), 3021–3029 (2014)
10. Alsubaie, A.: Improving critical infrastructure resilience with application to power distribution networks. University of British Columbia. Accessed (2016). https://open. library.ubc.ca/cIRcle/collections/24/items/1.0319263
11. Gao, H., Chen, Y., Yin, X., Liu, C.-C.: Resilience-oriented critical load restoration using microgrids in distribution systems. IEEE Trans. Smart Grid **7**, 2837–2848 (2016)
12. Ahmadi, H., Alsubaie, A., Martí, J.R.: Distribution system restoration considering critical infrastructures interdependencies. In: IEEE PES General Meeting—Conference & Exposition, pp. 1–5 (2014)
13. Bie, Z., Lin, Y., Li, G., Li, F.: Battling the extreme: a study on the power system resilience. In: Proceedings of the IEEE, vol. PP, no. 99, pp. 1–14 (2017)
14. D'Agostino, G., et al.: Methodologies for inter-dependency assessment. In: 5th International Conference on Critical Infrastructure (CRIS), Beijing, pp. 1–7 (2010)
15. Fioriti, V., D'Agostino, G., Bologna, S.: On modeling and measuring inter-dependencies among critical infrastructures. In: 2010 Complexity in Engineering, pp. 85–87, Rome (2010)
16. Martí, José R.: Multisystem simulation: analysis of critical infrastructures for disaster response. In: D'Agostino, G., Scala, A. (eds.) Networks of Networks: The Last Frontier of Complexity. UCS, pp. 255–277. Springer, Cham (2014). https://doi.org/10.1007/978-3-319-03518-5_12
17. Brown, R.E.: Electric Power Distribution Reliability. CRC Press, Boca Raton (2008)
18. Graham, R.L., Hell, P.: On the history of the minimum spanning tree problem. Ann. Hist. Comput. **7**(1), 43–57 (1985)
19. Sheng, Y., Qin, Z., Shi, G.: Minimum spanning tree problem of uncertain random network. J. Intell. Manuf. 1–10 (2014)
20. Verayiah, R., Ramasamy, A., Abidin, H.I.Z., Musirin, I.: Under voltage load shedding (UVLS) study for 746 test bus system. In: 3rd International Conference on Energy and Environment (ICEE), pp. 98–103, Malacca (2009)
21. Meier, R., Cotilla-Sánchez, E., Fern, A.: A policy switching approach to consolidating load shedding and Islanding protection schemes. In: 2014 Power Systems Computation Conference, pp. 1–7, Wroclaw (2014)
22. Verayiah, R., Ramasamy, A., Abidin, H.I.Z., Musirin, I.: Under voltage load shedding (UVLS) study for 746 test bus system. In: 2009 3rd International Conference on Energy and Environment (ICEE), pp. 98–103, Malacca (2009)
23. Safdarian, A., Farajollahi, M., Fotuhi-Firuzabad, M.: Impacts of remote control switch malfunction on distribution system reliability. IEEE Trans. Power Syst. **32**(2), 1572–1573 (2017)
24. Yusof, N.A., Mokhlis, H., Karimi, M., Laghari, J.A., Illias, H.A., Sapori, N.M.: Under-voltage load shedding scheme based on voltage stability index for distribution network. In: 3rd IET International Conference on Clean Energy and Technology (CEAT), pp. 1–5, Kuching (2014)
25. Cormen, M.L.A., Thomas, H., et al.: Greedy Algorithms. Introduction to Algorithms 1, pp. 329–355 (2001)
26. Hokstad, P.: Risk and Interdependencies in Critical Infrastructures: A Guideline for Analysis, pp. 67–79. Springer, Heidelberg (2012). https://doi.org/10.1007/978-1-4471-4661-2
27. Baran, M.E., Wu, F.F.: Network reconfiguration in distribution systems for loss reduction and load balancing. IEEE Trans. Power Deliv. **4**(2), 1401–1407 (1989)
28. Das, D.: A fuzzy multiobjective approach for network reconfiguration of distribution systems. IEEE Trans. Power Deliv. **21**(1), 202–209 (2006)

Public Tolerance Levels of Transportation Resilience: A Focus on the Oresund Region Within the IMPROVER Project

Laura Petersen[1(✉)], Laure Fallou[1], Elisabete Carreira[2],
and Andrei Utkin[2]

[1] EMSC, Arpajon, France
{petersen, fallou}@emsc-csem.com
[2] INOV, Lisbon, Portugal
elisabete.carreira@inov.pt

Abstract. Maintaining a minimum level of service and recovering quickly after a crisis event are key components of infrastructure resilience. While no consensus exists on the precise meaning of these two terms, one way to measure them is to examine public tolerances of service levels and recovery time. However, few studies have empirically investigated public tolerance levels. This paper sets out to address this gap by examining Swedish public tolerance levels of the transportation sector through the use of an online questionnaire and comparing the results to the change in habits following the change in service of the Oresund Crossing due to the implementation of border controls in 2016 in response to the migrant crisis. The findings suggest that the public are willing to tolerate service reductions. Furthermore, declared expectations are well reflected in the habits of Oresund Crossing users, demonstrating the resilience of citizens in crisis situations.

Keywords: Resilience · Infrastructure · Public tolerance

1 Introduction

Maintaining a minimum level of service and recovering quickly after a crisis event are key components of infrastructure resilience. While no consensus exists on the precise meaning of these two terms, one way to measure them is to examine public expectations of service levels and recovery time. While research often points to an "expectation gap" between what the public expect and what operators are capable of [1, 2], few studies have empirically investigated these aspects. The EU Horizon 2020 project IMPROVER (Improved risk evaluation and implementation of resilience concepts to critical infrastructure), makes use of Living Labs, or clustered regions of different types of infrastructure which provide specific services to a city or region. One such Living Lab is the Oresund region. This paper discusses the above expectation gap by examining Swedish public tolerance levels of the transportation sector through the use of an online questionnaire. The obtained results were then compared to the changes in population habits caused by an alternation in the Oresund Crossing service due to the

© Springer Nature Switzerland AG 2018
G. D'Agostino and A. Scala (Eds.): CRITIS 2017, LNCS 10707, pp. 13–24, 2018.
https://doi.org/10.1007/978-3-319-99843-5_2

migrant crisis. This paper first presents a brief literature review on public expectations of transportation operators in times of crisis. It then describes the Oresund Crossing case study. After which, the methodology of the questionnaires and case study are explained. This is followed by a presentation of the questionnaire results, and an overview of the public reaction to the Oresund Crossing service change, accompanied by a comprehensive discussion on the subject. The most important outcome of the work is stated in the conclusion section.

2   General Expectations of Transportation Operators in a Crisis

Overall, expectations for transportation infrastructure during and after a crisis appear high. Some minimum level of mobility is highly expected to be achieved, even if this requires a change in the means of transportation (for example bicycling instead of taking the subway), as was the case during the 2012 Hurricane Sandy when NYC subway users walked, biked or carpooled to maintain mobility [3]. There also appears to be an expectation for operators to help in long term recovery, as was made evident by survey results from victims of both the 2011 Great East Japan Earthquake and the 2010–11 Queensland Floods who had lost access to their private vehicles. They reported an expectation for public transportation to be available to make up for the loss of their private vehicles due to flood or tsunami waters [4, 5].

3   Background on the Oresund Crossing

The Oresund Crossing is a combined railway and roadway bridge across the Oresund strait between Sweden and Denmark, connecting Copenhagen, the Danish capital city, and the Swedish city of Malmö. As well as linking two large communities by road and rail, allowing commuters to live on one side and work in the other, the crossing (along with other bridges in Denmark) is the primary road and rail link between Scandinavia and mainland Europe [6]. The Oresund Institute, a non-profit Danish-Swedish organisation founded to promote integration in the Oresund Region, states that 95,900 people cross the Oresund Strait daily, both directions included, with 42,900 of them by car and 32,100 by train [7]. The BBC estimates that 20,000 commuters cross the bridge daily [8]. With a total population of 3.2 million people, the region is an excellent example of European cross-border collaboration and also includes the 6th largest air transportation hub in Europe (Copenhagen airport) [6].

In December 2015, due to the drastic increase in refugees and asylum seekers entering Sweden and Europe, commonly referred to as the ongoing "migrant crisis", the Swedish government made adjustments to its refugee policy and instituted a temporary (and thus Schengen compliant) 6-month program to check the documents of all travellers reaching its border by train, and a fraction of those arriving by car [9]. A fine of SEK 50,000 was established for travel companies serving clients without such identity documents [10]. In compliance with these requirements, the Øresundsbro Konsortiet, the company responsible for the Oresund Crossing infrastructure, as well as other transportation infrastructure operators, began identity checks. While originally stipulated for 6 months, Sweden extended the identity checks multiple times, finally ending them in May 2017 [8].

The main change in service was increased journey times. The BBC reports that the border control added an extra 30 min to the commute, whereas the Oresund Institute estimates that travel time increased by 10–60 min [10, 11]. Rail operators also reduced the daily number of trips between the two countries and there were fewer train departures in peak hours [10, 11]. However, it is difficult to get an overall picture of how the ID checks in conjunction with the internal Swedish border controls affected commuting across the Oresund region as it greatly depended on from and to where one was traveling. The commuters who work at the airport in Kastrup and get off at the first Swedish railway station in Hyllie experienced an increase in travel time of about ten minutes. On the other hand, the travel time increased by about 30–60 min for a commuter who works inside Copenhagen and lives in Lund. Furthermore, the Danish long-distance trains from Funen and Jutland ceased direct traffic to the Copenhagen airport soon after the Swedish identity checks were introduced. For motorists on the Oresund Crossing it is reported that ID checks generally operate without major delays. The same was observed for another alternative to the Oresund Crossing, the ferry route between Helsingborg and Helsingör, known under the trademark Scandlines Helsingborg-Helsingör.

4 Methodology

4.1 Research Questions

Specifically, three Research Questions emerged from the literature reviewed above:

1. What do Swedish citizens consider as an acceptable level of disruption to transportation infrastructure during a crisis?
2. How have Oresund region residents reacted to the change in service of the Oresund Crossing?
3. How do these declared expectations compare to the change in habits following the initiation of the ID checks at the Oresund Crossing?

An online questionnaire and case study-based study was designed to investigate these questions. Ethics approval was sought and obtained from the respective authorities prior to data collection.

4.2 Questionnaire

The target population for the questionnaire was adults aged 18 years and over who were familiar with the Oresund region. Convenience sampling was used. The questionnaire was translated into the three main languages spoken around the Oresund region (English, Danish, and Swedish). It was structured as follows: First, a brief description of the project was provided and participants were informed of their right to withdraw from the project at any time, as well as how all data would be handled during the project. For the purposes of this questionnaire, respondents were presented with the following definition of a disaster: "an event which has catastrophic consequences and significantly affects the quality, quantity, or availability of the service provided by the infrastructure." Regarding the minimum acceptable level of service, respondents were presented with four below normal service level scenarios. These were: Transportation for emergency services only; Alternative means (for example, trains as opposed to private car, ferry instead of bridge); Local diversion; or Reduced capacity or frequency of service (for example, trains going every half hour instead of every ten minutes). They had to state whether they were willing to accept the given reduction in service. Then they then had to choose the maximum amount of time they would be willing to tolerate a given disruption (from "years," "months," "weeks," "days," to "hours," or "not at all"). The questionnaire also asked about the participants' demographics. Data from the questionnaire was collected between 28 March 2016 and 30 April 2016. The questionnaire answers were translated back into English at the data entry stage. The questionnaire was disseminated through the IMPROVER consortium partners' contacts as well as through the Living Lab.

4.3   Questionnaire Sample Characteristics

A total of 88 participants completed the online questionnaire. 80 respondents were of Swedish nationality and 24 declared to live near the Oresund region. A variety of nationalities claimed to live in the Oresund region, including French, Italian, Russian, Icelandic, and Danish. The majority (66%) however were Swedish. Due to the dissemination method, this self-selected sample was not broadly representative of the Swedish population, nor of the Living Lab population. Sample characteristics of Swedish respondents showed that 51% of the respondents were men, 48% were women and 1% chose not to answer that question. Most were highly educated, with 71% reporting that they have a university degree or higher qualification. Both young and old people appeared to be underrepresented in the study. Respondents aged 18–24 accounted for only 4% of the total sample (for comparison, Swedish 15–24 year olds make up 12%), with 16% identifying themselves as aged 55 years and above (for Swedish population it is over 30%) [12].

4.4   Case Study Development

This preliminary study on the transportation infrastructure in the Oresund region examined a relatively recent event. As such, the event has yet to be duly addressed by sociologists. Therefore, the adapted methodology comprises the collection, synthesis, and subsequent analysis of news and other pertinent materials published on the Internet. The data was collected between November 2015 and May 2016. Due to language constraints of the researches, English was the search language. 24 newspapers were analysed. Key words were used to establish boundaries to our research. These included border ID checks, Oresund bridge, asylum seekers, refugee crisis, public reaction, reactions to change in service, commuters. Social media sites for relevant public entities that were created to deal with the introduction of border controls as well as social media accounts of transport entities (those intended to provide information to commuters) were also examined, as well as online reviews of the Oresund Crossing. Information was collected from the PR department of Øresundsbro Konsortiet. The same was done for the HH Ferries Group, the company that runs the ferry route Scandlines Helsingborg-Helsingör.

5   Questionnaire Results

Findings suggest that Swedish and Oresund region respondents were willing to tolerate service reductions in the transportation sector during crises (see Fig. 1). When presented with the four scenarios, no respondent selected "I would not tolerate any reduction in service." It turned out that *Local diversion* was the most tolerated option, as it was the most chosen option by both Swedish (93%) and Oresund region (88%) respondents. *Alternative means* was the next most selected, by 90% of Swedish and 79% of Oresund region respondents. *Reduced capacity* was chosen by 85% of Swedish respondents and 71% of Oresund region respondents. *Transportation for emergency services only* was the least chosen option by both Swedish (64%) and Oresund region (63%) respondents.

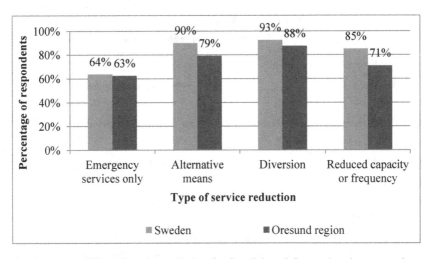

Fig. 1. Acceptability of service reduction for Swedish and Oresund region respondents

When asked for how long the respondents would be willing to tolerate the reduction in service, differences appeared among Swedish respondents (see Fig. 2). Most Swedish respondents were only willing to tolerate *Transportation for emergency services only* for days (47%). For *Alternative means*, Swedish respondents chose both months and weeks (35% each). Most Swedish respondents chose months for *Diversion* (38%) and for *Reduced capacity* (37%). Responses were similar for those who came from the Oresund region in regards to *Transportation for emergency services only* (divided equally for most responses between hours and days at 36% each) and

Alternative means where most (38%) chose months. However, there were larger differences for the other two service disruptions (see Fig. 3). Oresund region respondents were more willing to accept *Diversion* for months than the Swedish respondents (52% and 38% respectively). Most Oresund region respondents were willing to tolerate *Reduced capacity/frequency of service* for years (35%), whereas Swedish respondents were mostly willing to tolerate it for months (37%). No respondents selected "not at all" for either disruption.

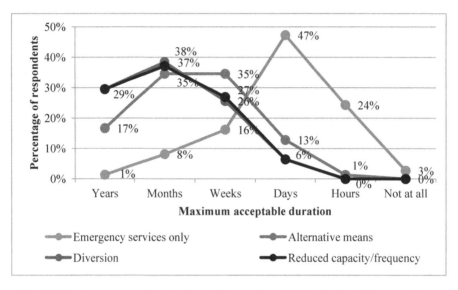

Fig. 2. Maximum acceptable duration of the service reduction for Swedish respondents

6   Public Reaction to Change in Service of the Oresund Crossing

6.1   Public Opinion

The initial reaction of the general public and, especially, commuters, appeared to be quite sharp, negative and disgruntled. According to Per Tryding, the deputy head of Chamber of Commerce and Industry of Southern Sweden (CCISS), the change made it difficult for employees to travel back and forth [13]. Some characteristic opinions given within the first week of implementation of the new border crossing regime [14, 15] include this comment from Ms. Sjolander, who has commuted from Malmö to Denmark for eight years: "I won't manage this for very long. I will have to look for another job." Another woman complained for her 14 year old daughter who commutes between her mother in Copenhagen and her father in Sweden every week, but goes to school in Copenhagen, and will have to add at least 30 min to her commute [14, 15]. These personal anecdotes are reflected in survey results from the Oresund Institute, which interviewed 400 commuters. It found that 39% were considering seeking employment

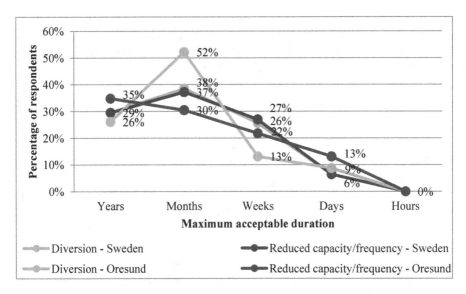

Fig. 3. Maximum acceptable duration for *Diversion* and *Reduced capacity/frequency of service* for Swedish and Oresund region respondents

in their country of residence, 26% were considering moving to the country of their employment, and that 16% were already in the process of either seeking employment or moving [16]. Despite these negative reactions to the change in service, the overwhelming majority of the latest reviews (as of June 2016) of the Oresund Crossing services were extremely positive, without even mentioning the border check inconveniences [17].

6.2   Using Alternative Means (Roads and Ferries)

Another way to study public opinion is to examine behavioural changes in regard to which infrastructure is being used after the implementation of the ID checks. There were 11% fewer passengers taking the train [11]. However, road traffic and ferry traffic increased. Road traffic demonstrated significant growth and for Q1 2016 the Oresund Crossing operation generated significant profit compared to the same period the previous year [16]. Many of the commuters were using ferry services rather than the Crossing due to the identity checks [20].

Road Traffic Using the Oresund Crossing
To avoid increased delays associated with the boarder control on the Oresund Crossing trains, many users switched to road. A popular alternative means for transport to work seemed to be replacing train travel with hired coaches as several companies started to provide them for their employees [15, 20]. Indeed, the coach traffic demonstrated the most significant growth in Q1 2016 when compared to Q1 2015 (see Fig. 4). Representatives of the Oresund Crossing said that they assume this increase as being a consequence of the ID checks [21]. Taxis and rental car use also demonstrated an

increase, along with the number of ride share Facebook groups [15]. However, these figures should be interpreted with caution as part of this growth was due to increased leisure traffic (demonstrated by the BroPas as seen in Table 1) and the fact that the Easter holiday fell in Q1 in 2016 and Q2 in 2015.

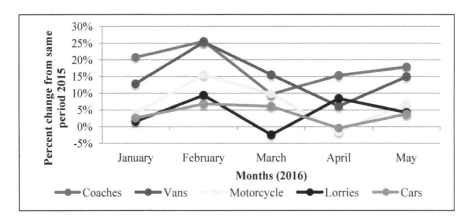

Fig. 4. Relative changes in the Oresund Crossing road traffic in the beginning of 2016 with respect to the same period of time in 2015 [22]

A more detailed analysis of the traffic composition and its dynamics is given in Table 1, from which it is clearly seen that *Commuters* have reduced, despite overall growth. The overall increase in *Business* further demonstrates the importance of hired coaches as a replacement for the train.

Table 1. Road traffic development for the period January–March 2016. Definitions for the type of payment can be found at https://www.oresundsbron.com/en/prices

Type of payment	Traffic per day 2016	Traffic per day 2015	Traffic development
Cash payment	2,207	2,188	0.9%
BroPas	4,824	4,278	12.8%
Commuters	5,895	5,969	−1.2%
Business	2,749	2,599	5.8%

Ferry Traffic

Another alternative to the Oresund Crossing is the ferry route Scandlines Helsingborg-Helsingör. While admitting that the introduction of ID controls put pressure on ferry operations, in the end of April 2016 the company reported significant traffic increase in Q1 2016 [23]. Once again, progress is partly attributed to the fact that Easter fell in Q1, but can also be attributed to the fact that, as stated earlier, the ferry ID checks generally operated without major delays. The number of departures grew moderately to almost 12,500 and there was a 4% increase in transported cars. Scandlines Helsingborg-Helsingör transported a total of almost 1.4 million passengers in Q1 2016, equalling a growth of 6%.

7 Discussion

7.1 Service Reductions Appear Well Tolerated by Swedish Respondents

The results indicate that the both Swedish and Oresund region residents were willing to tolerate service disruption in times of crisis. This appears to be in contrast to the "expectation gap" evoked in the literature. As demonstrated in the literature review, continued mobility was an expectation of the public, as most respondents expected *Transportation for emergency services only* to be a short term solution (days or hours only), while the other three service reductions presented appeared to be acceptable in the long term.

7.2 Oresund Region Respondents Appear More Willing to Accept Service Disruptions in the Long Term

At first look, it appeared as if Swedish respondents were more willing to tolerate service reductions than Oresund region respondents when asked about the acceptability of a given scenario. The difference between them went from 1 to 14 points, with Swedish respondents always being more willing to accept the scenario. The greatest difference in acceptability of the scenario was for *Reduced capacity or frequency of service*, which is what was happening at the time in the Oresund region with the Oresund Crossing train service. This could indicate that the residents of this region were dissatisfied with the changes in service. However, once the dimension of recovery was added and respondents were faced with how long they would be willing to tolerate a reduction in service, Swedish respondents appeared less accepting of the service disruptions in the long term than Oresund region respondents. A possible explanation for this is that the Oresund Region has many means of transport available, including both the road and train option on the Oresund Crossing, other bridges and ferries. As such, the Oresund region respondents may be able to more easily find an alternative means of travel, such as taking a ferry, than others. Another factor may be the relative newness of the Oresund Crossing, which was inaugurated on 1 July 2000. Many Oresund region residents then may share collective memory of the alternative routes that were once the only route available. When it comes to *Reduced capacity/frequency*, the most often chosen time frame was years for Oresund region respondents, compared to months for Swedish respondents, which could be a result of the change in service the Oresund Crossing had implemented. Perhaps the Oresund region respondents realised that they were indeed willing to tolerate Sweden's boarder control ID checks for longer than the originally planned six month period. More research would be necessary to verify these claims.

7.3 Quarterly Reports for Road and Ferry Transit Reflect Willingness to Use Alternative Means

The introduction of the border controls and ID checks at the Oresund Crossing had an immediate negative impact upon the service of the train, which led to increased journey times and reduced frequency of service. Although being significantly compromised, the service level never fell below the minimum level of acceptable for the majority of the train users, as the train Crossing was still actively used after the ID check introduction (only an 11% decrease). These users demonstrated resilience by tolerating increased journey times and reduced frequency of service.

Another manifestation of such resilience was by using alternative means. Despite being far from optimum, this process even resulted in a certain growth of the road traffic flow in Q1 2016 (with respect to Q1 2015). The ferry traffic seems to be one of the least affected by the border checks, due to its independency of other entities, low need in the third-party services, and inherent flexibility. The ferry service also demonstrated growth in number of passengers using its service, with several indications that they were doing so to avoid the train.

7.4   Limitations

The method we followed is not free from limitations. As discussed earlier, a self-selecting sample group was involved in the questionnaire study, which did not adequately represent the demographics of Sweden or the Oresund region. Furthermore, respondents may choose to answer in their own self-interest, claiming to tolerate less so as to not give the operator an excuse to perform any lower than absolutely necessary. The opposite, reporting that they are willing to tolerate more than they actually could handle in order to appear heroic, may also be true. The analysis of the Oresund Crossing case study presented here does not exhaust all related phenomena. Further progress in this research demands quite more complete technical and sociological data as well as more thorough analysis of this data.

8   Conclusion

After examining public expectations of the transportation sector in times of crisis, our findings suggest that these expectations are less high than was previously imagined. Swedish respondents appear to think that an acceptable level of disruption to transportation infrastructure includes *Diversion*, *Alternative means* and *Reduced capacity*, demonstrating their resilience. This willingness is quite high even in the long term. While Oresund region residents appeared to react negatively to the change in service of the Oresund Crossing, the same level of expected minimum service was also revealed in the case study findings. Most users of the Oresund Crossing train continued to take it, despite increased journey times and reduced frequency of service. Another way the Oresund region transportation infrastructure users demonstrated their resilience was by choosing alternatives to the Oresund Crossing train, either through increased use of the Oresund Crossing roadway or the Scandlines Helsingborg-Helsingör ferry. As such, the declared expectations in the questionnaire appear to reflect the actual habits of the Orseund region residents. While based on a small sample size, the differences in responses for Swedish and Oresund region residents with regard to the length of time they are willing to tolerate *Reduced capacity/frequency* (months vs. years, respectively) indicates that the Oresund region residents accepted the Swedish ID checks and their consequences on transportation infrastructure more easily. Nevertheless, it should be acknowledged that such an assessment is based on a self-selecting sample group that was not representative of the demographics in the populations studied. Perhaps, the analysis of the Oresund Crossing case study could also be more robust, by involving interviews/focus groups with citizens. Therefore, further work is needed to explore the perspectives of citizens who were not represented.

Future work within the IMPROVER project will consider the implications of these findings for infrastructure operators and efforts to build community disaster resilience within this Living Lab.

Acknowledgements. The IMPROVER project has received funding from the European Union's Horizon 2020 research and innovation programme under grant agreement No. 653390.

References

1. Buller, A.: Closing the Gap: Expectations versus Capabilities. PA Times, 10 July 2015. http://patimes.org/closing-gap-expectations-capabilities/. Accessed 14 Mar 2016
2. Iannucci, B., et al.: A Survivable Social Network. IEEE 978-1-4799-1535-4/13 (2013). http://repository.cmu.edu/cgi/viewcontent.cgi?article=1174&context=silicon_valley. Accessed 7 Apr 2016
3. Kaufman, S., Qing, C., Levenson, N., Hanson, M.: Transportation during and after Hurricane Sandy, pp. 1–36. Rudin Center for Transportation NYU, Wagner Graduate School of Public Service, November 2012
4. Nakanishi, H., Black, J., Matsuo, K.: Disaster resilience in transportation: Japan earthquake and tsunami 2011. Int. J. Disaster Resil. Built Environ. 5(4), 341–361 (2014). https://doi.org/10.1108/ijdrbe-12-2012-0039
5. Regional Australia Institute: From Recovery to Renewal: Case Study Reports, April 2013. http://www.regionalaustralia.org.au/wp-content/uploads/2013/06/RAI-Natural-Disasters-Report-Case-Studies.pdf. Accessed 21 Apr 2016
6. Ioannou, I., et al.: IMPROVER Deliverable 2.1 Methodology for identifying hazard scenarios to assess the resilience of critical infrastructure (2016)
7. Oresund Institute: Fact Sheet: The Effects of the ID- and Border Checks between Scania and Zealand, 1 November 2016. http://www.oresundsinstituttet.org/fact-sheet-the-effects-of-the-id-and-border-checks-between-scania-and-zealand/. Accessed 02 May 2017
8. BBC News: Sweden ends ID checks on 'The Bridge' with Denmark, 2 May 2017. http://www.bbc.com/news/world-europe-39784715. Accessed 09 May 2017
9. Traub, J.: The death of the most generous nation on earth. Foreign Policy, 10 February 2016. http://foreignpolicy.com/2016/02/10/the-death-of-the-most-generous-nation-on-earth-sweden-syria-refugee-europe. Accessed 21 Apr 2016
10. BBC News: Migrant crisis: Sweden border checks come into force, 4 January 2016. http://www.bbc.com/news/world-europe-35218921. Accessed 21 Apr 2016
11. Oresund Institute: Fakta: Effekterna av id- och gränskontroller mellan Skåne och Själland. Facts: The impact of identity cards and border controls between Scania and Zealand (2016). http://www.oresundsinstituttet.org/fakta-id-kontrollerna-over-oresund-forlanger-restiden-med-tag-till-sverige-med-mellan-10-och-50-minuter/. Accessed 22 Apr 2016
12. IndexMundi: Sweden Age Structure, 8 October 2016. http://www.indexmundi.com/sweden/age_structure.html. Accessed 09 May 2017

13. Christian, W.: Swedish border control costing Oresund region big time. CPH Post (2016). http://cphpost.dk/news/swedish-border-control-costing-oresund-region-big-time.html. Accessed 14 Apr 2016
14. Lisbeth, K.: Domino effect: Denmark follows Sweden on EU border checks. EUObserver (2016). http://euobserver.com/beyond-brussels/131702. Accessed 22 Apr 2016
15. Milne, R.: Oresund Bridge: barriers go up on corridor that unites Europe. Financial Times (2016). http://www.ft.com/cms/s/0/ba76c750-b5fb-11e5-8358-9a82b43f6b2f.html#axzz47h K9H8Uh. Accessed 26 Apr 2016
16. Savola, H.: Utvärdering av effekter av tillämpningen av förordning om vissa identitetskontroller. Evaluation of effects of the application of the Regulation on certain identity checks, 23 August 2016. http://www.oresundsinstituttet.org/wp-content/uploads/2016/09/20160923-Utvardering-av-effekter-av-tillampningen-av-forordning-om-vissa-identitetskontroller.pdf
17. Trip Advisor: Oresund Bridge: Overview, Trip Advisor's web page, continuously updated. https://www.tripadvisor.com/Attraction_Review-g189541-d548642-Reviews-Oresund_Bridge-Copenhagen_Zealand.html. Accessed 01 June 2016
18. Øresundsbro Konsortiet Q1 2016 result, Nasdaq: GlobeNewswire, 28 April 2016. https://globenewswire.com/news-release/2016/04/28/833940/0/en/%C3%98resundsbro-Konsortiet-Q1-2016-result.html. Accessed 01 June 2016
19. Radio Sweden: Danish politician: Sweden should pay for ID checks (2015). http://sverigesradio.se/sida/artikel.aspx?programid=2054&artikel=6335075. Accessed 15 Apr 2016
20. Ullman-Hammer, C.: Øresundsbro Konsortiet Q1 2016 result. Øresundsbro Konsortiet, 28 April 2016. https://cns.omxgroup.com/cdsPublic/viewDisclosure.action?disclosureId=708 905&messageId=887554. Accessed 04 May 2017
21. Holmqvist, S.: Taxi och hyrbilar ökar på Øresundsbron. Fokus Öresund, 10 March 2016. http://fokusoresund.com/se/2016/03/taxi-och-hyrbilar-okar-pa-oresundsbron/. Accessed 21 Apr 2016
22. Oresundsbron: Traffic Statistics 2016, Øresundsbron Web site. https://www.oresundsbron.com/en/traffic-stats. Accessed 11 May 2017
23. Rørbæk, H.: Easter traffic alleviated the effect of ID controls in Q1, Scandlines, Helsingborg-Helsingör, 27 April 2016. http://hhferriesgroup.com/wp-content/uploads/2016/04/Easter-traffic-alleviated-the-effect-of-ID-controls-in-Q1.pdf. Accessed 11 May 2017

Towards a Common Vocabulary for Crisis Management Scenarios

Jingquan Xie(✉), Betim Sojeva, Erich Rome, and Daniel Lückerath

Fraunhofer IAIS, Sankt Augustin, Germany
{jingquan.xie,betim.sojeva,erich.rome,
daniel.luckerath}@iais.fraunhofer.de

Abstract. Crisis management is a complex process, handling critical situations caused by natural or human-made hazards. In the response phase, crisis managers often have limited time to react on unexpected events. Hence, sufficient training during the preparedness phase of crisis management plays a vital role for correct behaviours under time pressure. Significant efforts in the research community have been invested to develop innovative IT-based crisis management training systems with one core idea in mind – create crisis scenarios with sufficient details for the targeted training purposes to better prepare crisis managers. Developing such scenarios is however a time-consuming process and involves contributing a vast amount of human efforts by crisis managers, domain experts and system engineers. Therefore, improved re-usability of well-developed and validated scenarios is of critical importance for crisis management training. To our best knowledge, a widely-accepted method to describe crisis scenarios in a machine understandable fashion is still missing – training systems are normally equipped with proprietary formats that cannot be easily shared with each other. This paper proposes a common machine-readable vocabulary to describe crisis scenarios. In addition, the corresponding software environment to support the generation and execution of crisis scenarios is also elaborated.

1 Introduction

Each crisis and emergency situation caused by either natural (earthquake) or human (terror-attack) events is unique and thus poses a challenge to responders and crisis management. Critical Infrastructures (CI) play crucial roles in crises and emergencies. Yet there is insufficient awareness of crisis management regarding the role of CI in such situations [5]. A widely used method to minimise the impacts of crisis situations and to better prepare crisis managers is to educate them via sufficient training. Information systems with distributed communication and simulation technology are playing an increasingly more important role in modern crisis management processes, especially during the preparedness phase. Useful scenarios for crisis management training must be as realistic as possible. This requires intensive communication between scenario developers

G. D'Agostino and A. Scala (Eds.): CRITIS 2017, LNCS 10707, pp. 25–36, 2018.
https://doi.org/10.1007/978-3-319-99843-5_3

and domain experts. The ability to reuse these scenarios is extremely important. During the past decades, a significant amount of efforts has been devoted in multiple security-related research projects to develop realistic scenarios to validate innovative crisis management methods. However, these independently developed valuable crisis scenarios cannot be easily shared and further developed in a collaborative way.

This paper proposes a common vocabulary called Scenario Description Language (SDL) for scenario developers to describe crisis scenarios in a machine understandable fashion focusing on the ease of scenario generation, execution and collaborative sharing. The rest of this work is organised as follows: Sect. 2 describes the essential elements of crisis scenarios that can be modelled with SDL. It is followed by Sect. 3 with a detailed explanation of the language SDL itself and Sect. 4 with an explanation of the ecosystem around SDL. One crisis scenario about cargo train derailment encoded in SDL is discussed in Sect. 5. Some related work is discussed in Sect. 6 and the whole paper is concluded by Sect. 7 with insights on potential future research directions.

2   Modelling Essential Elements of Crisis Scenarios in SDL

A crisis scenario contains different types of information that are relevant for crisis managers, organisation liaisons and on-site first responders. In order to achieve a certain level of usability of scenarios, detailed realistic and even real data needs to be collected and integrated into the scenario.

Storyline and Events. A storyline describes the dynamic behaviours of a crisis scenario. It consists of a sequence of pre-defined events with time stamps describing what could happen at a certain time point during the scenario execution. Events in the storyline of a scenario can be conditional. That means the pre-conditions to trigger an event can be different during the runtime of a scenario - and this results in different execution paths of a defined storyline at runtime. In particular, this is the case for scenarios involving decision making and execution of response actions. Depending on the courses of actions, the whole scenario may evolve in different directions.

Domain Models. A crisis scenario involves multiple domains like critical infrastructures, (e.g. power network, telecommunication system, and railway transportation, etc.), the weather conditions (e.g. wind, humidity, heavy rain, etc.), and threats (e.g. earthquake, flooding, derailment, etc.). To integrate these heterogeneous data sources into a single scenario is a big challenge. SDL uses the concept of Federated Simulation [8] to provide the dynamics of domain models. Each domain model is mapped to an Unified Resource Locator (URL), which can be uniquely identified in a distributed environment. Interface specifications between domain models and scenario executor are defined as part of the SDL ecosystem to enable the federation at runtime (see Fig. 1).

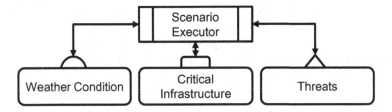

Fig. 1. Federation of domain models controlled by the scenario executor. Each federate exposes itself via an URL and implements the interface specification provided by SDL.

Resources. A crisis scenario may contain numerous categories of resources like rescue forces, police, hospitals, and ambulances, etc. Decision makers need to know the status (available or not, locations, etc.) of these resources for the forthcoming task at any time during crisis situations. Resource statuses are dynamically changing during scenario running. This information needs to be modelled in a scenario and monitored by the scenario executor to keep a consistent view of available resources for all participants of a crisis management training session (see the collaborative training in Sect. 4.2).

Mitigation and Response Actions. At certain time points of a crisis scenario, depending on the resilience of the affected technical systems, disruptions start to appear. Before serious consequences occur, like injuries of humans, some actions need to be performed to minimise or even eliminate the negative effects. SDL provides the capability of action modelling with parameters. A handful of candidate response actions against certain threats can be predefined in the scenario for runtime decision making. During scenario running, several response actions can be chosen by decision makers with adjustable parameters. The decision criteria are either based on the expertise of crisis managers, fixed regulations, check lists, or computer-based consequence analysis.

Consequence Analysis. Consequence Analysis (CA) is the entire computer-based process of assessing and evaluating impacts caused by threats and their cascading effects between critical infrastructures. Different criteria are available. For instance, the Cross Cutting Criteria of the 2008 Directive on European Critical Infrastructures [3] are early criteria that are recommended by the European Commission.

3   SDL – The Scenario Description Language

The Scenario Description Language is a declarative language based on JSON – the JavaScript Object Notation syntax. More precisely, SDL provides a JSON schema that can verify the validity of a serialised JSON object describing a crisis scenario. The major part of an SDL-encoded crisis scenario consists of the essential elements that are described in Sect. 2. Auxiliary information, like name of the scenario, can also be included to provide different kinds of meta data. In the following, the word SDL can mean the language itself or the SDL file that precisely describes a crisis scenario.

Simulation Time and Real Time. A clear understanding of *simulation time* and *real time* is essential for developing SDL-based crisis scenarios. Real time is the unrepeatable wall time that elapses. It exists in the daily life with the units of seconds, minutes and hours, etc. The simulation time, on the other hand, exists only in a simulated environment and is repeatable. A ratio between the real time and the simulation time can be defined to accelerate the scenario execution. It expects a positive integer value N, meaning the simulation time is N times faster than the real time. It is the basis to provide what-if analysis for a crisis scenario training, which is integrated in the SDL ecosystem.

Web-Oriented Design. By design, SDL takes the concept of distributed resource. Valid elements in SDL are considered as distributed resources that can be accessed via standard Web protocols like HTTP or HTTPS. With this idea in mind, numerous elements (like flooding simulators, weather information providers, etc.) in SDL are modelled as Web resources exposing RESTful web services based on the SDL specification. These Web resources are referenced in SDL-encoded scenarios for further aggregation and federation. The following is an example of integrating a power flow simulator in SDL:

```
"model": [{
    "domain":"power",
    "simulator":"sincal",
    "model_url":"<the url of the domain models>",
    "simulator_url":"<the url of the domain simulators>"
}, ...]
```

With this approach multiple data sources can be aggregated in a flexible way. The complexity of generating the required data is then hidden behind the RESTful endpoints. In addition, this schema provides a consistent way for the exchange of model elements: use the same element name and type in the federation model. For example, if a power substation failed in the power simulation, this information will be reflected in the railway simulation.

What-if Analysis. SDL hast built-in support for what-if analysis [7]. With what-if analysis, crisis managers are able to explore different courses of actions during training sessions and compare the impacts and consequences. The concept of conditional events in SDL is one of the core functionalities to support this feature. Each event comes with a `condition` attribute, which must be a set of statements that can be evaluated to TRUE or FALSE. For instance, the expression can be a legal JavaScript expression like `value>2` or a complex SQL query like the one below:

```
{
  "condition": "select count(1)>0 as result
    from (select sum(forces), destination, type, flag
          from ciprtrainer.actions where flag=1
          group by destination, type, flag) t
    where t.type='fra' and t.destination='Z8' and t.forces > 29"
}
```

In addition, it is common to have *periodic events* that occur in a crisis scenario based on a pre-defined interval in simulation time. For instance, an event can regularly trigger external discrete event simulators to provide heart beats for simulators. SDL provides built-in support for periodic events. At runtime, these event definitions are interpreted by the scenario executor and corresponding events will be generated. With this feature, cumbersome definitions of events with similar information at different time points in the storyline can be avoided. One example of periodic event definitions is presented below:

```
periodic_events: [{
    name:    OpenTrack step simulation,
    interval_sec: 300, // every 5 min a new event
    event:{
"type":"103", // identifies the type of the event
    payload: {
    command:step, // simulator specific parameter
"type":"opentrack",
    to:     $elapsed_sim_time_sec // an SDL built-in function
}
}
}, {// more periodic event definitions}]
```

A set of SDL built-in functions like $elapsed_sim_time_sec in the example above can be used to provide dynamic information at runtime. A complete list of the built-in functions that are currently available is summarised in Table 1.

Table 1. Built-in functions available for periodic event definitions in SDL. These functions can either return dynamic information by accessing the corresponding data sources.

Name of the function	Functional description
$elapsed_sim_time_sec	It returns an integer value representing the elapsed simulation time in seconds from the beginning of the training
$elapsed_sim_time_sec	It returns an integer value representing the elapsed real time in seconds
$wms_update_state	This function triggers the Web Map Service defined in SDL to update the spatial elements based on the scenario running
$wfs_update_state	Similar to $wms_update_state, it notifies Web Feature Service to be updated
$weather_update	This function returns the current weather information like wind direction, temperature, humidity, etc.

Internationalisation. Cross-border scenarios are becoming more important on the EU level, which raises the need of internationalisation of technical systems. SDL has built-in support for internationalisation by incorporating multilingual texts into a key-value structure. At runtime, the user is able to select the current system language and only the texts for that language will be used. For instance, a placeholder for the field `title` of an event definition can be introduced with the name $E001 as the key. Meanwhile, the real translations for different languages are encoded in a different section `internationalisation`:

```
{ "event_id": "E001",  "title": "$E001" }
...
"internationalisation": {
  "$E001": {
    "en": "A train derails in the city of Emmerich.",
    "de": "Ein Zug entgleist in Emmerich."  }}
```

With the unique key name, SDL is able to provide the right translation based on user selections. This approach has the advantage of flexibility and simplicity. Moreover, the translation section can be separated from the elements that uses these translation. Therefore, changing the structure of these elements, e.g. events defined in the storyline, does not require any change in the part containing translated texts. Even more, the translation can be stored outside of the SDL file. When translations of a specific language are needed, the scenario executor can process the SDL file beforehand and then laterally inject the translations into the GUI widgets.

4   SDL Ecosystem

SDL itself provides a common vocabulary to describe crisis scenarios in a machine understandable fashion. To maximise the productivity of using SDL in crisis management training, a complete ecosystem with sufficient tool support is essential:

- A runtime environment is required to execute the generated SDL and communicate with different RESTful endpoints integrated in the scenario.
- A graphical user interface with sophisticated GIS (Geographic Information System) support is introduced to visualise the results of scenario-based crisis management training.
- Handcrafting crisis scenarios in SDL is time consuming and error-prone. A tool called scenario editor is currently under development to facilitate the development of scenarios in SDL.

4.1   Scenario Executor

The scenario executor is a program that interprets a given SDL file. The core of the scenario executor includes functionalities like **start**, **stop**, **pause** and continue, etc. In addition, functionalities like load and clean are essential to manage the life cycle of scenario training. The pushEvent functionality instantiates pre-defined events and dispatches them to the event engine, which uses declarative dependency rules to handle dependencies and cascading effects. The scenario executor registers periodic events, conditional events and chronologically ordered storyline events based on the definitions in SDL. The available interface provided by the current implementation of the scenario executor is as follows:

```
interface {
    startSDL(): boolean; // starts the scenario
    stopSDL(): boolean; // stops the scenario
    pauseSDL(): boolean; // pauses the scenario
    continueSDL: boolean; // continues the scenario
    loadSDL(sdl: SDL): boolean; // loads the scenario
    clearSDL(): boolean; // clears the scenario
    pushSDLEvent(event: Event); // pushes storyline events
    loadTimeModel(time: TimeModel): boolean; // time ratio
}
```

4.2   Collaborative Graphical User Interface

An advanced graphical user interface with support for collaboration is essential for SDL to be adopted in crisis management training. CIPRTrainer (see Fig. 3) is an HTML5-based Web application that comes with SDL and fulfils the following requirements:

- **Collaborative training.** One trainer and multiple trainees are able to participate in a crisis training session from different geographical locations. During the training session they interact with each other by instantiating and executing actions in a simulated world. The current status of the scenario execution is kept up-to-date by pushing different events to the GUI. Thereby, a consistent image of the current scenario is synchronised transparently in a collaborative environment. In such a configuration, localisation of the software is also addressed. Trainees from different countries participating in a training will see their own language and eventually standard icons from their own countries.
- **Advanced what-if analysis.** What-if analysis enables the trainees to explore different courses of actions and compare the final impacts in terms of certain criteria defined in the consequence analysis. At any point in the training a trainee is able to roll back the whole training to a previous state caused by an action execution. In the collaborative environment, the clients of all other trainees get updated as well. So that they can collaboratively explore a set of different options to understand which course of actions is more optimised in terms of the number of casualties and economic loss.

- **Storyline visualisation.** As one of the core elements, the storyline in a training session is dynamically visualised and provides extremely useful information about what has happened until now (simulation time). Instantiated conditional events, executed actions and critical messages are presented in a specific *Timeline* GUI widget with chronological ordering. User functionalities like panning, zooming and filtering are all supported to provide a unique user experience.
- **Sophisticated GIS support.** A large part of the elements in a crisis scenario are spatial objects, i.e. they have either locations or are related to a region. Examples are the location of a derailment or an evacuation route. Sophisticated GIS support enables trainees to explore these objects in an intuitive fashion with background maps. Dynamic information, like operation states of spatial objects, is also visualised together with the spatial attributes.

4.3   Scenario Editor

The scenario editor is a tool that can facilitate and speed up the modelling process of a scenario. It is divided into three layers (as depicted in Fig. 2).

- The first layer deals with the scenario element creation, including location definition, availability of mitigation resources for emergency response, and event definitions (storyline, periodic and conditional events). The user can fill in necessary information in the different sections. The editor comes with a feedback functionality that enables the user to adjust invalid inputs.
- The second layer deals with technical issues for setting up the domain model configuration, database connection, and other services, like Web Mapping Services. Users have to take care that the given configurations are valid. Currently it is not planned for the scenario editor to check the validity of external services.
- Finally, the third layer of the editor functionalities include built-in modules that are capable of serialising SDL files based on the JSON schema. Automatic JSON validation transparently ensures the consistency of scenarios on the syntactic level.

5   Case Study

To demonstrate the capability of SDL and show how the ecosystem can facilitate scenario generation, execution, and visualisation, a minimalistic crisis scenario of cargo derailment is presented in this section.

The location where the derailment occurs is in the city Emmerich am Rhein in Germany. The complete scenario, which contains a short time period before the derailment happens, starts at 2015/03/05 10:28:00 local time. Auxiliary information like creator, scenario name, scenario description, etc. is also provided in the SDL.

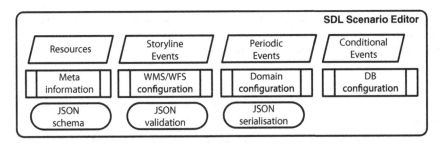

Fig. 2. The functional blocks of the scenario editor for SDL. It is organised in three layers for element management, configuration management and syntax management. The scenario editor provides high-level modelling capabilities for creating consistent SDL files complying to the JSON schema.

```
"meta": {
  "name": "$name",
  "url" : "<the URL via which the SDL can be retrieved>",
  "description": "$desc",
  "location": "Emmerich am Rhein, Germany",
  "creator name" : "<name of the creator>",
  "creator email" : "<email of the creator>",
  "basedate" : "2015/03/05 10:28:00 GMT+0100",
  ...
}
```

The information for the event engine is encoded in the section cep, which contains the RESTful endpoint URL of the event engine and the URL of the dependency rules. These rules are to be loaded by the rule engine at runtime during the initialisation phase.

```
"simulation time": 15, // 1 simulation sec means 15 real sec
"cep":{
  "engine url":"<the RESTful endpoint of the event engine>",
  "rule base":"<the URL of the rule base>"
}
```

Spatial objects that are relevant for the derailment scenario are defined in the SDL as well. Two types of spatial objects are needed for the derailment scenario: *line* and *point*. Other spatial types like *polygon* can also be provided for specific crisis scenarios.

```
"wfs": {
  "line url": "<the URL of the line features>",
  "point url": "<the URL of the point features>"
}
```

Domain simulation plays a central role in what-if enabled crisis management training. For the cargo derailment scenario, four simulations (flood, power, telecommunication, and railway) are defined:

```
"model": [
  {"domain":"flood", "simulator":"extern",
    "model":"<model URL>", "simulator":"<REST endpoint>"},
  {"domain":"power", "simulator":"sincal",
    "model":"<model URL>", "simulator":"<REST endpoint>"},
  {"domain":"telecommunication", "simulator":"ns-3",
    "model":"<model URL>", "simulator":"<REST endpoint>"},
  {"domain":"railway", "simulator":"opentrack",
    "model":"<model URL>", "simulator":"<REST endpoint>"}
]
```

Other SDL elements, like resources, decision makers, events, and actions can also be defined for this test scenario. Due to the page limits, the description of these elements will be provided in an extended version of this paper. With the SDL file, the scenario executor is able to initiate a training session and communicate with the collaborative graphical user interface. One of the screenshots during training session is illustrated in Fig. 3.

Fig. 3. The trainee view of the derailment scenario training session. The panel on the left hand side contains the available actions and the history actions. Operations like start, stop and continue are also provided. A trainee is able to select one action in the history and roll back to that point in time for conducting a what-if analysis. Various spatial objects are visualised on top of the background map, including an artificial power distribution network. Standard crisis management icons are adopted as overlays.

6 Related Work

Crisis management training [6] is a complex and costly task. Using a scenario-driven approach with computer simulation [1] and serious games [4] is proven to be an effective approach to improve training efficiency and flexibility while keeping the overall cost on a low level. The Military Scenario Description Language (MSDL) [9] is an XML-based language for developing military scenarios in an unambiguous way. It provides a common vocabulary and XML-based schema for exchanging scenario data in a networked environment for military use cases. The Coalition Battle Management Language (C-BML) [10] is another standard, which is a dedicated language for describing military scenarios focusing on expressing and exchanging plans, orders, requests, and reports across command and control (C2) systems [10]. Both standards provide a common vocabulary for specific domains. However, as a technology arisen in military, the default configuration lacks sufficient support for modelling civil crisis management processes, especially the ability to declaratively specify the dependencies between different involved domains. The CISO ontology [11] provides a formal foundation to describe various aspects of a crisis scenario. The common vocabulary SDL proposed in this work further extends the CISO approach by providing a set of pragmatic solutions and tool support. Several systems [2,12] have been proposed to handle collaborative training. An explicit approach to model scenarios as a first-class citizen in those systems is however still missing.

7 Conclusion and Outlook

Computer applications for advanced training or serious gaming aimed at improving the preparedness of crisis management staff often employ simulation of crisis scenarios. The formalism SDL presented in this paper can help to structure the information and data required for such simulations. Here, it is crucial finding the right level of abstraction for getting meaningful results while keeping the effort for this on a manageable level. Even when using SDL, the creation of complex and realistic scenarios remains a time-consuming task. Therefore, the adoption of a scenario representation scheme such as SDL would benefit from the availability of tools that facilitate and accelerate the creation of scenarios. For the training application that employed the derailment scenario, we used a graphical editor for creating static parts like resources (basically, for the ontology parts) and exported them to SDL. Other parts of the scenario have been created manually. The training application employed four different scenarios which we stored in a scenario database. Such a database helps to keep track of scenarios and their variations and it facilitates reusing scenario elements. Other proposed tools would be a timeline editor for quickly adjusting the scheduling of events, and on the implementation side, the use of a transcompiler could accelerate the execution. SDL also facilitated the usage of multiple languages, which allows for easy localisations of training applications. This, in turn, is beneficial for target users, since crisis management staff communicates most effectively in their mother tongues.

Acknowledgments. The research leading to these results was funded by the European Commission within the Seventh Framework Programme projects CIPRNet (grant agreement N° 312450) and PREDICT (grant agreement N° 60769). The authors thank all of the project partners for many constructive discussions and useful suggestions. The contents of this paper do not reflect the official opinion of the European Union. Responsibility for the information and views expressed herein lies entirely with the authors.

References

1. Benjamins, T., Rothkrantz, L.: Interactive simulation in crisis management. In: Proceedings of the 4th International Conference on Information Systems for Crisis Response and Management ISCRAM2007, pp. 571–580 (2007)
2. Chambelland, J.C., Raffin, R., Desbenoit, B., Gesquière, G.: SIMFOR: towards a collaborative software platform for urban crisis management. In: The IADIS Computer Graphics, Visualization, Computer Vision and Image Processing (CGVCVIP2011), Rome, Italy (2011)
3. European Council: COUNCIL DIRECTIVE 2008/114/EC of 8 December 2008 on the identification and designation of European critical infrastructures and the assessment of the need to improve their protection. Technical report, Official Journal of the European Union, (L 345/75) (2008)
4. Loreto, I.D., Mora, S., Divitini, M.: Collaborative serious games for crisis management: an overview. In: Enabling Technologies: Infrastructure for Collaborative Enterprises (WETICE), pp. 352–357. IEEE (2012)
5. Luiijf, E., Klaver, M.: Insufficient situational awareness about critical infrastructures by emergency management. In: Proceedings of the NATO Symposium on C3I for Crisis, Emergency and Consequence Management, Bucharest, 11–12 May 2009, RTO-MP-IST-086. NATO RTA (2009)
6. Robert, B., Lajtha, C.: A new approach to crisis management. J. Contingencies Cris. Manag. **10**(4), 181–191 (2002)
7. Rome, E., Doll, T., Rilling, S., Sojeva, B., Voß, N., Xie, J.: The use of what-if analysis to improve the management of crisis situations. In: Setola, R., Rosato, V., Kyriakides, E., Rome, E. (eds.) Managing the Complexity of Critical Infrastructures: A Modelling and Simulation Approach, pp. 233–277. Springer International Publishing, Cham (2016). https://doi.org/10.1007/978-3-319-51043-9_10
8. Rome, E., Langeslag, P., Usov, A.: Federated modelling and simulation for critical infrastructure protection. In: D'Agostino, G., Scala, A. (eds.) Networks of Networks: The Last Frontier of Complexity. UCS, pp. 225–253. Springer, Cham (2014). https://doi.org/10.1007/978-3-319-03518-5_11
9. Standard for Military Scenario Definition Language (MSDL) (2008)
10. Standard for Coalition Battle Management Language (C-BML) Phase 1 (2014)
11. Xie, J., Theocharidou, M., Barbarin, Y.: Knowledge-driven scenario development for critical infrastructure protection. In: Rome, E., Theocharidou, M., Wolthusen, S. (eds.) CRITIS 2015. LNCS, vol. 9578, pp. 91–102. Springer, Cham (2016). https://doi.org/10.1007/978-3-319-33331-1_8
12. Xie, J., Vullings, E., Theocharidou, M.: Towards the next generation training system for crisis management. In: 22nd TIEMS Annual Conference, vol. 22. TIEMS, The International Emergency Management Society (2015)

Analysis and Classification of Adaptation Tools for Transport Sector Adaptation Planning

Georgia Lykou, George Iakovakis, George Chronis, and Dimitris Gritzalis$^{(\boxtimes)}$

Information Security and Critical Infrastructure Protection Lab (INFOSEC),
Athens University of Economics and Business, Athens, Greece
{lykoug,giakovakis,p3120209,dgrit}@aueb.gr

Abstract. Climate change is an upcoming and unavoidable challenge that all critical infrastructures including transport sector will have to face. Although transport sector and its network substructures are typically designed to withstand weather-related stressors, shifts in climate patterns will greatly increase potential risks. The area of climate adaptation planning is still relatively new, however a variety of processes and methodologies for assessing and reducing the vulnerability to climate change are currently being developed. These processes require and benefit from the use of geospatial analyses, software tools and web portals. In this research, we have focused on climate-related adaptation planning. We provide detailed classification of a set of tools that can facilitate adaptation assessment and risk planning. Our goal is to present a multifaceted taxonomy and analysis of available Climate Change Adaptation tools which can support transport sector for risk management policies.

1 Introduction

Recent modeling studies indicate that climate change is inevitable and our society will have to deal with over coming decades. According to IPCC [1], global warming will have significant implications in climate, population and ecological health, economic development and social stability. Gradual global temperature increase, sea level rise and rainfall regimes along with the projected increase in frequency and intensity of extreme weather events will seriously challenge transportation substructures. Transport is characterized as a Critical Infrastructure (CI) that greatly supports the smooth functioning of society's prosperity and economy's viability worldwide [2]. Most transport substructures being built today are expected to last for decades or even centuries. Integrating adaptation into the design of new and upgraded substructures can enhance stability and life span, while minimizing unplanned outages, failures and maintenance costs [3].

In this research, we have focused on climate-related adaptation planning and we provide detailed information about a set of tools that facilitate adaptation assessment and risk management. Our goal was to present a detailed classification and analysis for adaptation tools which support transport sector.

© Springer Nature Switzerland AG 2018
G. D'Agostino and A. Scala (Eds.): CRITIS 2017, LNCS 10707, pp. 37–47, 2018.
https://doi.org/10.1007/978-3-319-99843-5_4

The term tool has been used to describe a wide variety of planning processes, policies, and analytic approaches, focusing on software and web-based applications that can help stakeholders to incorporate data geophysical, environmental or socioeconomic into the planning process.

The rest of the paper is structured as follows. Climate adaptation and planning process is presented in Sect. 2. Adaptation tools analysis takes place in Sect. 3, followed by a sort description for each one. The main contribution is in Sect. 4, where adaptation tools are analyzed and classified in several ways: (i) according to tool category and target audience; (ii) according to geographic scope, sectors affected and climate impacts; (iii) Adaptation Planning Steps; (iv) Software Tools Functionality & Mode of Use; and finally (v) Strengths and Weaknesses analysis. Section 5 concludes our analysis and classification results.

2   Climate Change Adaptation

Climate Change Adaptation is the evolutionary process of adjusting to new conditions, stresses and natural hazards that result from global warming effects. Thus, adaptation consists of actions responding to current and future climate impacts and vulnerabilities, not only protecting against negative impacts of climate change, but also building resilience and taking advantage of any benefits, it may bring [1]. According to UKCIP [4] adaptation responses and decisions can be categorized as measures and strategies that contribute to: (i) Build adaptive capacity with knowledge spread (i.e. research, data collection and monitoring, awareness raising); (ii) Create supportive social structures (i.e. organizational development, working in partnership), and supportive governance (i.e. regulations, legislation, and guidance); (iii) Identify adaptation actions which help to reduce vulnerability to climate risks, or to exploit opportunities. These three categories reflect the range of adaptation strategies from which a good adaptation assessment can be developed.

Although the field of climate adaptation planning is still relatively new, a variety of processes are emerging in order to assess and reduce vulnerabilities of CIs to climate change. Basic steps of Adaptation planning processes involve: (i) Scope problems, stressors & planning area, information gathering & data inventorying, build working groups and gain stakeholder involvement; (ii) Analyze information to elucidate patterns, relationships & potential future outcomes, conduct vulnerability, impact & risk assessment and set priorities; (iii) Establish vision and prioritize adaptation strategies, create action plan based on priorities and schedule implementation; (iv) Implement and evaluate the effectiveness of plan, seek funding, adjust to unexpected or novel issues or stressors, revise strategies and priorities as needed. Based on these basic steps, a variety of adaptation cycles exists in literature. Figure 1 shows the adaptation cycle defined in the Urban Adaptation Support Tool as consolidated and presented in the RAMSES project [5].

Conducting vulnerability and risk assessment is a key analytical step not only for CI protection, as already presented in [6,7], but also for adaptation

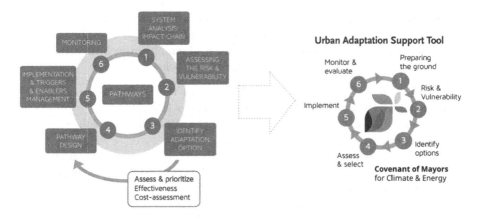

Fig. 1. Adaptation cycles developed in EU projects

planning. Climate change vulnerability assessments identify assets, which may be impacted. In addition, potential sources of vulnerability also consider the likelihood and consequences of potential climate change impacts. Due to the predictive nature of vulnerability and risk assessments, there is a degree of uncertainty in the results. It is important to understand and account for this uncertainty when considering management actions of adaptation, so decision support tools must incorporate data, analyze trends, project evolution and minimize uncertainty.

3   Climate Adaptation Tools Analysis

Transport has already dealt with extreme events causing interruptions, stemming from natural hazards and developed strategies to maintain resilience. In previous work [8] we have analyzed adaptation options for transport sector applied worldwide.

The purpose of Adaptation Tools development is to provide the information necessary for stakeholders involved to select appropriate measures and manage risk of their projects. Since there has been an increased demand by governments and international agencies for practical guidance on methods for adaptation assessment, there is a huge development of analytical tools, which are available to support communities, decision makers and stakeholders [9]. The emerging need for multi-model analysis has driven the creation of adaptation toolboxes, which describe the steps to be undertaken for adaptation and risk management process.

In our paper, we have extensively searched for open literature adaptation tools, in order to create a useful pool of tools that can be used for CIs adaptation assessment in transport sector. Although this selection of tools is not exhaustive, we have distinguished the ones who incorporate transport networks and related critical infrastructures. As a result, seventeen tools have been selected and analyzed in our paper. They allow for a broad range of aspects to be evaluated and provide supportive information for adaptation planning projects in transport sector. These seventeen tools are shortly presented below:

1. *Baltic Climate Toolkit*: is a methodology tool that guides the process of identifying vulnerabilities in the Baltic countries [10].
2. *Blue Spot Model*: is a methodology used to identify roadways vulnerable to flooding by using GIS environment [11].
3. *Climate Vulnerability Monitor*: assesses vulnerabilities and risks and contains information about projected climate related economic damages, deaths, environmental disasters on 184 countries [12].
4. *Climada*: uses numerical functions to model economic damages from natural hazards, based on scenario building [13].
5. *Climate Guide*: is developed for Finland, where scenarios are built concerning the water resources, potential energy demand and natural ecosystems [14].
6. *CommunityViz* is a decision support tool with variety of analytical models as well as visualization and mapping capabilities to support a variety of planning activities [15].
7. *Ecocities Spatial Portal:* is an interactive platform with spatial data and information for climate change vulnerabilities in Manchester [16].
8. *EconAdapt-Toolbox*: supports adaptation planning, builds the knowledge base on the economics of adaptation and provides practical information for decision makers [17].
9. *HAZUS-MH (HAZARDS US Multi-Hazard)*: is a risk-assessment methodology for analyzing potential losses from floods, hurricane winds, coastal surge, and earthquakes [18].
10. *MACC (Monitoring Adaptation Climate Change)*: leads project managers through the five steps of the guidebook Adaptation [19].
11. *MOWE-IT*: assists transport operators and authorities mitigating the impact of natural disasters and extreme weather phenomena on transport system performance [20].
12. NatureServe Vista: is a spatial decision support system for conducting cumulative effects assessment, mitigation planning, and conservation planning [21].
13. *ND-GAIN (Notre Dame Global Adaptation Index)*: follows a data-driven approach to show which countries are best prepared for global changes [22].
14. *Sea Level Rise and Coastal Flooding Impacts Viewer*: is a visualization tool for simulations and graphics of current and potential future conditions [23].
15. Stocktaking for National Adaptation: is a decision support tool for assessing the country's capacity to perform adaptation [24].
16. The Urban Adaptation Support Tool: is a methodology-guide, which takes decision makers gradually through the adaptation process [25].
17. UKCIP Adaptation Wizard: is a tool for adapting to climate change, by using a 5-step process, to assess vulnerability to current and future climate change [26].

4   Classification of Adaptation Tools

In this section, the main contribution of our paper is presented, where adaptation tools are analyzed and classified in several ways, aiming to facilitate stakeholders to understand which ones better fit to their adaption planning needs. In Sect. 4.1 tools are classified according to typology and target audience, in Sect. 4.2 classification is dealing with climate impacts and economy sectors affected, then in Sect. 4.3 tools are categorized according to adaptation planning steps. In Subsect. 4.4, software tools are further classified according to their functionality & mode of use. Finally, in Subsect. 4.5 Strengths and Weaknesses are evaluated.

4.1   Classification According to Type of Tool and Target Audience

The selected adaptation tools are classified, based on the following three broad categories: (1) *Informative Guidelines* offer informational databases on climate change and adaptation planning, through open libraries and repositories, supporting research and knowledge spread. (2) *Methodologies & Assessments* describe climate adaptation though a sequence of steps, to be followed in order to accomplish a specific task. Vulnerability and risk assessments are also included in this category, to evaluate threats and vulnerabilities. (3)*Software Tools* are

Table 1. Tools Categories and target audience

No	Name	Tool category			Target group
		Info guidelines	Method assess	Software tools	
1	Baltic	x	x		P - D - O
2	BlueSpot		x		O
3	ClimaVulM			x	P - O
4	Climada			x	D - O
5	ClimaGuide			x	O
6	ComViz			x	P - O
7	Ecocities			x	P
8	EconAdapt	x	x		D - O
9	HazusMH			x	D - O
10	MACC			x	O
11	MoweIt	x		x	P - O
12	NatureServe			x	P - D - O
13	ND-GAIN			x	P
14	SLR-CFI			x	P
15	SNAP		x		P - O
16	UKCIP			x	P - O
17	UrbanAdapt	x	x		O

those tools that offer a calculating platform to perform a specific task, model a problem and visualize provided information.

Each tool is designed to support different target audience and this information is presented in Table 1. Three main target groups are: (i) Designers & Engineers (D); (ii) Operators and Managers (O) and (iii) Policy Makers (P).

4.2 Classification of Adaptation Tools According to Sectors and Climate Impacts

In Table 2 examined tools have been classified based on geographic scope, affected economy sector and climate impacts. In terms of geographical coverage, there are tools that cover a Single State (S) or Multiple States (MS) like counties belonging to the same continent (EU, USA etc.) and finally those who have a Global (G) geographic scope. However, analysis resolution can focus on any specific vulnerable region, city, township or district. Sectors affected may be urban areas, agricultural activity, transport or energy sector and earth resources including water and other natural assets. In terms of climate impacts, there are various weather-related stressors that may impact transport substructure like flood, extreme heat or cold, storms and drought phenomena.

Table 2. Classification according to vulnerable sectors and climate impacts

No	Tool name	Geo scope	Vulnerable sector					Climate impacts				
			Urban	Transport	Agriculture	Energy	Resources	Flood	Heat	Cold	Storms	Drought
1	Baltic	MS	x	x	x	x	x	x	x			x
2	BlueSpot	G		x				x		x		
3	ClimaVulM	G		x	x	x	x	x			x	x
4	Climada	G	x	x		x	x	x		x	x	
5	ClimaGuide	S		x	x	x	x	x	x	x	x	x
6	ComViz	MS	x	x	x	x	x	x	x	x	x	x
7	Ecocities	MS	x	x		x	x	x	x			x
8	EconAdapt	G	x	x	x	x	x	x	x	x	x	x
9	HazusMH	MS	x	x			x	x			x	
10	MACC	G	x	x	x	x	x	x	x	x	x	x
11	MoweIt	MS		x				x	x	x	x	
12	NatureServe	G	x	x	x	x	x	x	x	x	x	x
13	ND-GAIN	G	x	x	x	x	x	x				x
14	SLR-CFI	MS	x	x			x	x				
15	SNAP	G	x	x	x	x	x	x	x	x	x	x
16	UKCIP	G	x	x	x			x	x	x	x	x
17	UrbanAdapt	MS	x	x		x		x	x	x	x	x

Analysis indicated that the majority of tools deal with all climate change impacts and all sectors approach. In addition, the most elaborated weather impact is flood. It is evident that multi sector combined with multi hazard approach tools are most developed, since they provide a holistic support for stakeholders to adaptation planning process.

Table 3. Tools classification according to adaptation planning steps

No	Tool name	Information engagement, Scoping	Vulnerability assessment	Scenario building	Adaptation planning	Implement & Monitor
1	Baltic	x	x		x	
2	BlueSpot		x			
3	ClimaVulM	x	x			
4	Climada		x	x	x	
5	ClimaGuide	x	x	x		
6	ComViz	x	x	x	x	
7	Ecocities	x	x	x		
8	EconAdapt	x	x			
9	HazusMH		x	x		
10	MACC				x	x
11	MoweIt	x		x		
12	NatureServe			x	x	
13	ND-GAIN	x	x			
14	SLR-CFI	x	x	x		
15	SNAP				x	x
16	UKCIP	x	x	x	x	x
17	UrbanAdapt	x	x	x	x	x

4.3 Classification of Adaptation Tools According to Adaptation Planning Steps

Another key characteristic of tools is how they support their users to planning process. Different tools perform different functions and are useful at different steps in climate adaption planning, which are: (i) Information, Engagement and Scoping, (ii) Vulnerability Assessment, (iii) Scenario Building, (iv) Adaptation Planning, and (v) Implementation & Monitoring. A key element for selecting the proper tool for a task is to have a well-identified planning process, so for each tool, we have examined which step of adaptation planning serves and results are listed in Table 3.

Results showed that the tools which have all steps planning approach are rather limited. In our research, we have found only two tools able to cover all five steps. These tools are Urban Adaptation Support tool and UKCIP Adaptation Wizard.

4.4 Software Tools Classification

Software tools are further classified according to functionality, mode of use and modeling algorithms, as presented in Table 4. They are web-based or standalone

Table 4. Software tools classified according to functionality and mode of use

No	Tool name	Software tool			Use mode		Modeling algorithms used
		Visualize	Modeling	DSS	Web based	Download	
1	ClimaVulM	x			x		Data visualization, WordPress, Javascript Framework (jquery)
2	Climada		x			x	Probabilistic model, Matlab functions
3	ClimaGuide	x			x		Environmental Data Visualization, OpenLayer maps and Javascript Frameworks (AlloyUI, YUI, jquery)
4	ComViz	x		x		x	3D Visualization, Realtime predictive model, decision tree
5	Ecocities	x			x		Environmental and Geophysical spatial data visualization on map, openlayer map, jquery
6	HazusMH		x			x	Predictive model
7	MACC		x			x	Excel based tool
8	MoweIt	x			x		Data Visualization, Javascript Frameworks and Google Maps
9	NatureServe			x		x	Decision tree, predictive model
10	ND-GAIN	x			x		Data visualization on maps, Javascript Framework (jquery, node.js, D3, backbone.js, underscore.js)
11	SLR-CFI	x			x		Env. Data Visualization on map

downloadable applications and they are further classified into three broad categories according to their functionality [9]: (1) *Visualization Tools* create simulations based on GIS and graphics to help stakeholders understand and envision potential consequences of different management decisions. They are easy to use and do not require specialized software or hardware. Increasingly, they are available via Internet. (2) *Modeling Tools* model current and potential future conditions of geophysical and socioeconomic processes. Being the most technically challenging tools, they often require GIS software, appropriate hardware, expertise and training. Models also require local data on the process being investigated. (3) *Decision Support Tools (DSS)* help develop scenarios of future conditions resulting from potential climate change effects and management decisions. They can help develop what if scenarios that allow users investigate a wide variety of management outcomes.

The majority of software applications, as presented in Table 4, integrate with existing GIS software and provide user-friendly interfaces and pre-assembled modeling functions. Most visualization tools are web based, while modeling and DSS tools are downloaded applications.

4.5   Strengths and Weaknesses of Adaptation Tools

Finally, after examining tools operation and technical characteristics, we have evaluated strengths and weaknesses of these selected tools, and results are presented in Table 5:

Table 5. Strengths and weaknesses analysis

No	Tool name	Main strengths	Main weaknesses
1	Baltic	Methodology easy to understand; Can be used as a model of regional adaptation planning	- Not enough data to make informed decisions; Example links stopped working
2	BlueSpot	All sectors and hazards; Suitable for new roads the planning phase; Potential to expand to other counties.	It requires extensive data related to precipitation, elevation etc. around the targeted road networks
3	ClimaVulM	Covers all countries worldwide; Financial analysis on clim.change; Policy development guidance & resource allocation	Data classifications of confidence levels; Uncertainty factor
4	Climada	Variety of simulated hazards; Simulation of natural catastrophes, costs and damages; Open source; Allows users to write their own modules	Some modules might not have been thoroughly tested, but core climada works without limitations; Uncertainty factor
5	ClimaGuide	Comprehensive tool; Wide range of climate related information; Can be combined with Baltic Climate Tool	Some parts of the tool are available in Finnish only; Local scope, only for Finland
6	ComViz	Interactive decision-support tool; Versatile, widely used well supported, and updated; Connects with Hazus-MH and Nat.ServVista	No built-in data and relatively little built-in modeling; Uncertainty factor; Not free, high cost to obtain
7	Ecocities	Wide variety of scenarios presented on a map; Template for vulnerability assessment; Can be combined with Urban Adaptation tool	It has a very limited scope, covering only the region of Manchester; Uncertainty factor
8	EconAdapt	Rich library of economics of CC adaptation; Detailed deliverables in adaptation process; Easy accessible	Some aspects of the toolbox do not seem to work properly; Uncertainty factor
9	HazusMH	Large-scale for planning, mitigation, emergency preparedness and response; Intuitive graphic and tabular formats; GIS software to map hazard and economic loss; Vehicle & traffic data	Components of default inventory data may not line up on maps, e.g. bridges and roads; Can run out of memory and fail during coastal floodplain delineation for complex regions
10	MACC	Useful manual and tutorial videos; The auto-generated indicator and progress charts; The charts and monitoring data can be exported	As with many Excel-based tools, formula can be deleted or altered; Uncertainty factor
11	MoweIt	Wide variety of information; Library of good practices and methodologies; Visualization tool for transport network	Not very detailed analysis on results calculations; Uncertainty factor
12	NatureServe	Covers integration and modeling assessment; Works with a variety of other tools; Number of conservation elements, objectives & multiple land-use.	Raster-based platform; Limited scale; The breadth of functions provided may lead to a slow learning curve; Uncertainty factor
13	ND-GAIN	A wide variety of sectors on almost every country; Comparison methods of countries and explanation; The tool is updated bi-annually	Incomplete measures of institutional and governmental capacity; Uncertainty factor
14	SLR-CFI	User friendly; GIS analysis for coastal areas; Visualizes impacts of sea; Diversity of information	Deficient inundation scenarios; Cannot customize outputs
15	SNAP	Can be used by a variety of stakeholders and in different projects	Requires preparation, conducted outside the tool and not supported
16	UKCIP	Captures information on weather events; Assesses organization vulnerability; Range of tools for adaptation strategy plans	Does not produce a tailor made climate adaptation strategy at the click of a button
17	UrbanAdapt	A complete methodology covering all steps; Feedback from user; Covers a wide range of different regions.	It is more focused on municipality-urban levels

5   Conclusion

Climate change adaptation has become a necessity for critical infrastructures. Research work has been done to investigate adaptation tools, suitable for transport sector, with emphasis on methodology assessments and supportive applications. Adaptation Tools are classified based on typology and target audience, activity sectors, climate impacts and adaptation planning steps. Moreover, the software tools are classified according to their functionality and mode of use. The majority of tools have been developed to deal with all climate change impacts and have an all sectors approach, in order to provide a holistic support for stakeholders to adaptation planning process. GIS functionality is incorporated into many decision-making and climate adaptation processes. Seeing that many of the questions raised by climate change planning are landscape-based, they are better addressed by geospatial visualization tools.

Out of the methodology tools examined, the Urban Adaptation Support Tool is a complete methodology-guide, which leads policy makers throughout all adaptation steps, covering all possible climate impacts and the majority of vulnerable sectors. It provides a comprehensive literature database for each step of the adaptation cycle. Also, UKCIP Wizard provides a variety of functionalities to help user plan his adaptation strategy and evaluate organization vulnerability to current and future climate. From software tools, Climada is the most advanced among European initiatives. It uses probabilistic modeling and projects vulnerabilities along with effectiveness evaluation of adaptation measures. From the US developed tools, we have distinguished the CommunityViz software which provides 3D real-time visualization, covers all steps in planning process and works as an interactive decision support tool. It is well maintained and can cooperate with other tools, like Hazus & NatureServeVista, which adds up in building adaptive capacity.

Finally, having examined strengths and weaknesses for each tool, we have collected main enforcing attributes like usability, modeling competencies, future projections and data visualization. On the other hand, scope limitations, missing data, broken links and information robustness are listed as main weaknesses. Last but not least, the uncertainty factor, which deals with climate projections, along with impact assessment ambiguity, is the main shortcoming for effective adaptation planning. As a result, adaptation tools should constantly improve their data robustness and modeling algorithms to avoid driving stakeholders to unnecessary measures, costs and complexity on adaptation policies and actions.

References

1. IPCC: Climate Change 2014: Impacts, Adaptation and Vulnerability, Part A: Global and Sectoral Aspects, Contribution of Working Group II to the 5th Assessment Report of the Intergovernmental Panel on Climate Change, p. 1132. Cambridge University Press, Cambridge (2014)
2. Committee on Climate Change and US Transportation: Potential Impacts of Climate Change on US Transportation. Special Report 290. National Academy of Sciences, USA (2008)

3. European Environment Agency: Adaptation of transport to climate change in Europe. EEA Report No 8/2014. EU (2014)
4. Willows, R.I., Connell, R.K.: Climate adaptation: risk, uncertainty and decision-making, p. 154pp. UKCIP Technical report, Oxford, UK (2003)
5. Mendizabal, M., et al.: RAMSES Transition Handbook & Training Package. RAMSES (Reconciling Adaptation, Mitigation and Sustainable Development in Cities), FP7, EU, February 2017
6. Stergiopoulos, G., Kotzanikolaou, P., Theocharidou, M., Lykou, G., Gritzalis, D.: Time-base critical infrastructure dependency analysis for large-scale and cross-sectoral failures. IJCIP **12**, 46–60 (2016)
7. Stergiopoulos, G., Vasilellis, E., Lykou, G., Kotzanikolaou, P., Gritzalis, D.: Critical infrastructure protection tools: classification and comparison. In: Proceedings of the 10th International Conference on Critical Infrastructure Protection, USA (2016)
8. Lykou, G., Stergiopoulos, G., Papachrysanthou, A., Gritzalis, D.: Protecting transport from climate change: analysis & classification of adaptation options. In: Proceedings of the 11th International Conference on Critical Infrastructure Protection, USA, March 2017
9. Rozum, J.S., Carr, S.D.: Tools for Coastal Climate Adaptation Planning: A Guide for Selecting Tools to Assist with Ecosystem-Based Climate Planning. NatureServe, Arlington (2013)
10. Baltic Climate for Spatial Research and Planning, Baltic Climate Toolkit. https://toolkit.balticclimate.org/en/the-project
11. SWAMP (Storm WAter prevention Methods to Predict) Blue Spot Model. https://toolkit.balticclimate.org/en/the-project
12. DARA: Climate Vulnerability Monitor. http://daraint.org/climate-vulnerability-monitor/climate-vulnerability-monitor-2012/
13. Bresch, D.N.: Climada. https://github.com/davidnbresch/climada/wiki
14. Climate Guide: Climate Change Impacts in Finland. http://ilmasto-opas.fi/en/datat
15. Placeways LLC and the Orton Family Foundation, CommunityViz. http://communityviz.city-explained.com/communityviz/
16. EcoCities: The Bruntwood Initiative for Sustainable Cities, The Ecocities Spatial Portal. www.ppgis.manchester.ac.uk/ecocities/
17. Pan-European Consortium: Led by the University of Bath, EconAdapt. http://econadapt.eu/
18. US Department of Homeland Security FEMA: HAZUS-MH: Hazards-United States-Multi-Hazard. https://www.fema.gov/hazus
19. MACC: Monitoring Adaptation to Climate Change. http://climate-adapt.eea.europa.eu/metadata/tools/monitoring-adaptation-to-climate-change-macc
20. MOWE-IT: Management of Weather Events in the Transport System. http://www.mowe-it.eu/
21. NatureServe: NatureServe Vista. http://www.natureserve.org/conservation-tools/natureserve-vista
22. ND-GAIN: Notre Dame Global Adaptation Index. http://index.gain.org/
23. NOAA Coastal Services Center: Sea Level Rise and Coastal Flooding Impacts. https://coast.noaa.gov/digitalcoast/tools/slr.html
24. AdaptationCommunity.net: SNAP: Stocktaking for National Adaptation Planning. http://www.adaptationcommunity.net/knowledge/mainstreaming/tools/snap/
25. Mayors Adapt, Urban Adaptation Support Tool. climate-adapt.eea.europa.eu/tools/urban-ast/
26. Environmental Change Institute and University of Oxford, UKCIP Adaptation Wizard. http://www.ukcip.org.uk/wizard/

Timing-Based Anomaly Detection in SCADA Networks

Chih-Yuan Lin$^{(\boxtimes)}$, Simin Nadjm-Tehrani$^{(\boxtimes)}$, and Mikael Asplund

Department of Computer and Information Science, Linköping University, Linköping, Sweden
{chih-yuan.lin,simin.nadjm-tehrani,mikael.asplund}@liu.se

Abstract. Supervisory Control and Data Acquisition (SCADA) systems that operate our critical infrastructures are subject to increased cyber attacks. Due to the use of request-response communication in polling, SCADA traffic exhibits stable and predictable communication patterns. This paper provides a timing-based anomaly detection system that uses the statistical attributes of the communication patterns. This system is validated with three datasets, one generated from real devices and two from emulated networks, and is shown to have a False Positive Rate (FPR) under 1.4%. The tests are performed in the context of three different attack scenarios, which involve valid messages so they cannot be detected by whitelisting mechanisms. The detection accuracy and timing performance are adequate for all the attack scenarios in request-response communications. With other interaction patterns (i.e. spontaneous communications), we found instead that 2 out of 3 attacks are detected.

Keywords: SCADA · Industrial Control System (ICS)
Anomaly detection · Traffic periodicity

1 Introduction

A SCADA system is an Industrial Control System (ICS) that operates public and private industrial processes including critical infrastructures. Such systems are becoming increasingly dependent on information and communication technologies and being connected to the Internet. This poses new challenges related to cyber security while allowing improved flexibility and ease of use of the systems.

Being less protected and more sensitive to software updates (or malware protection updates) than a typical office environment makes additional security measures in ICS necessary. Also, ease of exposure to cyber attacks once the physical levels of security is breached (e.g. insider attacks) requires a new look at how to protect these critical environments.

Compared with standard information and communication systems, SCADA systems exhibit more stable and persistent communication patterns since the communications are triggered by polling mechanisms. Typically, a master device requests data from field devices such as Programmable Logical Controller (PLC)

© Springer Nature Switzerland AG 2018
G. D'Agostino and A. Scala (Eds.): CRITIS 2017, LNCS 10707, pp. 48–59, 2018.
https://doi.org/10.1007/978-3-319-99843-5_5

or Remote Terminal Unit (RTU) periodically in order to provide a real-time view of the industrial processes. This makes anomaly detection based on timing a potentially viable approach to detect unknown adverse events such as those potentially caused by insider threats.

The published literature regarding timing variation detection in SCADA systems mostly aims at flooding-based attacks, recognizable as dramatic changes of the network throughput [1–3]. Some works also focus on directly modeling the inter-arrival times of periodic messages. These Intrusion Detection Systems (IDS) usually deploy relaxed detection thresholds to avoid high false positive rates. However, there are many attacks that only cause subtle changes on every single inter-arrival period in between communication messages. For example, TCP sequence prediction attacks can be difficult to recognize with existing techniques. To our knowledge, there is no SCADA-specific IDS that has successfully detected this kind of attacks.

In this paper, we propose a solution for timing-based anomaly detection in SCADA networks by monitoring statistical attributes of traffic periodicity. Our approach uses sampling distribution of the mean and the range to model the inter-arrival times of repeated messages in the same master-PLC/RTU flow. This approach has been widely used in statistical process control area to monitor the stability of processes. The contributions of this paper are:

- Analyzing the periodicity of SCADA traffic collected from real and emulated systems and showing that the traffic periodicity exists in both the request and response direction including some asynchronous events.
- Presenting three attack scenarios being formed of only valid requests/ responses but breaking the traffic periodicity.
- Exploring the sampling distribution approaches for timing-based anomaly detection and showing that the proposed IDS can detect the timing-based attacks through changes of mean and dispersion in request/response inter-arrival times event though the change is small in every single inter-arrival time.

The rest of the paper is organized as follows. Section 2 provides the background. Section 3 presents the related work. Section 4 describes the threat model. Section 5 elaborates the proposed IDS. Section 6 describes how the attacks are generated for testing and evaluates the detection results. We conclude this paper in Sect. 7.

2   Background

This section provides an overview of SCADA protocols and their communication modes. It also presents a brief introduction of sampling distribution of sample mean and sample range.

2.1 SCADA Protocols

The communication between the master device and field devices relies on SCADA-specific protocols built upon different communication technologies like serial communication and TCP/IP. In this work, we analyze three different protocols: Modbus, Siemens S7 and IEC 60870-5-104. These protocols are widely used in SCADA systems but allow different communication modes.

- Modbus: There are several Modbus protocols: Modbus RTU and Modbus ASCII are used in serial communication, often RS232. Modbus TCP is used for TCP communication. In this paper, we use a dataset based on Modbus RTU for testing and refer to it as simply Modbus. The Modbus protocol uses a synchronous request-response communication mode. The SCADA master initiates requests/commands stating the request type and starting address. The field device then responds by sending the requested data.
- Siemens S7: We use the S7-0x32 proprietory protocol on top of TCP/IP stack and refer to it as S7 in the rest of the paper. In addition to the synchronous communications, S7-0x32 PLCs may asynchronously send messages from predefined memory areas, called Parameter Items, under certain conditions. Moreover, S7 protocol allows requesting multiple Parameter Items in one message.
- IEC 60870-5-104: This is a standardized application layer protocol built upon TCP/IP stack. The protocol allows balanced/unbalanced communications. In the unbalanced mode, only the master can initiate communications to field devices. On the contrary, both the master and field devices can initiate communications in the balanced mode. This protocol allows both synchronous and asynchronous messages. The field devices can send Spontaneous and Periodic messages from predefined addresses, called Information Object Address (IOA). We will refer to the IEC 60870-5-104 protocol as IEC104 in this paper.

2.2 Sampling Distribution of Sample Mean and Sample Range

Sampling distribution of sample mean and sample range are two metrics widely used in statistical process control to monitor the stability of a production process. In these cases, quality assurance staff take a few sample sets of a certain attribute from produced products (e.g., weight of bottles) and calculate the sample mean and sample range for each sample set $X = \{x_1, \ldots, x_W\}$.

The sample mean is defined as $\bar{X} = \sum x_i / W$. It can provide a measure of central tendency. The distribution of $\bar{X}$ is called sampling distribution of the sample mean. For a finite number of sample means $\bar{X}_j, j = 1, \ldots, k$, one can compute their center of distribution as $\bar{\bar{X}} = \sum \bar{X}_j / k$ and standard deviation $\sigma_{\bar{X}}$ by the Central Limit Theorem (CLT). Based on CLT, for any population with mean μ and standard deviation σ, $\bar{X}$ tends toward being normally distributed with

$$\mu_{\bar{X}} = \mu \tag{1}$$

$$\sigma_{\bar{X}} = \frac{\sigma}{\sqrt{W}} \tag{2}$$

when the sample size increases.

The sample range $R_j = max(X_j) - min(X_j)$ can state the natural variation in a process. The distribution of R_j for finite sets of X_j is called sampling distribution of the sample range. The center of this distribution is $\bar{R} = \sum R_j/k$. People in this area usually assume the population they take samples from follows a normal distribution. Under this assumption, one can estimate the σ_R with $\bar{R}$ and sample size. However, we do not make any specific assumption on the distribution of the population. Instead we use Eq. (4) in Sect. 5.2 to estimate it.

Sample mean and sample range display variations from their historical distribution when the process is stable. If the variations exceed predefined thresholds, Upper Limitation (UL) and Lower Limitation (LL), it means the system conditions changed. In this paper, we use mean and range to model the message inter-arrival times. For the sake of simplicity, we refer to the sampling distribution of the sample mean and the sample range as the *mean model* and the *range model* in the rest of the paper.

3 Related Work

IDSs that exploit the overall timing attributes such as average packet inter-arrival time and bytes sent in a certain time interval are an active research area. Barbosa et al. [4,5] investigated the use of spectral analysis methods to uncover traffic periodicity. Udd et al. [6] propose and implement the TCP sequence prediction attack for the IEC104 protocol but this attack is not detected by their IDS, which uses average inter-arrival times of packets grouped by their header type. Other works presented so far are mostly validated with flooding/DDoS attacks [1,2]. The main limitation of these approaches is the "semantic gap". These approaches demonstrate that traffic patterns can be used for anomaly detection but provide little insights about which packets caused the anomalies.

To enhance the detection ability for more attack types, IDSs exploiting deep packet inspection technologies and timing models have been proposed. Sayegh et al. [3] model the inter-arrival times between signatures (i.e., a sequence of packets) and validate their approach with large amount of injected signatures. Barbosa et al. [7] propose an approach to model the period of repeated requests in an orderless group. The authors evaluate this approach with Modbus and MMS[1] datasets without attacks and set relaxed thresholds to avoid high false positive rates. This makes it difficult to detect subtle changes within a single period.

More recently, sequence-aware intrusion detection systems are subject of interest. Yang et al. [8], Goldenberg and Wool [9], and Kleinmann and Wool [10–12] use deterministic finite automata to model the message sequences of IEC104, Modbus TCP and S7 respectively. Casselli et al. [13] model the sequence of messages in discrete-time Markov chains in order to detect sequence attacks. These approaches model the order of messages. As a result, they cannot detect timing changes if the order of messages are not changed in the attack.

---

[1] https://www.iso.org/standard/28059.html.

4   Threat Model

Our work focuses on attacks composed of valid messages, which cannot be detected by simple whitelisting. This section introduces three attack scenarios and the expected violation of the mean and range models. This is to provide an intuition for our approach to anomaly detection.

4.1   Flooding-Based Attacks

Bhatia et al. [1] propose and implement a Modbus flooding attack. It disrupts the operation of normal commands by sending a huge amount of same commands with different instruction values to the same address on the targeted PLC. In Report to the President's Commission on Critical Infrastructure Protection[2], a similar attack scenario is described. An attacker can cause water hammer effect and damage the system by rapidly opening and closing the major control valves on the water pipeline. These attacks rely on many repetitions of specific messages in a short time, and thus cause decreased average message inter-arrival time and violate the mean model as illustrated in Fig. 1. Blue points represent the sample mean in a sliding window containing four inter-arrival times (i.e., sample size = 4).

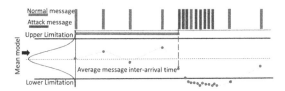

Fig. 1. Illustration of how a flooding attack violates the mean model (Color figure online)

4.2   Injection Attacks

Due to lack of authentication mechanisms in many SCADA networks, an attacker can easily capture, modify, and inject a message into the network. Morris et al. [14] provide an overview of different injection attacks in their work. Figure 2 illustrates the timing changes on the mean and range attributes caused by a single message injection.

4.3   TCP Sequence Prediction

TCP sequence prediction is an attempt to spoof a trusted host and inject a series of packets in a TCP session. Udd et al. [6] present a SCADA-specific TCP sequence prediction attack. In this work, the attacker can be someone who knows

---

[2] https://resources.sei.cmu.edu/library/asset-view.cfm?assetid=12731.

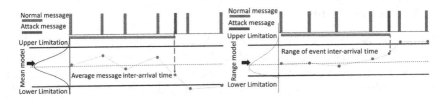

Fig. 2. Illustration of how a single injection attack violates the mean and range model

the traffic periodicity (e.g., an insider). Since the connection in SCADA networks can last for a long time, the attacker can insert a series of packets with predicted sequence numbers just before the real packets come. As a result, the network equipment considers the real packets as TCP retransmission packets and drops them. However, an attack packet may also be dropped if it comes later than the real packet. Figure 3 presents the changes on range attributes.

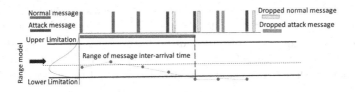

Fig. 3. Illustration of how the TCP prediction violates the range model

5 Proposed Intrusion Detection System

The proposed system contains three main modules: first, the extractor module extracts timestamps of events (i.e., messages having same features) in the same master-PLC/RTU flow. Second, the learner module builds the mean and range models and defines their thresholds. Finally, the detector module runs the testing data and raises alarms when the event inter-arrival times depart from learned models. Figure 4 illustrates the workflow of the experiments. The solid rectangles are IDS modules. The extractor is written is Python and the others are in R language.

Fig. 4. System components used in our experiment workflow

5.1   Extractor Module

Based on the assumption that the master device periodically reads/writes data from certain memory addresses in a PLC/RTU, the extractor module identifies unique sets of request-response events from two attributes: request type and requested addresses. For the asynchronous events, the extractor only uses their addresses. Each of the attributes can contain a number of features. For example, the requested addresses of S7 comprise the Item Count (number of Parameter Items) and the locations of Parameter Items. The Extractor then outputs the event sets, together with their timestamps, in a protocol-independent text file.

5.2   Learner Module

The learner module is responsible for constructing the mean and range models of event inter-arrival times and setting detection thresholds.

Mean Model. For every event set $E = \{e_1, \ldots, e_{m+1}\}$, there exists a corresponding set of inter-arrival times $T = \{t_1, \ldots, t_m\}$ in the learning dataset. Instead of computing $\bar{X}$ as described in Sect. 2, we use CLT to construct the mean model based on Eqs. (1) and (2). Since the μ and σ are unknown, we estimate them with the mean and standard deviation of the subpopulation T.

$$\mu \approx \bar{T} = \frac{1}{m} \sum_{i=1}^{m} t_i \tag{3}$$

$$\sigma \approx S_T = \sqrt{\frac{1}{m-1} \sum_{i=1}^{m} (t_i - \bar{T})^2} \tag{4}$$

We set detection thresholds, UL and LL, as $\mu_{\bar{X}} \pm N\sigma_{\bar{X}}$, where N is a performance parameter called threshold level. Note that the LL needs to be positive to provide detection ability since all the inter-arrival times are positive.

$$\mu_{\bar{X}} - N\sigma_{\bar{X}} > 0 \tag{5}$$

Equations (1), (2), and (5) imply that the LL is positive when the sample set size $W > (\frac{N\sigma}{\mu})^2$.

Range Model. We continue with the selected sample size W and event set E. For every $W + 1$ events, there exists a set of inter-arrival times $T^j = \{t_1^j, \ldots, t_W^j\}, j = 1 \ldots, \left\lfloor \frac{m+1}{W+1} \right\rfloor$. We calculate the sample range R_j and $\bar{R}$ as described in Sect. 2 and use Eq. (4) to estimate σ_R. The UL is defined as $\bar{R} + N\sigma_R$ but we set LL as the smallest event inter-arrival time in the learning period since the range model can be asymmetric.

5.3   Detector Module

During the detection phase, the module uses a sliding window which has the same window size as the sample size W. The module calculates the sample mean and sample range in each window and raises an alarm if the mean or range is outside the UL-LL interval. We consider an alarm as a true positive if there is at least one attack event in the window. Otherwise, the alarm would be considered a false positive.

6   Evaluation

To evaluate the effectiveness of proposed IDS, we implement and test the attacks stated in Sect. 4. This section contains the description of datasets and the results regarding the detection accuracy and timing performance of our approach.

6.1   Datasets

The experiments use three datasets: (1) An emulated S7 traffic from 4SICS[3] ICS Lab with real Siemens devices, (2) A Modbus system log from real control networks for building ventilation systems provided by the company Modio, and (3) An IEC104 traffic from the virtual SCADA network RICS-EL that is developed in our project, emulating an electricity utility network extending FOI Cyber Range And Training Environment (CRATE)[4], as shown in Table 1.

We use the first 1/10 of data for learning and the remaining for testing. We find that the request-response events (X-req/X-res) come in pairs and have identical $\bar{T}$ and S_T rounded up to first decimal place. In addition, these events have lower Variance to Mean Ratio (VMR) compared with spontaneous events.

Table 1. Overview of datasets and event sets used for experiments

	Duration	# of Events	Event set	# of Events	$\bar{T}$ [s]	S_T [s]
S7	14 h	106378	S-req	53189	1.0	0.014
			S-res	53189	1.0	0.014
Modbus	5 days	161062	M-req1	5984	59.9	2.8
			M-res1	5984	59.9	2.8
			M-req2	1197	297.9	25.1
			M-res2	1197	297.9	25.1
IEC104	24 h	61714	I-Spont	16831	4.9	2.9

---

[3] https://download.netresec.com/pcap/4sics-2015/4SCICS-GeekLounge-151022. pcap.
[4] Swedish Defense Research Agency (https://www.foi.se).

Figure 5 illustrates the extracted events from the learning period for the three datasets. The Y axes indicate the sequence number of events in each event set and X axes present the arrival times of these events. In S7 traffic, there exists only one pair of request-response event sets, S-req and S-res, which are presented as blue and red circles. In Modbus traffic, the extractor identifies 97 pairs of event sets in a master-PLC flow. These 97 pairs of event sets are further grouped by their sizes. The group 1 and 2 event sets present a persistent communication pattern, in which we select one event set in each group and refer to them as listed in Table 1. Though group 3 event sets contain too few events for learning, by manual examination, their events actually arrive around every 12 h. By contrast, IEC104 traffic lacks persistent request-response periodicities. The request-response events only exists in a short period of time (from 4300–4800 s) and there is a rate change between 4400–4500 s. Most of the communications are spontaneous events and only event sets from IOA 10091 and 10092 show persistent and stable communication patterns. We select the 10091 event set for testing and refer to it as I-spont. Other spontaneous events are either not persistent (IOA 10001, IOA 5005) or not stable (IOA 10010-10017).

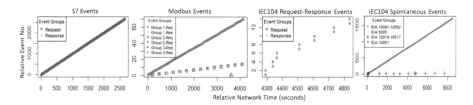

Fig. 5. Event arrival times of identified event sets for S7, Modbus and IEC104 data (Color figure online)

6.2   Attack Generation

We implement an attack generator in Python to insert synthetic events for attacks presented in Sect. 4. The generator divides testing data into many segments (see below) and inserts an attack in each segment. This section presents how to insert an attack for each attack type.

- Flooding-based Attack: We identify that the shortest event period in all our datasets is about 1 s. We generate synthetic flooding attack events every 100 ms with some random variations. The variations are produced from Gaussian distribution with standard deviation of 10 ms. An attack lasts for 1 min. A segment is 20 min long for S7 dataset and 100 min long for the others.
- Injection Attack: The generator inserts one event in the beginning of every segment with the random variations sampled from the same Gaussian distribution as above. It also adopts the same setting of segments as above.
- Prediction Attack: The generator uses the learned $\bar{T}$ and S_T of inter-arrival times. It attempts to insert one malicious event in the time that is one S_T

ahead of $\bar{T}$. An attack repeats the insertion 100 times in series. A malicious event will be accepted only when it arrives earlier than the original event. Otherwise, it will be discarded silently. A segment is 1000 events long.

6.3 Detection Accuracy

We present the detection accuracy using True Positive Rate (TPR), False Positive Rate (FPR) and Overall Detection Rate (ODR). TPR is defined as number of true alarms divided by number of windows with attacks, FPR is defined as number of false alarms divided by number of windows without attacks, and ODR is number of detected attacks divided by number of attacks.

There are two tunable parameters in the proposed IDS, sample/window size (W) and threshold level (N). We do the following experiments with $W = 5$ and $N = 4$ for the S7 and Modbus datasets; $W = 5$ and $N = 3$ for IEC104 dataset. Figure 6 shows the FPRs of range detector under different settings when we run the S7 test data without any inserted attacks. The FPRs in other datasets are similar. This shows stable FPRs over different sample sizes.

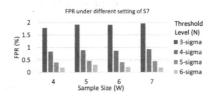

Fig. 6. False positive rates observed when tunning the W parameter (S7 data)

Table 2 is a summary of the detection performance in percentage (%). The results average the measures over segments. For the flooding attack, the mean model performs well (i.e., has high TPR) for all the datasets as we expected. To our surprise, the range model also has over 99% TPRs on flooding attack in the Modbus and IEC104 datasets. This is because the event inter-arrival times and ranges in Modbus and IEC104 datasets are in the order of seconds. However, the event inter-arrival times of flooding attack are in the order of milliseconds. Therefore, the revised range after the attack in milliseconds become lower than LL. For the injection attack, both the mean and range model perform well on request-response event sets. However, it is difficult to detect a single injected event in IEC104-spont events due to the high VMR. For the prediction attack, only the range model can be used to detect this kind of event as expected and its TPR is a bit lower since the IDS spends more time to detect an attack (see next section). However, it still shows a high ODR. All of the cases have FPR under 1.4%.

6.4 Timing Performance

The Mean-Time-to-Detection (MTTD) measurement is based on Average Number of Events (ANE). More specifically, it records the time when the IDS raises

Table 2. Detection performance

	Flooding					Injection					Prediction				
	Mean		Range			Mean		Range			Mean		Range		
	TPR	FPR	TPR	FPR	ODR	TPR	FPR	TPR	FPR	ODR	TPR	FPR	TPR	FPR	ODR
S-req	99.9	0.01	59.1	0.8	100	96.2	0.01	100	0.8	100	0.1	0	90.6	0.8	99.8
S-res	99.9	0.2	56.4	1.1	100	96.6	0.2	99.5	1.1	100	0.2	0.2	91	1.1	99.5
M-req1	99.8	0	99.6	1.1	100	83.3	0	83.3	1.1	100	0	0	92.8	1.3	99.1
M-res1	99.8	0	99.6	1.1	100	83.3	0	83.3	1.2	100	0	0	91.9	1.4	99.1
M-req2	99.8	0	100	0	100	83.1	0	100	0	100	4.9	0	100	0	100
M-res2	99.8	0	100	0.3	100	83.1	0	100	0.3	100	4.9	0	100	0.3	100
I-spont	99.8	0.4	98.1	1.1	100	2.4	0.4	3.7	1.1	13.3	2.8	0.4	72.4	1.1	92.8

its first alarm for an attack and counts how many events have passed since the beginning of the attack. ANE averages the measurements over segments. The MTTD is therefore defined as $ANE \times Avg\_period$. The Avg_period is 100 ms for flooding attacks and learned $\bar{T}$ of each dataset for the other attacks. Table 3 shows the ANE and MTTD for different attacks. Most of the time, the proposed IDS can detect attacks immediately but prediction attacks take longer time to detect on average.

Table 3. Average number of event and mean-time-to-detection for different attacks

	Flooding		Injection		Prediction	
	ANE	MTTD	ANE	MTTD	ANE	MTTD
S-req	0.05	5 ms	0.025	25 ms	5.72	5.7 s
S-res	0.05	5 ms	0.025	25 ms	5.72	5.7 s
M-req1	0.4	40 ms	0.08	4.8 s	5	299.5 s
M-res1	0.08	8 ms	0.08	4.8 s	5	299.5 s
M-req2	0.08	8 ms	0.08	23.8 s	4	1190.8 s
M-res2	0.08	8 ms	0.08	23.8 s	4	1190.8 s
I-spont	3.87	387 ms	3	14.7 s	5	24.5 s

7   Conclusions

SCADA traffic exhibits persistent and stable communication patterns. This paper studied three attack scenarios formed by valid requests only and then proposed an anomaly detection system, which uses sampling distribution of sample mean and sample range to model the timing of repeated events. We tested and evaluated the proposed IDS with Modbus, S7, and IEC104 traffic. The proposed IDS performs well in all the request-response events, resulting in over 99% for overall detection rate and less than 1.4% for false positive rates. However, it is difficult to detect a single injected message on spontaneous events due to the high VMR of the inter-arrival times.

Acknowledgement. This work was completed within RICS: the research centre on Resilient Information and Control Systems (www.rics.se) financed by Swedish Civil Contingencies Agency (MSB). The authors would also like to thank the support by Modio.

References

1. Bhatia, S., Kush, N., Djamaludin, C., Akane, J., Foo, E.: Practical Modbus flooding attack and detection. In: Proceedings of the Twelfth Australasian Information Security Conference, AISC (2014)
2. Valdes, A., Cheung S.: Communication pattern anomaly detection in process control systems. In: IEEE Conference on Technologies for Homeland Security, HST (2009)
3. Sayegh, N., Elhajj, H.I., Kayssi, A., Chehab, A.: SCADA Intrusion Detection System based on temporal behavior of frequent patterns. In: 17th IEEE Mediterranean Electrotechnical Conference (2014)
4. Barbosa, R.R.R., Sadre, R., Pras, A.: A first look into SCADA network traffic. In: IEEE Network Operations and Management Symposium, NOMS (2012)
5. Barbosa, R.R.R., Sadre, R., Pras, A.: Towards periodicity based anomaly detection in SCADA networks. In: IEEE Conference on Emerging Technologies & Factory Automation (2012)
6. Udd, R., Asplund, M., Nadjm-Tehrani, S., Kazemtabrizi, M., Ekstedt, M.: Exploiting Bro for intrusion detection in a SCADA system. In: Proceedings of the 2nd ACM International Workshop on Cyber-Physical System Security, CPSS (2016)
7. Barbosa, R.R.R., Sadre, R., Pras, A.: Exploiting traffic periodicity in industrial control networks. Int. J. Crit. Infrastruct. Prot. **13**, 52–62 (2016)
8. Yang, Y., McLaughlin, K., Sezer, S., Yuan, Y., Huang, W.: Stateful intrusion detection for IEC 60870-5-104 SCADA security. In: IEEE PES General Meeting (2014)
9. Goldenberg, N., Wool, A.: Accurate modeling of Modbus/TCP for intrusion detection in SCADA systems. Int. J. Crit. Infrastruct. Prot. **6**(2), 63–7 (2013)
10. Kleinmann, A., Wool, A.: Accurate modeling of the siemens S7 SCADA protocol for intrusion detection and digital forensic. J. Digit. Forensics Secur. Law **9**(2), 4 (2014)
11. Kleinmann, A., Wool, A.: A statechart-based anomaly detection model for multi-threaded SCADA systems. In: Rome, E., Theocharidou, M., Wolthusen, S. (eds.) CRITIS 2015. LNCS, vol. 9578, pp. 132–144. Springer, Cham (2016). https://doi.org/10.1007/978-3-319-33331-1_11
12. Kleinmann, A., Wool, A.: Automatic construction of statechart-based anomaly detection models for multi-threaded SCADA via spectral analysis. In: Proceedings of the 2nd ACM Workshop on Cyber-Physical Systems Security and Privacy (2016)
13. Caselli, M., Zambon, E., Kargl F.: Sequence-aware intrusion detection in industrial control systems. In: Proceedings of the 1st ACM Workshop on Cyber-Physical System Security, CPSS (2015)
14. Morris, T.H., Gao, W.: Industrial control system cyber attacks. In: Proceedings of the 1st International Symposium for ICS & SCADA Cyber Security Research (2013)

Operational Resilience Metrics
for a Complex Electrical Network

Alberto Tofani[1]([✉]), Gregorio D'Agostino[1], Antonio Di Pietro[1],
Giacomo Onori[2], Maurizio Pollino[1], Silvio Alessandroni[3], and Vittorio Rosato[1]

[1] ENEA Casaccia Research Centre, Via Aguillarese 301, 00123 Rome, Italy
{alberto.tofani,antonio.dipietro,
maurizio.pollino,vittorio.rosato}@enea.it
[2] Department of Engineering, University of RomaTre, Rome, Italy
[3] Areti SpA, Piazzale Ostiense 2, 00154 Rome, Italy
silvio.alessandroni@areti.it

Abstract. The Electrical Distribution Network is a Critical Infrastructure which plays a primary role in citizen life. Resilience is a relevant property to be achieved as it allows the network to withstand all types of perturbations affecting its functions and allowing to provide its service with continuity. Resilience comes out from a combination of a number of specific properties related to both intrinsic network technologies and to operator's management skills. This work reports on the results obtained by using a model for estimating Resilience applied to a real network (the electrical distribution network of the city of Roma) which accounts for most of the parameters influencing the effective resilience of the network. Results confirm that the model can appropriately handle a real network and provide valuable insights to electrical operators.

Keywords: Resilience metrics · Electrical distribution network
(Inter)dependency · Cascading failures

1 Introduction

Resilience is a relevant systemic property allowing to measure the capability of a system (embedded and interacting with other technological and/or social systems) to withstand a perturbation (due to faults, natural or anthropic disruptive events) which, causing physical damages, or simply disconnecting one or more elements, might produce a reduction (or the loss) of all, or of a part of, the service that it delivers [1,2].

The assessment of the impact of a perturbation on a Critical Infrastructure (CI) cannot disregard the estimate of the effects that the induced reduction (or loss) of service produces on related systems. Cascading perturbations can back-propagate and have negative feedbacks which could also reduce initial network restoration capabilities. A typical example of connected CI are the electrical and telecommunication networks: the first needs the second to tele-control its

© Springer Nature Switzerland AG 2018
G. D'Agostino and A. Scala (Eds.): CRITIS 2017, LNCS 10707, pp. 60–71, 2018.
https://doi.org/10.1007/978-3-319-99843-5_6

elements from a remote Control Room, while the second needs the energy supplied by the first to deploy its services (among which the tele-control service offered to the electrical network). They are often labelled as interdependent systems.

However further properties affect the resilient behavior of a network [3,4], some of them depending on the employed technologies, others on the operator management efficiency:

1. the topology of the network which has much to do with its robustness and functionality. For an Electrical Distribution Network (EDN) the term topology encompasses both the graph structure of the network and the position of the switches along the distribution lines. Both properties have an impact in determining the overall resilient response of the network;
2. the presence along the distribution network of a number of tele-controlled CI elements which could be reached from a Remote Control Room in case of problems and/or of automatic elements enabling a rapid decoupling of the faulted branch from the rest of the line. The lower the number of such units, the weaker is the remote controllability of the system and longer the required restoration times;
3. efficiency in the remote control of the network. This can be achieved by redundant connections to telecommunication networks or private (and secure) wired communication networks;
4. the efficiency with which restoration procedures are carried out and, ultimately, the efficiency of the whole emergency management (i.e. the times needed to carry out the different restoration actions);
5. the amount of technical resources available on the field when manual interventions on CI elements are needed.

The purpose of the present work is manifold:

- Developing a model enabling the estimate of the Resilience of a EDN, by appropriately taking into account all issues (1–5) above;
- Performing a measurement of the current resilience of a real CI (the EDN of the city of Roma) and to test the model capability of producing Resilience estimate on the network when specific improvements in one of the issues (1–5) above are applied;
- Open the way to a more general model where perturbation effects are spread over a larger number of connected networks. In this first attempt, EDN is only connected to the part of telecommunication network allowing telecontrol operation of EDN nodes. In a more general model (under elaboration), other networks (gas, water distribution) will be connected to the EDN and the telecommunication networks, and the overall effects of perturbations spreading over all the networks appropriately inserted into the resilience metrics.

Next sections will be devoted to the definition of the resilience model; to the description of the algorithm (RecSim) allowing the simulation of the effects of a perturbation on the EDN and of all the actions which are carried out to completely restore the electrical service; to present the obtained results; to draw some conclusions and prompting new ideas for further activities.

2   Operational Definition of Resilience

Let us assume to have an EDN characterized by its topology, with nodes N and links L corresponding to electrical stations and electrical lines, respectively. Electrical stations are either Secondary Stations (SS) containing medium-to-low tension transformers and Primary Stations (PS) containing high-to-medium tension transformers. Let us also assume that each element of EDN is **remotely tele-controlled** or **not tele-controlled**. All PS are tele-controlled, while only a fraction of SS are tele-controlled. Electrical stations are assumed to be in one of the three functional states:

- **on** (when it is physically intact and its functionalities are available)
- **disconnected** (when it is still physically intact but functionally unavailable)
- **damaged** (when it is physically damaged and thus functionally unavailable)

PS are assumed to be always in the **on** state. Each tele-controlled node is related to a telecommunication Base Transceiver Stations (BTS) enabling the tele-control functionality: in turn each BTS is energetically supplied by one EDN node (these EDN nodes do not usually coincide). The EDN-BTS dependency map for the city of Roma has been identified thanks the collaboration of the electrical distributor and the telecommunication operators.

Let us assume that there is a function of the states of all the elements of the EDN, call it F, such as

$$F(N, L, t) = 0 \quad \forall t \tag{1}$$

if all elements N and L are in **on** state and all tele-control functionalities are active. Let us now introduce a perturbation function P that can change the state of one EDN element from the **on** state to one of the other possible states. In such a case

$$P : F(N, L, t) \rightarrow F'(N, L, t) \tag{2}$$

where $F'(N, L, t) > 0$ for $t \in [0, T]$ and zero elsewhere. For the sake of simplicity, we will apply the perturbation P only to SS. Time T represents the time when all elements have been repaired and the network comes back to its fully functional state F. Perturbation P, in principle, could affect one (or more) electrical station and bring it (or them) from the **on** state to **disconnected** or the **damaged** states. Throughout this work, perturbation P will act on one SS at a time, bringing it from the **on** to the **damaged** state. The damage of a SS consequent to the introduction of P produces a sequence of perturbations on the network. These consist in the disconnection of other nodes along the line due to instantaneous opening of protection switches. The **damaged** node is replaced by a Power Generator (PG) to ensure electrical continuity to the node's customers. It will not be repaired in the time space of the simulation but its function restored through the settlement of a PG. The disconnected nodes, in turn, are reconnected either through a tele-control operation (if available) or by dispatching technical crews to provide manual reconnection. All such interventions require specific times which are considered when defining a restoration sequence of interventions.

We measure the impact of the perturbation P on the EDN by measuring a Key Performance Indicator (KPI) which is currently used by the italian Energy Authority to estimate the level of service continuity of an EDN. Such KPI is expressed as the number of disconnected customers n_i of the i-th EDN node times the duration τ_i of its disconnection. Such a value is expressed in terms of *kilominutes* (i.e. 10^3 min). Thus if the damage of the i-th SS of the network will result in the disconnection of m SS, each for a time τ_j, the overall KPI outage metrics will be measured in terms of Γ_i

$$\Gamma_i = \sum_{j=1}^{m} n_j \tau_j \tag{3}$$

If we identify the KPI with the integral of the perturbation effects of P on F as in Eq. 2, we can write:

$$\int_0^T F'(N, L, t)dt = \Gamma_i \tag{4}$$

Γ_i thus represents the extent of the consequences that the damage of a EDN element (the i-th node) can produce, by using an official KPI as metrics. Larger the value of Γ_i, weaker the capability of the network to withstand the perturbation in terms of consequences that the EDN customers will suffer. As the value of Γ_i depends on all the issues (1–5) above described, it would not be inappropriate to correlate the value of Γ_i with the inverse of the Resilience concept $\mathbf{R}$. In other terms

$$\mathbf{R}^{-1} \propto \Gamma_i \tag{5}$$

We can generalize the concept by checking the EDN behavior versus all possible perturbations. The overall operational network Resilience will be thus associated to the value of the integral of the distribution function of all the Γ_i values $(D(\Gamma))$ resulting to the failure of each one of the N nodes of the EDN (normalized with respect to the total number of nodes N):

$$\mathbf{R}^{-1} \propto \frac{\int D(\Gamma)d\Gamma}{N} \tag{6}$$

Lower the integral of Eq. 6, higher the operational Resilience of the EDN network. The RecSim algorithm enables to carry on such a "crisis game" consisting in the estimate of all Γ_i resulting from the application of the perturbation P to each of the nodes of the EDN and in the evaluation of the distribution $D(\Gamma)$. Each "crisis game" is carried out by fixing specific input conditions (1–5) to the network. We can then repeat the crisis game by modifying one or more input parameters in a way to appreciate the effect of such modification in improving the EDN Resilience.

3 The RecSim Algorithm

The Fig. 1 shows the input of the RecSim simulator and its output (i.e. the consequence of a perturbation P in term Γ_i). In particular, the Fig. 1 highlights the relationships among the simulator input and the resilience properties of points (1–5) introduced in Sect. 1. RecSIM inputs are:

- *Network topology* - expressed as the EDN graph and the perturbation P represented by the SS in brought in the **damaged** state. In this work, perturbation P is introduced by the user. However, the node brought in the **damaged** state can also result from the analysis of external perturbation (i.e. weather forecast) and result from an over-threshold probability of damage of a node induced by a natural hazard (like e.g. in the CIPCast platform, see [5]);
- *SCADA system* - expressed in terms of the set Ω of SS that can be remotely tele-controlled;
- *Efficiency of SCADA system* - expressed in terms of the functioning status of the BTS providing communication service to the EDN (BTS_{st}) and in terms of tlc_t, the time needed to perform a remote operator action (using the EDN SCADA functionalities);
- *Efficiency of restoration procedures* - expressed in terms of the time needed by an emergency crew (a) to reach a damaged SS (tr_t), (b) to perform a manual reconnection action (m_t) and (c) to set in place a PG to feed the users of the **damaged** SS (or of other SS which will result to be isolated and thus needing a PG as they were **damaged**). The input time values represent "mean" values as they have been provided by the electrical operator. RecSim perform simulations by using these values as mean values of a flat distribution from which time values to be used in the simulation are randomly extracted;
- *Technical resources* - expressed in terms of the number C of technical crews available in the field. The number of available PGs is assumed to constitute an unlimited resource. Further development of the algorithm will consider the finiteness of available PGs.

The details of the RecSIM algorithm have been reported in [6] where a prototypical JAVA implementation of the simulator has been presented. The current version of RecSim presents a number of improvements: (1) the implementation is able to treat with EDN topology where each medium-tension distribution line has, in general, a tree-like structure, (2) the new algorithm is more efficient as it circumscribes the portion of the EDN interested by the cascading effects, (3) the implementation uses an efficient Python library (Networkx [7]) allowing to represent and study complex networks. Such a library provides data structures for representing many types of graphs (simple, directed, with parallel edges and self-loops etc.) and, in addition, it provides a number of algorithms for calculating network properties (e.g. shortest paths, betweenness centrality, clustering) and (4) the use of Python has allowed the easy integration of the RecSim module in different platforms (i.e. CIPCast workflow, Areti online platform).

The output of RecSim is represented by the value of the impact of the damage scenario (represented by the perturbation P and by its cascading effects) on the

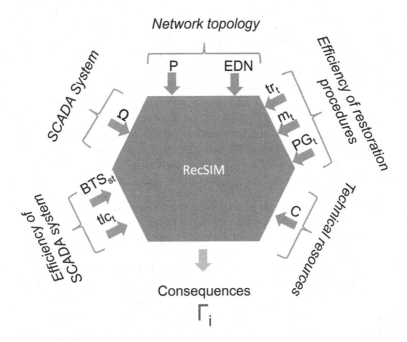

Fig. 1. The RecSim simulator

EDN, considering all the actions performed (in series or in parallel, as many technical crews were simultaneously available): (a) the **damaged** node and, whenever the case, the isolated node substitution with a PG; (b) the manual reconnection of **disconnected** nodes by the available technical crews and (c) the automatic reconnections made through remote telecontrol operations. These actions restores the EDN in a normal operating status. Upon these actions, all users are supposed to be reconnected to the grid. As previously said, **damaged** SS are just substituted by a PG and, at the end of the simulation, they are still in the **damaged** state although their function is guaranteed by the PG. The impact of P is thus computed using the Eq. 3.

4   Results

RecSim has been used to study the behavior of the whole EDN of the metropolitan area of Rome (Roma Capitale). This network contains $N = 13980$ SS and by $M = 74$ PS. Perturbation P affects only SS, bringing them from the **on** to the **damaged** state. The input parameters in the RecSim simulation are thus the following:

– the network topology, in terms of the position of the switches along the distribution lines. This has been defined as in the *"normal" configuration* as provided by the electrical operator;

- the available tele-control: whereas all PS are tele-controlled, not all SS are tele-controlled. A constant, small fraction of tele-controlled SS are supposed to be "physiologically" not-controllable (due to maintenance of the telecommunication network or to other possible causes);
- the number of technical crews available on the field;
- the number of available PG: this is considered as an unlimited resource (technical crews have as many PG available as they need);
- the typical times for the interventions: average times for each possible type of interventions (as provided by the electrical operator) are input in the model. The times needed by each intervention in the simulation are randomly extracted by a flat distribution having input times as average values.

We have performed several simulations where we have varied some of the input parameters to estimate the effects on the resulting EDN Resilience value. In the first set of simulations (S1) we have varied the number of available technical crews on the field.

Simulation results consist in the distribution of Γ values resulting from the damage, one at a time, of each SS in the EDN. The value of the integral of $D(\Gamma)$ (see Eq. 2) is then used to provide the overall Resilience of the network.

Table 1 reports the parameters used for the S1 simulations, which results are shown in Fig. 2 and reported in Table 2. It is worth recalling that, as $X \equiv R^{-1}$, larger the value of X lower the Operational Resilience. An increase of X thus represents a reduction of Operational Resilience of the EDN.

Table 1. Parameters used for S1 simulations

Model parameters S1 simulations	
Network topology	Normal configuration
Number of technical crews available on the field	$2, 4, 6, 8$
Time for tele-control operation (tlc_t)	$5 \pm 2 \, \text{min}$
Time for technical intervention on-site ($travel_t$)	$45 \pm 10 \, \text{min}$
Time for installing an electrical generator (pg_t)	$180 \pm 20 \, \text{min}$
Fraction of tele-controllable SS being not tele-controllable	0.4%

Figure 2 shows the log-log behavior of the $D(\Gamma)$ distribution of $kmin$ for the two limiting values of the number of available technical crews (note that, for confidentiality reasons, the scale values of $kmin$ have been omitted). Results show the presence of a large number of cases where the damage of a single SS node does not produce a significant effect while there is a certain number of SS whose damage will result in large consequences (large Γ values). As the simultaneous number of SS to be restored is always quite small, the effect of increasing the number of technical crews does not produce significant improvements (see results shown in Table 2) where, for convenience, the score with 4 technical crews available is considered as a baseline. Whereas moving from 2 to 4 technical crews

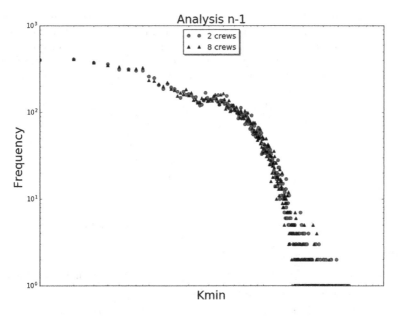

Fig. 2. $D(\Gamma)$ distribution of the estimated consequences for each single perturbation affecting the network (the perturbation brought one SS into a *damaged* state). The scale on the abscissa has not been shown, as agreed with the electrical operator, for confidentiality reasons.

produces a sizable Resilience improvement, the further increase of this number to 6 and 8 does not provide any appreciable resilience improvement.

Other simulations have been carried out to analyse the performances of the EDN in different conditions which allowed us to vary other input parameters:

- the effects of *low traffic* and *high traffic*, in a way to reproduce the effects of traffic congestions (S2 and S3 simulations, respectively). These effects are reproduced by reducing (or dilating) the characteristic averages times needed for the different types of interventions.
- the effects of *SCADA system availability* to simulate the EDN performance problems on the tele-control system are present (S4 simulation set). This problem can have different causes as for example telecommunication network problems (i.e. in these cases the SCADA components are working properly but there is no communication between the control room and the EDN elements) or SCADA components failures. The electrical operator constantly monitors the availability of the network SCADA system. A *low SCADA system availability* condition represents the case when the fraction of not-controllable SS is twice as much as in normal conditions (i.e. 0.8% with respect to the "physiological" 0.4% see Table 1).

Tables 3 and 4 report the parameters used for the S2 and S3 simulations.

Table 2. The table reports the results considering the case 4 technical crews as the referring point (i.e. in these experiments the availability of 4 technical crews is considered the base condition). The results are showed in term of relative increase/decrease of to the integral of the Γ with respect to the referring point (this also to comply with the request of the electrical operator of preventing the disclosure of absolute values.

No. of technical crews	R^{-1}
2	$X \sim +2.2\%$
4	X
6	$X \sim -0.2\%$
8	$X \sim -0.4\%$

Table 3. Parameters used for S2 (*low traffic*) simulation

Model parameters S2 simulations	
Network topology	Normal configuration
Number of technical crews available on the field	4
Time for tele-control operation (tlc_t)	$5 \pm 2\,\text{min}$
Time for technical intervention on-site ($travel_t$)	$35 \pm 10\,\text{min}$
Time for installing an electrical generator (pg_t)	$160 \pm 20\,\text{min}$
Fraction of tele-controllable SS being not tele-controllable	0.4%

Table 4. Parameters used for S3 (*high traffic*) simulation

Model parameters S3 simulations	
Network topology	Normal configuration
Number of technical crews available on the field	4
Time for tele-control operation (tlc_t)	$5 \pm 2\,\text{min}$
Time for technical intervention on-site ($travel_t$)	$60 \pm 10\,\text{min}$
Time for installing an electrical generator (pg_t)	$220 \pm 20\,\text{min}$
Fraction of tele-controllable SS being not tele-controllable	0.4%

Tables 3, 4 and 5 report the input settings used to compare the EDN resilience in the mentioned different operational/environmental conditions. Table 6 reports the results of the different experimental settings. In order to show the relative increase/decrease of the integral of the $D(\Gamma)$ (S2–S4 simulations are compared to the S1 simulation results when the same number of 4 technical crews available on the field has been considered).

Results provide evidence that traffic might have a relevant impact on the operational resilience of the EDN. However "traffic" is just a metaphor to indicate the need of a rapid deployment of the technical crews on the field. Manual

Table 5. Parameters used for S4 (*low SCADA system availability*) simulation.

Model parameters S4 simulations	
Network topology	Normal configuration
Number of technical crews available on the field	4
Time for tele-control operation (tlc_t)	5 ± 2 min
Time for technical intervention on-site ($travel_t$)	45 ± 10 min
Time for installing an electrical generator (pg_t)	180 ± 20 min
Fraction of tele-controllable SS being not tele-controllable	0.8%

Table 6. Operational resilience score for the different operational/environmental conditions of the EDN network

Comparative results	R^{-1}
Normal conditions (S1 with 4 technical crews)	X
Low traffic (S2)	$X \sim -13\%$
High traffic (S3)	$X \sim +19\%$
Low SCADA system availability (S4)	$X \sim +20\%$

restoration times could be reduced by an optimized technical crews fleet management, and by a wise assignment of intervention to the technical crew closer to the point where the intervention is needed. This could be easily realized by a GPS tracking of the crews and their automatic assignment during emergency procedures.

5   Conclusions

In this work we have proposed a methodology to assess the operational resilience of an electrical distribution network. The RecSim algorithm is able to simulate the operational management of the distribution power grid. RecSim simulates the behaviour of the protection devices and automatic devices in the network as well as the operator actions. These actions are performed using either the SCADA system or the response teams. Considering the functioning status of the SCADA system and supporting telecommunication devices, RecSim performs the simulation, taking into account the dependencies of the operational management of the network on the internal SCADA system and the telecommunication domain. On the other hand, the simulator accounts also for the dependencies on the urban viability infrastructure by configuring specific simulation parameters. Results confirm that the RecSim model is capable to handle very large and complex urban distribution networks and to deal with a number of different properties of the network which contribute to its overall resilience to perturbations.

This work reports on the results collected in the analysis of perturbations consisting in the damage of a single SS ($n-1$ case) only. In particular, results show how the operational resilience changes with the operational/environmental settings. For the $n-1$ case, the operational resilience substantially decreases/increases by varying the fraction of non functioning SCADA system devices and/or BTS and by varying the parameters used to simulate urban congestion. For instance, the operational resilience decrease of the 20% if the number of not available tele-controlled devices are doubled with respect to the normal conditions. Decreasing of a factor ~0.2 the mean time needed by a response team to reconnect a disconnected SS, the operational resilience will increase of a factor ~0.13. Similarly, if we increase by a factor ~0.2 the same parameter, the operational resilience decreases by a factor ~0.19. The results show how, for the $n-1$ case, the operational resilience does not significantly depend on the number of the available technical crews as the simultaneous number of SS to be reconnected is usually quite small. We are currently analyzing the single SS responses in order to highlight the SS's which mostly contribute to the resilience and those which mostly weaken it. In a future work we will simulate more severe perturbations to the network, by simultaneously producing damages to two SS (located along the same distribution line, $n-2$ case). That further analysis will emphasize the role played by the configurational parameters and will further highlight the presence of those SS which strengthen the network and those which weaken the overall resilient response.

Acknowledgments. This work was developed from

- the FP7 Network of Excellence CIPRNet, which is being partly funded by the European Commission under grant number FP7-312450-CIPRNet. The European Commissions support is gratefully acknowledged;
- the Italian national project RoMA (*Resilience enhancement Of a Metropolitan Area* SCN-00064).

Responsibility for the information and views expressed herein lies entirely with the authors. The authors wants to further acknowledge the support and the contributions of several colleagues during the course of the CIPRNet and RoMA projects: Erich Rome and Jingquan Xie (IAIS, Fraunhofer Institute, Bonn), Luca Pelliccia and Roberto Baccini (Telecom Italia SpA).

References

1. www.cipedia.eu
2. Arghandeh, R., et al.: On the definition of cyber-physical resilience in power systems. Renew. Sustain. Energy Rev. **58**, 1060–1069 (2016)
3. Willis, H.H., Loa, K.: Measuring the Resilience of Energy Distribution Systems. RAND Corporation, Santa Monica (2015). https://www.rand.org/pubs/research_reports/RR883.html
4. Kwasinski, A.: Quantitative model and metrics of electrical grids resilience evaluated at a power distribution level. Energies **9**, 93 (2016). https://doi.org/10.3390/en9020093

5. Di Pietro, A., Lavalle, L., Pollino, M., Rosato, AV., Tofani, A.: Supporting decision makers in crisis scenarios involving interdependent physical systems. In: Emergency Management Society (TIEMS) (2015)
6. Tofani, A., Di Pietro, A., Lavalle, L., Pollino, M., Rosato, V., Alessandroni, S.: CIPRNet decision support system: modelling electrical distribution grid internal dependencies. J. Pol. Saf. Reliab. Assoc. Summer Saf. Reliab. Semin. **6**(3), 133–140 (2015)
7. Hagberg, A.A., Schult, D.A., Swart, P.J.: Exploring network structure, dynamics, and function using NetworkX. In: Varoquaux, G., Vaught, T., Millman, J. (eds.) Proceedings of the 7th Python in Science Conference, SciPy 2008, Pasadena, CA USA, pp. 11–15, August 2008

The Influence of Load Characteristics on Early Warning Signs in Power Systems

Steffen O. P. Blume[1] and Giovanni Sansavini[2]([⊠])

[1] Future Resilient Systems, Singapore-ETH Centre, ETH Zürich,
Singapore, Singapore
[2] Risk and Reliability Engineering Laboratory, Department of Mechanical
and Process Engineering, ETH Zürich, Zürich, Switzerland
`sansavig@ethz.ch`

Abstract. Critical infrastructure systems like the power system are in danger of abrupt transitions into unstable and oftentimes catastrophic regimes. These critical transitions occur due to the modification of certain control parameters or an external forcing acting on the dynamical system. Bifurcation analysis can help to characterize the critical threshold beyond which systems become unstable. Moreover, some systems emit early warning signs prior to the critical transition, detectable from small-scale signal fluctuations triggered by the stochasticity of the external forcing. We present here our analysis of a time-domain dynamical power system model subjected to an increasing load level and small-scale stochastic load perturbations. We confirm previous findings from other literature that the autocorrelation of system signals increases, as the load level approaches a critical threshold characterized by a Hopf bifurcation point. Furthermore, we analyze the effects of load homogeneity and load connectivity on early warning signs. We assert that load connectivity does not influence autocorrelation coefficients. In addition, we show that changes in load homogeneity shift the location of the critical threshold.

1 Introduction

Power systems have been prone to extreme failure cascades and blackout events, that were initiated by single component or operator faults [1]. These events happened despite contingency tolerances that were expected to account for an acceptable degree of component failure. Critical infrastructure systems like the power system could face similar or more severe failure events, if they are continually pushed into critical conditions that render them even more susceptible to small disturbances. They therefore need to be equipped with early warning tools that can alert about possible critical thresholds before contingencies.

In this work we focus on anticipating such critical thresholds and associated critical transitions in power systems. Critical transitions in various dynamical systems have been extensively studied and comprehensively reviewed and summarized in [2,3]. The works in [2,3] show that: (i) Complex dynamical systems exhibit generic characteristics prior to a critical transition; (ii) The generic

© Springer Nature Switzerland AG 2018
G. D'Agostino and A. Scala (Eds.): CRITIS 2017, LNCS 10707, pp. 72–83, 2018.
https://doi.org/10.1007/978-3-319-99843-5_7

character across various types of systems suggests that these transitions are related to bifurcations, governed by universal laws of complex dynamical systems; (iii) In certain cases, systems emit early warnings signs that the critical transition is imminent, such as an increase in the autocorrelation of time series measurements; and (iv) The response of networked systems under stressed conditions depends on the internal characteristics of the systems, such as homogeneity and connectivity of their components.

As opposed to studying the internal characteristics of the systems, the goal of this work is to assess the effects of external stressor characteristics on the system behaviour and early warning signs. By way of addressing this goal, this work expands on existing works on power system models and established early warning signs. We extend the analysis by studying the effect of load characteristics on the system response and corresponding changes in autocorrelation of bus voltage measurements.

The test case is a stochastic time-domain dynamical simulation of the 39-bus New England power system model. We define two controllable parameters to adjust load characteristics: load homogeneity adjusts the distribution of the total load across all load buses of the system, whereas load connectivity alters the coupling strength between stochastic perturbations superimposed on the linear load profile of each network bus. As the load level gradually increases, we measure the autocorrelation of voltage magnitude signals at network buses to detect changes that can signal a critical transition. In addition, we aim to identify differences in these early warning signs depending on different adjustments of load homogeneity and connectivity.

This work is structured as follows. First, we give a description of the current general knowledge about critical transitions and point to the existing work particularly in the field of power system models. We further explain our approach and procedure used to simulate the power system. Furthermore, we explain the definitions of load homogeneity and load connectivity. Next, we present and discuss the results, followed by conclusions.

2   Critical Transitions and Early Warning Signs

This work studies critical transitions that are related to bifurcations. Bifurcations occur because a certain forcing or control parameter modifies the characteristics and state of the dynamical system [4–6]. Once the forcing exceeds a critical threshold, i.e. the bifurcation point, the system transitions abruptly into a different, possibly unstable, state. While there exists a myriad of different types of bifurcations [4,6,7], this work only addresses Hopf bifurcations. Hopf bifurcations describe the qualitative change from a stable equilibrium into a regime influenced by strong adverse oscillations that can drive the system out of stability.

It has been shown that bifurcation points are, in certain cases, preceded by early warning signs that indicate the imminent critical transition [3,4,8–11]. In addition, these early warning signs give evidence to the behaviour of a system before the critical transition occurs. One characteristic behaviour is known as critical slowing down. It refers to the fact that the rates of change of system state variables start to reduce with increasing proximity to the critical transition, hence making it less responsive to perturbations and slower in returning to a stable equilibrium.

Most physical systems face constant irregular stochastic perturbations, resulting in small-scale fluctuations in system time series signals. These fluctuations contain patterns that can be decomposed into standard signal quantities, such as autocorrelation. An increase in autocorrelation can give strong indication of critical slowing down. Since recovery rates start to reduce near the bifurcation point, every new state will be more and more like its past state, creating an increase in autocorrelation [3,12].

2.1 Early Warning Signs in Power Systems

Many works [7,13–24] have studied bifurcations in power system models, some of which have looked at early warning signs [20–24]. Out of these five works, three have addressed early detection of critical transitions from simulated time-series dynamical data [21–23]. The analyses focus on critical slowing down prior to a critical transition and the commonly associated early warning signs, such as increase in autocorrelation and variance.

The study in [21] finds evidence of critical slowing down prior to a critical transition in power system models and a real-world example by observing lag-1 autocorrelation and variance of bus voltage magnitude signals. Following earlier work on closed-form analytical expressions for autocorrelation functions and variance of state variables in small test systems [22], the same authors develop their work further by treating a power system model for the 39-bus New England test case [23]. Their findings are an increase in autocorrelation and variance in bus voltage magnitude and line current signals prior to a Hopf bifurcation.

2.2 Gaps

Critical transitions together with the early warning signs that precede them are influenced by numerous system parameters. Among those, systemic characteristics such as the homogeneity and connectivity of system components affect how a system responds to stressors and eventually undergoes a critical transition [3]. In this work, therefore, we aim to address the effect of the external stressor characteristics on critical transition behaviour.

3 Approach

The study considers a dynamical time-domain simulation of a power system. The system is gradually brought under increased stress by introducing a linear load ramp that increases over time. With every time step and hence increase in load, the simulation uses a discrete time step integration approach to solve the system of equations. In addition, load increases are superimposed with small stochastic fluctuations.

Due to the stochasticity of the loads, the system equations are expressed in terms of a set of m-dimensional stochastic differential algebraic equations (SDAE's), that can be generally represented in the following form [25]:

$$\dot{x} = f(x, y, \eta, \dot{\eta})$$
$$0 = g(x, y, \eta) \tag{1}$$
$$\dot{\eta} = \alpha(x, y, \eta) + b(x, y, \eta)\xi$$

where f ($f : \mathbb{R}^{m_x} \times \mathbb{R}^{m_y} \times \mathbb{R}^{m_\eta} \times \mathbb{R}^{m_\eta} \to \mathbb{R}^{m_x}$) are differential equations, and g ($g : \mathbb{R}^{m_x} \times \mathbb{R}^{m_y} \times \mathbb{R}^{m_\eta} \to \mathbb{R}^{m_y}$) are algebraic equations that govern the power system mechanics[1]. The variables x ($x \in \mathbb{R}^{m_x}$) are differential state variables (i.e., machine transient voltages, rotor speeds, and rotor angles), whereas y ($y \in \mathbb{R}^{m_y}$) are algebraic variables (i.e., bus voltage magnitudes and phases, machine currents and voltages, and electrical and mechanical torques). Stochastic terms are given by η. The component α ($\alpha : \mathbb{R}^{m_x} \times \mathbb{R}^{m_y} \times \mathbb{R}^{m_\eta} \to \mathbb{R}^{m_\eta}$) is the drift, and b ($b : \mathbb{R}^{m_x} \times \mathbb{R}^{m_y} \times \mathbb{R}^{m_\eta} \to \mathbb{R}^{m_\eta} \times \mathbb{R}^{m_w}$) represents the diffusion of the stochastic differential equations (SDE's), governed by the stochastic process w ($w \in \mathbb{R}^{m_w}$). The variable ξ denotes white noise.

3.1   Load Modelling

We define a stochastic load ramp superimposed with stochastic fluctuations, such that the time-dependent active and reactive load components at each load bus n and iteration i are

$$p_{L_{n,i}} = p_{L_{n,0}}\lambda_i + \eta_{p_{n,i}} = p_{L_{n,0}} + \sigma^2 \xi_{n,i}$$
$$q_{L_{n,i}} = q_{L_{n,0}}\lambda_i + \eta_{q_{n,i}} = q_{L_{n,0}} + \sigma^2 \xi_{n,i} \tag{2}$$

where the variables $p_{L_{n,0}}$ and $q_{L_{n,0}}$ are the initial ($t_0 = 0$) active and reactive loads at load bus n, respectively. The load level λ_i is given in terms of $\lambda_i = (1 + k_t t_i)$, where k_t is a fixed parameter to adjust the ramp rate. Additionally, loads are perturbed by stochastic noise components, based on the stochastic load model presented in [25]. We define the stochastic perturbations $\eta_{p_{n,i}}$ and $\eta_{q_{n,i}}$ in terms of Gaussian white noise processes with zero mean and variance equal to σ^2. The variable $\xi_{n,i}$ is a Gaussian random number ($\xi \sim \mathcal{N}(0,1)$) sampled at every iteration step i.

---

[1] In case of the 10-machine 39-bus New England power system model used here, the system of equations consists of 85 differential and 138 algebraic equations: 4 differential and 4 algebraic equations for each of the G generators ($G = 10$); 5 differential and 2 algebraic equations for every generator with a turbine governor and voltage regulator ($G^* = 9$); 2 algebraic equations for each of the $N_b = 39$ network buses; and 2 algebraic equations for the synchronous reference frequency and rotor angle; Thus $m_x = (4G + 5G^*)$ differential equations and $m_y = (4G + 2G^* + 2N_b + 2)$ algebraic equations. Stochastic perturbations in both the active and reactive components of each of the $N = 19$ loads result in $m_\eta = 2N$.

3.2   Definition of Load Connectivity and Homogeneity

The connectivity ζ between the random noise component of the stochastic perturbations is defined such that

$$\xi_{n,i} = \zeta \xi_i' + \sqrt{1 - \zeta^2} \xi_{n,i} \tag{3}$$

where $\xi_{n,i}$ is the Gaussian noise sampled for each load bus n, and ξ_i' is a Gaussian prior sampled only once at each integration step i.

Homogeneity, h, parameterises the load distribution and is defined such that the active and reactive loads are

$$
\begin{aligned}
p_{L_n} &= p_{L_n}' (1 - h) + h \frac{p_{tot}}{N} \\
q_{L_n} &= q_{L_n}' (1 - h) + h \frac{q_{tot}}{N}
\end{aligned}
\tag{4}
$$

where N is the total number of load buses. The variables p_{tot} and q_{tot} are the total active and reactive loads summed over all load buses, respectively. A fully homogeneous load distribution is equivalent to a uniform allocation of loads, where all loads are equal in magnitude. In contrast, a non-homogeneous load distribution assumes the original default load values (i.e., p_{L_n}' and q_{L_n}') for the given power system model. Note that independent of the value for h, the total consumed power remains the same.

4   Case Study

We investigate early-warning signs of imminent critical transitions by applying the methodology in Sect. 3 to the 10-machine 39-bus New England power system test case in [26]. The stochastic time-domain dynamical simulation is implemented using the open-source Matlab®-based Power System Analysis Toolbox (PSAT) [27]. Most of the data for the 39-bus test case is gathered from [26]. The model is refined by including torque damping coefficients that are adopted from a similar system [28]. Additionally, turbine governor data is included into the simulations, and given in Table 1.

Our approach uses a linearly increasing continuous load ramp with a ramp rate of 1/90 min^{-1} (i.e., $k_t = 5400^{-1}$ [s^{-1}]). This is equivalent to doubling the load after 1.5 h and is considered slow enough to not create machine transients that could distort the signals of interest [21]. At the same time that loads are increased, they are perturbed by small-scale stochastic variations as described in Sect. 3.1. The variance of the stochastic white noise perturbations is set to $\sigma^2 = 1.4 \times 10^{-6}$. The simulation integration time step is equal to 0.01 s.

The stochastic simulation is evaluated ten times at each of the 25 test sites given by the combinations of load homogeneity, $h = \{0.0, 0.25, 0.5, 0.75, 1.0\}$, and load connectivity $\zeta = \{0.0, 0.25, 0.5, 0.75, 1.0\}$. The work in [21] uses low-pass Gaussian Kernel Smoothing to filter out the slow trends in the voltage magnitude signals, due to the load ramp. The resulting residual was used to determine the early indicators. Here, the stochastic signals are detrended using a deterministic base case. The deterministic solution only assumes the linear load ramp without any stochastic load perturbations. Given the voltage signal outputs from a stochastic simulation run and the deterministic solution, the effects of the slowly increasing load ramp can be filtered out by subtracting the deterministic signals from the stochastic signals.

The autocorrelation coefficients are computed over a rolling window of 270 s length[2], which captures both low-frequency changes and avoids correlated signal components being concealed by uncorrelated noise [21]. The standard equations for determining the sample autocorrelation of time-series signals [29] can be found in the appendix (c.f. (8)). The window is moved over the entire signal by approximately 100 steps. The autocorrelation time lag is chosen as 0.2 s, which is in line with comparable works [23]. With an integration step size of 0.01 s, the 270 s window and the 0.2 s time lag hence correspond to 27,000 and 20 data points, respectively. All simulations are implemented in PSAT and executed on the high-performance computing cluster, EULER, of ETH Zürich.

5 Results and Discussion

As the system loads increase, generators compensate for the system frequency and bus voltage changes by elevating the mechanical turbine power output, hence injecting more electrical power into the system. At a sudden point, however, the system responses, measured in terms of bus voltages and generator controls, transition into a state of strong unstable drifts and oscillations. The system condition further aggravates, as loads further increase. Eventually, the system model becomes numerically unstable, and the power system reaches an unrecoverable break-down.

5.1 Identifying the Bifurcation Point

The sudden point at which the system transitions into the unstable state is characterized by a Hopf bifurcation. The system state matrix, A_s, can be determined from the Jacobian entries of the linearized SDAE system as

$$A_s = f_x - f_y g_y^{-1} g_x \tag{5}$$

where f_x, f_y, g_x and g_y correspond to the partial derivatives of the differential and algebraic equations in Eq. (1). By eigenvalue analysis of the power system state matrix, we find that a complex eigenvalue pair moves across the imaginary axis into the right half plane at the moment when the system transitions into aggravating oscillations. This behaviour is evidence of a Hopf bifurcation [4].

The autocorrelation of the bus voltage magnitude signals measures patterns in the stochastic system response. The identification of characteristic changes, which consistently affect the system variables prior to the bifurcation, may provide early warning signs of the approaching critical transition.

---

[2] The load level increases by 0.05 within the 270 s window.

5.2   Aggregate Metrics

Autocorrelation curves are determined on the residuals of the voltage magnitude signals for each of the 39 network buses 10 times for each of the 25 test sites. The distribution of the autocorrelation coefficients is characterised according to the following definitions. The first metric for the set of autocorrelation values is their median, henceforth denoted as $\tilde{R}$ (i.e., $\tilde{R}_v$ denotes the median of the autocorrelation coefficients of bus voltage magnitudes). The second metric, denoted as the scaled percentile range (SPR), measures the spread of the set of correlation values. It is given by the difference be- tween the values adjacent and still within the minimum and maximum bounds, b_l and b_u, defined by

$$
\begin{aligned}
b_l &= q_1 - w(q_3 - q_1) \\
b_u &= q_3 + w(q_3 - q_1)
\end{aligned}
\tag{6}
$$

where q_1 and q_3 are the 25th and 75th percentile (i.e., first and third quartile) of the set of correlation values, respectively. The variable w is chosen as 1.5, which corresponds to approximately $\pm 2.7\sigma$ or 99.3% of the samples included, if the data are normally distributed. Data beyond the bounds defined in Eq. (6) are considered outliers. Hence, the SPR becomes

$$
SPR = \max_{j:R_j \leq b_u} R_{v_j} - \min_{j:R_j \geq b_l} R_{v_j}
\tag{7}
$$

The smaller the SPR is, the more the correlation values converge, reducing the spread around the median.

5.3   Early Warning Signs

Increase in autocorrelation has been identified as one of the key indicators for critical slowing down. We aggregate all of the measurable autocorrelation coefficients into two metrics, the median and scaled-percentile range (SPR), to study the effects of load homogeneity and connectivity on the early warning signs.

The Effect of Load Homogeneity. Five different curves are displayed in Fig. 1, each corresponding to a different load homogeneity. Every curve in Fig. 1 represents the average of the autocorrelation median, $\tilde{R}_v$, over all five connectivities for each homogeneity level. The shaded bands represent the scaled-percentile range SPR_{R_v}, which is also averaged over all five connectivity levels. It measures the span between minimum and maximum autocorrelation coefficients that are not considered outliers, according to the criterion defined in Sect. 5.2.

  The curves terminate at the breakdown point, shortly after the system passes the Hopf bifurcation point, which is marked by the circles in Fig. 1. The curves show that the load homogeneity influences the location of the bifurcation and break-down point. The shift of the bifurcation point is however not consistent with the change in homogeneity. Although different gradients in the spatial stress

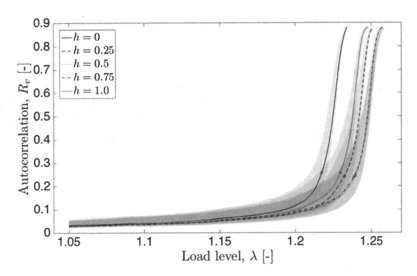

Fig. 1. Autocorrelation R_v and scaled-percentile-range (SPR_{R_v}) of bus voltage magnitude signals for five different load homogeneity levels. The SPR is shown as bands around the median. Circles plotted onto the curves mark the Hopf bifurcation point. Curves are averaged over all values of connectivity.

distribution thus alter the point where a system becomes unstable and eventually collapses, an increase in stress homogeneity, as it is defined here, does not necessarily result in a consistent shift of the bifurcation point.

In addition, the curves climb sharply upward, starting just prior to the Hopf bifurcation point. They continue to rise until the system has become irrecoverably unstable and the system breaks down. The increase in autocorrelation median confirms previous findings that the autocorrelation of system state variables increases, as dynamical systems approach a critical transition. It indicates that the voltage responses at network buses exhibit increasingly similar and dominant patterns over time - the behavior known as critical slowing down. Moreover, the SPR narrows as the system goes past the Hopf bifurcation point towards collapse, indicating that the system responses at different locations start to express similar autocorrelation patterns near and beyond the critical threshold.

The shift in the location of the critical threshold due to changes in load homogeneity also affects the shape of the autocorrelation curves in Fig. 1. However, while the bifurcation and breakdown point shift distinguishably, the onset of an observable change in autocorrelation is not distinctive enough between different load homogeneities. At a given distance from the critical threshold the autocorrelation curves do not shift by the same margin as the bifurcation points. Due to the sharp rise in autocorrelation near the bifurcation point, different curves are only discernible moments prior to the bifurcation point. Without knowledge of the underlying load distribution, early warning signs deduced from an increase in autocorrelation may therefore deem the system more stable and safer that it actually is.

The Effect of Load Connectivity. The stronger the connectivity, the more similar load fluctuations at different network buses become, although they remain to be stochastically varying over time. Figure 2 depicts curves of the autocorrelation median and SPR versus the proximity to the bifurcation point for different load connectivities. The curves represent the average over the five load homogeneity levels. The horizontal axis gives the proximity to the bifurcation point, which is marked by the zero datum.

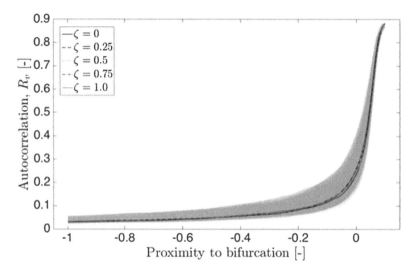

Fig. 2. Autocorrelation R_v and scaled-percentile-range (SPR_{R_v}) of bus voltage magnitude signals for five different load connectivity levels. The SPR is shown as bands around the median. The 0 tick mark indicates the Hopf bifurcation point. Curves are averaged over all values of homogeneity.

The connectivity of load fluctuations does not markedly affect the autocorrelation, according to Fig. 2. Connectivity modulates the coupling (i.e., correlation) between the stochastic load perturbations across network buses, without influencing the degree to which individual loads may be correlated with past samples over time. Consequently, the autocorrelation coefficients of voltage signal responses are expected not to show any sensitivity on the load connectivity.

6   Conclusion

In this work we analysed different load scenarios to assess their influence on early warning signs of critical transitions in power systems. We find that:

1. The autocorrelation coefficients of different bus voltage signals can be aggregated into two standard metrics, significantly reducing the number of metrics otherwise generated.
2. As has previously been established in other works, we confirm that the autocorrelation increases prior to and beyond a Hopf bifurcation point, irrespective of the scenarios considered in this analysis. The increase in autocorrelation occurs system-wide.
3. Load connectivity does not influence autocorrelation coefficients.
4. Load homogeneity shifts the location of the critical threshold, while the onset of an observable change in autocorrelation and the value of the autocorrelation coefficient at a given distance from the critical threshold does not shift by the same margin. Without knowledge of the underlying load distribution, early warning signs may therefore deem the system more stable and safer that it actually is.

Acknowledgements. We would like to thank the IT Services at ETH Zürich for the provision of computing resources and access of the EULER cluster. This research was conducted under the Future Resilient Systems program at the Singapore-ETH Centre and funded by the National Research Foundation of Singapore.

Appendix

Since this analysis deals with discrete signals, an estimate of the autocorrelation for lag k of a signal with length N is obtained from [29]

$$\hat{R}[k] = \frac{1}{N-k} \frac{\sum_{i=1}^{N-k} (x_i - \bar{x})(x_{i+k} - \bar{x})}{s^2} \tag{8}$$

where $\bar{x}$ is the sample mean of the signal and s^2 is the unbiased sample variance.

Table 1. Maximum turbine output for 10-machine 39-bus New England test case. The following control variables are equal for all generators: Droop ($R = 0.04$ p.u.), Minimum turbine output ($p^{\min} = 0.0$ p.u.), Governor time constant ($T_S = 0.5$ s), Transient gain time constant ($T_3 = 3.0$ s)

Generator no	Max. turbine output, $p^{\max}$ [$p.u.$]	Generator no	Max. turbine output, $p^{\max}$ [$p.u.$]
2	7.5	7	8.5
3	9.75	8	8.0
4	9.5	9	12.45
5	7.65	10	3.75
6	9.75		

References

1. Glavitsch, H.: Large-scale electricity transmission grids: lessons learned from the European electricity blackouts. In: Voeller, J.G. (ed.) Wiley Handbook of Science and Technology for Homeland Security, vol. 3, no. 4, pp. 1–20 (2009)
2. Scheffer, M., et al.: Early-warning signals for critical transitions. Nature **461**(7260), 53–59 (2009)
3. Scheffer, M.: Anticipating critical transitions. Am. Assoc. Adv. Sci. **338**(6105), 344–348 (2012)
4. Strogatz, S.H.: Nonlinear Dynamics and Chaos: With Applications to Physics, Biology, Chemistry, and Engineering. Westview Press, Boulder (2015)
5. Kuehn, C.: A mathematical framework for critical transitions: bifurcations, fast-slow systems and stochastic dynamics. Phys. D Nonlinear Phenom. **240**(12), 1020–1035 (2011)
6. Kuznetsov, Y.A.: Elements of Applied Bifurcation Theory, 3rd edn. Springer, New York (2004). https://doi.org/10.1007/978-1-4757-3978-7
7. Ajjarapu, V., Lee, B.: Bifurcation theory and its application to nonlinear dynamical phenomena in an electrical power system. IEEE Trans. Power Syst. **7**(1), 424–431 (1992)
8. Chisholm, R.A., Filotas, E.: Critical slowing down as an indicator of transitions in two-species models. J. Theor. Biol. **257**(1), 142–149 (2009)
9. Lade, S.J., Gross, T.: Early warning signals for critical transitions: a generalized modeling approach. PLoS Comput. Biol. **8**(2), e1002360 (2012). https://doi.org/10.1371/journal.pcbi.1002360
10. Ghanavati, G., Hines, P.D.H., Lakoba, T.I.: Investigating early warning signs of oscillatory instability in simulated phasor measurements. arXiv, pp. 1–5 (2013)
11. Kuehn, C., Zschaler, G., Gross, T.: Early warning signs for saddle-escape transitions in complex networks. Sci. Rep. **5**, 13190 (2015)
12. Ives, A.R.: Measuring resilience in stochastic systems. Ecol. Monogr. **65**(2), 217–233 (1995)
13. Alvarado, F., Dobson, I., Hu, Y.: Computation of closest bifurcations in power systems. IEEE Trans. Power Syst. **9**(2), 918–928 (1994)
14. Vournas, C.D., Pai, M.A., Sauer, P.W.: The effect of automatic voltage regulation on the bifurcation evolution in power systems. IEEE Trans. Power Syst. **11**(4), 1683–1688 (1996)
15. Rosehart, W.D., Cañizares, C.A.: Bifurcation analysis of various power system models. Int. J. Electr. Power Energy Syst. **21**(3), 171–182 (1999)
16. Carreras, B.A., Lynch, V.E., Dobson, I., Newman, D.E.: Critical points and transitions in an electric power transmission model for cascading failure blackouts. Chaos **12**(4), 985–994 (2002)
17. Lerm, A.A.P., Cañizares, C.A., Silva, A.S.: Multiparameter bifurcation analysis of the South Brazilian power system. IEEE Trans. Power Syst. **18**(2), 737–746 (2003)
18. Mendoza-Armenta, S., Fuerte-Esquivel, C.R., Becerril, R.: A numerical study of the effect of degenerate Hopf bifurcations on the voltage stability in power systems. Electr. Power Syst. Res. **101**, 102–109 (2013)
19. Ren, H., Watts, D.: Early warning signals for critical transitions in power systems. Electr. Power Syst. Res. **124**, 173–180 (2015)
20. Hines, P., Cotilla-Sanchez, E., Blumsack, S.: Topological models and critical slowing down: two approaches to power system blackout risk analysis. In: 44th Hawaii International Conference on Systems Sciences, pp. 1–10 (2011)

21. Cotilla-Sanchez, E., Hines, P.D.H., Danforth, C.: Predicting critial transitions from time series synchrophasor data. IEEE Trans. Smart Grid **3**(4), 1832–1840 (2012)
22. Ghanavati, G., Hines, P.D.H., Lakoba, T.I., Cotilla-Sanchez, E.: Understanding early indicators of critical transitions in power systems from autocorrelation functions. IEEE Trans. Circuits Syst. I Regul. Pap. **61**(9), 2747–2760 (2014)
23. Ghanavati, G., Hines, P.D.H., Lakoba, T.I.: Identifying useful statistical indicators of proximity to instability in stochastic power systems. IEEE Trans. Power Syst. **31**(2), 1360–1368 (2016)
24. Chevalier, S., Hines, P.: System-wide early warning signs of instability in stochastically forced power systems. arXiv, January 2016
25. Milano, F., Zárate-Miñano, R.: A systematic method to model power systems as stochastic differential algebraic equations. IEEE Trans. Power Syst. **28**(4), 4537–4544 (2013)
26. Pai, M.: Energy Function Analysis for Power System Stability, 1st edn. Kluwer Academic Publishers, Norwell (1989)
27. Milano, F.: An open source power system analysis toolbox. IEEE Trans. Power Syst. **20**(3), 1199–1206 (2005)
28. Pal, B., Chaudhuri, B.: Robust Control in Power Systems. Springer, New York (2005). https://doi.org/10.1007/b136490
29. Box, G.E.P., Jenkins, G.M., Reinsel, G.C.: Time Series Analysis: Forecasting and Control, 4th edn. Wiley, Hoboken (2008)

DMA Optimal Layout for Protection of Water Distribution Networks from Malicious Attack

Simeone Chianese[1], Armando Di Nardo[1,2], Michele Di Natale[1],
Carlo Giudicianni[1(✉)], Dino Musmarra[1],
and Giovanni Francesco Santonastaso[1]

[1] Dipartimento di Ingegneria, Università degli Studi della Campania
"Luigi Vanvitelli", via Roma 9, 81031 Aversa, Italy
{simeone.chianese,armando.dinardo,michele.dinatale,
carlo.giudicianni,dino.musmarra,
giovannifrancesco.santonastaso}@unicampania.it
[2] Istituto Sistemi Complessi (Consiglio Nazionale delle Ricerche), via dei
Taurini 19, 00185 Rome, Italy

Abstract. Water distribution networks (WDNs) are among the most important civil networks, because they deliver drinking and industrial water to metropolitan areas, supporting economic prosperity and quality of life. Therefore, they constitute critical infrastructures (CIs) as systems whose operability are of crucial importance to ensure social survival and welfare. In the last years, extreme natural events and intentional malicious attacks have shown that global safeguard of systems cannot be ever performed. In this regard, critical infrastructure protection (CIP) strategies should be focused both on the prevention of these events and on the procedures for the functioning recovery and damage limitation. In this paper, starting from previous works of the authors, the impact of an intentional contamination attack to water distribution network and a possible strategy to mitigate the user risk have been studied, simulating the introduction of potassium cyanide with a backflow attack into water system. As protection technique, the water network partitioning (WNP) has been adopted in order to improve the management and also to reduce the extent of damage showing a dual use-value. WNP reveals to be an efficient way to protect water networks from malicious contamination, through the closure of gate valves by a remote control system creating semi-independent District Meter Areas (DMAs). The study also investigates the possibility to identify *a priori* the most critical point of a water distribution network for the malicious attack through a novel procedure based on topological metric. The methodology, tested on a real medium size water network in Italy, shows very interesting results in terms of mitigation risk.

Keywords: Critical infrastructure · Water protection
Water network partitioning

© Springer Nature Switzerland AG 2018
G. D'Agostino and A. Scala (Eds.): CRITIS 2017, LNCS 10707, pp. 84–96, 2018.
https://doi.org/10.1007/978-3-319-99843-5_8

1 Introduction

Nowadays societies are strongly dependent on infrastructure systems – such as communication, banking, health, energy, water supply, etc. – that support economic prosperity and human life, wherein inoperability can lead to great impact on the quality of life [1, 2]. These infrastructure systems continually face threats and natural or manmade disasters that cause significant physical, economic and social disruption. For these reasons, the operators of infrastructure systems continuously work on improving safety and security. Generally, these systems are arranged in very large networks and show complex behaviour which makes difficult to analyse all possible failure scenarios. Therefore, if total security cannot be achieved, more efforts must be focused for planning effective strategies for functioning recovery and disaster limitation. In order to better realize these aims, a necessary step is represented by modelling the complex behaviours that Critical Infrastructures (CIs), as systems of systems, can exhibit [3].

Water distribution networks (WDNs) are important civil infrastructure, because they deliver water to metropolitan areas ensuring the living beings life and supporting economic prosperity. In the last years, also water systems are considered as complex infrastructure, in particular as a multiple interconnected link-node planar, spatially organized, weighted graph, with n nodes (such as pipe intersections, water sources and nodal water demands) and m links (pipes and valves) [4, 5]. They belong to the class of networks with nodes occupying precise positions into Euclidean space with edges being real physical connections and strongly constrained by their geographical embedding [6, 7], like other spatially organized urban infrastructure systems [8, 9].

WDNs are exposed to different potential sources of contamination both accidental and intentional [10]. Accidental contamination is related to occasional bad source water quality, malfunctioning chlorine stations, pipe breaks, and leak repairs, whereas malicious attacks are represented by the intentional introduction of a contaminant into the network [11–13], i.e. through a backflow attack that occurs when a pump system is utilized to overcome the local pressure at the insertion point [14]. Terrorist contamination attacks in water distribution networks can have disastrous consequence and many countries after 11 September 2001 adopted guidelines [15]. A malicious act may consist of the introduction of chemical, biochemical, microbiological, or radioactive contaminants [13]. Different papers deal with the ability of common sensors to detect noticeable changes in water quality when a contaminant is present [16], with the optimal positioning of measurement stations and the identification of point source contamination [17].

As reported in Di Nardo et al. [13], only three main actions can be performed when a WDS contamination is identified: (1) alert users not to use the contaminated water; (2) close the sector of the network to limit health risks; and (3) remove the contaminant. The implementation of an early warning system (EWS) is crucial for the first action with a good distribution of fast warning sensors over the network [18]. The effectiveness of the second action depends on the possibility of closing pipes, to disconnect network sectors after an alert of the EWS [13, 19].

Water sectors can be designed, respecting the criteria of 'dual-use value' [13], defining a water network partitioning (WNP) that divides the water network in district meter areas (DMAs) [20] aiming to improve the management and control of water systems [21]. For this purpose, Di Nardo et al. [13] highlighted that: (a) user protection increases with an increasing number of DMAs controlled by a EWS; (b) the WNP reduces the extent of the risk because several introduction points would be needed to produce a wide negative impact on the whole network; (c) the WNP allows easier protection measures to be activated because a small part of the network can be disconnected.

Generally, WNP is carried out in two main steps [22]: (a) *clustering*, aimed at defining the number, the shape and the dimension of the sub-regions and the definition of the boundary edges between clusters; (b) *dividing*, so the physical division of the system, that consists in the selection of boundary pipes on which insert gate-valves or flow-meters.

For the investigation described in this paper, the clustering phase has been carried out exploiting the property of the Laplacian matrix [23] using a spectral algorithm [24], while the dividing phase has been achieved minimizing a proper Objective Function (OF) taking into account hydraulic performance with a Genetic Algorithm.

This study analyses the advantages of defining DMAs for network protection that are compatible with hydraulic performance. The intentional contamination was modelled by the introduction of potassium cyanide in a tub that is used for a backflow attack into a water system [25]. The weakest points for such deliberate contaminant delivery was also defined by a combinatorial hydraulic simulation. The *a priori* identification of the most critical point was defined through a novel procedure based on weighted topological metric (eigenvector centrality) from complex network theory [26] in order to define *a priori* the most critical points and the parts of system on which to focus monitoring to reduce the malicious attacks. The procedure was tested on a real medium size water distribution network of Italy, that serves the city of Villaricca, near to Naples. The results show a significant reduction of risk for users.

2 Proposed Methodology

The proposed methodology is arranged in different phases synthetically described in the following sub-sections.

2.1 Malicious Attack

The malicious contamination has been described in Di Nardo et al. [13, 25] and uses the back-flow attack methodology. In particular, potassium cyanide is introduced into the water system through a single point by overcoming the local pressure and disseminates it into the network affecting progressively the areas surrounding the introduction point. The insertion point consists in a bathroom tub of a house in which the cyanide is pumped. The malicious attack is carried out in two times (from 7.00 am to 8:00 and from 9.00 am to 10:00 am) since in two hours it is possible to refill the tub and mix cyanide. The lethal concentration of potassium cyanide in water for a user whose bodyweight is 70 kg is 200 mg/l.

The backflow attack was simulated by means of water quality simulation module of EPANET 2 [27] that allows to model the transport of a dissolved species travelling along pipes.

2.2 Critical Points Identification

The most critical points in terms of negative effects for the users, measured as the total number of exposed users (N_{eu}), the number of exposed users that ingest more than the lethal dose LD_{50} (N_{eu50}) and the length of contaminated pipes L_{ep}, are computed in two different way:

(a) through a full analysis of all possible positioning of a malicious attack in the network (identifying the worst network node);
(b) through the computation of the weighted *eigenvector centrality* [26].

The investigation of the effectiveness of the second way is very interesting because it can allow to provide a simple tool to identify *a priori* the most critical points in the network without water quality simulation which require many information about water network and contaminant.

In particular, the eigenvector centrality, a topological local metric, is a good measure of node-centrality, and so it can be used to identify an intrinsic importance of nodes. In other terms, the centrality of some nodes does not only depend on the number of its adjacent nodes, but also on their value of centrality. Bonacich [26] defined the centrality $c(v_i)$ of a node v_i as positive multiple of the sum of adjacent centralities, that in matrix notation become:

$$Ac = \lambda c \tag{1}$$

Evidently, this equation can be solved by the definition of eigenvalues and eigenvectors of A. From the set of different eigenvectors, only that associate to the maximal eigenvalue can provide a centrality measure [26] and it is called *principal eigenvector* and an entry $c(v_i)$ eigenvector-centrality of node v_i.

In this study, in order to take into account also hydraulic aspects in the definition of node "centrality" improve the effectiveness of *eigenvector centrality*, the network graph was considered undirected and weighted with the pipe flow.

2.3 Clustering Phase

Water distribution network can be modelled as a graph $G = (V, E)$, where V is the set of n vertices v_i (the junctions and the delivery nodes) and E is the set of m edges e_l (the pipes). In this way, it is possible to apply the clustering algorithm of complex network theory. It is important to highlight that a k-way graph clustering problem consists in partitioning V vertices of G into k subsets, $P_1, P_2, \ldots, P_k$ such that:

- $\bigcup_1^k P_k = V$ (the union of all clusters P_k must contain all the vertices v_i);
- $P_k \cap P_t = \emptyset$ (each vertex can belong to only one cluster P_k);

- $\emptyset \subset P_k \subset V$ (at least one vertex must belong to a cluster and no cluster can contain all vertices);
- $1 < k < n$ (the number k of clusters must be different from one and from the number n of vertices).

Generally, the graphs are considered undirected and weighted, where weights express the strength of the link between elements. In this regard it is possible to take into account proximity and/or similarity between elements during the definition of the sub-graphs.

Optimal graph clustering can be achieved with many procedures, widely reported in [22, 28], with the aim of minimizing the number of boundary edges and simultaneously balancing the number of nodes in each cluster.

In this paper, a recently proposed procedure for WDN, based on spectral clustering [4], was adopted, which allows automatically defining the optimal network sub-regions layout with similar number of nodes n_i and by an edge cut set with the smallest number of pipes N_{ec} in order to improve the subsequent dividing phase, reducing the investment device cost and the hydraulic potentially deterioration. The number of clusters was defined through the *eigengap approach* [29]. According to the above said approach, six clusters were defined as optimal number of sub-regions. In particular, the clustering phase has been carried out with the normalized spectral clustering according to Shi and Malik [24]. Such a clustering procedure is based on the eigenvalues of the graph Laplacian matrix $L\ nxn$ [29], which is the difference between the diagonal matrix $D_k\ nxn$ with the connectivity degrees of the nodes ($D_k = \text{diag}(K_i)$ and K_i is the degree of a node v_i) and the adjacency matrix $A\ nxn$ (where elements $a_{ij} = a_{ji} = 1$ indicate that there is a link between nodes i and j and $a_{ij} = a_{ji} = 0$ otherwise). The used spectral clustering methods solves the relaxed version of the NCut problem defining the set of edge-cuts (or boundary pipes) N_{ec} of the water network.

In order to measure the quality of the clustering phase, the following metrics have been calculated: the *silhouette* S_h (ranging from -1 to 1, with highest value when the layout is good); the *number of edge-cuts* N_{EC} (lower value are preferable since minimize the hydraulic deterioration and initial device investment in the second dividing phase) and the *balanced index* I_B (it represents the standard deviation of the total number of nodes of the six clusters so lower value is preferable since it indicate a more balanced districts).

2.4   Dividing Phase

The clustering phase provides the edge-cut between clusters, i.e. the set of N_{ec} boundary pipes along which gate valves or flow meters must be installed. First, the number N_{fm} of flow meters to insert in the network is chosen, so that the remaining boundary pipes $N_{bv} = (N_{ec} - N_{fm})$ are closed by inserting gate valves. In order to simplify the water budget computation, N_{fm} is kept as low as possible [30]. Established the number of flow meters and gate valves, it is necessary to define which pipes have to be closed between all the possible combinations N_{DL} of water network partitioning layouts that are expressed by the binomial coefficient:

$$N_{DL} = \binom{N_{ec}}{N_{fm}} \tag{2}$$

Since the number N_{DL} is such a huge that it is often computationally impossible to investigate all the solution space also for a small water distribution network, an optimization technique has been developed, in order to find the optimal device position on the boundary pipes; in particular, the following Objective Function [28] was maximized:

$$OF = \max \gamma \sum_{i=1}^{n} Q_i H_i \tag{3}$$

it represents the total node power P_N, where Q_i and H_i are the water demand and the hydraulic head of the i-th node.

Objective Function (OF) was maximized thought a Genetic Algorithm (using the Genetic Toolbox of MATLAB©) with the following simulation parameters: each individual of the population is a sequence of N_{ec} binary chromosomes corresponding to the pipes belonging to the edge-cut set. Each chromosome assumes value 1 if a gate valve will be inserted in the j-th pipe, value 0 otherwise if a flow meter will be inserted. The GA was carried out with 100 generations of a population consisting of 500 individuals with a crossover percentage $P_{cross} = 0.8$, and a mutation rate $P_{mut} = 2\%$.

Further, the OF is constrained by the following expression, which imposes a minimum service level for the users:

$$constraint = (h_{min} \geq h^*) \tag{4}$$

where h_{min} is the minimum nodal pressure head and h^* is the network design pressure.

Some Performance Indices (PIs) were also computed to compare different scenarios and to help operators to choice the better solution in a Decision Support System; specifically:

- resilience index I_r [31], which quantify the overall performance of the network

$$I_r = \frac{\sum_{i=1}^{n_n} Q_i(h_i - h^*)}{\sum_{R=1}^{n_R} Q_R H_R - \sum_{i=1}^{n_n} Q_i h^*} \tag{5}$$

with n_n is the number of demand nodes, n_R the number of reservoirs, Q_i and h_i the demand and the head of the i-th node, Q_R and H_R the discharge and the pressure head of the generic R-th source point, and h^* the design pressure head of the network i.e. the minimum required pressure to guarantee water demand at nodes;
- the resilience deviation I_{rd} [28], which quantify the percentage reduction of energy resilience of partitioned network, I_r, compared with the resilience of the original network, I_r^*

$$I_{rd} = 1 - \frac{I_r}{I_r^*} \tag{6}$$

- the mean, h_{mean} min, h_{min}, and the max h_{max} node pressure indices;
- $N_{eu,p}$ and $N_{eu50,p}$ refer, respectively, to the number of exposed users and the users that ingest more than the lethal dose of the p-th district (or sector) of the network.

Clustering and Dividing phases allow to obtain an optimal water network partitioning (WNP) with a number of DMAs previously chosen by the operators.

3 Case Study

The proposed methodology was tested on a real medium-sized water distribution network, serving the town of Villaricca, located near Naples (Italy), with about 30,000 inhabitants [21]. Table 1 summarises the main characteristics.

Table 1. Main characteristics of the Water Distribution Network of Villaricca

n [-]	m [-]	n_R [-]	$L_{p,TOT}$ [km]	h_{min} [m]	h_{mean} [m]	h_{max} [m]	I_r [-]	h^* [m]
196	249	3	34.71	25.11	36.54	45.94	0.524	25.00

The network consists of n = 199 nodes (considering also the three reservoirs) and m = 249 links.

The hydraulic performances of the un-partitioned water distribution network of Villaricca, reported in Table 1, are good in terms of nodal pressure head, with h_{max} and h_{mean} and h_{min} higher than the design pressure head $h^* = 25$ m (the pressure head required to satisfy water demand at all nodes).

At first, the most critical points are reported in the Table 2, computed, as reported in the previous Sect. 2.2, in the two different way thought a full analysis of all possible positioning of a malicious attack in the network and through the computation of the weighted *eigenvector centrality*. The Table 2 reports the first 5 most critical points in terms of the negative impact measured by N_{eu50}. In this case study, and with a pipe weight equal to water flow, only the node 104 is in both sets. This is an interesting result but not yet useful and further investigation have to be achieved.

Table 2. Most critical point identification

Water quality simulation	Weighted eigenvector centrality
104	145
159	100
126	141
127	104
19	78

Additional information about the worst nodes as insertion point, cyanide concentrations, and other simulation details are not reported for evident safety reasons.

To analyse the effectiveness of water network partitioning and DMA sectorization to protect the water network from malicious attack, different scenarios were analysed:

- S_{WDN} = Water distribution network with no districts;
- S_{OWNP} = Optimal Water Network Partitioning with $k = 6$ DMAs;
- S_{WNSk} = Water Network Sectorization through the isolation of DMA_k.

The network hydraulic performance of WDN are reported in the Table 1. Results for the optimal water network partitioning with $k = 6$ DMAs are reported in the Table 3, in which clustering, dividing and hydraulic performance are also included. It is clear that the clustering layout is good since the $S_h = 0.705$, the $I_B = 11.44$ and the $N_{EC} = 16$ (about 6.5% of total number of pipes).

Table 3. Characteristics of the Water Network Partitioning of Villaricca with $k = 6$ DMAs

S_h [-]	I_b [-]	N_{ec} [-]	N_{fm} [-]	N_{bv} [-]	h_{min} [m]	h_{mean} [m]	h_{max} [m]	I_r [-]	I_{rd} [%]
0.705	11.44	16	7	9	25.42	35.23	47.78	0.462	11.83

It is important to highlight that the clusters must preserve the internal continuity so every node of a clusters must be linked at least to another node of the same cluster. For the continuity check, it has been exploited an important property of the Laplacian matrix [4, 29], namely the multiplicity m_a of its zero eigenvalue, that is equal to the number of connected sub-graphs of the network. So, in the case study since the number of clusters has been chosen to be $k = 6$, the multiplicity of the zero eigenvalue must to be $m_a = 6$. If $m_a > 6$, it would mean that the network has been divided into more than six sub-graphs.

After the clustering phase, the dividing phase has been carried out, computing the hydraulic performance metrics described above. As shown in Table 3, the number of flow meters has been to $N_{fm} = 7$, which is the minimum possible number that guarantees the hydraulic performance of the network in order to simplify the computation of the water budget and the identification of water losses. Clearly, the number of gate valves is equal to the difference $N_{bv} = N_{ec} - N_{fm}$.

The hydraulic performance of the partitioned water network show that from an energy point of view they are preserved with a slight reduction of the level of service for the users (Table 3).

Table 4. Contamination results for un-partitioned and partitioned WDN of Villaricca

Network	N_{eu} [-]	N_{eu50} [-]	L_{ep} [m]
S_{WDN}	9,970	5,063	13,906
S_{OWNP}	4,258	4,078	8,112

The results in Table 4 show a significant reduction of N_{eu} (about 57%), a less (but also important) reduction of N_{eu50} (about 20%). In terms of total contamination length, L_{ep}, the reduction was about 42%. This preliminary comparison shows that, even if the partitioning of network was carried out only to improve the management of the system, it can reduce, in a significant way, the negative consequence of a malicious attack preserving the hydraulic performance and so confirming the dual-use value of the partitioning as proposed in Di Nardo et al. [13].

The Fig. 1 shows the comparison between the effect of malicious contamination for the Villaricca network (S_{WDN}) without districts (a) and for the partitioned network (S_{OWNP}) (b).

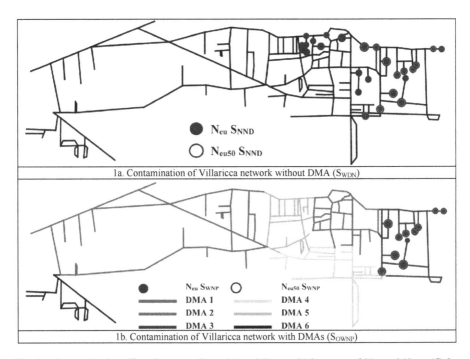

Fig. 1. Contamination effects between S_{WDN} (a) and S_{OWNP} (b) in terms of N_{eu} and N_{eu50} (Color figure online)

In Fig. 1, DMAs are indicated with different colors and the contaminated nodes are indicated with different colors and symbols (blue and full circle for the exposed users N_{eu} and red and empty circle for exposed users that ingest more than the lethal dose N_{eu50}), as explained in the legend of the figure. In particular, the diameter of each circle is proportional to the number of exposed users, the higher the diameter, the larger is N_{eu} or N_{eu50} corresponding to the node. The comparison shows as the cyanide contamination is spatially reduced in terms of pipe extension only defining six DMAs for the network. In this way, with a water network partitioning, the contaminant is limited only to DMA3 and not, as in S_{WDN}, in three DMAs (DMA2, DMA3, DMA4). This mitigation result was obtained in passive way, because no actions were activated on the network.

The study also analyses different scenarios consisting into the total closure of the contaminated DMA (water network sectorization S_{WNS}) with the isolation of a single district at 8.00 am, in the case of a single malicious attack from 7:00 am to 8:00 am, and with the insolation of the same district at 10:00 am, in the case of a double malicious attack, the first from 7.00 am to 8.00 am and the second from 9:00 am to 10:00 am. As reported in the previous studies [13, 25], the closure of the contaminated DMA one hour (at 8.00 am) or three hours (at 10.00 am) after the beginning of the malicious attack is a reasonable hypothesis for a water network equipped with an early warning system, that alerts the authorities which order the isolation of the district. The effect of water network sectorization ($SWNS_k$), for each district, in the case that the contamination starts from the most critical point of each DMA, are reported in Tables 5 and 6. In particular, the results of the isolation at 8.00 am (attack from 7:00 to 8:00 am), and the results of the isolation at 10.00 am (two attacks, from 7:00 to 8:00 am and from 9:00 to 10:00 am) are reported in Tables 5 and 6, respectively. In both Tables, the number of total users for each district is indicated with N_u.

Table 5. Simulation results for each WNS scenario of Villaricca with DMA closure at 8.00 am

DMA Isolation	N_u [-]	N_{eu} [-]	N_{eu50} [-]	L_{ep} [m]
S_{WNS1}	7,930	3,134	0	5,072
S_{WNS2}	8,042	569	0	5,508
S_{WNS3}	4,258	3,222	0	4,468
S_{WNS4}	5,539	3,604	0	4,533
S_{WNS5}	4,955	1,803	0	4,720
S_{WNS6}	570	161	92	1,612

As reported in the Table 5, even if the contamination starts from the most critical point of each district, the early warning system, allowing the closure of the corresponding district after an hour from the beginning of the malicious attack, provides an almost total protection of the network in terms of number of users that consumed more than the LD_{50} (N_{eu50}) with a minimum reduction of 98.2% for S_{WNS6}, with respect to S_{WDN}. Also in terms of exposed users N_{eu}, although the mitigation is lower, the reduction ranges from 63.85% (S_{WNS4}) to 98.40% (S_{WNS6}). The highest N_{eu50} was found for the attack in the district $k = 6$, which is the DMA with the lowest number of

Table 6. Simulation results for each WNS scenario of Villaricca with DMA closure at 10.00 am

DMA Isolation	N_u [-]	N_{eu} [-]	N_{eu50} [-]	L_{ep} [m]
S_{WNS1}	7,930	3,497	1,014	7,495
S_{WNS2}	8,042	5,519	2,196	6,162
S_{WNS3}	4,258	4,078	788	7,983
S_{WNS4}	5,539	3,604	676	4,923
S_{WNS5}	4,955	3,605	788	7,604
S_{WNS6}	570	455	455	3,068

total users (N_u). This result can be explained by considering that attacking all single districts with an equal amount of contaminant, the lower the number of users the higher the dose ingested. Therefore, since district $k = 6$ is the DMA with the lowest number of total users, it is reasonable to find, in the scenario S_{WNS6}, the highest N_{eu50} after only one hour from the attack. Also with a larger delay in the early warning (so with a district isolation at 10.00 am), as reported in Table 6, the simulation results are good

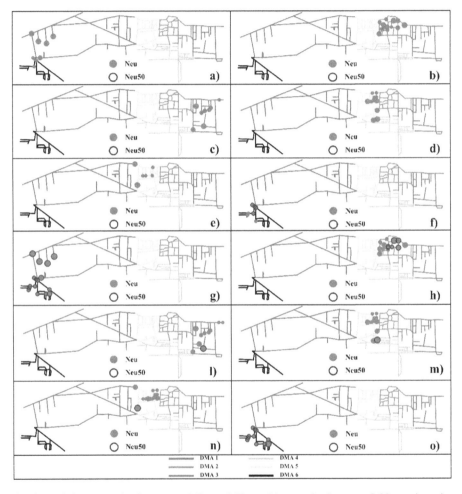

Fig. 2. Isolation scenarios in terms of N_{eu} and N_{eu50}: (a) scenario S_{WDS1} at 8:00 am, insertion point in DMA1; (b) Scenario S_{WDS2} at 8:00 am, insertion point in DMA2; (c) scenario S_{WDS3} at 8:00 am, insertion point in DMA3, (d) scenario S_{WDS4} at 8:00 am, insertion point in DMA4; (e) scenario S_{WDS5} at 8:00 am, insertion point in DMA5; (f) scenario S_{WDS6} at 8:00 am, insertion point in DMA6; (g) scenario S_{WDS1} at 10:00 am, insertion point in DMA1; (h) S_{WDS2} at 10:00 am, insertion point in DMA2; (i) scenario S_{WD3} at 10:00 am, insertion point in DMA3; (l) scenario S_{WD4} at 10:00 am, insertion point in DMA4; (n) scenario S_{WDS5} at 10:00 am, insertion point in DMA5; (o) scenario S_{WDS6} at 10:00 am, insertion point in DMA6 (Color figure online)

but, of course, worse than the ones obtained with a closure at 8.00 am. In the case of double attack, in terms of exposed users N_{eu} the range is from 44.64% (S_{WNS2}) to 95.44% (S_{WNS6}) and for N_{eu50} the range is from 56.62% (S_{WNS2}) to 91.00% (S_{WNS6}). In this case, the contamination starts from a single DMA but, with more time before the closure, it can diffuse easier in the other DMAs contaminating more users.

Finally, all the isolation scenarios were reported in Fig. 2.

By comparing Figs. 1 and 2, it is possible to observe a very different contamination condition of the network, since results reported in Fig. 1 were obtained by considering the most critical insertion point for the whole network, while results reported in Fig. 2 were obtained by considering the most critical insertion points for each DMA. In Fig. 2, it is evident the significant reduction of contaminated users.

4 Conclusion

This paper deals with a novel *a priori* definition, through a topological approach and, specifically, by the use of the weighted eigenvector centrality, of the critical points of a network, in terms of intentional contamination. This approach could be interesting because it is independent from the specific contamination event and it requires a simpler hydraulic model of contamination. The first preliminary results are encouraging but more studies are required. Moreover, the paper highlights the effectiveness of dual-use value of water network partitioning, allowing to improve the water management and to mitigate the effect of intentional contamination of the water distribution network, at the same time. The protection is wide with a significant reduction both in terms of number of exposed users and users that ingest more than the lethal dose, with respect to those of the original network without partitioning. An improvement of the protection occurs with the district isolation both after one or three hours from the malicious attack.

References

1. Bashan, A., Berezin, Y., Buldyrev, S.V., Havlin, S.: The extreme vulnerability of interdependent spatially embedded networks. Nat. Phys. **9**(10), 667–672 (2013)
2. Edwards, M.: Critical Infrastructure Protection. IOS Press, Amsterdam (2014)
3. Eusgeld, I., Kroger, W., Sansavini, G., Schlapfer, M., Zio, E.: The role of network theory and object-oriented modeling within a framework for the vulnerability analysis of critical infrastructures. Reliab. Syst. Saf. **94**(5), 954–963 (2009)
4. Di Nardo, A., Di Natale, M., Giudicianni, C., Greco, R., Santonastaso, G.F.: Water supply network partitioning based on weighted spectral clustering. In: Cherifi, H., Gaito, S., Quattrociocchi, W., Sala, A. (eds.) Complex Networks & Their Applications V. SCI, vol. 693. Springer, Cham (2017). https://doi.org/10.1007/978-3-319-50901-3_63
5. Facchini, A., et al.: Complexity science for sustainable smart water grids. In: Rossi, F., Piotto, S., Concilio, S. (eds.) WIVACE 2016. CCIS, vol. 708, pp. 26–41. Springer, Cham (2017). https://doi.org/10.1007/978-3-319-57711-1_3
6. Boccaletti, S., Latora, V., Moreno, Y., Chavez, M., Hwang, D.U.: Complex networks: structure and dynamics. Phys. Rep. **424**, 175–308 (2006)

7. Di Nardo, A., Di Natale, M., Giudicianni, C., Greco, R., Santonastaso, G.F.: Complex network and fractal theory for the assessment of water distribution network resilience to pipe failures. Water Sci. Technol.: Water Supply (2017). https://doi.org/10.2166/ws.2017.124

8. Carvalho, R., Buzna, L., Bono, F., Gutierrez, E., Just, W., Arrowsmith, D.: Robustness of trans-European gas networks. Phys. Rev. E **80**, 016106 (2009)

9. Newman, M.E.J.: The structure and function of networks. SIAM Rev. **45**, 167–256 (2003)

10. US EPA 2009: National Primary Drinking Water Regulations. US Environmental Protection Agency, Washington, DC. EPA 816-F-09-004

11. Nilsson, K.A., Buchberger, S.G., Clark, R.M.: Simulating exposures to deliberate intrusions into water distribution systems. J. Water Resour. Plann. Manag. **131**(3), 228–236 (2005)

12. Clark, R.M., Chandrasekaran, L., Buchberger, S.B.: Modeling the propagation of waterborne disease in water distribution systems: results from a case study. In: 8th WSDA Symposium, Cincinnati, OH (2006)

13. Di Nardo, A., Di Natale, M., Musmarra, D., Santonastaso, G.F., Tzatchkov, V., Alcocer-Yamanaka, V.H.: Dual-use value of network partitioning for water system management and protection from malicious contamination. J. Hydroinform. **17**, 361–376 (2015)

14. Kroll, D.: Protecting world water supplies against backflow attacks. Water Wastewater Int. **25**(2), 4 (2010)

15. US EPA 2003: Response Protocol Toolbox: Planning for and Responding to Drinking Water Contamination Threats and Incidents

16. Hall, J., et al.: On-line water quality parameters as indicators of distribution system contamination. J. Am. Water Works Assoc. **99**(1), 66–67 (2007)

17. Ostfeld, A.: The battle of water sensor networks (BWSN): a design challenge for engineers and algorithms. J. Water Resour. Plann. Manag. **134**(6), 556–568 (2008)

18. Kroll, D., King, K.: Methods for evaluating water distribution network early warning systems. J. Am. Water Works Assoc. **102**(1), 79–89 (2010)

19. Grayman, W.M., Murray, R., Savic, D.A.: Effects of redesign of water systems for security and water quality actors. In: Starrett, S. (ed.) Proceedings of the World Environmental and Water Resources Congress, Kansas City (2009)

20. WRC/WSA/WCA: Engineering and Operations Committee. Managing Leakage: UK Water Industry Managing Leakage. Rep. A-J. WRC/WSA/WCA, London (1994)

21. Di Nardo, A., Di Natale, M.: A heuristic design support methodology based on graph theory for district metering of water supply networks. Eng. Optim. **43**(2), 193–211 (2011)

22. Perelman, L.S., Allen, M., Preis, A., Iqbal, M., Whittle, A.J.: Automated sub-zoning of water distribution systems. Environ. Model Softw. **65**, 1–14 (2015)

23. Fiedler, M.: Algebraic connectivity of graphs. Czech. Math. J. **23**, 298 (1973)

24. Shi, J., Malik, J.: Normalized cuts and image segmentation. IEEE Trans. Pattern Anal. Mach. Intell. **22**, 888–905 (2000)

25. Di Nardo, A., Di Natale, M., Guida, M., Musmarra, D.: Water network protection from intentional contamination by sectorization. Water Resour. Manag. **27**(6), 1837–1850 (2013)

26. Bonacich, P.: A technique for analyzing overlapping membership. In Costner, H. (ed.) Sociological Methodology, pp. 176–185. Jossey-Bass, San Francisco (1972)

27. Rossman, L.A.: EPANET2 Users Manual. US EPA, Cincinnati, Ohio (2000)

28. Di Nardo, A., Di Natale, M., Santonastaso, G.F., Venticinque, S.: An automated tool for smart water network partitioning. Water Resour. Manag. **27**(13), 4493–4508 (2013)

29. Von Luxburg, U.: A tutorial on spectral clustering. Stat. Comput. **17**, 395–416 (2007)

30. Di Nardo, A., Di Natale, M., Giudicianni, C., Santonastaso, G.F., Tzatchkov, V., Varela, J. M.R., Yamanaka, V.H.A.: Water supply network partitioning based on simultaneous cost and energy optimization. Procedia Eng. **162**, 238–245 (2016)

31. Todini, E.: Looped water distribution networks design using a resilience index based heuristic approach. Urban Water **2**(2), 115–122 (2000)

Role of Urban Interactions and Damage in Seismic Resilience of Historical Centers

Anna Bozza$^{(\boxtimes)}$ ⓘ, Domenico Asprone ⓘ, Fulvio Parisi ⓘ,
and Gaetano Manfredi ⓘ

University of Naples Federico II, Via Claudio 21, 80125 Naples, Italy
anna.bozza@unina.it

Abstract. Historical centers are places where local identity principles and contemporary dynamics of urbanization coexist. They conserve cultural heritage, hence the presence of many historical assets makes these places highly vulnerable and exposed.

Accordingly, historical centers need to be managed in order to guarantee proper resilience levels. This is paramount in light of the increasing rate of occurrence of adverse natural and man-made events, above all earthquakes.

This study proposes a methodology, that enables to model any urban environment as a complex network. Different urban components and their interrelations can be considered, and rigorous mathematical measures can be performed. These measures quantify the efficiency of urban functioning.

Reiterating such measures before and after an event occurrence, and in each stage of the recovery of an urban context, enables to compute a unique resilience indices.

The real case study of the inner city Naples is proposed to show the methodology. Results are discussed with regards to seismic scenario analysis for different intensity levels. Hence, the trend of the resilience indices against the event magnitude is observed, in case different recovery strategy are simulated.

Keywords: Disaster resilience · Urban networks · Earthquakes

1 Introduction

Disaster resilience is understood as the capability of a system to withstand negative impacts and recover efficiently in the face of an adverse event. This concept is crucial when dealing with urban environments and, in particular, with those holding vulnerable assets, namely historical centers. These are typically characterized by building agglomerations, that are spatially distributed over a network of narrow streets, that makes them more exposed and vulnerable.

Current studies on disaster resilience highlight the importance of considering urban complexity, as the whole of the interrelations between people, physical assets and stakeholders. Accordingly, the present study adopts an experimental framework to model urban environments as complex networks including physical and social urban components [1–4]. The methodology is implemented for the real case study of the historical center of the city of Naples (Italy), namely the Quartieri Spagnoli area.

G. D'Agostino and A. Scala (Eds.): CRITIS 2017, LNCS 10707, pp. 97–106, 2018.
https://doi.org/10.1007/978-3-319-99843-5_9

Seismic scenarios are simulated with 5 different earthquake intensity, in terms of the peak ground acceleration (PGA), according to the local hazard.

Two different recovery scenarios are simulated for each seismic event. The former is focused on the restoration of the network connectivity between couple of residential buildings. The latter is focused on the restoration of the scholar urban service, namely the connectivity each residential building and each school building.

Hence, efficiency indices are calculated, to assess the urban functioning before and after the earthquake occurrence, and in each stage of the recovery. Finally, the damage level is assessed with reference to each seismic intensity, and resilience is computed. Two alternative resilience indices are calculated, being respectively dependent or independent on the initial level of damage suffered by the urban network.

The trend of resilience indices is investigated against the damage level, so as to provide a prompt estimate of the expected resilience level of the urban area in case of earthquake.

The proposed curves can be potentially used as a support to decision makers in the medium-long term in peacetime or after an extreme event occurrence. Accordingly, when no event has occurred diverse damage levels and recovery strategies can be simulated to study the resilience level exhibited. As a result, disaster managers can forecast damage scenarios, assess actual resilience and eventually plan for enhancing resilience through mitigation actions.

On the other hand, in case a disaster has occurred, local officers might use the methodology proposed to promptly recognize the effective urban resilience level. Consequently, they can be able to univocally choose the best strategy, which can guarantee the higher resilience level.

2   Resilience of the Inner City Naples

2.1   HSPN Modelling

In this paper, resilience is understood as the engineering one, in the sense of ecosystems. Hence, quantifying resilience represents the final phase of a complex process, that starts from the modelling of the urban environment investigated.

Such modelling accounts for complex dynamics, that typically characterize a city. Hence, single urban components are considered and also mutual interrelations, to finally model a complex network.

In addition, the city model also accounts for the human component of a city, by means of a physical abstraction of the buildings they live in. Hence, citizens are computed to the final network by assuming 1 citizen each 30 m^2 of each residential buildings. The number of inhabitants is then calculated for each building within the network, by knowing the number of storeys and the mean square meters of the floor area.

Finally a hybrid social-physical network (HSPN) is modelled according to Cavallaro et al. [1]. Physical and social urban components are integrated, and also mutual interrelations are included, being represented by the street links connecting them.

The HSPN of the inner city Naples, namely the Quartieri Spagnoli area, is modelled within this paper to provide a real case study.

The Quartieri Spagnoli area is a 0.80 km^2 wide area, whose building portfolio is mainly constituted by medium- and high-rise masonry buildings (600 residential buildings and 17 schools). The area have about 30,000 inhabitants.

The Quartieri Spagnoli's HSPN is a quite regular lattice, characterized by the presence of 615 door-links, 547 street links and 1,009 nodes (617 buildings and 395 street junctions). It exhibits the typical features of historical city centers in Italy and in Europe (Fig. 1).

(a)

(b)

Fig. 1. City map (a), residential HSPN (b) of the Quartieri Spagnoli area (Naples, Italy)

2.2   Generating Seismic Scenarios

City damages are simulated by assuming structural vulnerability to be uniformly distributed on the territory and imposing diverse extreme seismic scenarios. The damage state is computed to the HSPN in a deterministic fashion, by simulating five diverse earthquake severity levels, in accordance to the seismic hazard of the Naples area and with reference to five different return periods, T_r.

Table 1 following show the simulated earthquake intensities, whose reference intensity measure is the peak ground acceleration (PGA). For each scenario the mean damage, d, suffered by the Quartieri Spagnoli area is assessed in a systemic fashion. Essentially, fragility curves are integrated according to the buildings' structural typology and the probability of street interruption is also computed. Hence, damaged buildings are identified by means of the random methodology outlined in Bozza et al. [4].

Table 1. Seismic scenario simulated according to different return periods for the Naples area.

Return period, T_r	PGA [g]	d [%]
2475	0.51	85
975	0.39	60
475	0.30	30
201	0.22	15
104	0.18	3

The random methodology is iterated depending on the building typology observed, namely for residential and school buildings.

Hence, the efficiency of the urban network is evaluated, in terms of its capability to connect couples of residential buildings and also each residential building and each school, namely citizen-citizen, E_{cc}, and citizen-school efficiency, E_{cs}. Equations (1) and (2) following show the formulas for the two specific case analysis:

$$E_{cc} = \frac{1}{H_{tot} \cdot (H_{tot} - 1)} \cdot \sum_{i \in B} H_i \cdot \left((h_i - 1) + \sum_{j \in (B \setminus I)} H_j \cdot \frac{d_{ij}^{eucl}}{d_{ij}} \right) \tag{1}$$

$$E_{cs} = \frac{1}{S_{tot} \cdot H_{tot}} \cdot \sum_{i \in S} S_i \cdot \left(h_i + \sum_{j \in (B \setminus I)} H_j \cdot \frac{d_{ij}^{eucl}}{d_{ij}} \right) \tag{2}$$

With reference to Eq. (1), i, j are the identification number (ID) of the building nodes, H_{tot} is the number of the citizens living in the studied area, H_i and H_j are the number of citizens living in building i and in building j. B identifies the set of the building nodes, d_{ij} is the shortest path's length and d_{ij}^{eucl} is the Euclidean distance, between node i and j. h_i is the number of citizens, whose residences have zero distance from building i and belong to the set I.

Accordingly, Eq. (2) performs a summation over the set S identifying the set of the school nodes. In this case, S_{tot} represents the summation of the total number of users using the facilities that supply the school service, and weights their importance in the HSPN. S_i is the number of citizens, which benefit from the school service supplied by the facility building i belonging to S.

Citizen-citizen and citizen-school efficiency is evaluated on the whole HSPN before the event occurrence. Hence, seismic scenarios are simulated. Accordingly, damaged building nodes and street links are considered to be subjected to usage restrictions, hence they are inactive within the HSPN. Inactive nodes and links are removed from the HSPN and efficiency in the aftermath of the earthquake is evaluated. Hence, the functionality of the disrupted network is evaluated.

Paralleling this, citizens living in each damaged building, and users of the school service, are considered to be reallocated.

As a case in point, at this stage a recovery strategy is designed and simulated to restore the urban functionality. In particular, in this study, a "status quo down-up" strategy is implemented [1], that leads the urban context to recover its pre-event configuration. In both the case analysis, and for each seismic scenario, the strategy is implemented in a discrete fashion and efficiency is assessed in each stage.

2.3   Resilience Assessment

Efficiency is evaluated before and after the event occurrence, and in each stage of the recovery, thus enabling to define the recovery function. This is defined as a time-independent variables, that returns the residual urban efficiency.

The recovery function is defined as a function of the reallocated citizens, c, normalized to the total number of the inhabitants of the urban area. It can be differently evaluated, according to the approach selected to quantify resilience. In fact, two alternative resilience indices are proposed, in this study: the former being fully normalized with respect to the observed damages, the latter being dependent on the initial damage state. Accordingly, the functional form adopted for the recovery function can be respectively Eq. (3) or Eq. (4):

$$y_1(c) = \frac{E(c) - E^{post}}{E^{pre} - E^{post}} \tag{3}$$

$$y_2(c) = \frac{E(c)}{E^{pre}} \tag{4}$$

Where E^{pre} represents the urban efficiency before the earthquake occurs, E^{post} represents urban efficiency after the event, and $E(c)$ is the urban efficiency in the specific stage examined, namely when c citizens have been reallocated.

Finally, resilience is quantified according to the following (Eq. (5)):

$$R = \int_0^1 y(c) \cdot dc \tag{5}$$

Where $y(c)$ can be replaced by Eq. (3) or (4).

Time is deliberately not taken into account, in order to avoid including further uncertainties in the assessment process. In fact, resilience is typically affected by decision making processes, that depend on the time, money and human and material resources' availability. Consequently, may issues might arise, being substantially related to time and money, and that cannot be specifically considered.

In keeping with this, there are studies in the literature [5, 6], that approach resilience by totally removing its dependence on time.

Resilience calculated according to the two approaches proposed, is defined in different interval of definition. When damage independence is assumed involved variables are fully normalized and resilience is defined in [0, 1]. On the other hand, when damage dependence is assumed resilience has got unity as an upper bound, but it will never tend to the zero value.

3   Results and Discussion

An important result that can be drawn from this study is the relationship that exists between the resilience indices, R, and the damage level observed on the urban context after the seismic event. The trend of the resilience indices is observed against the damage, in order to monitor the urban capability to recover from an external stress when changing its magnitude.

Resilience indices are evaluated as a function of both the recovery function defined. In particular, the damage independent resilience is evaluated by integrating the function $y_1(c)$ over the recovery process simulated. The resulting indices is defined as R_{DI}. Paralleling this, also the damage dependent resilience indices is evaluated, by using the alternative functional form of the recovery function, namely $y_2(c)$. such indices is indicated as R_{DD}.

The trend of both the indices are illustrated following in Figs. 2 and 3, for the case study of the Quartieri Spagnoli area. Both the simulated recovery strategies are analyzed, namely the citizen-citizen and the citizen-school recovery strategy.

Essentially, it can be observed that the resilience indices tend to decrease with the increasing magnitude of the seismic event. This outcome is highlighted in both the case analysis of citizen-citizen and citizen-school recovery strategy.

Diverse level of damages can be observed in the two cases, because of the different number of structures affected by the event. In fact, in case resilience of the residential network is observed, fragility curves are evaluated almost on the entire built environment (600 buildings) within the area. Consequently, a higher number of street links are likely to become unusable, and after the event the urban network is observed to be seriously disconnected.

Conversely, in case citizen-school connectivity is observed, a lower number of buildings is assumes to be seriously damaged. Hence, a lower number of citizens have to be relocated and also a lower number of street links become inaccessible.

It can be also observed that the average value of the resilience indices is higher in the case of damage dependent resilience, with respect to the damage independent. This is because of the direct correlation with initial level of damage suffered by the urban network, that highly influences the indices. As a consequence, damage dependent resilience seems to be less unbiased than the damage independent indices.

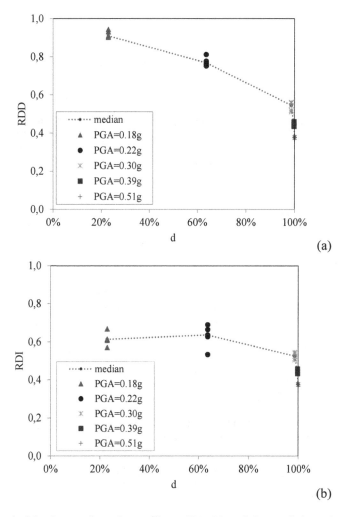

Fig. 2. Trend of the damage dependent resilience, R_{DD} (a), and damage independent resilience, R_{DI} (b), against 5 diverse damage levels (corresponding to diverse PGAs) in the case of citizen-citizen recovery strategy

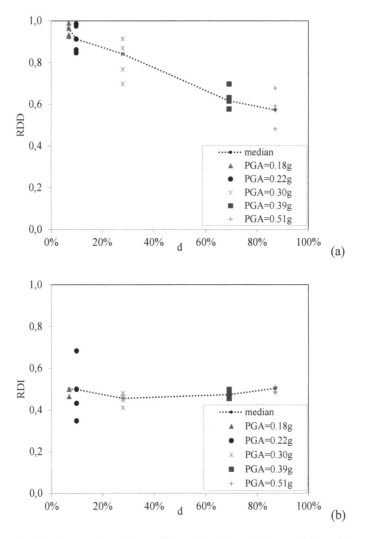

Fig. 3. Trend of the damage dependent resilience, R_{DD} (a), and damage independent resilience, R_{DI} (b), against 5 diverse damage levels (corresponding to diverse PGAs) in the case of citizen-school recovery strategy

4   Conclusions

Physical and social components are tightly correlated within contemporary cities. Hence, in case an extreme event occurs, it has got the potential to impact the whole urban society. An extreme event can be even more detrimental in case it impacts a historical center, that holds a huge quantity of assets representing the social identity. Accordingly, building resilient cities against catastrophic events is nowadays a major issue.

In this paper, the correlation between urban resilience and the damage level observed after a seismic event is investigated. Resilience is quantified according to the methodology proposed by Bozza et al. [4] and Cavallaro et al. [1], to quantify the resilience of urban centers as their copying capacity against earthquakes. In addition, two alternative resilience indices are developed, being the former dependent on the damage level after the event, and the latter fully normalized with respect to it.

The urban context investigated is modelled as a complex network, accounting for physical components and also for inhabitants (HSPN). Hence, scenario analysis are performed for the real case study of the Quartieri Spagnoli area, by simulating five different earthquake intensity.

Experimental results show a decreasing trend of the resilience indices with respect to the increasing damage level. The observed drop of such indices results to be higher in the case damage dependent resilience is observed. This is because of the higher variability of this indices caused by its direct dependence on the initial level of damage. In fact, being R_{DD} highly influenced by the network damage, causes also a higher standard deviation of the observed results.

Accordingly, despite results in terms of the damage dependent and the damage independent resilience indices being very similar against the seismic magnitude simulated, R_{DI} seems to be unbiased. Hence, higher reliability is observed for the R_{DI} indices. Consequently, such indices has got the potential to be applied in order to compare different urban topologies and also different event typologies. In fact, different hazards and related structural vulnerability can be easily integrated within the proposed framework, by using specific fragility curves, as is also in Bozza et al. [4].

This study proposes a novel approach for the purposes of the resilience quantification, that enables to evaluate disaster resilience and city robustness to structural damages according to a human-centric perspective. Damages suffered by a urban context are, in fact, evaluated as the decay of the city's state of service after the occurrence of an adverse event in an integral fashion. Furthermore, the proposed approach can be valuable to be integrated within current traditional practices for disaster management. Developing preliminarily resilience curves against the damage level with respect to a certain event, can potentially support local institutions in forecasting the urban capability to recover. In addition, the methodology provides the chance for simulating different scenarios and also recovery strategies, that enable to observe the urban behavior. As a consequence, also the best recovery strategies to restore the urban functionality after the occurrence of an extreme event can be recognized. Paralleling, the corresponding resilience level can be assessed, so as to promptly implement the most feasible strategy, that enables to maximize resilience for the investigated urban center.

References

1. Cavallaro, M., Asprone, D., Latora, V., Manfredi, G.: Assessment of urban ecosystem resilience through hybrid social–physical complex networks. Comput.-Aided Civil Infrastruct. Eng. **29**(8), 608–625 (2014)
2. Bozza, A., Asprone, D., Manfredi, G.: Developing an integrated framework to quantify resilience of urban systems against disasters. Nat. Hazards **78**(3), 1729–1748 (2015)
3. Ouyang, M., Dueñas-Osorio, L., Min, X.: A three-stage resilience analysis framework for urban infrastructure systems. Struct. Saf. **36**, 23–31 (2012)
4. Bozza, A., Asprone, D., Parisi, F., Manfredi, G.: Alternative resilience indices for city ecosystems subjected to natural hazards. Comput.-Aided Civil Infrastruct. Eng. (2017). https://doi.org/10.1111/mice.12275
5. Bozza, A., Asprone, D., Fiasconaro, A., Latora, V., Manfredi, G.: Catastrophe resilience related to urban networks shape: preliminary analysis. In: proceedings of the 5th ECCOMAS Thematic Conference on computational methods in structural dynamics and earthquake engineering, COMPDYN 2015, Crete, Greece (2015)
6. Franchin, P., Cavalieri, F.: Probabilistic assessment of civil infrastructure resilience to earthquakes. Comput.-Aided Civil Infrastruct. Eng. **30**(7), 583–600 (2015)

Towards Blockchain-Based Collaborative Intrusion Detection Systems

Nikolaos Alexopoulos$^{(\boxtimes)}$, Emmanouil Vasilomanolakis$^{(\boxtimes)}$,
Natália Réka Ivánkó, and Max Mühlhäuser

Telecooperation Group, Technische Universität Darmstadt, Darmstadt, Germany
{alexopoulos,vasilomano,max}@tk.tu-darmstadt.de,
nataliareka.ivanko@stud.tu-darmstadt.de

Abstract. In an attempt to cope with the increased number of cyber-attacks, research in Intrusion Detection System IDSs is moving towards more collaborative mechanisms. Collaborative IDSs (CIDSs) are such an approach; they combine the knowledge of a plethora of monitors to generate a holistic picture of the monitored network. Despite the research done in this field, CIDSs still face a number of fundamental challenges, especially regarding maintaining trust among the collaborating parties. Recent advances in distributed ledger technologies, e.g. various implementations of blockchain protocols, are a good fit to the problem of enhancing trust in collaborative environments. This paper touches the intersection of CIDSs and blockchains. Particularly, it introduces the idea of utilizing blockchain technologies as a mechanism for improving CIDSs. We argue that certain properties of blockchains can be of significant benefit for CIDSs; namely for the improvement of trust between monitors, and for providing accountability and consensus. For this, we study the related work and highlight the research gaps and challenges towards such a task. Finally, we propose a generic architecture for the incorporation of blockchains into the field of CIDSs and an analysis of the design decisions that need to be made to implement such an architecture.

1 Introduction

Nowadays, cyber-attacks are increasing in both their numbers and sophistication. In particular, recent attacks such as the case of the so-called Wannacry malware [15], highlight the need for protection, especially in the realm of critical infrastructures. To cope with such challenges, research in cyber-security has focused on more collaborative approaches that are broadly referred to as CIDSs [33]. CIDSs attempt to create an improved and holistic picture of the monitored networks via, as their name implies, collaboration among participants.

Nevertheless, a number of research challenges remain unsolved with regard to CIDSs. First, one of the most important aspects of such systems is the trust establishment (and management) of the participants. That is, the techniques that the system employs to ensure that the collaborative monitoring units trust each other, as well as methods for quantifying the quality of the exchanged

© Springer Nature Switzerland AG 2018
G. D'Agostino and A. Scala (Eds.): CRITIS 2017, LNCS 10707, pp. 107–118, 2018.
https://doi.org/10.1007/978-3-319-99843-5_10

alert data. In addition, a fair and public approach that provides accountability among the monitors of the CIDS is also a topic that has not been touched until now. Lastly, methods for providing consensus in a distributed environment and specifically in the CIDS scenario are yet to be explored.

Recently, there has been a spike in the interest around blockchains in the context of several industry applications, including critical infrastructures. Apart from, the now established, use of blockchains among financial institutions [12], identity schemes secured by blockchain technology have been discussed, with many startups offering such solutions [28]. Furthermore, critical services, such as healthcare providers [18,29], national and state authorities [36], land registries [20], and the energy sector [17,27], are considering incorporating distributed ledgers (i.e. blockchains) in their workflows. They take advantage of the immutability and consensus properties of these designs, in order to secure their respective systems.

In this paper, we introduce the idea of utilizing blockchain technology as a mechanism for improving CIDSs. In particular, we argue that certain functionality and properties of blockchains can be of significant benefit for collaborative intrusion detection; namely for the improvement of trust between monitors, for providing accountability and as a consensus mechanism. For this, we carefully study the related work and highlight the research gaps and challenges towards such a task. Finally, we propose a generic architecture for the incorporation of blockchains into the field of CIDSs.

The rest of this paper is organized as follows. First, Sect. 2 provides some background knowledge with regard to both CIDSs and blockchains. Section 3 discusses the related work in the intersection of CIDSs and blockchain technologies. Section 4 proposes a number of requirements for CIDSs with regard to the need for trust and fairness during collaboration. Sections 5 and 6 discuss our proposed CIDS architecture and the various design considerations, respectively. Finally, Sect. 7 concludes this paper and summarizes our future directions.

2   Background

In this section, we present necessary background information with regard to blockchains and CIDSs.

2.1   Collaborative Intrusion Detection

There has been a lot of work in the area of CIDS over the last years [33]. The majority of it has been focusing on novel architectures and collaborative detection techniques. In more detail, CIDSs can be classified with regard to the network placement of their monitors to: *centralized, hierarchical* and *distributed.* Due to various fundamental disadvantages of centralized and hierarchical CIDSs (e.g., scalability and the existence of a Single Point of Failure (SPoF)) [33], this paper focuses mainly on distributed systems. In this class, a number of such systems have been proposed in the literature, e.g. [22,34,38]. However, most of these proposals deal with the construction of sophisticated architectures, hence not addressing other challenging topics. For instance, validating and managing trust between monitors (see Sect. 3.1), or creating consensus when exchanging alert data, have not been tackled in sufficient extent in the state of the art.

2.2 Blockchains

Despite recent media, corporate, and research coverage, there is no standard definition for blockchain technology - or simply blockchains - yet. It can be described as a distributed data structure, which is shared and replicated between the participants of a peer-to-peer network. The data structure itself is built from a back-linked list of blocks, where each block is identified by its cryptographic hash and also contains the hash of the previous block. This property establishes a cryptographic link between blocks, creating a so-called "blockchain" [1] that all participants can examine, yet without being able to tamper with. Due to this fact, blockchains are considered an implementation of a shared *secure distributed ledger*, where the participants can read from - most of the time without any constraints - and write to, when only specific constraints are met.

Regarding the control of these permissions, current blockchain implementations fall into three categories: *public, consortium* and *private* [26]. In the case of *public* blockchains, such as Bitcoin [25] and Ethereum [37], everyone can read and maintain the ledger, i.e. there is no membership mechanism in place.

Meanwhile, in *consortium* blockchains, such as Hyperledger[1][8], a predefined consortium of peers is responsible for maintaining the chain. In *private* blockchains, such as Monax[2], a single entity controls the system, i.e. there is no consensus process.

The process of updating the blockchain takes place via a protocol, which achieves consensus, i.e. gives guarantees that all participants agree on a uniform view of the ledger that contains only valid transactions, ensuring the integrity and consistency of the ledger [3]. This protocol may vary a lot and depends on both the type of the blockchain implementation and the threat model. To offer guaranteed security properties, public blockchains design the consensus part to be either computationally hard (Proof-of-Work) or based on the possession of a scarce resource within the system (Proof-Of-Stake). On the other hand, consortium and private blockchains apply some kind of Byzantine [19] or benign fault tolerant algorithms, such as PBFT [10] or SIEVE [9], to cope with malicious nodes. For an overview of Bitcoin and other cryptocurrencies, we refer the reader to [7].

3 Related Work

This section discusses the related work in the field of CIDSs, emphasizing in trust management, as well as in the field of blockchains.

---

[1] https://www.hyperledger.org.

[2] https://monax.io.

3.1 Building Trust in CIDSs

Beyond the fundamental (architectural-level) research on CIDSs, some work has been done lately with regards to trust management. In more detail, researchers have proposed trust management mechanisms to cope with both the *insider attack* problem[3] as well as to enhance the overall quality of the collaboration [31].

Specifically, trust management in CIDSs can be distinguished based on the overall goal of the respective (trust) mechanism. In this context, computational trust is most commonly applied to quantify the trust levels between monitoring nodes. That is, if a monitor is compromised or starts disseminating false information, its trust score will decrease and eventually some response action will take place (e.g., blacklisting). Another approach is to attempt to quantify the quality of the alert data (rather than the source of it). In such a scenario, the trust model attempts to measure the quality of the alerts themselves or assign a reputation score to certain parameters of an alert (e.g., to the IP address of an adversary) [4].

The majority of the work proposed in this area makes use of computational trust mechanisms, based on various mathematical models, to measure the trustworthiness of the monitors [14,16]. In particular, the basic concept is that a monitor can utilize its own old experiences, with respect to its communication with other monitors, and via the usage of certain computational trust methods (e.g., Bayesian statistics) can infer (with a certain probability and confidence) the amount of trust it can place on others. Nevertheless, to the best of our knowledge, no work has been done towards providing CIDSs with strong accountability and consensus properties.

3.2 Blockchains as a Means of Collaboration

There has been a recent explosion of interest around blockchains and several industry applications have been proposed in the last five years. Each application is developed for a special use case, thus requires a different blockchain implementation, which has to provide custom, unique characteristics. For example, there are specific implementations, which were developed to enhance privacy by enabling different parties to use the system, meanwhile keeping the stored data completely private [39]. Other implementations use cryptographic identity schemes, which offer full anonymity and unlinkability between the transactions [28]. Due to these versatile properties, various industries have started to investigate the potential of this technology.

In the energy sector, blockchain can facilitate a peer-to-peer market, where machines buy and sell energy automatically, according to predefined criteria [23,24]. For example, prosumers with solar panels can record their output in the blockchain and sell it to other parties via smart contracts. Moreover,

---

[3] This refers to the case where a monitor, which is part of the CIDS, turns malicious and attempts to attack or misguide other monitors of the system.

Azaria et al. [2] propose a novel, decentralized record management system to handle and store medical data by using blockchains to ensure data integrity and to enforce access control policies.

These applications have demonstrated that the combination of IoT and blockchains can lead to rewarding results [11]. All of them benefit from the fact that this technology allows peers to communicate with each other in a verifiable manner without trusting each other and without any trusted intermediary; while being able to preserve their anonymity and guarantee the integrity of their data.

4   Requirements

As a first step of any system design attempt, it is very important to clearly articulate the requirements of the goal system. Thus, in accordance with the related work in [31,33], we specify the requirements for an effective and trustworthy CIDS:

- **Accountability:** Participating parties should be held accountable for their actions.
- **Integrity:** The integrity of the alert data is very important for detecting attacks over time as well as for post-mortem analysis (e.g., during forensic analysis).
- **Resilience:** The system should not have SPoFs and should not depend on small groups of participants.
- **Consensus:** The system should be able to reach consensus on the quality of individual alert data and on the trustworthiness of each participant.
- **Scalability:** The system should be able to scale to a large number of participants/monitors and also handle churn.
- **Minimum Overhead:** The communication and computation overhead should be kept as low as possible.
- **Privacy:** Participants should be able to reserve their right to privacy and selectively disclose alert data as they wish. However, at the same time, the accountability and integrity requirements should still hold.

In this section, we specified seven requirements for a successful CIDS design. These requirements will guide our design choices and argumentation, for the rest of this paper. However, the requirements presented above are not orthogonal regarding the design decisions they favor. That is, there are inherent trade-offs between them (e.g. accountability vs. privacy). These trade-offs are further explored in Sect. 6.

5   A Blockchain-Based Architecture for CIDSs

To satisfy the requirements of Sect. 4, we propose the utilization of a secure distributed ledger, as e.g. implemented by blockchain technology, to secure the exchange of alerts between the collaborating nodes.

As a simple example, raw alert data generated by the monitors are stored as transactions in a blockchain, replicated among the participating nodes of the network. For an insight into the options regarding the nature of the actual data stored in the blockchain (e.g. alert hashes, bloom filters) see Sect. 6. The nodes involved, run a consensus protocol to guarantee the validity of the transactions before adding them in a block. This process guarantees that only well-formed alerts are included in the blockchain, that alert data transactions are tamper-resistant, and that each participating entity has a global view of the alerts.

This way, the participants are held *accountable* for their actions, as the latter are transparent to the network. Furthermore, the *integrity* of the data is guaranteed and the system has no *SPoF*, as it can tolerate as many byzantine failures as the underlying consensus protocol. The communication *overhead* of the construct can be managed e.g. by storing hashes of the alert data in the blockchain instead of the raw data. This way, a node would be able to verify the integrity of the alerts it receives by comparing their hash value with the corresponding hashes that are stored on the chain. There are a multitude of design considerations, like the one mentioned above towards the realization of such a system. In this section, we focus on the proposed generic architecture, while in Sect. 6, we explore the design space of a possible implementation.

The proposed architecture for a blockchain-based distributed CIDS can be seen in Fig. 1. The participating nodes in the blockchain network are either monitor units, analysis units, or perform both tasks simultaneously, which is the most general case. Communication between the nodes takes place in two logical layers, namely the *Alert Exchange layer* and the *Consensus layer*.

In the *Alert Exchange layer*, the implemented CIDS performs the alert data dissemination process. Specifically, the participating nodes exchange or collect alert data with respect to their role as monitors or analysis units. The exact communication mechanism in use is determined by the needs of the CIDS. For example, a flooding or gossiping [13] protocol can be used to disseminate data in the Alert Exchange layer of a distributed CIDS, while on-demand data exchange is also an option.

Second, there is a *Consensus layer*, where a subset (not necessarily proper) of peers, e.g. only the analysis units, run a consensus protocol, and agree on which transactions should be included in the ledger. The most basic scenario is one in which all members of the CIDS participate in the consensus protocol, and all alert data is stored in the blockchain. The connection between the two layers, the result of the Consensus layer, and the properties of the underlying blockchain construct, together enforce strict accountability of the participants and guarantee data integrity.

Furthermore, if required, it is possible to keep specific alert data confidential among a subset of peers. For instance, there might be a scenario, where specific alerts contain confidential information, which should not be revealed to anyone outside a specific corporation. In this case, the nodes who should have access to these specific alerts, can participate in a separate collaborative network and create a separate blockchain for it. The specific alert data can be encrypted in

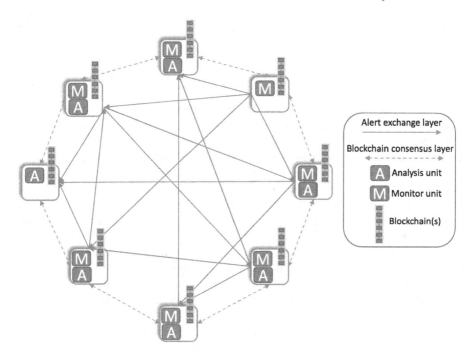

Fig. 1. Generic architecture of a blockchain-based CIDS.

both layers as well as in the distributed ledger, and the keys will be available only to the participating nodes. This way, peers that do not belong to this collaborative group, and do not hold the specific secret key, cannot view alert data exchanged and processed among the certified participants. As a result, peers are able to collaborate in multiple groups without revealing any confidential alert information to external nodes, while still staying on the same CIDS network.

6   Design Considerations

In Sect. 5, we proposed a general architecture for a trustworthy CIDS. However, there are a number of design and implementation choices regarding the realization of this architecture. Using blockchains as the basis of the design, inherently offers a degree of accountability, integrity and resilience to our system. Nevertheless, note that the choice of the type of blockchain and consensus algorithm to use, affects the degree to which these requirements are satisfied. Other characteristics, such as the scalability of the network, the communication overhead and the privacy of the participants, might depend on the distributed ledger type (w.r.t. the implemented consensus algorithm) or the data format via which the alerts are exchanged. Note that each combination of these alternatives provides unique characteristics to a CIDS, which enables us to design the system architecture tailored to the real world application.

In this section, we recount the aforesaid alternatives while focusing on the trade-offs between them, with respect to the requirements laid out in Sect. 4.

Governance of Distributed Ledger: In general, both public (permissionless) and corporate (permissioned) blockchain designs provide authenticity, integrity and resilience to the system, via guaranteeing a global, partially ordered view of alert transactions. However, they have their own advantages and disadvantages. Public blockchains provide an uncontrolled network, which everybody can freely join, and where every peer can read from and update the distributed ledger. General-purpose CIDSs, especially cyber incident monitors and network telescopes, e.g., [30,32], can benefit considerably from these advantages. The stored alert data are integrity-protected and available to everybody, while the participants remain accountable for their actions. These properties can provide high quality data for the scientific community to examine attacks, create statistics, or gather data to train another CIDS. Nevertheless, a major shortcoming is the possible transaction cost that a peer has to pay in order for her alert to be included in a public Proof-of-Work blockchain, e.g. in Bitcoin a peer can store 80 bytes of data using the "OP_RETURN" [5] transaction script, with a transaction fee of a couple of USD.

In consortium blockchains, access permissions are more tightly controlled and rights to modify or even read the blockchain state are restricted to a specific set of users. For example, the consensus is controlled by a pre-selected set of nodes. In this case, the validators are known and any risk of a lot of malicious peers joining the system (e.g. due to a sybil attack) and destroying the accuracy of the CIDS is mitigated. Additionally, if a peer starts to behave maliciously, e.g., starts sending fake alerts, the organization can easily change the rules of the blockchain and revert the fake transactions. This makes consortium blockchains a better choice for institutions and groups of institutions who do not want to reveal the alert data publicly and want to keep the system's participants under control.

Consensus: Apart from the issue of who is able to view and add alert data (in the form of transactions) to the blockchain, the selection of the consensus algorithm and of the peers that take part in it, is of great importance. Especially in corporate blockchain designs, there is the possibility to choose a subset of peers, i.e., super-peers, that will be responsible for running the consensus algorithm; hence, offering integrity guarantees to the system. Apart from that, the consensus algorithm that is selected will greatly affect the security guarantees of the system. We have already presented several options, including Proof-of-Work, Proof-of-Stake and traditional byzantine fault-tolerant designs in Sect. 2. The choice of the consensus algorithm defines the adversary model of the system, i.e., the ratio of honest and malicious peers in the CIDS. Furthermore, each approach comes with a different scalability potential, e.g., practical byzantine fault tolerant (PBFT) designs will generally be less scalable (in terms of the peer population) than Proof-of-Work or Proof-of-Stake based ones [35].

Data on/off the Ledger: Another question that rises is related to the alert data and their granularity during the sharing process, in each of the two communication layers (*Alert Exchange* and *Blockchain Consensus*). For this, there are various strategies that can be considered in a CIDS; each one having its own advantages and disadvantages. For instance, exchanging raw alert data can provide the deepest level of granularity. However, this comes with a major communication overhead. In addition, considering the large amount of data that a local IDS generates, such an approach would not scale. Another approach is to instead only share compact representations of alert data. For instance, in [21, 34] researchers have proposed the exchange of bloom filters [6] containing such a mapping of alerts. Such approaches fulfill a number of requirements, namely the minimal overhead, privacy and integrity. Nevertheless, when only exchanging aggregated/compact versions of the alerts the accuracy of the system might be decreased.

Our proposal is to use a compact representation, e.g. bloom filters, for the communication in the *Consensus layer*, in order to decrease the overhead and size of the blockchain construct. On the other hand, in the *Alert Exchange* layer, where data exchange can potentially take place on demand, exchanging raw data would offer the highest level of accuracy to the system.

Data Encryption: The norm in both public and corporate blockchain networks is that the transactions can be observed by all participating peers, a fact which could give away information that should not be revealed, e.g., sensitive corporate information. Therefore, in some CIDS usage scenarios, it is important to provide a mechanism that protects the privacy of the participating parties with respect to alert data and confidential information (exchanged in the *consensus layer*). One solution can be encrypting the alert data by using symmetric key cryptography and making the keys available only to the participants who should have the right to read them[4]. This allows every peer to stay on the same network, but be able to decrypt and examine only the alert data which they are certified to access. However, this would produce overhead in the form of key management and distribution. Nevertheless, as described in the previous paragraph, another approach is to only exchange compact representations of the alert data (e.g., bloom filters or hashes). In such a case the problem of over-sharing is mitigated.

In general, there are numerous considerations when designing a blockchain-based CIDS. In this section, we gave an overview of the most challenging ones and presented the trade-offs between them. There is no generic optimal solution to making decisions about the considerations presented above. The specific requirements of a CIDS, such as the expected number of peers, the expected alert volume, the required privacy level, etc., will guide these decisions.

---

[4] An asymmetric approach, e.g., with a Public Key Infrastructure (PKI), is also possible, however a lot of overhead would be expected in the key distribution and maintenance process.

7   Conclusion and Future Work

To cope with the increase and the sophistication of cyber-attacks in critical infrastructures, there is a demand for collaboration between the defenders. In order to practically improve the area of collaborative intrusion detection, there is a need for constructing a trusted and accountable environment for the participating monitors. In this paper, we presented a generic architecture for the creation of such a CIDS, and explained how blockchain technology can be incorporated. In addition, we identified the open research challenges and discussed the various directions of this research area.

With regard to our future work, we plan to demonstrate the feasibility of a blockchain-based CIDS via implementing a proof of concept. In more detail, we are currently implementing such a system based on the architecture presented in this paper and by taking into account the design considerations of Sect. 6. We plan to evaluate our approach by examining whether the introduction of a blockchain adds overhead to the system, and if yes how much. Another challenge is the incorporation of computational trust mechanisms in our design, with the goal of increasing the trustworthiness of the overall system even further. In conclusion, we believe that *by-design* secure collaborative platforms, such as the ones offered by the various implementations of secure distributed ledgers, can increase the performance and durability of CIDSs, and in turn offer better protection to critical infrastructures.

Acknowledgments. This work has received funding from the European Union's Horizon 2020 Research and Innovation Program, PROTECTIVE, under Grant Agreement No 700071. This work has also been funded by the DFG within the RTG 2050 "Privacy and Trust for Mobile Users" and within the CRC 1119 CROSSING.

References

1. Antonopoulos, A.M.: Mastering Bitcoin: Unlocking Digital Cryptocurrencies. O'Reilly Media, Inc., Sebastopol (2014)
2. Azaria, A., Ekblaw, A., Vieira, T., Lippman, A.: Medrec: using blockchain for medical data access and permission management. In: International Conference on Open and Big Data (OBD), pp. 25–30. IEEE (2016)
3. Baliga, A.: Understanding Blockchain Consensus Models. Technical report. Persistent Systems Ltd. (2017)
4. Bartoš, V., Kořenek, J.: Evaluating reputation of internet entities. In: Badonnel, R., Koch, R., Pras, A., Drašar, M., Stiller, B. (eds.) AIMS 2016. LNCS, vol. 9701, pp. 132–136. Springer, Cham (2016). https://doi.org/10.1007/978-3-319-39814-3_13
5. bitcoinwiki: OP_RETURN (2017). https://en.bitcoin.it/wiki/OP_RETURN
6. Bloom, B.H.: Space/time trade-offs in hash coding with allowable errors. Commun. ACM **13**(7), 422–426 (1970)
7. Bonneau, J., Miller, A., Clark, J., Narayanan, A., Kroll, J.A., Felten, E.W.: Sok: research perspectives and challenges for bitcoin and cryptocurrencies. In: 2015 IEEE Symposium on Security and Privacy (SP), pp. 104–121. IEEE (2015)

8. Cachin, C.: Architecture of the hyperledger blockchain fabric. In: Workshop on Distributed Cryptocurrencies and Consensus Ledgers (2016)
9. Cachin, C., Schubert, S., Vukolić, M.: Non-determinism in byzantine fault-tolerant replication. arXiv preprint arXiv:1603.07351 (2016)
10. Castro, M., Liskov, B., et al.: Practical byzantine fault tolerance. In: OSDI, vol. 99, pp. 173–186 (1999)
11. Christidis, K., Devetsikiotis, M.: Blockchains and smart contracts for the internet of things. IEEE Access **4**, 2292–2303 (2016)
12. Coindesk: Seven asian banks investigating bitcoin and blockchain tech. http://www.coindesk.com/7-asian-banks-investigating-bitcoin-and-blockchain-tech/
13. Demers, A., et al.: Epidemic algorithms for replicated database maintenance. In: Proceedings of the sixth annual ACM Symposium on Principles of distributed computing, pp. 1–12. ACM (1987)
14. Duma, C., Karresand, M., Shahmehri, N., Caronni, G.: A trust-aware, P2P-based overlay for intrusion detection. In: International Conference on Database and Expert Systems Applications (DEXA 2006), pp. 692–697. IEEE (2006)
15. Ehrenfeld, J.M.: Wannacry, cybersecurity and health information technology: a time to act. J. Med. Syst. **41**(7), 104 (2017)
16. Fung, C.J., Zhang, J., Aib, I., Boutaba, R.: Dirichlet-based trust management for effective collaborative intrusion detection networks. IEEE Trans. Netw. Serv. Manage. **8**(2), 79–91 (2011)
17. Grid, T.: http://transactivegrid.net/
18. Halamka, J.D., Lippman, A., Ekblaw, A.: The potential for blockchain to transform electronic health records (2017). https://hbr.org/2017/03/the-potential-for-blockchain-to-transform-electronic-health-records
19. Lamport, L., Shostak, R., Pease, M.: The Byzantine generals problem. ACM Trans. Program. Lang. Syst. (TOPLAS) **4**(3), 382–401 (1982)
20. Lantmäteriet, Landshypotek Bank: SBAB, Telia company, ChromaWay, Kairos Future: The land registry in the blockchain - testbed. Technical report (2017)
21. Locasto, M.E., Parekh, J.J., Keromytis, A.D., Stolfo, S.J.: Towards collaborative security and P2P intrusion detection. In: IEEE Workshop on Information Assurance and Security, pp. 333–339. IEEE (2005)
22. Locasto, M.E., Parekh, J.J., Stolfo, S., Misra, V.: Collaborative distributed intrusion detection. Technical report, Columbia University (2004)
23. Mihaylov, M., et al.: Virtual currency for trading of renewable energy in smart grids. In: European Energy Market (EEM), 11th International Conference on the, pp. 1–6. IEEE (2014)
24. Mihaylov, M., Jurado, S., Van Moffaert, K., Avellana, N., Nowé, A.: Nrg-x-change- a novel mechanism for trading of renewable energy in smart grids. In: SMART-GREENS, pp. 101–106 (2014)
25. Nakamoto, S.: Bitcoin: A peer-to-peer electronic cash system (2008)
26. Okada, H., Yamasaki, S., Bracamonte, V.: Proposed classification of blockchains based on authority and incentive dimensions. In: Advanced Communication Technology (ICACT), 2017 19th International Conference on, pp. 593–597. IEEE (2017)
27. Rutkin, A.: Blockchain-based microgrid gives power to consumers in new york. New Scientist (2016). https://www.newscientist.com/article
28. Shrier, D., Wu, W., Pentland, A.: Blockchain & infrastructure (identity, data security). Technical report, (2016). http://cdn.resources.getsmarter.ac/wp-content/uploads/2016/05/MIT_Blockchain_Infrastructure_Report_Part_Three_May_2016.pdf

29. Suberg, W.: Factom's latest partnership takes on us healthcare (2015). https://cointelegraph.com/news/factoms-latest-partnership-takes-on-us-healthcare
30. Ullrich, J.: Dshield internet storm center (2000). https://www.dshield.org/
31. Vasilomanolakis, E., Habib, S.M., Milaszewicz, P., Malik, R.S., Mühlhäuser, M.: Towards trust-aware collaborative intrusion detection: challenges and solutions. In: Steghöfer, J.-P., Esfandiari, B. (eds.) IFIPTM 2017. IAICT, vol. 505, pp. 94–109. Springer, Cham (2017). https://doi.org/10.1007/978-3-319-59171-1_8
32. Vasilomanolakis, E., Karuppayah, S., Kikiras, P., Mühlhäuser, M.: A honeypot-driven cyber incident monitor: lessons learned and steps ahead. In: International Conference on Security of Information and Networks, pp. 158–164. ACM (2015)
33. Vasilomanolakis, E., Karuppayah, S., Mühlhäuser, M., Fischer, M.: Taxonomy and survey of collaborative intrusion detection. ACM Comput. Surv. **47**(4), 33 (2015)
34. Vasilomanolakis, E., Krügl, M., Cordero, C.G., Mühlhäuser, M., Fischer, M.: Skipmon: A locality-aware collaborative intrusion detection system. In: Computing and Communications Conference (IPCCC), IEEE 34th International Performance, pp. 1–8. IEEE (2015)
35. Vukolić, M.: The quest for scalable blockchain fabric: Proof-of-work vs. BFT replication. In: Camenisch, J., Kesdoğan, D. (eds.) iNetSec 2015. LNCS, vol. 9591, pp. 112–125. Springer, Cham (2016). https://doi.org/10.1007/978-3-319-39028-4_9
36. Walport, M.: Distributed ledger technology: beyond blockchain. UK Government Office for Science (2016)
37. Wood, G.: Ethereum: a secure decentralised generalised transaction ledger. Ethereum Project Yellow Paper 151 (2014)
38. Zhou, C.V., Karunasekera, S., Leckie, C.: A peer-to-peer collaborative intrusion detection system. In: International Conference on Networks, pp. 118–123. IEEE (2005)
39. Zyskind, G., Nathan, O., Pentland, A.: Enigma: decentralized computation platform with guaranteed privacy. arXiv preprint arXiv:1506.03471 (2015)

Analysis of Cybersecurity Threats in Industry 4.0: The Case of Intrusion Detection

Juan E. Rubio$^{(\boxtimes)}$, Rodrigo Roman, and Javier Lopez

Department of Computer Science, University of Malaga,
Campus de Teatinos s/n, 29071 Malaga, Spain
{rubio,roman,jlm}@lcc.uma.es

Abstract. Nowadays, industrial control systems are experiencing a new revolution with the interconnection of the operational equipment with the Internet, and the introduction of cutting-edge technologies such as Cloud Computing or Big data within the organization. These and other technologies are paving the way to the Industry 4.0. However, the advent of these technologies, and the innovative services that are enabled by them, will also bring novel threats whose impact needs to be understood. As a result, this paper provides an analysis of the evolution of these cyber-security issues and the requirements that must be satisfied by intrusion detection defense mechanisms in this context.

Keywords: Industry · Control systems · Internet · IoT · Cloud
Big data · Critical infrastructure · Intrusion detection · IDS

1 Introduction

Traditionally, industrial facilities and critical infrastructures have been governed by SCADA (Supervisory Control and Data Acquisition) systems, which provide real-time data and remote management of the devices that are deployed over the production cycle, like Programmable Logic Controllers (PLCs) or field devices. However, these systems are now experiencing a growing interconnection with other services to share information and uptake new business processes. This is a consequence of the standardization of the software and hardware used in control systems, mainly caused by the adoption of Ethernet or TCP/IP and wireless technologies like IEEE 802.c or Bluetooth in this context.

Yet it seems this is only the beginning of the evolution of industrial ecosystems. Following with this tendency, the so-called fourth Industrial Revolution, or Industry 4.0 [1], is being heralded by the integration of communication technologies as novel as the Internet of Things or Cloud/Fog Computing to the current control and automation systems. Other concepts, such as the creation of virtual representations of entities (virtualization) and the acquisition and analysis of operational information (big data), are also under consideration. This evolution

G. D'Agostino and A. Scala (Eds.): CRITIS 2017, LNCS 10707, pp. 119–130, 2018.
https://doi.org/10.1007/978-3-319-99843-5_11

will facilitate the deployment of innovative industrial services such as "digital twins", "cloud-based manufacturing", and "digital workers", amongst others.

While the integration of IT and OT (operational technology) environments has several major benefits, it has also facilitated the emergence of several IT attack vectors in industrial ecosystems [2]. It is then to be expected that the number and impact of these cyber-security threats will also increase in future industrial environments. However, due to the lack of analyses on this subject, it is essential to study and understand the cyber-security threats caused by the previously mentioned enabling technologies and innovative services, plus their influence on the creation of specific intrusion detection systems.

For this purpose, in this work we will carry out a study of this nature, applying the following methodology: in Sect. 2 we will review the main enabling technologies included under the concept of Industry 4.0, identifying the local security threats against those areas and their most representative attack vectors in Sect. 3. Having understood the issues associated to the enabling technologies, Sect. 4 will focus on the security threats associated to the most innovative Industry 4.0 services. Finally, Sect. 5 will make use of the previous results to provide an overview of the additional requirements that must be fulfilled by intrusion detection systems in the context of the industry of the future. Note that, due to the lack of available space, only the most relevant references have been included.

2   Industry 4.0 Technologies

The Industry 4.0 refers to the digitization of all components within the industry. This concept is not mature due to a lack of agreement on the set of technologies considered and the different interests of the actors involved (e.g., researchers, standardization committees, governments). However, it can be defined from a technical perspective as the combination of productive processes with leading technologies of information and communications. This allows all the elements that conform the productive processes (suppliers, plant, distributors, even the product itself) to be digitally connected, providing a highly integrated value chain [1].

To better understand the innovations that Industry 4.0 introduces in the existing infrastructure, we must pay attention to its architectural changes. The ISA-95 standard defines five levels of operations in the industrial automation, in the form of a pyramid: this way, the productive process itself is located in the base (level 0), whereas those devices that interact with it (i.e., PLCs) are set in level 1. On top of these (level 2) we find the devices that control the production process (i.e., SCADAs, HMIs), and those that control the workflow (i.e., MES systems), represented at level 3. Lastly, the highest level contains the infrastructure of logistics, inventory, ERP or planning.

In traditional industrial environments, the information processing infrastructure follows the pyramidal structure reflected by this standard. One of the objectives of researchers in the field of Industry 4.0 is to analyze how to change this pyramid to a model that provides a more dynamic and reconfigurable decentralized infrastructure [3], as depicted in Fig. 1. By creating well defined services and

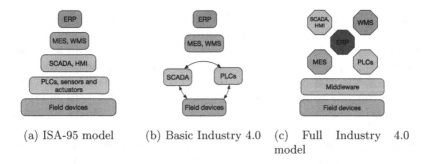

(a) ISA-95 model   (b) Basic Industry 4.0   (c) Full Industry 4.0 model

Fig. 1. ISA-95 pyramid and evolution towards Industry 4.0

interfaces, in which each element of the ecosystem has a specific functionality and purpose, it would be possible to redefine the structure of an industrial environment through various configurations, enhancing new services and optimizing existing ones [4]. The following is a summary of the most common conceptual features that this new model would enable:

- **Interoperability.** The application of the technologies that belong to the Industry 4.0 would ensure an interoperability between each of the elements of the productive processes.
- **Virtualization.** Within industry 4.0, it would be possible to create a virtual copy of each of its elements.
- **Decentralization.** Each of the elements of Industry 4.0 might be able to intelligently make decisions for itself, in conjunction with other elements, or globally.
- **Capabilities in real time.** The ecosystem would allow the acquisition and analysis of data in real time.
- **Service orientation.** The elements of Industry 4.0 would be able to abstract their functionality into a service-oriented architecture, and would also be able to consume services offered by other assets. In addition, these services would be indexed and easily accessible by authorized entities.
- **Modularity.** An Industry 4.0 environment would not function in a monolithic way, but would allow adaptation to new requirements by integrating new modules and extending or replacing existing modules.
- **Interactivity.** Industry 4.0 operators at all levels would be able to interact with various physical and logical elements in a simple and effective way.

These principles can be accomplished by a set of enabling technologies that can be summarized into four areas: Industrial Internet of Things, Cloud and Fog computing, Big Data and Virtualization.

Firstly, the goal of the **Internet of Things** (IoT) paradigm is to massively interconnect the objects that surround us – the "things" – using standardized interfaces, allowing them to produce and consume services. Applied to the industrial context, the so-called Industrial Internet of Things (IIoT) vertically integrates all the components within the architecture, ranging from control systems to machines or even the product itself. Moreover, due to their interconnection capabilities, all entities could interact with each other at an horizontal level, enabling decentralized interactions such as monitorization (between operators and machinery) and decision making (between the machines themselves). There are other concepts that are related to the IoT, such as Cyber-Physical systems (CPS), that can also be applied to this context. Note that CPS focus on feedback between systems (i.e., looping) in a more local environment, while IIoT assumes a greater global connectivity.

Cloud computing can be considered as another of the pillars of Industry 4.0 for a variety of reasons. On the one hand, it carries on the analytic procedures with the data provided by the industrial process, retrieved by IIoT devices. On the other hand, it provides support for the delegation of production processes and control to the cloud – enabling new productive processes (e.g. product customization) and innovative services such as "Cloud-based manufacturing" [5]. However, there are various situations, such as management of swarms of robots, where the cloud might not the most suitable solution due to its inherent features (high latency and jitter, lack of local contextual information). For this very purpose, it can be possible to apply emerging paradigms such as *Fog Computing* [6], which focus on the deployment of cloud-like services at the edge of the network.

Third, Industry 4.0 will facilitate the evolution of industrial decision making processes, mainly due to the multiple sources of information that will be available to both operators and systems alike. In order to distill all this information and extract both business and operational intelligence, it is necessary to conduct advanced data analytics procedures. This area includes both the analysis of information at a more local level (e.g., the independent optimization of the operation of a machine based on its interactions with other elements of the production line) and the concept of **Big Data** - the processing of all information provided by entities of the industrial ecosystem, looking for added value services such as monitoring the operation of the ecosystem entities, process optimization, and the identification of anomalies.

Lastly, we can highlight a group of technologies whose target is to change the way of designing and interacting with the production chain, that we will refer to as **Virtualization**. One of these consists in the creation of virtual representations (e.g. 3D abstractions [7]) of all machines and components involved in the production process. This is facilitated by the previously mentioned enabling technologies, and it will allow the creation of novel services based on the concept of "digital twins", where it will be possible to conduct simulations to prevent failures and optimize the production line. Aside from this paradigm, the introduction of modern Human-Machine Interfaces (HMI) can also be included in this category, that make use of augmented and virtual reality devices that ultimately make the operations easier and more flexible for the workers. In addition, the use of advanced robots (autonomous, mobile, modular, multifunctional, etc.) also contribute to improve the performance of certain tasks within the production chain.

3 Landscape of Cyber-Security Threats of Industry 4.0 Enabling Technologies

There are various researchers that have identified the most impactful threats that affect current industrial infrastructure ecosystems. Examples include social engineering, malware infection, compromising Internet-connected components, and insider threats [8]. Still, while these threats are also applicable to Industry 4.0 environments, it is necessary to understand the threats that might arise due to the integration of the enabling technologies introduced in Sect. 2. For this very purpose, this section will provide a taxonomy of such threats. The taxonomy described here has been created according to the IETF standard 7416 [9], that proposes an analysis of security issues whose classification is based on their effect on the main security services: availability, integrity, confidentiality and authentication. Nevertheless, it is important to note that many of the threats affect several of these services. An overall summary of the main threats of each technology, which have been extracted from the current literature, is presented in Table 1.

Industrial Internet of Things. In terms of security, IIoT's main concerns are the privacy protection, authentication and control of access to heterogeneous resources, information management, etc. which are aggravated due to the scarcity of computational resources and autonomy that they present. This causes that most attacks are perpetrated against their *availability*, this is, the exhaustion of the node resources (processing, memory or battery) by overloading them with traffic and repetitive requests (cf. [10]). Nodes can also be physically or remotely compromised by exploiting vulnerabilities or running malware that can put the data *confidentiality* and *integrity* under risk: on the one hand, by exposing sensitive information (e.g., node internal status), as well as intellectual property or personal information retrieved by wearable devices. On the other hand, by manipulating information of all kinds: firstly, the routing information (i.e., neighbor states, available links), which allows the attacker to influence other nodes within the production chain. Secondly, the sensing data itself, that can be potentially falsified when appropriate encryption mechanisms are not applied. In this sense, the node identity misappropriation is also considerable (e.g., with Man-in-the-Middle attacks), which opens the door to other types of attacks. This is the main *authentication* issue, that appears as a consequence of ineffective access control mechanisms to IoT devices.

Cloud/Fog Computing. As it gains interest among the organizations to externalize multiple services (at remote – Cloud – or close – Fog – locations) along the product life cycle, it is crucial to ensure the security and privacy protection of data from internal or external attackers [11]. Again, the most common attack goes against its *availability*, by means of a Denial of service (DoS) attacks against the cloud services. Another example is a service theft attack, where the attacker use the cloud services at the expense of other clients, exploiting vulnerabilities of the underlying hypervisor. Data *integrity* is threatened in presence of malware (e.g., replacing legitimate virtual machines with malicious ones in order to read and manipulate information), and *confidentiality* problems arise when putting trust in the service provider, who has total access to the stored data. Also concerning confidentiality, side-channel attacks must be also mentioned, where malicious virtual machines analyze certain shared features such as the amount of shared memory used. As for *authentication* problems, the major issue appears through social engineering or phishing, where attackers host websites in the cloud that imitate the appearance of legitimate services. It is important to remark the difficulty for the cloud provider to detect such behavior in its servers, since they are also required to not be able to access the data hosted by its clients, for privacy reasons. However, it is necessary to apply robust control access policies, agreed by both client and provider.

Big Data. As the industry processes huge amounts of information about their business, usually through cloud computing resources, it becomes critical to securely store and manage this bulk of data by means of preventive, detective and administrative mechanisms. Such data is characterized by its volume (huge amount), velocity (speed of generation) and variety (multiple formats), and is usually processed in a parallel way by a distributed network of nodes in charge of running MapReduce operations [12]. It is hence difficult to know where the computation takes place and equally tricky to ensure the security of all components (e.g., databases, computing power, etc.), so small weaknesses can put the *availability* of the entire system or its data at risk [13]. As for *confidentiality* and *integrity*, data can be exposed or modified if encryption or integrity measures are not respectively applied, which is frequent in this context to improve efficiency. Data input validation is thereby essential to protect the information during its transmission from several sources (e.g., the corporative network, field devices, the web, etc.). In addition, Big Data also has privacy implications when data is analysed massively, which can draw accurate conclusions about the infrastructure or behaviour patterns of workers within the organization. *Authentication* problems also arise with the unauthorized access to sensitive data (by both insiders or external attackers) spread over multiple nodes. Therefore, it is crucial to introduce security services such as granular access controls, real time monitoring of devices, exhaustive logging procedures, and others.

Virtualization. For the creation and integration of the virtualization technologies in the industry of the future, it is necessary to create standards for the secure information exchange between the physical assets and their virtual representations in order to achieve interoperability among all the interfaces [14]. Again, in terms of *availability*, the multiplicity of devices (each one with its own vulnerabilities) and technologies in this context complicates the assurance of fault-tolerance and the realization of multi-platform user interfaces (e.g., augmented/virtual reality glasses, smartphones). Regarding the *integrity*, the representation of the cyber-physical world also implies the synchronization of coherent data among virtual and real endpoints (e.g., control commands and 3D coordinates) to avoid producing incorrect predictions or dysfunctions in those resources. This information used in simulations could also be leaked due to various reasons (e.g. unsecure execution environments, workers lacking the necessary training), posing a threat to *confidentiality*. In addition, privacy must be taken into account, as the location of operators should be tracked in order to propagate information efficiently. Moreover, *authentication* issues exist with the dissemination of information over multiple platforms and the virtualization of services, blurring the barriers of data protection and easing its access by unauthorized entities, which is aggravated with the use of smartphones and similar devices that are easily breakable. It is thereby necessary to establish trust management procedures when sharing critical information, as well as strict control over the data produced by collaborating partners.

Table 1. Main cyber-security threats of Industry 4.0 enabling technologies

	IIoT	Cloud/fog	Big data	Virtualization
Availability	Exhaustion of resources (traffic, requests)	Network flooding, service theft	Multiple points of failure	Multiple points of failure
Confidentiality	Exposure of sensitive information	Data accesss by the provider, side-channel attacks	Lack of cryptography, privacy issues when massively analyzing data	Simulations information leakage
Integrity	Data or routing information manipulation	Malicious VMs	Untrusted mappers, lack of integrity measures	Disparity between physical and virtual parameters
Authentication	Identity misappropriation	Phishing	Lack of fine-grain access controls to nodes and tables	Lack of AAA services to access data from heterogeneous devices

4   Cyber-Security Threats in Industry 4.0 Innovative Services

In the previous section we have introduced the security threats that affect the main enabling technologies of Industry 4.0. Yet it is also vital to review what are the threats that could affect the most innovative services of this novel industrial ecosystem. The reason is simple: while these services inherit the threats of their enabling technologies, there are also various novel threats that arise due to their particular features. For this analysis, whose results have been obtained through an expert review of the available Industry 4.0 state of the art, we will continue following the IETF standard 7416 [9]. We also provide an overall summary of the main threats of each service in Table 2.

Novel Infrastructures. The gradual transition to more decentralized architectures shown in Sect. 2 is bringing a more heterogeneous and complex environment, where any element could (theoretically) interact and cooperate with any other element. Besides the potential dangers of unresponsive components, from the point of view of *availability* this transition means that not only a malicious insider could target any element, but also that a DoS attack could be launched from any element of the infrastructure. In terms of *integrity*, we need to consider that an adversary can alter the overall global behaviour (e.g. process workflows) by tampering with local decision makers. This is related to the *confidentiality* issues, where malicious attacks against local entities might expose high-level behaviour. Finally, regarding *authentication* threats, as the barriers between the different subsystems are blurred, it is necessary to deploy adequate security policies that can limit the damage caused by unauthorized accesses. However, the expected complexity of such policies will surely result on misconfigured systems, which can be exploited by adversaries.

Retrofitting. It is possible to bring the benefits of the Industry 4.0 to legacy systems by deploying and connecting new technologies to older subsystems [15]. Still, these deployments also bring additional security issues that need to be considered. The existence of a parallel subsystem (e.g. a monitoring system) might bring certain *availability* and *integrity* issues: not only the components that serve as the bridge between the old and the new can become a single point of failure, but also the new technologies could be used to launch attacks against the legacy elements. *Confidentiality* threats also exist, as the new technologies usually act as a "sensing layer" that can expose information about the status and behaviour of the monitored industrial processes. As for the impact of *authentication* threats, it mostly depends on the granularity of the integration of the novel subsystems: black-box interfaces limit the amount of information that can be retrieved from internal subcomponents.

Industrial Data Space. One of the goals the Industry 4.0 is to create common spaces for the secure exchange of information between industrial partners [16]. The creation of such cooperative spaces could bring additional threats from the point of view of *availability* and *integrity*: the existence of DoS attacks that interrupt the information flow at critical times, or tainted components generating bogus data, will probably affect other elements – opening the door to potential cascade effects. *Confidentiality* is also especially important in this context: it is essential to assure that the information exchanged by partners does not facilitate the extraction of competitive intelligence. Still, misconfigurations and other internal attacks might open the door to more serious information leaks. *Authentication* threats are also aggravated in this cooperative space, as unauthorized accesses can have a wider impact in the extraction of valuable information.

Cloud Manufacturing. One of the tenets of this paradigm is the creation of cloud-based industrial applications that take advantage of distributed manufacturing resources [17]. This distribution of resources creates certain threats that have been already described in the context of the novel digital architectures:

from DoS attacks that can be launched from anywhere to anywhere (*Availability*), to the manipulation of the distributed components (*Integrity*). The main difference here is the nature of these threats, such as malicious VMs targetting the hypervisors, DoS against the cloud/fog servers or the network connection, etc. *Confidentiality* threats also become more critical, as the cloud infrastructure not only contains sensitive data, but also sensitive business processes as well. Finally, the complexity in the management of these kind of cloud-based infrastructures also opens more opportunities for *authentication* attacks.

Agents. There are already various proof-of-concepts related to the integration of agents in manufacturing, such as workflow planners to self-organising assembly systems [18]. But there are dangers associated to the deployment of agents in an industrial environment, too. A malicious agent can behave like a piece of malware, affecting the *availability* of other industrial elements. Besides the *integrity* of the agents themselves, we also have to consider how other manipulated elements can exert a (in)direct influence over the behaviour of the agents. By tampering with the environment that surrounds the agent, or even the agent itself, it is possible to launch several *confidentiality* attacks that aim to extract the information flow that goes to the agent, and the information created by the agent itself. Finally, without a proper *authentication* infrastructure, malicious/manipulated agents will tamper with the overall workflow.

Other Enhanced Interactions. As aforementioned, Industry 4.0 enabling technologies such as virtualization allow the creation of novel services such as "digital twins" (virtual representations of subsystems) and "digital workers" (interaction with advanced HMI). Yet there are certain threats related to the actual usage of such technologies and services that need to be highlighted here. These enhanced systems can be manipulated by their human operators, effectively increasing the damage caused by an insider: a malicious digital worker could perform several attacks such as launching DoS attacks (*Availability*), interfering with the decision making processes (*Integrity*), extracting confidential information (*Confidentiality*), and executing privilege escalation attacks (*Authentication*). On the other hand, these enhanced systems can become attackers themselves, causing damage in subtle ways. For example, a malicious attacker could manipulate the HMI to force the worker to perform an incorrect action – and pin the blame on him.

5   Intrusion Detection in Industry 4.0

The analyses performed in the previous section have shown that Industry 4.0 threats are inherently more complex than the threats that target traditional industrial environments. Since networks and interactions are no longer compartmentalized, the attack surface increases – not only in terms of vulnerable entities, but also in terms of potential attackers and attack strategies (e.g. behavioral attacks). Besides, as the number of elements and business processes increases, the existence of misconfigured elements does so as well. Moreover, the opportunities for collaboration also increase the amount of information that is available to

Table 2. Main cyber-security threats of Industry 4.0 innovative services

	Dig. arch.	Retrofitting	Data space	Cloud manuf.	Agents	Others
Availability	Wide attack surface	Single point of failure	Cascade effects	Wide attack surface	Agents as malware	Denial of service
Confidentiality	Global data in local context	Exposure of sensing layer	Information leakage	Business processes leakage	Agent data in local context	Information leakage
Integrity	Behavior manipulation	Cross-cutting attacks	Cascade effects	Manipulation of components	Tampered data/agents	Disrupt decision making processes
Authentication	Complexity and misconfiguration	Fake legacy/sensing layers	Bigger scope of attacks	Management issues	Attacks from/to agents	Privilege escalation

an adversary in case he controls a section of the system. These threats have considerable influence on how intrusion detection systems (IDS) must be designed, deployed and managed in these kind of contexts. In particular, given the threats described in the previous sections, an IDS should comply with several requirements that are described below.

- **Coverage.** Due to the extended attack surface, the IDS must be able to cover all potential interactions and elements of an Industry 4.0 deployment. In addition, it must be able to be easily upgraded with new detection algorithms.
- **Holism.** The IDS must be able to consider not only the different parts of the system – including users, configurations, interactions, potential points of failure and cascade effects, and the like – but also their interactions as a whole, mainly due to the cooperative nature of their elements and the interactions between all actors.
- **Intelligence.** Beyond traditional protocol analysis and information correlation mechanisms, the IDS should take into consideration the existence of more advanced attacks and incorporate more advanced detection techniques such as behavioral analysis.
- **Symbiosis.** The IDS should closely interact not only with other protection mechanisms, such as prevention systems and forensics, but also with other relevant Industry 4.0 services, such as "digital twins".

Notice that these requirements are also desirable for traditional industrial ecosystems, yet such requirements are very difficult to enforce in those contexts – mainly due to the inherent industrial features and necessary trade-offs (e.g. avoid false alarms that can put the production line in jeopardy, minimize the impact of the IDS components in the operational network, etc [19]). Still, the cooperative, dynamic and complex nature of Industry 4.0 ecosystems require that IDS subsystems must interact more closely with the industrial components, in order to detect attacks before their impact becomes too severe.

Understandably, and also due to the specific features of industrial ecosystems, the actual state of the art on IDS for the current industrial ecosystems (cf. [19]) do not fully cover the previously mentioned requirements, and do not consider the services mentioned in Sect. 4. Besides, there are few or no components that search for anomalies in the behavior of Industry 4.0 essential protocols, such as OPC-UA; and the concepts of symbiosis and exchange of security information in this context are still in its infancy.

As for the creation of IDS mechanisms for the industry of the future, there is no need to start from zero: there are various elements in the state of the art that can be adapted and/or enhanced to fulfill the previously presented requirements. For example, there are various platforms that provide event correlation and knowledge extraction from a holistic perspective, although most of such platforms focus on a more centralized architecture. Precisely, there are also agent-based architectures that validate the behavior of the monitored systems [20].

Moreover, there are various preliminary works that could serve as a foundation for the more advanced features required by Industry 4.0 IDS, such as the dynamic deployment of honeypots adapted to the requirements of the system, the automatic identification of critical elements, and the interaction with physical simulation systems in order to detect anomalies [21].

6   Conclusions

In this article we have provided an overview of the threats and requirements that are related to the enabling technologies and innovative services of Industry 4.0. As cyber-attacks against industrial ecosystems are increasing, the integration of novel technologies will create new avenues to exploit. Therefore, it is crucial to take these novel threats into consideration and further study how to apply the highlighted requirements in the design of intrusion detection mechanisms for the industry of the future.

Acknowledgments. This work has been funded by the Spanish Ministry of Economy, Industry and Competitiveness through the SADCIP (RTC-2016-4847-8) project. The work of the first author han been partially financed by the Spanish Ministry of Education under the FPU program (FPU15/03213).

References

1. Davies, R.: Industry 4.0. digitalisation for productivity and growth. European Parliamentary Research Service, Briefing (2015)
2. ICS-CERT. Overview of cyber vulnerabilities, June 2017. https://ics-cert.us-cert. gov/content/overview-cyber-vulnerabilities
3. Leitão, P., Barbosa, J., Papadopoulou, M.-E.Ch., Venieris, I.S.: Standardization in cyber-physical systems: the ARUM case. In: IEEE International Conference on Industrial Technology (ICIT 2015), pp. 2988–2993 (2015)
4. Colombo, A.W., Karnouskos, S., Bangemann, T.: Towards the next generation of industrial cyber-physical systems. In: Colombo, A.W., et al. (eds.) Industrial Cloud-Based Cyber-Physical Systems, pp. 1–22. Springer, Cham (2014). https:// doi.org/10.1007/978-3-319-05624-1_1

5. Xu, X.: From cloud computing to cloud manufacturing. Robot. Comput.-Integr. Manuf. **28**(1), 75–86 (2012)
6. Chiang, M., Zhang, T.: Fog and IoT: an overview of research opportunities. IEEE Internet Things J. **3**(6), 854–864 (2016)
7. Moreno, A., Velez, G., Ardanza, A., Barandiaran, I., de Infante, Á.R., Chopitea, R.: Virtualisation process of a sheet metal punching machine within the industry 4.0 vision. Int. J. Interact. Des. Manuf. (IJIDeM) **11**, 365–373 (2016)
8. Federal Office for information Security. Industrial control system security: Top 10 threats and countermeasures 2016, June 2017. https://www.allianz-fuer-cybersicherheit.de/ACS/DE/_/downloads/BSI-CS_005E.pdf?__blob=publicationFile&v=3
9. Tsao, T., Alexander, R., Dohler, M., Daza, V., Lozano, A., Richardson, M : A security threat analysis for the routing protocol for low-power and lossy networks (RPLs). Technical report (2015)
10. Zhang, K., Liang, X., Lu, R., Shen, X.: Sybil attacks and their defenses in the internet of things. IEEE Internet Things J. **1**(5), 372–383 (2014)
11. Khalil, I.M., Khreishah, A., Azeem, M.: Cloud computing security: a survey. Computers **3**(1), 1–35 (2014)
12. Dean, J., Ghemawat, S.: Mapreduce: simplified data processing on large clusters. Commun. ACM **51**(1), 107–113 (2008)
13. Upadhyay, G.M., Arora, H.: Vulnerabilities of data storage security in big data. IITM J. Manag. IT **7**(1), 37–41 (2016)
14. Brettel, M., Friederichsen, N., Keller, M., Rosenberg, M.: How virtualization, decentralization and network building change the manufacturing landscape: an industry 4.0 perspective. Int. J. Mech. Ind. Sci. Eng. **8**(1), 37–44 (2014)
15. Stock, T., Seliger, G.: Opportunities of sustainable manufacturing in industry 4.0. Procedia CIRP **40**, 536–541 (2016)
16. Industrial Data Space Association. Industrial data space: Reference architecture, June 2017. http://www.industrialdataspace.org/en/
17. Dazhong, W., Greer, M.J., Rosen, D.W., Schaefer, D.: Cloud manufacturing: Strategic vision and state-of-the-art. J. Manuf. Syst. **32**(4), 564–579 (2013)
18. Wang, S., Wan, J., Zhang, D., Li, D., Zhang, C.: Towards smart factory for industry 4.0: a self-organized multi-agent system with big data based feedback and coordination. Comput. Netw. **101**, 158–168 (2016)
19. Rubio, J.E., Alcaraz, C., Roman, R., Lopez, J.: Analysis of intrusion detection systems in industrial ecosystems. In: 14th International Conference on Security and Cryptography (SECRYPT 2017) (2017)
20. HeSec. HeSec Smart Agents, June 2017. http://he-sec.com/products/
21. McParland, C., Peisert, S., Scaglione, A.: Monitoring security of networked control systems: it's the physics. IEEE Secur. Priv. **12**(6), 32–39 (2014)

De-Synchronisation Attack Modelling in Real-Time Protocols Using Queue Networks: Attacking the ISO/IEC 61850 Substation Automation Protocol

James G. Wright[1]([envelope]) and Stephen D. Wolthusen[1,2]

[1] School of Mathematics and Information Security, Royal Holloway,
University of London, Egham TW20 0EX, UK
james.wright.2015@live.rhul.ac.uk
[2] Norwegian Information Security Laboratory,
Norwegian University of Science and Technology, Trondheim, Norway
stephen.wolthusen@rhul.ac.uk

Abstract. Applications developed for Supervisory Control And Data Acquisition (SCADA) protocols in several domains, particularly the energy sector, must satisfy hard real-time constraints to ensure the safety of the systems they are deployed on. These systems are highly sensitive to Quality of Service (QoS) violations, but it is not always clear whether a compliant implementation will satisfy the stated QoS of the standard. This paper proposes a framework for studying a protocol's QoS properties based on a *queuing network* approach that offers a number of advantages over state machine or model-checking approaches.

The authors describe the framework as an instance of a network of M/M/1/K of queues with the block-after-service discipline, to allow for the analysis of probabilistic packet flows in valid protocol runs. This framework allows for the study of denial of service (DoS), performance degradation, and de-synchronisation attacks. The model is validated by a tool allowing automation of queue network analysis, and is used to demonstrate a possible breach of the QoS guarantees of the ISO/IEC 61850-7-2 substation automation standard with a de-synchronisation attack.

Keywords: Queue networks · ISO/IEC 61850 · Quality of service
Protocol analysis · De-synchronisation attack

1 Introduction

The methods that are used to secure SCADA technologies are being stretched as they are being incorporated into Smart Grid (SG) communication standards. To maintain the safety of the physical distribution infrastructure, stringent QoS requirements that govern how instructions and data are transmitted and processed across the network must be maintained by the implementer of the SG's

© Springer Nature Switzerland AG 2018
G. D'Agostino and A. Scala (Eds.): CRITIS 2017, LNCS 10707, pp. 131–143, 2018.
https://doi.org/10.1007/978-3-319-99843-5_12

communications network. Any delays in transmission could potentially lead to the disruption and damage of the physical distribution network. The imbalance of maintaining the QoS requirements over the security promises laid out in the communications standards in a SG cyber-physical system could lead to the safety of physical infrastructure still being compromised. This is due to malicious actors being able to force the communications network into either an undesirable state, or being allowed to send malicious commands. Whilst both the academic and industrial research communities are now focusing on solving these new security challenges, there is very little focus dedicated to checking if the security and QoS promises made by SCADA protocols hold true. It is important that the communications standards have rigid security definitions as the networks they will be deployed on will be made up of devices supplied by different manufactures, who may have different interpretations of the standard, as well as the infrastructure itself being required to run uninterrupted on a time scale of decades. Alongside this the communications network will be distributed across a wide area network, which provides an adversary with ample attack vectors to undermine the security of the cyber infrastructure. A benefit of securing the protocols is that it could prevent some of the attacks that have already been implemented against SG technologies using these standards [2].

The focus of this work is to describe and demonstrate the effectiveness of a framework developed by the authors to analyse distributed communications models, that are being incorperated into SCADA standards. The authors have pursued a new framework because the standards that govern communications networks provide a large number of communications models, whose permutations of use would make the searchable space of potential attacks close to boundless [13]. Also SG standards are more flexible on the acceptable behaviour within a communication models than their cryptographic counterparts, so traditional model checking frameworks would find it difficult to detect undesirable behaviours in their communications models.

The framework uses queuing networks to model the flow of both regular and malicious packets between the stages of the state machine representing a possible protocol run. The model can analyse how an adversary interacts with the semantic steps of either the client or server machines in a run that involves, theoretically, as many communication models as the user of the framework needs in attempt to drive it into a undesirable state. Each queue in the network is truncated to allow for a more realistic modelling of buffer sizes of the state machine, so that packets can be prevented from travelling through the network if all of its recipient queues are full. This inclusion allows DoS attacks against a run to be encapsulated in any model computed by the framework. The framework also allows the user to model attacks against the semantics of synchronization of state machines in a protocol run. In its current form the framework provides a global view of the run, showing the user the mean total number of packets in each stage of the run. The mean total number of packets can be used to derive a range of performance metrics that allow the user to analyse the effects that an attack will have on a specific part of the protocol run. The framework can also be reconfigured to look at attacks at the packet level of the network.

The author's are primarily using the framework to investigate the promiseses of IEC 61850 substation automation standard, which has stringent QoS requirements governing communications network. These stringent requirments provide a fertile development ground for the discovery of bespoke attacks, that only arise in networks with distributed communication topologies. As well as this, the generation of any potential solutions for these undesired behaviours must be efficient enough meet the QoS of the protocol. The real-time nature of the protocol means that the communications networks of the SG are easily susceptible performance degradation and attacks against the security promise of availability. However, the way in which framework has been developed means that any attacks discovered, and their potnetial solutions, can be applied to other SCADA and distributed communications standards. Using the framework the authors have discovered an attack against IEC 61850's control communication model [12]. In this attack the adversary alters the rate of processing of one of the queues in the state machine of a protocol run, which increases the probability that the server's state machine will go down the timeout path of the run. As the server's state machine doesn't announce that it has timed out, the client continues sending request for the server to follow. This will eventually lead to a de-synchronisation of state between the client and server, and will force both machines to reset the run.

The remainder of this paper proceeds as follows: Sect. 2 describes the current research on how DoS and timing attacks affect SGs, along with how queuing theory has been used to model DoS attacks. Section 3 goes onto to describe the mathematical formalism used in the framework. Then Sect. 4 describes the de-synchronisation attack demonstrated in the framework. Before giving a conclusions and a direction for future work in Sect. 5.

2   Related Works

Many different frameworks have been developed over the years to model the security promises of cryptograpic standards. The underlying principle of each varies; the main ones being belief logics, theorem proving and state exploration, along with an array of different model checkers [17].

The main use of the queing theory formalism in the security domain has been to describe DoS attacks. It is a suitable formalism for this type of attack, as DoS scenarios can be modeled without much abstraction. This is due to how queuing theory calculates the efficency of a series of objects being processed in a queue according to a specific set of rules. These rules can easily be translated to represent a processor with a specific memory allocation. Despite this natural affinity, seemingly little research has been persued in the modelling DoS attacks using queuing theory. Most of the research describes various packet level scenarios with either a single $M/M/1$ queue or an open Jackson network, which is a network of $M/M/1$ queues. Relying on $M/M/1$ limits what the user can discern from the framework, as a queue of this type can hold an infinite number of objects. Given this underlying assumption, all that can be discerned from these models is the degradation of the queues performance. It doesn't tell the user at what point the system being modelled will fail to meet its promise of avaliability. However, Xiao-Yu *et al.* [22] does use a $M/M/c/K$ queue to investigate SIP INVITE request flooding scenario. Their solution is to create a queue that deals only with INVITE requests. Kammas *et al.* [8] created an open Jackson network of $M/M/1$ queues to model virus propagation across a network. Their state space included the internal transitions of state of each node, as well as the global state of the network. Wang *et al.* [23] developed a mathematical model, using embedded two dimensional Markov chains, to allow the user to generate different probability distributions for any distribution of acceptance rates. Their model also allows for the separate analysis of the malicious packets properties from the normal traffic's.

There has been some research into how DoS attacks will affect SG communication networks. Hurst *et al.* [6] developed a mathematical framework to help security practitioners to evaluate the scale of the damage their communication network would suffer if they were attacked by various types of distributed DoS attacks. Liu *et al.* [10] demonstrated that a DoS attack against load frequency controls can affect the stability of the power grid. Li *et al.* [9] studied the time delay suffered by critical communication packets on an IEC 61850 communications network, when either the physical or application layer is flooded with malicious messages. There seems to have been no other research into how a DoS attack could be used against the IEC 61850 standard. One potential solution to this problem is to use flock based behavioural transitions rules to make sure the packets avoid denying a node availability to the network [24]. Ansilla *et al.* [1] developed a hardware based algorithm to deal with SYN flooding on SG networks. Srikantha & Kundur [18] developed a game theoretic approach to deal with DoS attacks. Their solution is a system that provides each node in the communication network with a reputation score, which, if a node is compromised, automates the rerouteing process to exclude that node from the communications topology.

Clock synchronisation protocols are a fertile group of standards investigation of de-synchronisation attacks. There have been various analyse of the security vulnerabilities of the Network Time Protocol (NTP)/Precision Time Protocol (PTP) protocols, where a taxonomy of the various attack vectors against the network show how an andversary would be able to either manipulate or control the network [4,7,11]. Each taxonomy has proposed various countermeasures, such as introducing the Confidentiality Integrity Authentication triad into this domain or basing the protocol on the peer-to-peer network paradigm. Ullmann & Vogler [21] performed an analysis on the consequence of a delay attack against both the NTP and PTP protocols. They proved that a delay in a sync message would affect all the client clocks, and a delayed request message would only affect the client that sent the message. They proposed implementing a Secure Hash Algorithm on the protocol to mitigate these attacks. Tsang & Beznosov [20] created a qualitative taxonomy of attacks against the PTP protocol. They laid out how an adversary could potentially misuse certain messages in the protocol to create undesirable effects, while suggesting countermeasures for most of them. Mizrahi [14] developed some game theoretic strategies to prevent delay attacks against NTP. Moussa *et al.* [15] who produced a detailed analysis of the consequences of a delay attack in a SG substation environment. They also provided a mathematical model to counter delay attacks.

3 Mathematical Theory of the Framework

The framework uses a network of truncated $M/M/1/K$ queues to create a probabilistic state exploration methodology for checking the promises of a protocol. The $M/M/1/K$ provides a more realistic model than the $M/M/1$ queues because it imposes a limit, K, on the length of the queue, so when the queue is full it will no longer accept any packets. This allows the user to model attacks against the availability of a step in a protocol run. Also, using a network of $M/M/1/K$ provides the user with the versatility of being able to model different layers of abstraction of the system, as it can be set up to represent the flow of packets over the communications network, as well as the semantics of a protocol run. When the formalism is used to describe the semantic flow of run each queue represents an action that a state machine can perform. The framework adapts the work of Osorio & Bierlaire [16], which describes the state of an individual queue in a $M/M/c/K$ network, to describe the global state of the network.

The assumptions made by the framework are;

- Each queue obeys the first-in-first-out (FIFO) discipline for processing packets.
- If the queue is blocked, it uses the blocked-at-service discipline.
- The process time and time between successive unblocking are each assumed to follow an exponential distribution. However, the effective probability distribution describing the rate at which packets pass through a queue isn't an exponential distribution.
- That the transition between states is memoryless.

The rest of the this section is dedicated to describing the mathematical formalism used by the framework to create models. It first gives a brief overview of continuous time Markov Chains (CTMC) that are used to find the probabilities of certain events occurring within the network. The next section describes how the physical properties of each queue in the network are calculated. Then the state space that is used to generate the transition rate matrix is described, before, finally, going over the various performance metrics the framework provides. The below description focuses on the assumptions and set up for the semantic flow protocol runs.

3.1 Probability for Queuing Theory

As the state of the queuing network is memoryless, the probability of a transition happening between states can be described using CTMC [5]. To find the vector

of the probabilities of the state that the network will be in, the global balance
equation must be solved. The assumptions used in solving this equation are that
the system:

- It is independent of time.
- It is independent of the initial state vector.

If the CTMC are ergodic, then an unique steady state probability vector, $\boldsymbol{\pi}$,
exists that is independent of any initial probability vector. This means the global
balance for each state can be described by the conservation of probability flux
in and out of the state:

$$\sum_{j \in \mathscr{I}} \pi_j q_{ji} = \pi_j \sum_{j \in \mathscr{I}} q_{ij} \tag{1}$$

where π_j is the probability of being in a state, q_{ij} is the rate of transmission
between state i and j, and $\mathscr{I}$ is the state space. Rearranging equation (1) it can
be represented in the matrix form:

$$0 = \pi Q \tag{2}$$

where Q is the transition matrix. The steady state vector can be found by solving
the system of linear equations described in (2), using the boundary condition:

$$\sum_{i \in \mathscr{I}} \pi_i = 1 \tag{3}$$

which states that the sum of all the probabilities of being in a given state is one.

3.2   The Mathematical Description of the Topological Space

The first step that the framework must do is to calculate the parameters that
govern how each queue in the network performs. For this framework that is
being developed there are a few built in assumptions that provide bounds for
the calculations. Packets in a queue can be in one of three states, being processed,
a, waiting to be processed, w, or blocked b. For queues in the model's network
$a + b \leq c$, where the number of servers of a queue. It is assumed that $c = 1$
in this framework. The next assumption of the framework is $a + b + w \leq K$,
where K is the maximum capacity of packets in each queue in the network.
Another assumption when using the framework to model a semantic protocol
run is that a packet cannot return to a queue behind it in the network topology.
This guarantees that the model doesn't break causality, as protocol runs are
assumed to have unidirectional flow of time built into them.

Before calculating the endogenous parameters of each queue in the network,
the user must set up a series of exogenous parameters for each node. These are:

- K_i: The maximum capacity of each queue.
- μ_i: The service rate of each queue
- γ_i: The external arrival rate to a queue, if it is at the starting edge of the
  network.

- $\phi(i,1)$: The average number of distinct target queues that are blocking a packet at each queue. If a queue is at the concluding edge of the network this term is not required. A method for approximating this value is given in Osorio & Bierlaire [16].
- p_{ij}: The probability of packet transitioning from queue i to queue j once processed.

Once these have been set, the rest of the parameters describing the queues' behaviour can be solved by using the following set of non-linear simultaneous equations. The first equation calculates the probability that a queue is full. It is a standard result for $M/M/1/K$ queues. The probability that a queue is full is given by:

$$P(N_i = K_i) = \frac{(1 - \rho_i)\rho_i^{K_i}}{1 - \rho_i^{K_i+1}} \tag{4}$$

where $\rho_i = \frac{\lambda_i}{\mu_i^{eff}}$ is the traffic intensity [5]. In the steady state approximation $\rho < 1$. This equation calculates the total arrival rate into the queue, including those that are lost:

$$\lambda_i = \frac{\lambda_i^{eff}}{1 - P(N_i = K_i)} \tag{5}$$

This is the effective arrival rate of only the packets that are processed by the queue:

$$\lambda_i^{eff} = \gamma_i(1 - P(N_i = K_i)) + \sum_j p_{ji}\lambda_j^{eff} \tag{6}$$

$\mathscr{P}_i$ is the probability that of being blocked at a queue:

$$\mathscr{P}_i = \sum_j p_{ij}P(N_j = K_j) \tag{7}$$

The following equation is the approximation that presents the common acceptance rate of all the queues that a queue can send a packet to:

$$\frac{1}{\widetilde{\mu_i^a}} = \sum_{j \in \mathscr{I}+} \frac{\lambda_j^{eff}}{\lambda_i^{eff}\mu_j^{eff}} \tag{8}$$

The effective service rate of a queue, which includes time being blocked, is given by:

$$\frac{1}{\mu_i^{eff}} = \frac{1}{\mu_i} + \frac{\mathscr{P}_i}{\widetilde{\mu_i^a}\phi(i,1)} \tag{9}$$

3.3   The Description Probabilistic View of the Protocol Run

Once all of the queue's parameters have been discerned, a transition rate matrix, Q, can be generated for the transitions between all the possible states in the state space. Once that is done π can be calculated and the marginal probability of an event happening can be calculated.

Currently the framework allows the user to calculate the most likely path across a protocol run. The state space for this view is given by.

$$\mathscr{I} = \{(k_1, \ldots, k_N) \in \mathbb{N}^N\} \tag{10}$$

There are three types transitions that can occur in this state space.

Initial state s	New state t	Rate q_{st}	Conditions
$(i, \ldots)$	$(i+1, \ldots)$	λ_i	$p_{0i} \neq 0$ & $N_i \leq k_i - 1$
$(\ldots, i)$	$(\ldots, i-1)$	μ_i^{eff}	$p_{0i} \neq 0$ & $N_i \geq 1$
$(\ldots, i, \ldots, j, \ldots)$	$(\ldots, i-1, \ldots, j+1, \ldots)$	μ_i^{eff}	$p_{ij} \neq 0$ & $N_i \geq 1$ & $N_j \leq k_i - 1$

1. Flow into the network.
2. Flow out of the network.
3. Packet transmission between states.

Q is then used to find the steady state vector for this CTMC.

The marginal probabilities that can be calculated in this view is the likelihood that a specific queue has k packets. It is calculated by summing the probability of all the states that have k packets in the queue of interest:

$$\pi_i(k) = \sum_{k_i = k \in \mathscr{I}} \pi(k_1, \ldots, k_N) \tag{11}$$

3.4   Performance Metrics

Below are various performance metrics that can be applied to the marginal probabilities produced by this mathematical formalism.

Performance metric	Equation
Traffic intensity	$\rho_i = \sum_{k=1}^{k} \pi_i(k)$
Throughput	$\lambda_i = \sum_{k=1}^{k} \pi_i(k)\mu_i^{eff}$
Total throughput	$\lambda = \sum_{i=1}^{N} \lambda_{0i}$
Mean number of packets	$\bar{k}_i = \sum_{k=1}^{k} k\pi_i(k)$
Mean queue length	$\bar{q}_i = \sum_{k=c_i}^{k} (k - c_i)\pi_i(k)$
Mean response time	$\bar{T}_i = \frac{\bar{k}_i}{\lambda_i}$
Mean wait time	$\bar{W}_i = \bar{T}_i - \frac{1}{\mu_i^{eff}}$
Mean number of visits	$e_i = \frac{\lambda_i}{\lambda}$
Relative utilisation	$x_i = \frac{e_i}{\mu_i^{eff}}$

4   Results

This section describes de-synchronisation attack against the IEC 61850's control model that has been discovered using the framework described in Sect. 3.

4.1   De-Synchronisation Attack

The attack developed using the framework shows that an adversary can cause the client's and server's state machines to become de-synchronised. The adversary achieves this by either increasing or decreasing the rate at which the server receives the $oper - req[TestOK]$ in the Select Before Operate (SBO) control model, described in section 19.2.2 of IEC 61850-7-2 (shown in a truncated form in Fig. 1). The adversary can cause this disruption of state because the standard can be interpreted as not requiring the server to send out a *timeout* message to the client. Whilst this is happening the client still thinks the run is following the operation request branch of the protocol run, and will expect an update that will never arrive. This is a legitimate interpretation of the standard that devices will have to be prepared for, due to the QoS promise of interoperability of all devices regardless of manufacturer. This attack vector provides the adversary the ability to create doubt over the state of any logical node that has *"data object instances of a Controllable common data class and whose ctlModel DataAttribute that is not set to status-only"* [12]. This includes safety equipment, such as circuit breakers, whose response to an emergency situation have to be completed within $5ms$ [19]. If the disruption caused by the de-synchronisation of states causes a control command to violate the QoS requirements, the adversary can cause physical damage to the distribution network.

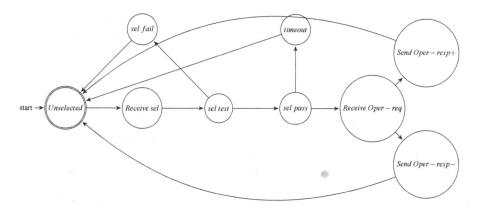

Fig. 1. A truncated version of the server side of the SBO version of the control communication protocol run described in section 19.2.2 of IEC61850-7-2.

The adversary in this result is the same the symbolic one described by Dolev-Yao [3]. The adversary in this model is an omnipotent and omnipresent party on the communications network who *"can intercept messages before they reach their intended destination, it can modify and reroute them, possibly with invalid sender fields"*.

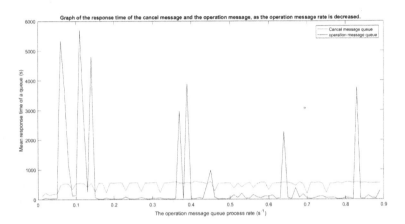

Fig. 2. The graph shows the mean response time a queue dealing with *timeout* and receiving the $oper - req[TestOK]$ message as the adversary changes the processing rate of the $oper - req[TestOK]$.

Figure 2 shows that adversary can increase the mean response time of the protocol run receiving the $oper - req[TestOK]$ message by several orders magnitude by altering the processing rate of queue accepting those packets. The dramatic increase in the response time to receiving the packets increases the probability that the protocol run will take the *timeout* path, which would cause the desynchronisation. In this analysis no other variables were altered. The analysis also used the truncated form of the protocol run depicted in Fig. 1.

5   Conclusion

The above analysis has shown that the explicit QoS requirements of IEC 61850 are not upheld throughout specification. This has been shown using a framework that allows the user to look at how specific adversarial interactions with a protocol run can undermine certain performance metrics in the data stream. The de-synchronisation attack allows an adversary to cause confusion as to the state of a physical device on the SG's communication network. This could cause physical damage to the cyber-physical system if the client's communications are delayed due to having to reset its state machine, and begin the protocol again when it is dealing with safety equipment. This attack could be prevented by having the standard declare that the server broadcast that the session has timed out, so the client can revert back to the previous known state without having to query the server to find out what state it is in.

Future versions of the framework will allow for greater resolution in describing this attack, as it will give the user the ability to calculate the probability that the protocol run will go down a certain path.

Progressing onwards, the authors plan to further develop the framework by allowing the user to see the possible internal states of each queue. The two possible views are a module that allows for the probability of the specific packet ordering to be calculated, and a module to see whether the packets are blocked, processing, or waiting. These modules will be added so adversaries with less knowledge and capabilities can be modelled. They will also add a calculation parameter to the non-linear equations that calculates the probability that a blocked packet will drop out of the network after a certain period of time. After this the aim is to develop more performance criteria for other types of undesirable metrics in the communication network so that more attacks against the security and QoS promises of IEC 61850 can be discovered in the other communication models in the standard. Once the development of the framework is complete, the development of new attacks will be undertaken. The ultimate aim of the authors is to produce attacks that have a more realistic adversary, one that isn't omnipresent in the communications network, and develop a framework in such a way that it can warn SG managers if they are under attack.

Acknowledgments. This work is supported by an EPSRC Academic Centres of Excellence in Cyber Security Research PhD grant. The authors would like to thank Joshua Robinson and Ela Kasprsky for their help in understanding some of the mathematical concepts used in this paper.

References

1. Ansilla, J.D., Vasudevan, N., JayachandraBensam, J., Anunciya, J.D.: Data security in smart grid with hardware implementation against DoS attacks. In: International Conference on Circuit Power and Computing Technologies, ICCPCT 2015, pp. 1–7 (2015)
2. Cherepanov, A.: WIN32/INDUSTROYER: A New Threat for Industrial Control Systems. Technical report, ESET, 12 June 2017
3. Dolev, D., Yao, A.: On the security of public key protocols. IEEE Trans. Inf. Theory **29**(2), 198–208 (1983)
4. Gaderer, G., Treytl, A., Sauter, T.: Security aspects for IEEE 1588 based clock synchronization protocols. In: IEEE International Workshop on Factory Communication Systems, WFCS 2006, Torino, Italy, pp. 247–250. Citeseer (2006)
5. Gross, D., Shortle, J.F., Thompson, J.M., Harris, C.M.: Fundamentals of Queueing Theory, 4th edn. Wiley-Interscience, New York (2008)
6. Hurst, W., Shone, N., Monnet, Q.: Predicting the effects of DDoS attacks on a network of critical infrastructures. In: IEEE International Conference on Computer and Information Technology; Ubiquitous Computing and Communications; Dependable, Autonomic and Secure Computing; Pervasive Intelligence and Computing, 2015, pp. 1697–1702, October 2015
7. Itkin, E., Wool, A.: A security analysis and revised security extension for the precision time protocol. In: IEEE International Symphosium on Precision Clock

Synchronization for Measurement, Control, and Communication, ISPCS 2016, pp. 1–6 (2016)

8. Kammas, P., Komninos, T., Stamatiou, Y.C.: A queuing theory based model for studying intrusion evolution and elimination in computer networks. In: The Fourth International Conference on Information Assurance and Security, pp. 167–171, September 2008

9. Li, Q., Ross, C., Yang, J., Di, J., Balda, J.C., Mantooth, H.A.: The effects of flooding attacks on time-critical communications in the smart grid. In: 2015 IEEE Power Energy Society Innovative Smart Grid Technologies Conference (ISGT), pp. 1–5, February 2015

10. Liu, S., Liu, X.P., Saddik, A.E.: Denial-of-Service (dos) attacks on load frequency control in smart grids. In: IEEE PES Innovative Smart Grid Technologies Conference ISGT **2013**, pp. 1–6 (2013)

11. Malhotra, A., Goldberg, S.: Attacking NTP's authenticated broadcast mode. SIGCOMM Comput. Commun. Rev. **46**(2), 12–17 (2016)

12. TC 57 Power Systems Management and Associated Information Exchange. Communication Networks and Systems for Power Utility Automation - Part 7–2: Basic Information and Communication Structure - Abstract Communication Service Interface. IEC standard 61850-7-2. Technical report, International Electrotechnical Commission (2010)

13. Mitchell, D.L., Durgin, N.A., Lincoln, P.D., Mitchell, J.C., Scedrov, A.: Undecidability of bounded security protocols. In: Workshop on Formal Methods and Security Protocols (1999)

14. Mizrahi, T.: A game theoretic analysis of delay attacks against time synchronization protocols. In: 2012 IEEE International Symposium on Precision Clock Synchronization for Measurement, Control and Communication, pp. 1–6, September 2012

15. Moussa, B., Debbabi, M., Assi, C.: A detection and mitigation model for PTP delay attack in a smart grid substation. In: IEEE International Conference on Smart Grid Communications, SmartGridComm 2015, pp. 497–502, November 2015

16. Osorio, C., Bierlaire, M.: An analytic finite capacity queueing network model capturing the propagation of congestion and blocking. Eur. J. Oper. Res. **196**(3), 996–1007 (2009)

17. Patel, R., Borisaniya, B., Patel, A., Patel, D., Rajarajan, M., Zisman, A.: Comparative analysis of formal model checking tools for security protocol verification. In: Meghanathan, N., Boumerdassi, S., Chaki, N., Nagamalai, D. (eds.) CNSA 2010. CCIS, vol. 89, pp. 152–163. Springer, Heidelberg (2010). https://doi.org/10.1007/978-3-642-14478-3_16

18. Srikantha, P., Kundur, D.: Denial of service attacks and mitigation for stability in cyber-enabled power grid. In: 2015 IEEE Power Energy Society Innovative Smart Grid Technologies Conference (ISGT), pp. 1–5, February 2015

19. TC 57 Power systems management and associated information exchange. Communication networks and systems for power utility automation - Part 5: Communication requirements for functions and device models. IEC standard 61850-5. Technical report, International Electrotechnical Commission (2013)

20. Tsang, J., Beznosov, K.: A security analysis of the precise time protocol (short paper). In: Ning, P., Qing, S., Li, N. (eds.) ICICS 2006. LNCS, vol. 4307, pp. 50–59. Springer, Heidelberg (2006). https://doi.org/10.1007/11935308_4

21. Ullmann, M., Vgeler, M.: Delay attacks - implication on NTP and PTP time synchronization. In: 2009 International Symposium on Precision Clock Synchronization for Measurement, Control and Communication, pp. 1–6, October 2009

22. Wan, X.Y., Li, Z., Fan, Z.F.: A SIP DoS flooding attack defense mechanism based on priority class queue. In: 2010 IEEE International Conference on Wireless Communications, Networking and Information Security, pp. 428–431, June 2010
23. Wang, Y., Lin, C., Li, Q., Fang, Y.: A queueing analysis for the denial of service (DoS) attacks in computer networks. Comput. Netw. **51**(12), 3564–3573 (2007)
24. Wei, J., Kundur, D.: A flocking-based model for DoS-resilient communication routing in smart grid. IEEE Global Communications Conference, GLOBECOM 2012, pp. 3519–3524, December 2012

Assessing Urban Rail Transit Systems Vulnerability: Metrics vs. Interdiction Models

Stefano Starita[1], Annunziata Esposito Amideo[2(✉)], and Maria Paola Scaparra[2]

[1] Warwick Business School, University of Warwick, Coventry, UK
Stefano.Starita@wbs.ac.uk
[2] Kent Business School, University of Kent, Canterbury, UK
{ae306,M.P.Scaparra}@kent.ac.uk

Abstract. Urban rail transit systems are highly vulnerable to disruptions, including accidental failures, natural disasters and terrorist attacks. Due to the crucial role that railway infrastructures play in economic development, productivity and social well-being of communities, evaluating their vulnerability and identifying their most critical components is of paramount importance. Two main approaches can be deployed to assess transport infrastructure vulnerabilities: vulnerability metrics and interdiction models. In this paper, we compare these two approaches and apply them to the Central London Tube to identify the most critical stations with respect to accessibility, efficiency and flow measures.

Keywords: Critical infrastructures · Vulnerability analysis
Interdiction

1 Introduction

Railway infrastructures have been repeatedly affected by disasters, either natural or man-made. On July 7 2005, a series of coordinated suicide bomb attacks in the London tube severely disrupted underground services, caused more than 50 casualties and injured hundreds [4]. More recently, Euston Station, one of London's principal interchange points, was closed due to a fire that triggered a power cut, leading to a massive transportation system disruption all over the UK [11]. In March 2017, London Bridge Rail and Tube stations were closed down as a preventive measure in response to a security alert prompted by a suspicious vehicle: the stations were evacuated, many trains cancelled, and travellers experienced major disruptions for several hours [10]. Given these threats and the huge number of people relying on railway transport (the number of passenger journeys in the UK during 2016–17 has reached a peak of 1.7 billions [17]), it is paramount to develop appropriate techniques to assess railway infrastructure vulnerabilities so as to plan for efficient protection strategies.

Railway infrastructures are network-based systems composed of stations (the nodes) and connections among them (the links). We assess railway infrastructure

G. D'Agostino and A. Scala (Eds.): CRITIS 2017, LNCS 10707, pp. 144–155, 2018.
https://doi.org/10.1007/978-3-319-99843-5_13

vulnerability through the identification of the most critical stations in the network, i.e., those whose disruption may damage the system the most. According to the intergovernmental panel on climate change (IPCC) *vulnerability encompasses a variety of concepts and elements including sensitivity or susceptibility to harm and lack of capacity to cope and adapt* [14]. Vulnerability can be generally defined as *the performance drop of an infrastructure system under a given disruptive event* [18], and can be assessed through either metrics or optimization models. For instance, [16] describes four different metrics to evaluate vulnerability: maximal flow, shortest path, connectivity, and system flow. More recently, [3] discusses several vulnerability indices such as network importance [12] and robustness [19] to assess road networks vulnerability. The main rational behind these methods is to use metrics to devise a ranking among the system components, which can then be used to prioritize mitigation measures.

Optimization models offer an alternative approach to assess infrastructure criticalities. Specifically, network interdiction models identify optimal ways to disrupt network operations, by removing nodes and edges. Seminal papers in this area were introduced for military purposes and aimed at identifying critical set of arcs to disrupt network flow [25] or shortest paths [8]. A few decades later, interdiction models were extended to service and supply chain systems, to identify critical facilities with respect to system costs and demand coverage [6]. Many recent interdiction models focus on network connectivity and cohesiveness measures [1,2,9]. For a comprehensive review of interdiction models, the reader can refer to [7,21].

In this paper, we argue that interdiction models are a more effective and accurate tool to identify critical components than static rankings based on vulnerability measures. The latter, in fact, fail at capturing component interactions after a disruption and often result in an underestimation of possible disruption extents. In fact, if for example the most critical component according to a given vulnerability metric fails, the ranking of the other components may change and should be reevaluated. Interdiction models are able to capture this interdependency and therefore identify the real sets of most critical components.

To prove our claim, we consider different vulnerability measures recently proposed in the literature to assess rail transport systems vulnerability [18,22]. We then propose some interdiction models and test both approaches on the Central London Tube.

The remainder of this paper is organized as follows. Vulnerability metrics and interdiction models are described in Sect. 2. In Sect. 3, a vulnerability analysis of the Central London Tube is performed using both methods and the obtained results are critically analyzed. Section 4 offers some conclusive remarks, along with further research developments.

2 Vulnerability Assessment Approaches

Vulnerability metrics and interdiction models used to identify critical network nodes can be broadly grouped into three categories according to the performance criterion they focus on: *connectivity*, *path length*, and *flow*.

In the following, the railway network is represented as a directed graph $G(N, A)$, where N is the set of $n = |N|$ stations and A the set of links.

2.1 Vulnerability Metrics

Connectivity-Driven Metrics

Node Degree (ND): For a given node, the degree is the number of edges incident to that node. This metric has been frequently used for power grid systems [24]. It can also be used to estimate the importance of a station. In fact, stations with a high degree represent interchange stations which are critical to the overall transport system.

Network Accessibility (NA): A measure of the fraction of nodes that are connected after a disruptive event [18]. It is sometimes referred to as *Pairwise Connectivity* [2] and can be computed as follows :

$$NA = \frac{1}{n(n-1)} \sum_{i=1}^{n} n_{disr}^{i} \tag{1}$$

where n_{disr}^{i} is the number of nodes that can be reached from node i after the occurrence of a disruptive event.

Path Length-Driven Metrics

Network topological efficiency (E): The average of the reciprocals of the length of each shortest path in the network [22], computed as:

$$E = \frac{1}{n(n-1)} \sum_{s,d=1}^{n} \frac{1}{SP_{sd}} \tag{2}$$

where SP_{sd} is the length of the shortest path connecting node s to node d.

Node Vulnerability (NV): The disruption of a station has a negative impact on the network topological efficiency E, which can be measured as follows [22]:

$$NV(i) = e(i) = e(o) - e'(i) \tag{3}$$

where $e(o)$ is the topological efficiency before the disruption and $e'(i)$ is the topological efficiency after the removal of node i.

Node Betweenness (NB): The number of times a node is part of a shortest path.

Flow-Driven Metrics

Passenger Flow Influence (PFI): The total amount of flow that is affected when a node i is disrupted, which is computed as in [22]:

$$PFI = \sum OF_i + DF_i + IF_i \tag{4}$$

where OF_i, DF_i, and IF_i are the generated, attracted, and intercepted flow for node i, respectively.

2.2   Interdiction Models

The interdiction models use the following additional notation.

Sets, Indices and Parameters
- $P(sd)$, indexed by p, is the set of paths connecting nodes s and d
- $N(p)$ is the set of nodes in path p
- l_p is the length of path p
- β_{sd} is an arbitrarily large constants defined for each (s, d) pair
- LP_{sd} is the length of the longest path connecting s and d
- K_{sd} is a constant defined for each (s, d) pair to normalise the objectives
- D is the maximum number of nodes to be removed from the network
- f_{sd} is the amount of passenger flow travelling from s to d
- $\alpha \in [0, 1]$ is a factor used to weight different objectives

Variables
- X_i is equal to 1 if node i is disrupted, 0 otherwise
- Z_{sd} is equal to 1 if there is no connection between s and d, 0 otherwise
- Y_{sd} is the length of the shortest non-disrupted path from s to d

The Path Interdiction Problem (PIP)
We propose a bi-objective interdiction model which addresses connectivity and path length (or equivalently travel time) issues in an integrated manner. The evaluation of path lengths, in fact, cannot prescind from the evaluation of connectivity: if a path between two nodes no longer exists after a disruption, this needs to be captured in a path-length based model.

$$[\text{PIP}(\alpha)] \ \max \sum_{s \in N} \sum_{d \in N} (\alpha Z_{sd} + (1 - \alpha) K_{sd} Y_{sd}) \tag{5}$$

$$\text{s.t.} \ \sum_{i \in N} X_i \leq D \tag{6}$$

$$Z_{sd} \leq \sum_{i \in N(p)} X_i \qquad \forall s, d \in N, p \in P(sd) \tag{7}$$

$$Y_{sd} \leq (1 - Z_{sd}) LP_{sd} \qquad \forall s, d \in N \tag{8}$$

$$Y_{sd} \leq \sum_{i \in N(p)} \beta_{sd} X_i + l_p \qquad \forall s, d \in N, p \in P(sd) \tag{9}$$

$$Z_{sd} \in \{0, 1\} \qquad \forall s, d \in N \tag{10}$$

$$Y_{sd} \geq 0 \qquad \forall s, d \in N \tag{11}$$

$$X_i \in \{0, 1\} \qquad \forall i \in N \tag{12}$$

The objective function (5) aims at maximizing a linear combination of the total number of disconnected s-d node pairs and the total length of the shortest non-disrupted paths connecting s-d pairs. Parameter K_{sd}, used to normalise the objectives so that they have similar magnitude, is set equal to $\frac{1}{LP_{sd}}$. With this setting, $K_{sd}Y_{sd}$ assumes value between 0 and 1, in line with the connectivity variables Z_{sd}. Constraints (6) state that the number of disrupted nodes cannot exceed a threshold D. Constraints (7) guarantee that an s-d pair can be disconnected (i.e. $Z_{sd} = 1$), only if at least one node i on each path connecting s to d is disrupted. Constraints (8) link connectivity and path variables. In particular, if there is no connection between s and d ($Z_{sd} = 1$), then the variable Y_{sd} is forced to zero and pair s-d is not included in the computation of the second objective. Otherwise, if s and d are connected ($Z_{sd} = 0$), the length of the path p from s to d is at most equal to the one of the longest path connecting them (e.g. the constraint has no effect). Constraints (9) guarantee that, if none of the nodes i belonging to a path p connecting s to d is disrupted, then Y_{sd} cannot exceed the length of path p; otherwise, the right hand side of (9) is increased so that the constraint has no effect (we set $\beta_{sd} = LP_{sd}$). Finally, (10), (11) and (12) define the domains of the connectivity, path and interdiction variables, respectively.

The parameter α can be varied to give more emphasis to the connectivity objective or to the path-length objective. Specifically, if $\alpha = 0$, priority is given to the path lengths of the connected components, whereas for $\alpha = 1$, the model reduces to a pure connectivity-based interdiction model. By considering intermediate values, it is possible to generate and evaluate different trade-off solutions.

The Flow Interdiction Problem (FIP)

An interdiction model that considers flow disruption is the FIP model introduced in [15]. FIP uses the amount of post-disruption unserved demand to evaluate the impact of disruptive events.

$$[\text{FIP}] \ \max \sum_{s \in N} \sum_{d \in N} f_{sd} Z_{sd} \tag{13}$$

$$\text{s.t.} \ \sum_{i \in N} X_i \leq D \tag{14}$$

$$Z_{sd} \leq \sum_{i \in N(p)} X_i \qquad \forall s,d \in N, p \in P(sd) \tag{15}$$

$$Z_{sd} \in \{0,1\} \qquad \forall s,d \in N \tag{16}$$

$$X_i \in \{0,1\} \qquad \forall i \in N \tag{17}$$

The objective function (13) maximizes the total amount of disrupted flow across all the network s-d node pairs. Constraint (14) and (15) have the same meaning as in PIP. Constraints (16) and (17) are binary constraints for the connectivity and interdiction variables, respectively.

3   London Underground: A Case Study

In this section, we present a vulnerability analysis of the Central London Tube using the vulnerability metrics and interdiction models discussed in Sect. 2. The network (Fig. 1) has 51 stations, 178 directed arcs and 10 different lines. Travelling time data and the origin-destination flow matrix were obtained from the

Transport for London (TfL) website. All the possible paths for each origin-destination pair were computed as in [20], by considering a 10-min interchange delay to account for a line change.

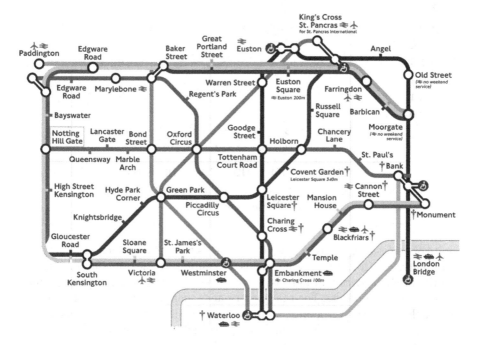

Fig. 1. Central London tube map

3.1   Static Ranking vs. Optimization

Each metric ND, NA, NV, and NB was used to rank the network nodes (we refer to this process as static ranking). Up to 10 nodes in each ranking were then removed incrementally from the network so as to evaluate the impact of multiple, simultaneous losses on three performance measures: accessibility, efficiency, and passenger flow. The results were then compared with the results obtained with PIP(0), PIP(1) and FIP. Although PIP was also solved for other values of α so as to generate more solutions on the Pareto front [13], the most interesting results were found for $\alpha = 0$ and 1. The other results are not reported for the sake of brevity.

Figure 2 shows the impact of increasingly removing nodes on the network accessibility, as defined by (1). The figure clearly indicates that static rankings overestimate network accessibility. Even when only 2 nodes are removed, none of the metric-based approaches is able to identify the two most critical nodes (Green Park and Oxford Circus). The analysis also highlights that the node degree (ND),

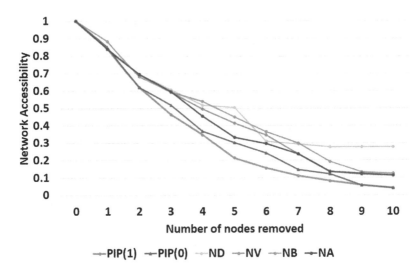

Fig. 2. Network accessibility

in spite of being a connectivity-based measure, is not a good indicator of network accessibility loss (it almost always yields accessibility values significantly higher than the other metrics and models). Interdiction models, as expected, produce the most accurate results. For this performance measure, the pure connectivity model PIP(1) is overall the best approach and significantly outperforms all the metrics. For example, if 5 nodes are disrupted simultaneously, the efficiency can be as low as 0.2 (as identified by PIP(1)). However, three out of the 4 metrics return a value greater than 0.4, which is double the real worst-case value. One metric (NA) returns a value of about 0.32, which is also an overestimate.

Figure 3 displays similar results when we consider the impact of disruption on network efficiency, as defined by (2). Even in this case, the most critical nodes identified by the static rankings are not the ones which, if lost, have the greatest impact on the network efficiency. For this performance measure, the difference between the two interdiction models is less significant.

To summarise, these two analyses suggest that if vulnerability is assessed in terms of accessibility or efficiency deterioration, PIP(1) is the most suitable tool among the ones investigated in this paper. Among the vulnerability metrics, NA finds the most accurate worst-case loss estimates.

In the last analysis, we measure the impact of nodes disruption on passenger flow loss. As for FIP, we assume that the passenger flow between two nodes is entirely lost if there is no connection. Figure 4 compares the total flow loss returned by the PFI static ranking and by the FIP model. The other metrics and PIP are excluded from the analysis as they do not consider the flow in any way. The graph shows that for any number of loss greater than 2, PFI yields significantly lower flow loss than FIP, with gaps between the two approaches reaching

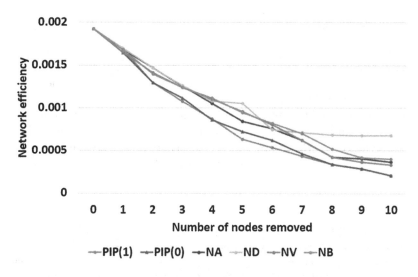

Fig. 3. Network efficiency

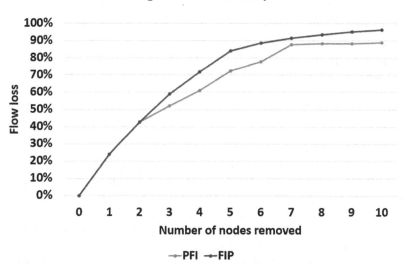

Fig. 4. Network demand loss

as far as 12%. In this example, a 12% difference means that PFI underestimates flow losses by roughly 100,000 passengers.

Overall, these graphs suggest that the difference between static rankings and interdiction models can be substantial, and that the use of metrics is only suitable to identify the first one or two most vulnerable nodes.

3.2 Metrics Comparison

In this section, we analyse in more details the solutions obtained by the different approaches. Table 1 lists the ten most critical stations, ranked according to the different vulnerability metrics. The stations which appear in all the metric rankings are displayed in bold. The table suggests only a minor overlapping across the metrics. Only four stations are always present, however their position within the ranking is quite different. For instance, St Pancras is the station with the highest node degree in the network given that it provides interchange among six lines. However, it is ranked only 7th according to the node betweenness.

Table 1. Ten most critical stations for each metric

NA	ND	NV	NB	PFI
Baker street	St Pancras	Green park	Oxford circus	BankMonument
St Pancras	Baker street	Bond street	Bond street	Oxford circus
Green park	Oxford circus	Oxford circus	Green park	St Pancras
Bond street	Embankment	Baker street	Tottenham court road	Green park
BankMonument	Farringdon	St Pancras	Holborn	Waterloo
Oxford circus	Green park	Holborn	Baker street	Victoria
Holborn	Edgware Road	BankMonument	St Pancras	Baker street
Embankment	Barbican	Embankment	BankMonument	Bond street
Marble arch	Euston square	Tottenham court road	Westminster	Euston
Warren street	Great portland street	Leicester square	Marble arch	Warren street

To estimate the most critical stations using the interdiction models, we solve PIP(1), PIP(0) and FIP with $D = 1, ..., 10$ and count how many times a station appears in the optimal solution. The 10 most frequently disrupted stations are listed in Table 2. Results show a more significant overlap with 9 stations appearing in all rankings. Nonetheless, the frequency and associated ranking order clearly show non negligible variations.

To further analyse these results, Fig. 5 shows the 10 most frequently disrupted stations on the London tube map. The figure shows that both central and peripheral stations are considered vulnerable. The Piccadilly line is the most vulnerable, with 4 stations (South Kensington, Green Park, Leicester Square and St Pancras) identified by all models and one (Holborn) identified by both PIP(0) and PIP(1). Interestingly, Victoria station only appears in the FIP solutions. This station is a rather large station, intercepting a significant portion of passenger flow due to its connections with the railway network and airports. PIP(0) and PIP(1) instead select Holborn station, whose central position makes it more crucial when accessibility and connectivity are considered.

Table 2. Ten most frequently disrupted stations for each optimization model

PIP(1)		PIP(0)		FIP	
Station	Disr.	Station	Disr.	Station	Disr.
Green park	9	Green park	10	BankMonument	10
Oxford circus	9	Oxford circus	9	St Pancras	8
St Pancras	8	BankMonument	8	Embankment	7
BankMonument	7	Embankment	7	Green Park	7
Embankment	6	Holborn	6	Oxford circus	7
Baker Street	5	Notting Hill Gate	5	Leicester square	5
Notting hill gate	5	Baker street	4	Notting hill gate	3
Holborn	3	St Pancras	3	Victoria	3
South Kensington	2	South Kensington	2	Baker street	2
Leicester square	1	Leicester square	1	South Kensington	2

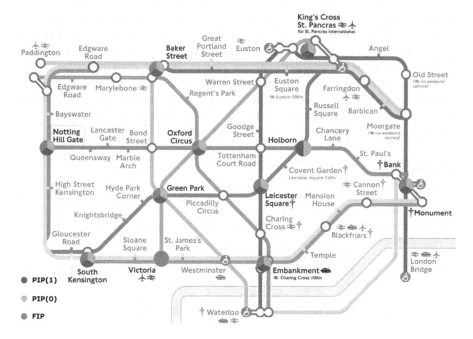

Fig. 5. Map of the ten most frequently disrupted stations for each optimization model

4 Conclusion and Future Developments

In this paper, we discussed and compared two alternative approaches to evaluate urban rail transit systems vulnerability: vulnerability metrics and interdiction models. The approaches have been tested on a real case study based on the central London Underground network, to identify the most critical stations with respect to three performance criteria: accessibility, efficiency and passenger flow. The analysis revealed significant discrepancies in the results obtained with the two approaches and highlighted that vulnerability metrics tend to underestimate the real impact of disruptive events. This is mainly due to their inability to capture the interaction among system components after a disruption. On the contrary, interdiction models are able to identify the most vulnerable network components, even in the event of multiple, simultaneous losses. Hence, they represent a more reliable tool for assessing vulnerability and supporting the development of cost-efficient mitigation strategies.

Several lines of research can be pursued in the future. Firstly, the impact of disruption on other performance criteria (e.g. cohesiveness [23]) or a combination of criteria could be considered. Secondly, while we have assessed railway infrastructure vulnerability through the identification of the most critical network nodes, an analogous investigation should be carried out to evaluate the impact of disruptions of network links. Thirdly, similar studies should be carried out to assess the vulnerability of other infrastructure networks (e.g. road networks, energy grids, telecommunication networks). Finally, in order to plan effective protection strategies, interdiction models like the ones discussed in this paper should be embedded into bi-level programs, i.e. hierarchical optimisation models which mimic a game between two players. In fact, although interdiction models are fundamental for the identification of network vulnerabilities, protection strategies relying solely on them often lead to sub-optimal solutions [5]. Finally, cutting-edge solution algorithms should be devised to solve such complex optimisation models and enable their applicability to real-world infrastructures.

References

1. Addis, B., Di Summa, M., Grosso, A.: Identifying critical nodes in undirected graphs: complexity results and polynomial algorithms for the case of bounded treewidth. Discret. Appl. Math. **161**(16), 2349–2360 (2013)
2. Arulselvan, A., Commander, C.W., Elefteriadou, L., Pardalos, P.M.: Detecting critical nodes in sparse graphs. Comput. Oper. Res. **36**(7), 2193–2200 (2009)
3. Balijepalli, C., Oppong, O.: Measuring vulnerability of road network considering the extent of serviceability of critical road links in urban areas. J. Transp. Geogr. **39**, 145–155 (2014)
4. 7/7 London bombings: What happened on 7 July 2005? (2015). CBBC Newsround. Accessed 23 June 2017
5. Cappanera, P., Scaparra, M.P.: Optimal allocation of protective resources in shortest-path networks. Transp. Sci. **45**(1), 64–80 (2011)
6. Church, R.L., Scaparra, M.P., Middleton, R.S.: Identifying critical infrastructure: the median and covering facility interdiction problems. Ann. Assoc. Am. Geogr. **94**(3), 491–502 (2004)
7. Esposito Amideo, A., Scaparra, M.P.: A synthesis of optimization approaches for tackling critical information infrastructure survivability. In: Havarneanu, G., Setola, R., Nassopoulos, H., Wolthusen, S. (eds.) CRITIS 2016. LNCS, vol. 10242, pp. 75–87. Springer, Cham (2017). https://doi.org/10.1007/978-3-319-71368-7_7
8. Fulkerson, D.R., Harding, G.C.: Maximizing the minimum source-sink path subject to a budget constraint. Math. Program. **13**(1), 116–118 (1977)
9. Granata, D., Steeger, G., Rebennack, S.: Network interdiction via a critical disruption path: branch-and-price algorithms. Comput. Oper. Res. **40**(11), 2689–2702 (2013)

10. Gillett, F.: London Bridge station: commuters warned of major disruption on trains for rest of evening. Evening Standard (2017). Accessed 23 June 2017
11. Harley, N.: Fire at Euston Station continues to cause rail disruption. The Telegraph (2017). Accessed 23 June 2017
12. Jenelius, E., Petersen, T., Mattsson, L.G.: Importance and exposure in road network vulnerability analysis. Transp. Res. Part A: Policy Pract. **40**(7), 537–560 (2006)
13. Kim, I.Y., de Weck, O.L.: Adaptive weighted-sum method for bi-objective optimization: pareto front generation. Struct. Multidiscip. Optim. **29**(2), 149–158 (2005)
14. Mach, K., Mastrandrea, M.: In: Field, C.B., Barros, V.R. (eds.) Climate Change 2014: Impacts, Adaptation, and Vulnerability. Cambridge University Press, Cambridge and New York (2014)
15. Matisziw, T.C., Murray, A.T.: Modeling st path availability to support disaster vulnerability assessment of network infrastructure. Comput. Oper. Res. **36**(1), 16–26 (2009)
16. Murray, A.T.: An overview of network vulnerability modeling approaches. GeoJournal **78**(2), 209–221 (2013)
17. Office of Rail and Road: Statistical releases (2017). Accessed 23 June 2017
18. Ouyang, M., Zhao, L., Hong, L., Pan, Z.: Comparisons of complex network based models and real train flow model to analyze Chinese railway vulnerability. Reliab. Eng. Syst. Saf. **123**, 38–46 (2014)
19. Scott, D.M., Novak, D.C., Aultman-Hall, L., Guo, F.: Network robustness index: a new method for identifying critical links and evaluating the performance of transportation networks. J. Transp. Geogr. **14**(3), 215–227 (2006)
20. Starita, S., Scaparra, M.P.: Passenger railway network protection: a model with variable post-disruption demand service. J. Oper. Res. Soc. **69**(4), 1–18 (2017)
21. Sullivan, J., Aultman-Hall, L., Novak, D.: A review of current practice in network disruption analysis and an assessment of the ability to account for isolating links in transportation networks. Transp. Lett. **1**(4), 271–280 (2009)
22. Sun, D.J., Zhao, Y., Lu, Q.C.: Vulnerability analysis of urban rail transit networks: a case study of Shanghai, China. Sustainability **7**(6), 6919–6936 (2015)
23. Veremyev, A., Prokopyev, O.A., Pasiliao, E.L.: An integer programming framework for critical elements detection in graphs. J. Comb. Optim. **28**(1), 233–273 (2014)
24. Wang, J.W., Rong, L.L.: Cascade-based attack vulnerability on the US power grid. Saf. Sci. **47**(10), 1332–1336 (2009)
25. Wollmer, R.: Removing arcs from a network. Oper. Res. **12**(6), 934–940 (1964)

Automatically Generating Security Models from System Models to Aid in the Evaluation of AMI Deployment Options

Michael Rausch[1]([✉]), Ken Keefe[1], Brett Feddersen[1], and William H. Sanders[2]

[1] Information Trust Institute, University of Illinois at Urbana-Champaign,
Urbana, IL, USA
{mjrausc2,kjkeefe,bfeddrsn}@illinois.edu
[2] Department of Electrical and Computer Engineering,
University of Illinois at Urbana-Champaign, Urbana, IL, USA
whs@illinois.edu

Abstract. System architects should use security models to gain insight into how different design choices impact the overall security of a system. However, it is often difficult for those who do not possess a security modeling background to construct such models. To overcome this challenge we present a case study that demonstrates a novel approach that uses an ontology-assisted model generator to automatically create ADVISE security models from intuitive hand-built system models. More specifically, we consider a case study of a hypothetical utility that wishes to select the most cost-effective of several different intrusion detection system approaches to defend its *Advanced Metering Infrastructure* (AMI) deployment. We construct an AMI-focused ontology that consists of system model elements, security model elements, and the mapping between the two. We then use the ontology in conjunction with the generator to create security models from a system model. Finally, we discuss the benefits of the use of the approach relative to previous approaches, including an explanation of how it significantly eases the burden of creating complex security models for users without prior security modeling experience.

Keywords: Automatic model generation · Security · Forecasting
Risk assessment · ADVISE · Smart grid · AMI · Möbius

1 Introduction

Architects of new cyber-physical infrastructure must make many decisions when designing a system that will impact its overall security. There are two major approaches for evaluating the impact of different design choices on system security: (1) consultation with security experts, and (2) construction and analysis of rigorous security models.

The two approaches may be used jointly and complement one another, though both suffer limitations. Security experts may make assumptions that are not

© Springer Nature Switzerland AG 2018
G. D'Agostino and A. Scala (Eds.): CRITIS 2017, LNCS 10707, pp. 156–167, 2018.
https://doi.org/10.1007/978-3-319-99843-5_14

explicit, and thus their decisions are not easily auditable; further, experts often rely on experience and intuition to make decisions, rather than on rigorous scientific approaches. From a practical perspective, there is also a significant shortage in the number of qualified security experts, with some estimating that more than 200,000 cybersecurity-related positions are unfilled [11]. On the other hand, security models make assumptions explicit and are easily auditable and scientifically rigorous, but they are also difficult and time-consuming to construct, especially for domain experts who do not have a background in modeling or security.

We propose a novel approach that allows those with no security modeling background to construct simple and intuitive system models that may be used to automatically generate relevant, rigorous security models to support the evaluation of a system. Following this approach, a user would (1) use a tool with an intuitive graphical user interface to develop a system model, (2) select the types of adversaries that should be considered in the analysis, and (3) choose the metrics the security model should compute. Next, the complete user-defined model would be given to a model generator, which would leverage a predefined ontology to construct a relevant ADversary VIew Security Evaluation (ADVISE) model [3]. The security model would then be executed to calculate the metrics, and the results would be presented to the user to aid in the evaluation of designs. We have implemented this approach in the Möbius tool [13].

We explain the approach through a case study of a hypothetical utility that has an *Advanced Metering Infrastructure* (AMI) deployment and seeks to select the most cost-effective *intrusion detection system* (IDS) approach to monitor and defend it. An AMI is a cyber-enhanced power grid that gives a utility a more fine-grained ability to observe its network, and more remote control over the network components. Different IDS deployment approaches, including both centralized and distributed ones, may be used to defend an AMI. We show how a system architect can easily and automatically create security models to calculate security estimates to be used to inform the design choices among the IDS options.

The remainder of the paper is organized as follows. In Sect. 2 we provide a brief overview of AMI deployments and IDS approaches. Section 3 explains the model generation approach, while Sect. 4 demonstrates the approach by working through a case study of a hypothetical AMI deployment. Finally, Sect. 5 provides a concluding discussion.

2   System Information

Utilities are increasingly upgrading the power grid by incorporating smart meters and other computerized components to form AMI deployments that enhance the ability to monitor and remotely control the grid. These upgrades will allow utilities to be more efficient and cost-effective; the Electric Power Research Institute estimates that utilities will gain billions of dollars in benefits by constructing smart grids [4].

While many network topologies may be used, we shall limit our discussion in this paper to one representative case. In this deployment, the smart meters are connected to one another and to a *data concentrator unit* (DCU) via a *neighborhood area network* (NAN), which is a wireless mesh network. The DCU collects readings from the smart meters and sends them via the *wide area network* (WAN) to a centralized server on the utility's back-end network, where they may be observed by network operators. The utility may also send control commands in the reverse direction to the smart meters or to other AMI components.

The AMI deployments are critical infrastructure that must be effectively protected to ensure that people continue to receive power. However, the increasing networking and computerization of the power grid are potentially introducing new vulnerabilities [1,2,5]. A utility may choose to defend its AMI deployment by employing defenses, e.g., IDSes, commonly used to protect more traditional cyber networks.

In general, an intrusion detection system monitors and logs network traffic and processes on machines and alerts the network operators if it detects suspicious behavior. Different IDS deployment approaches will give different levels of benefit in terms of coverage and have different costs, and these must be carefully weighed before an appropriate choice may be made. In this paper, we consider two IDS deployment approaches — centralized and distributed — in addition to the trivial case of having no IDS, which shall serve as a baseline. The centralized approach places the intrusion detection system in the utility network, so that network traffic going to and from the centralized server may be monitored. This approach is relatively cheap, but suffers from the limitation that it cannot observe any of the traffic between the smart meters at the NAN level. The distributed approach is to embed the IDS directly into each smart meter. The approach provides greater traffic coverage than the centralized approach and thus may be able to detect more attacks, or alert at an earlier stage of an attack. In addition, it enables direct detection of attacks on the smart meters themselves. However, it will also cost more, since the per-unit cost of each IDS-enabled smart meter will be higher. The utility must carefully choose among the three IDS options, and should use security models to help make a decision.

3   Generating Security Models from General System Models in Möbius

We present a novel approach to automatically generate security models from system models, which we have implemented in the Möbius modeling tool. At a high level, a modeler will use component types defined in an ontology to construct a simple system model, choose adversaries of concern, and select security metrics to be calculated. The user-defined system model is used as input to the model generation algorithm. This algorithm relies on the ontology to provide mappings between system model elements and security model elements. The algorithm will output a security model, which may be executed to obtain the user-defined security metrics.

Our approach for automatically generating security models is novel, though the concept has been considered previously. Groundbreaking work in this area was presented in [12], though that approach was found to scale poorly. An approach for scalable security model generation is given in [8], but it is intended for analysis of existing systems and does not support analysis of systems in the design stage, in contrast to the approach described in this paper. The approach shown in [6] is perhaps closest to our method, though that method does not use an ontology and it is not immediately clear how it could be extended to support state-based security models, like ADVISE.

3.1 Ontology

The ontology is the key to the model generation approach. All of the component types and relationships between them, in both the system model and the security model, are drawn from the ontology.

Formally, the ontology can be defined as the tuple

$$<C, R, F, M, I, A, S>,$$

where:

- C is the set of all possible system model component types.
- R is the set of all possible pairwise relationships, $r(C_d, C_r)$, from components of types from C_d to components of types from C_r, with $C_d, C_r \subset C$.
- F is the set of security model fragments, $fragment_x \in F$. Since the generated security models conform to the ADVISE formalism, the model fragments may include attacks along with access, knowledge, skill, and system state variables, and the precondition/effect relationships between them. For more on ADVISE, see Sect. 3.4.
- M is the set of mappings that can be made based on a component's type to infer a security model fragment, $m(c_u, fragment_x) \in M$. For example, if there is a physical device in the system and the adversary gains physical access to it, he or she may try to damage it. This is expressed as $fragment_1 = pAttck, pAccss, dmg, precond(pAttck, pAccss), effect(pAttck, dmg) \in F$, $physicalDevice \in C$ and $m(physicalDevice, fragment_1)$.
- I is the $inheritance$ relationship between $c_u, c_v \in C$. If $i(c_u, c_v) \in I$, then we say that component type c_u $inherits$ from c_v, i.e., c_u is a specialized type of c_v. For example, if the $smartmeter$ component type inherits from the $meter$ type, $i(smartmeter, meter) \in I$. Inheritance is transitive and multiple inheritance is supported. Attributes and mappings are inherited, e.g., $[m(physicalDevice, fragment_1) \in M] \wedge [i(meter, physicalDevice) \in I] \implies m(meter, fragment_1)$.
- A is the set of all adversary profiles.
- S is the set of security metrics to be calculated.

The ontology should be constructed by experts who have experience with the system domain, modeling, and security; the typical user will not have to learn the details of the ontology or modify it. Once defined, the ontology may be used to construct models of many different systems and system configurations.

3.2   General System Model

To begin, a user builds a model of the system using a graphical user interface tool. The model resembles a UML-style diagram. The user drags and drops predefined system component types from a menu onto a canvas to define instances of the component type, and then forms connections between the components to describe the relationships between the components. Smart meters, DCUs, servers, and networks are examples of components, while *NetworkConnection* is an example of a relationship. Components can contain attributes, which may be editable by the user. At this stage, the user also selects the types of adversaries of concern, and customizes the base adversary profiles. Finally, the user selects the security metrics of interest that should be calculated by the security model (e.g., damage to the system as the result of an attack, or the probability of detecting the adversary).

3.3   Generator

The purpose of the generator is to construct a security model, which may be executed to calculate security-relevant metrics from the user-defined system model along with the corresponding ontology. At its core, the generation algorithm is simple. First, the type of each instance defined in the system model is determined, and then the mapping function is applied to find the corresponding security model fragments.

Next, once found, the security model fragments are stitched together to form a whole, and the model elements are pruned if doing so does not affect the results obtained by executing the model. During fragment stitching, each state variable in a model fragment is compared to state variables in other fragments. If it is found that the state variables are equivalent, they may be combined, joining the fragments. As an example, consider two fragments, f_1 and f_2. Now, f_1 consists of an attack $InstallWirelessJammerOnNAN1$ that has an effect on a state variable called $WirelessJammerAccessOnNAN1$, while f_2 consists of an attack $JamWirelessSignalOnNAN1$ with a precondition state variable called $WirelessJammerAccessOnNAN1$. Both fragments contain the state variable $WirelessJammerAccessOnNAN1$, and so may be linked together to form an attack chain that expresses the idea that a wireless jammer must be installed before a wireless jamming attack can be accomplished. Similarly, security model elements (i.e., attack steps and state variables) may be pruned without affecting the model execution results if a path from the fragment to a goal does not exist.

3.4   Security Model

We developed the generator and ontologies to support the creation of ADVISE security models, though in theory it should be possible to use this approach to generate security models in other modeling formalisms.

Each model in ADVISE consists of an *Attack Execution Graph* (AEG) and an *adversary profile*, which together form one atomic submodel in Möbius. The full resulting model may then be executed to obtain the security results. The formalism is explained briefly here; for more details, consult [7].

Formally, an AEG is defined by the tuple

$$<A, S, C>,$$

where A is a set of attack steps, S is a set of state variables, and the relation C defines the set of directed connecting arcs from $p \in S$ to $a \in A$, and from $a \in A$ to $e \in S$, where p and e are precondition and effect state variables, respectively.

An attack step $a \in A$ is defined by the tuple

$$<B, T, P, O>,$$

where B is a Boolean precondition that must be satisfied before the adversary may attempt the attack, T is the time to complete an attack, P is the cost the adversary incurs for attempting the attack, and O is the set of outcomes that may occur if the attack is attempted. Each outcome has a probability of occurrence, and, if selected, a specified effect on the system state.

The attacker model describes the initial state of the attack execution graph (the starting value of every state variable), as well as some further adversary characteristics, such as the payoff the adversary receives for achieving a goal, the cost the adversary incurs if it is detected, and the adversary's ability to forecast the future (modeled by defining an upper limit on the longest chain of attack steps the adversary may consider when forming attack plans).

The model is executed once the AEG and adversary profile have been defined. During model execution, the adversary first uses a competitive Markov decision process to select the optimal attack, given the system state, that will maximize the accumulated net profit (as described in [9]); then, one of the attack's outcomes is randomly selected according to its probability of occurrence, and its effect is applied to the model state. This process repeats until the end of the simulation, at which time the results are presented to the user. These results may be used to inform security-related decisions regarding the design of cyber systems.

4   Demonstration of Approach

To show the effectiveness of the novel model generation approach described in Sect. 3, we present a case study of a hypothetical utility that is deciding whether to select a centralized or distributed IDS approach to protect its AMI, or to do without any IDS at all, as described in Sect. 2. The utility is primarily concerned with attacks from malicious customers, insiders, and terrorist organizations. The utility wishes to estimate the amount of damage to the system and the probability of detecting the adversary for each possible pairing of adversary and IDS approach. The estimate will help the utility evaluate the cost-effectiveness of each IDS approach. However, the employees of the utility do not possess prior knowledge of security modeling and are not capable of easily constructing a security model by hand. We show how an effective security model that can calculate the metrics of interest may be automatically constructed from a simple system model that a domain expert would be comfortable building by hand.

4.1 AMI Ontology

The AMI-focused ontology we created for this case study defines the system model elements, the security model elements, and the mapping between them. Since the ontology provides the type definitions allowable in the system model, it must be created before the system model. We shall be as complete as possible in the explanation of the ontology that we created for this case study, but space limitations prevent us from giving a full description.

First, we defined the type information used to create the system model. The base component type object in the ontology, *Thing*, is the parent of both *PhysicalThing* and *NonPhysicalThing*. Both the *Computer* and *Meter* types are children of the *PhysicalThing* type. The *Computer* type is the parent of the *DCU* type and the *BackendServer* type, which is in turn the parent of the *BackendServerIDS* type. The *Network* type and the *Wireless* type are children of the *NonPhysicalThing* type. The *WAN* type is a child of the *Network* type, while the *WirelessNAN* type is a child of both the *Network* and *Wireless* types. The *DedicatedDeviceIDS* is the child of both the *Computer* and *Wireless* types. Finally, the *SmartMeter* type is the child of three parents (the *Computer* type, the *Meter* type, and the *Wireless* type), while the *SmartMeterWithIDS* type is the child of the *SmartMeter* type. The *NetworkConnection* relationship is the only relationship defined, and signifies that a direct network link exists between the two items that share this relationship.

Next, we defined the AMI-focused attack steps and state variables that are used to help generate the security model. We primarily followed [5,10] to come up with the relevant list of attack steps and state variables. There are 17 attack steps in our ontology, and, at a high level, they may be broken into several major categories: (1) attack steps the adversary may attempt in order to gain control of a smart meter, through either a physical exploit or a remote exploit; (2) attack steps the adversary may perform to gain the ability to route traffic in the AMI, which in turn could be used to perform routing attacks and Byzantine attacks; (3) attack steps to form a botnet and perform resource exhaustion attacks; (4) attack steps meant to jam wireless communication in the NAN; and (5) low-tech physical attacks on the AMI infrastructure. Relevant AEG state variables, such as skill in various attacks, access to various parts of the AMI, and knowledge of how things operate internally, are also defined.

Following the definition of system model and security model elements, the appropriate relationships between ontology elements were defined. The AEG state variables were given roles as prerequisites or effects of various attacks, e.g., the *BotnetOnNAN* access is the effect of the *CreateBotnet* attack and the prerequisite of the *ResourceExhaustion* attack. Similarly, each attack and AEG state variable was associated with at least one system model component to which it may be applied, e.g., the *ResourceExhaustion* attack was applied to the *DCU* system model component type, and each one of that attack's prerequisite and

effect state variables was associated with either the *DCU* component type itself
or one of its ancestors, or was defined to be global. Finally, relevant adversary
profiles and metrics were defined in the ontology. With the ontology thus completed, any system modeler can use the component types defined in the ontology
to create instances of those types and relationships between them in a hand-built
system model.

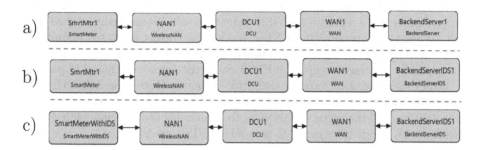

Fig. 1. Graphical representations of the system models in Möbius. The models (a), (b),
and (c) represent the system with no IDS, a centralized IDS, and a distributed IDS,
respectively.

4.2 System Model

Next, we constructed a separate system model of the AMI for each IDS approach.
Graphical representations of the system models are shown in Fig. 1. We modeled
the AMI at a high level, both for ease of explanation of the approach and because
the metrics we were interested in calculating did not require a model with more
detail. Additional detail could be added if required for the accurate calculation
of different security metrics, if that level of detail is supported by the ontology.
We note that multiple smart meters are present in the modeled AMI, though
only one is shown graphically. Multiple smart meters are defined by setting the
NumMeters attribute of the smart meter instance represented in the graphical
model to the desired number (100 in our model).

After we created the system model, we completed the remaining steps. First,
we defined goals that the adversaries could attempt to accomplish: remain undetected, steal electricity, damage equipment, or interrupt service. Second, we
applied the baseline adversary profiles defined in the ontology to the model
and customized them. Third, we applied two metrics defined in the ontology,
the *Undetected* metric and the *MonetaryDamage* metric, which calculate (1) the
probability that the utility will detect the adversary during the attack and (2)
the amount of damage and lost revenue the utility would suffer as a result of
the attack, respectively. Finally, we paired the system model with each defined
adversary, along with the metrics of interest, to create a complete configuration.
From a configuration, we automatically generated an ADVISE security model

consisting of an AEG and an adversary profile. The end-to-end process of auto-matically generating an ADVISE security model took on the order of minutes, as opposed to the hours it would have taken to create an ADVISE model of comparable size and complexity by hand.

4.3   ADVISE Security Models

For each of the 9 configurations (one for each pairing of IDS approach and adver-sary) we generated a separate ADVISE security model. We manually verified that each automatically generated ADVISE model was correct given the definitions in the ontology and hand-built system model. An example of an AEG that was automatically generated is given in Fig. 2. Since the ontology is based in part on the attack step and state variable definitions found in [9,10], the AEGs that we automatically generated closely resemble the AEGs presented in those publica-tions. It is beyond the scope of this work to explain the security model in detail; consult [9,10] for specifics on AMI-focused ADVISE models.

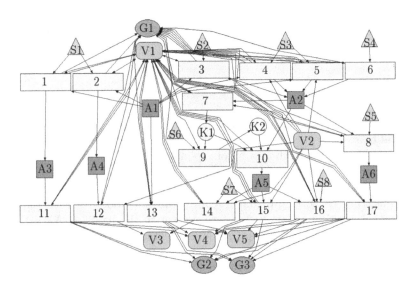

Fig. 2. The AEG generated from the *AMI with a Centralized IDS* system model paired with the Insider adversary. The gray blocks labeled $V1$, $V2$, $V3$, $V4$, and $V5$ are the *Undetected*, *Centralized_IDS*, *StealElectricity*, *InterruptService*, and *DamageEquipment* state variables, respectively. The names corresponding to the other labels may be found in Table 1.

4.4   Results

We executed each of the models to obtain estimates of the monetary value of the amount of damage and lost revenue the utility could expect at the end of

Table 1. Labels and their corresponding names for attack steps or adversary state variables from Fig. 2.

Label	Attack step name	Label	State variable name
1	NAN1_InstallLongRangeJammer	A1	NAN1_PhysicalAccess
2	NAN1_InstallShortRangeJammer	A2	NAN1_NumCompromisedMeters
3	NAN1_InstallMaliciousSmartMeter	A3	NAN1_LongRangeJammerAccess
4	SmrtMtr_PhysicalSmrtMtrExploit	A4	NAN1_ShortRangeJammerAccess
5	SmrtMtr_MassMtrCompromise	A5	NAN1_RoutingCapability
6	SmrtMtr_RemoteSmrtMtrExploit	A6	NAN1_BotnetAccess
7	NAN1_CollectCryptoKeys	G1	UndetectedGoal
8	NAN1_CreateBotnet	G2	DamageEquipmentGoal
9	NAN1_AnalyzeTraffic	G3	InterruptServiceGoal
10	NAN1_GainRoutingCapability	K1	NAN1_CryptoKeys
11	NAN1_MajorJammingAttack	K2	NAN1_TrafficKnowledge
12	NAN1_MinorJammingAttack	S1	NodeInstallationSkill
13	NAN1_PhysicalAttack	S2	SmartMeterInstallationSkill
14	NAN1_MinorRoutingAttack	S3	PhysicalSmartMeterExploitSkill
15	NAN1_MajorRoutingAttack	S4	RemoteSmartMeterExploitSkill
16	NAN1_ByzantineAttack	S5	BotnetShepherdSkill
17	DCU1_ResourceExhaustionAttack	S6	TrafficAnalysisSkill
		S7	RoutingAttackSkill
		S8	ByzantineAttackSkill

an attack and the probability of detecting the adversary as the attack was in progress. These results are presented in Table 2. The results are similar to those presented in [9,10], which is not surprising since the ontology that was used to generate these security models was informed by the security models in those publications. We could have calculated additional security metrics (e.g., the costs and payoffs of the adversary given the chosen sequence of attack steps), but chose not to do so since a full analysis of the security model is outside the scope of this paper. The calculated results give insight that will aid decision-makers in choosing the most cost-effective IDS. Supplied with the estimates this model provides of the various IDSes, along with cost information provided by the IDS vendors, a system architect can make an informed choice in selecting the most cost-effective IDS.

5   Discussion and Conclusion

In this paper we presented a novel approach a modeler may employ to automatically create security models from hand-built system models that are used as input to an ontology-assisted model generator. These security models may then be executed to obtain results that may be used to gain insight into the

Table 2. Cost incurred by the utility as a result of the actions of each adversary and the probability of detecting an adversary during an attack, given a particular IDS. Italicized results indicate that the adversaries did no damage because they did not attempt to attack the system.

IDS	Adversary	Monetary Damage	Damage Error	Prob. of Detect. Adv.	Detection Error
None	Insider	$11.6M	+/− $440K	0.62	+/− 0.03
	Customer	$380	+/− $5	0.05	+/− 0.01
	Terrorist	$1.2M	+/− $120K	1	+/− 0
Centralized	Insider	$3M	+/− $100K	0.62	+/− 0.03
	Customer	*$0*	*+/− $0*	*0*	*+/− 0*
	Terrorist	$1.2M	+/− $120K	1	+/− 0
Distributed	*Insider*	*$0*	*+/− $0*	*0*	*+/− 0*
	Customer	*$0*	*+/− $0*	*0*	*+/− 0*
	Terrorist	$1.2M	+/− $120K	1	+/− 0

system and support design decisions. We demonstrated the effectiveness of this approach with a case study of a utility that has an AMI deployment and is deciding whether to protect its infrastructure with a centralized IDS or a distributed IDS, or to forgo an IDS. We found that the process of automatically building a security model by first hand-building a system model was much easier and faster than hand-building a security model of similar complexity and size. This is a promising result that may enable security modeling at scale and with a minimal learning curve by those who use the approach.

Some argue that quantitative security models (like those automatically generated by the approach explained in this paper) may not improve the security of systems, in part because the results may be misinterpreted by modelers and because the initial parameters and assumptions of the model are difficult to obtain or justify [14]. However, we believe that quantitative security models can improve security by offering a level of scientific rigor that is vitally needed to supplement the intuition of experts. The dangers of misinterpretation may be minimized by clearly explaining the results and their limitations. Estimates of initial parameters and assumptions may be explored via sensitivity analysis, which can identify the parameters that are the most important ones to obtain accurately, either from historical data or consultation with experts.

In the future, we plan to extend the approach so that it can generate reliability, availability, and performability models in addition to security models, all from the one base system model, so that different aspects or perspectives of the system may be easily modeled to obtain quantitative results useful for the evaluation of systems.

Acknowledgments. The work described here was performed, in part, with funding from the Maryland Procurement Office under Contract No. H98230-14-C-0141. The authors would like to thank Jenny Applequist for her editorial assistance.

References

1. Krishna, V.B., Lee, K., Weaver, G.A., Iyer, R.K., Sanders, W.H.: F-DETA: a framework for detecting electricity theft attacks in smart grids. In: 46th Annual IEEE/IFIP International Conference on Dependable Systems and Networks, pp. 407–418 (2016)
2. Federal Bureau of investigation cyber intelligence section: smart grid electric meters altered to steal electricity (2010). http://krebsonsecurity.com/wp-content/uploads/2012/04/FBI-SmartMeterHack-285x305.png
3. Ford, M., Keefe, K., LeMay, E., Sanders, W., Muehrcke, C.: Implementing the ADVISE security modeling formalism in Möbius. In: Dependable Systems and Networks, 43rd Annual IEEE/IFIP International Conference on 2013. pp. 1–8. June 2013
4. Gellings, C.: Estimating the costs and benefits of the smart grid: a preliminary estimate of the investment requirements and the resultant benefits of a fully functioning smart grid. Technical report, Electric Power Research Institute, March 2011
5. Grochocki, D., et al.: AMI threats, intrusion detection requirements and deployment recommendations. In: Smart Grid Communications (SmartGridComm), IEEE Third International Conference on 2012, pp. 395–400. November 2012
6. Ivanova, M.G., Probst, C.W., Hansen, R.R., Kammüller, F.: Transforming Graphical System Models to Graphical Attack Models, pp. 82–96. Springer International Publishing, Cham (2016), https://doi.org/10.1007/978-3-319-29968-6_6
7. LeMay, E.: Adversary-driven state-based system security evaluation. Ph.D. thesis, University of Illinois at Urbana-Champaign, Urbana, Illinois (2011)
8. Ou, X., Boyer, W.F., McQueen, M.A.: A scalable approach to attack graph generation. In: Proceedings of the 13th ACM conference on Computer and communications security, pp. 336–345. ACM (2006)
9. Rausch, M.: Determining cost-effective intrusion detection approaches for an advanced metering infrastructure deployment using ADVISE. Master's thesis, University of Illinois at Urbana-Champaign (2016)
10. Rausch, M., Feddersen, B., Keefe, K., Sanders, W.H.: A comparison of different intrusion detection approaches in an advanced metering infrastructure network using ADVISE, vol. 9826, pp. 279–294. Springer International Publishing (2016), https://doi.org/10.1007/978-3-319-43425-4_19
11. Setalvad, A.: Demand to fill cybersecurity jobs booming, March 2015. http://peninsulapress.com/2015/03/31/cybersecurity-jobs-growth/
12. Sheyner, O., Haines, J., Jha, S., Lippmann, R., Wing, J.M.: Automated generation and analysis of attack graphs. In: Proceedings Security and privacy, 2002 IEEE Symposium on 2002, pp. 273–284. IEEE (2002)
13. Möbius team: Möbius documentation. University of Illinois at Urbana-Champaign, Urbana, IL (2014), https://www.mobius.illinois.edu/wiki/
14. Verendel, V.: Quantified security is a weak hypothesis: a critical survey of results and assumptions. In: Proceedings of the 2009 Workshop on New Security Paradigms Workshop, pp. 37–50. NSPW 2009, ACM, New York, NY, USA (2009). https://doi.org/10.1145/1719030.1719036

A Gamified Approach to Participatory Modelling of Water System Risks

Alex Coletti[1] , Antonio De Nicola[2] , Giordano Vicoli[2] ,
and Maria Luisa Villani[2](✉)

[1] SMRC, Ashburn, VA, USA
acoletti@smrcusa.com
[2] ENEA-CR Casaccia, Via Anguillarese 301, 00123 Rome, Italy
{antonio.denicola,giordano.vicoli,marialuisa.villani}@enea.it

Abstract. Modelling risks related to critical infrastructures requires integrated and multi disciplinary competencies of experts, stakeholders, and users who are often located in different places and have limited time to be involved in a strenuous knowledge elicitation project. In this context we propose a gamified and participatory modelling approach to boost engagement of people involved in risk assessment related to critical infrastructures. The approach is supported by a risk management system based on the ICE-CREAM framework, including the CREAM (CREAtivity Machine) software for computational creativity and the ICE (Innovation through Collaborative Environment) mobile app developed for iOS. Insights on risk assessment of water systems are also discussed.

Keywords: Critical infrastructure · Gamification
Ontology · Participatory modelling · Risk assessment · Water systems

1 Introduction

Inherent complexity of critical infrastructures, such as the water system, requires several competencies in figuring out the impact of a hazard on them and the related aftermath. For instance, in case of a flood contamination of the water distribution system, experts on physical, chemical and biological conditioning of water, geologists, city planners, and water distribution company managers could be involved to provide their perspective on the crisis situation and on the way to recover from it.

Collecting multi-disciplinary knowledge related to critical infrastructure risks from experts, stakeholders, and users (knowledge contributors in the following) and building a shared understanding of such knowledge could be a difficult problem to solve as this requires involving them in endless and strenuous workshops. Such people are usually front-line employees often involved in daily activities that do not leave time. Furthermore, they are not stimulated to attending such events. Hence a novel engaging approach to elicit knowledge is needed.

© Springer Nature Switzerland AG 2018
G. D'Agostino and A. Scala (Eds.): CRITIS 2017, LNCS 10707, pp. 168–180, 2018.
https://doi.org/10.1007/978-3-319-99843-5_15

In this context we propose a gamified approach to collecting and defining new risks related to critical infrastructures by means of a gamified and participatory modelling approach. The first objective is to involve knowledge contributors in a flexible and engaging experience which allows to collect information on critical infrastructure risks. Then we aim at specifying risks at different levels of formalization including a set of intuitive conceptual models, i.e. risk mini-models (RMM)s [10], and a domain ontology. In particular we propose a risk management system based on the ICE-CREAM framework, which enhances the CREAM (CREAtivity Machine) software for computational creativity [10] with ICE (Innovation through Collaborative Environment), i.e. a gamified and easy-to-use mobile application for participatory modelling.

According to [15], gamification is the use of game design elements in non-game contexts. It aims at motivating and increasing user activity and it is used in different contexts, such as training in enterprises. To the best of our knowledge using a gamified approach to elicit and model risks from a group of people is a novel application of gamification.

The rest of the paper is organized as follows. Section 2 presents the related work in the area. Section 3 describes the water systems case study, the risk management system based on ICE-CREAM, the method applied to build the water systems ontology, and some details on the computational creativity approach. Section 4 presents the methodological underpinnings and game mechanics used for the gamified elicitation and modelling of water system risks. The ICE mobile app is described in Sect. 5 and, finally, Sect. 6 closes the paper by discussing the opportunities provided by our proposal.

2   Related Work

Modelling risks requires several competences of multiple stakeholders. Participatory approaches are recognized by the scientific community as a valuable means to elicit knowledge and integrate the different perspectives of stakeholders [20]. Along this line, [17] presents a participatory study dealing with flood risk, vulnerability and adaptive capacity and [11] presents a vulnerability assessment support system for collaborative definition of risks. [14] is a collaborative application to collect data concerning cascading effects of the impact of a hazard on critical infrastructures. Then [22] presents a system which enhances a collaborative platform for risk detection and resolutions in three manufacturing plants with creativity support. With all of these works we share the goal of involving and engaging experts in a collaborative activity to improve knowledge elicitation and with [22] we share the opinion that creativity support is needed. However, with respect to them, we leverage the existence of domain-specific ontologies which is the fundamental element of the ICE-CREAM framework.

Gamification is now considered a valuable means to increase motivation of users (e.g. employees) [23]. [18] presents a literature review of empirical studies on gamification according to a framework based on motivational affordance, psychological outcome and behavioral outcome. Then [24] presents a method to design gamification. Gamification is currently used in real contexts, as demonstrated by simulation tools such as the climate change negotiation game [6], by the gamified training for cyber defence presented in [7], and by the gamified risk management approach for enterprises in [8]. Furthermore, a gamified environment to improve decision maker awareness of cyber threats for critical infrastructures is described in [13] and an approach proposing a game for ethnographic analysis of security risks for cyber-physical systems is being developed in the Multi-faceted metrics for ICS Business Risk Analysis (MUMBA) project [4]. An example of a software platform providing gamification services to enterprises is Badgeville [2].

Concerning the state of the art of technological frameworks for risk analysis, they generally implement quantitative methods, but there is an increasing interest in on-line decision systems realized by linking available quantitative resources (e.g., models, historical data and standards) to semantics to allow for integration of knowledge with qualitative local experiences [16]. Our work is also positioned in this line as our creative process is a means to building a new knowledge base for risk analysis of water systems, as described in Subsect. 3.1. Another relevant work in this area is the CORAS platform for risk assessment of security critical systems [21], which is the result of a EU-funded project and introduces the field of model-driven risk assessment. Similarly to the works in model-driven engineering, CORAS proposes modelling methods and high-level graphical notations to support risk analysts in describing risks and related aspects, such as threat scenarios, to the purpose of analysis.

3   Risk Elicitation and Assessment for Water Systems

The work presented in this paper is part of a wider research activity aimed at realizing a novel risk management software system to support informed risk assessment of critical infrastructures, where risks are elicited by means of creative processes by the various stakeholders of infrastructures.

Our main case study is provided by water systems, in particular it is based on the result of the Vulnerability Assessment Support System (VASS) experiment [11], which was conducted under a grant by the National Oceanic and Atmospheric Administration U.S. Department. This was a qualitative vulnerability assessment where focus groups of expert stakeholders identified and discussed about thirty-five risks affecting community water systems in two sites of the East coast of the United States. The VASS experiment demonstrated that qualitative risk-ranking approaches can provide managers, policymakers, and stakeholders with key understanding of the risks of a system, and deliver the knowledge necessary for the formulation of realistic resilience plans. During execution of the experiment, experts recognized the lack of software tools to adequately support the required activities.

3.1 The ICE-CREAM-Based Risk Management System

The findings of the VASS experiment lead us to the design of a new knowledge-based system to assist various stakeholders in the collaborative work of risk identification and assessment. The distinguishing features of such a system are: (a) the definition and use of a formal model, the Vulnerability Upper Model (VUM) [9], for conceptual representation of risks, and the organization of the related information in a Water Systems ontology, to ensure logical coherence of risk definitions, to avoid redundancies, and to allow for automatic interpretation and reasoning; (b) a methodology for a VUM-based ontology engineering, to support and ease risk knowledge evolution; (c) the use of computational creativity methods to automatically suggest new risk definitions that can be possibly discussed and validated by the stakeholders [10]; (d) a collaboration tool to support gamified risk elicitation activities by the stakeholders where users interaction is facilitated by a mobile application.

The overall architecture of such a knowledge-based system, applied to water system risks, is shown in Fig. 1. This comprises design tools for the preparation and setup of the knowledge base, and of run time tools where such knowledge is exploited to search for and identify new risks through collaborative processes by water system stakeholders. Specifically, at design time, an initial VUM-based water system risk ontology is created by using an Ontology Management System (OMS), like Protégé [26], as described in Subsect. 3.2. Such an ontology can be enriched with contextual information, in the form of rules, derived from the specific water system at hand (such as geographic information, organization/business, ...). Finally, one or more VUM-based patterns, defining the structure of the semantic risk descriptions, are formally designed by using some modelling tool. In this work, patterns correspond to VUM sub-models and are defined by means of the OMS. Indeed, a system risk is represented by one or more semantic risk description fragments, called risk mini-models (RMM), each obtained through a specialization or instantiation operation of a VUM-based pattern with more detailed information. RMMs are created and validated by the water system stakeholders through the ICE application, on the basis of the information supplied by CREAM. Validated risk models contribute to enrich the VUM-based ontology.

In the following, we present the VUM, with the main aspects of the VUM-based risk ontology engineering approach, and the computational creativity methods to generate risk mini-models, which were already presented in [10]. Instead, the ICE application is described in details in Sect. 5.

3.2 Water System Ontology Engineering

The VUM is a conceptual representation of a general risk definition concerning a complex technological system, and provides the blueprints on how a detailed VUM ontology may be built. Indeed, this model was validated on water system risks by using the free-text descriptions that resulted from the VASS experiment,

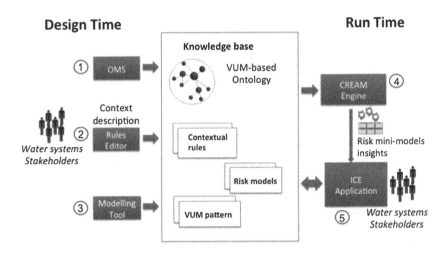

Fig. 1. ICE-CREAM system for risk assessment consisting of the Ontology Management System (OMS), the rules editor, the VUM-based pattern Modelling Tool, the CREAtivity Machine (CREAM), the Innovation through Collaborative Environment (ICE) Application, and the Knowledge Base

mainly related to the effect of climate change on the frequency distribution of natural hazards.

In the VUM, *hazards* are characterized by their set of *severity* metrics defined by specific properties such as time, duration, location, and intensity. Individual hazards of defined severity property can be associated with collections of likely *threats* meaningful for selected *system aspects* of the assessment. *Threat* and *system risk* concepts differentiate between the threats a hazard can pose to a system when likely *vulnerability* conditions make the threats significant to risk estimates. This way the system risk can be defined according to vulnerability and severity parameters within the *system aspect*. In turn, both *system risk* and *vulnerability* concepts are properties of the system. The *system* concept defines all the user interfaces with the participating *stakeholders*, who not only control the system through its interfaces, but, when the system fails to function within operational conditions, they are themselves affected by its risk.

The risk descriptions of the VASS experiment were turned into conceptual models, by defining domain-specific concepts through subsequent refinements of the core VUM abstract concepts. Indeed, the basic mechanism to refine the VUM is the specialization relationship that allows the introduction of new concepts whenever they can be associated with more abstract ones. As an example, in the VUM-based water system ontology, the (natural) *environment aspect* at the top of the core VUM organizes all *hazard* entities according to suitable general categories (e.g. climatological, ecosystem/habitats, geological, hydrological and weather).

3.3 Computational Creativity Approach

Our solution for automatic suggestion of risk mini-models leverages methods from *computational creativity*, a subfield of Artificial Intelligence devoted to defining computational systems that create artifacts and ideas [12]. In our application, we modelled risk mini-model detection as a search process within a space consisting of the VUM ontology constrained by contextual rules, which is updated and refined by accounting for the risk definitions produced by the users through the ICE tool and validated by the risk analysts.

In our system, risk mini-models can be generated by means of the CREAtivity Machine (CREAM) by linking abstract ontological models (i.e., patterns) to domain-specific concepts, exploiting entity and object property specialization relations of an ontology. For this application, a VUM pattern is linked with a set of the most specific concepts of the water system VUM ontology, preserving the semantics of the pattern, and according to the contextual rules. This method, that uses a SPARQL engine [1], is explained in detail in [10]. Given a VUM pattern, the output of CREAM can be: (*a*) a risk mini-model fully created by the system; (*b*) a risk mini-model obtained by automatic completion of a partially specified risk mini-model; or (*c*) an alternative risk mini-model of a given one, that may be selected based on some criteria such as concept similarity/dissimilarity. These functions are made available to users by means of the ICE application.

A basic VUM pattern includes the following concepts: System risk, System, Hazard, Threat, Severity, Vulnerability and Stakeholder. Its aim is to identify threats and system vulnerabilities related to a given system risk, from the perspective of different stakeholders.

The following is an example of a risk mini-model generated from the ontology and the basic VUM pattern. *A flood caused by unpredictably fast snow melting rate, transports surface pollutants (possibly including antibiotics from farming) into surface waters. Germs with resistance to water treatment measures in the drinking water system, colonize the treated water tank. Due to the presence of unsanitary water in the system, low immune system consumers are affected.*
SystemRisk: FloodPollutesSurfaceWaters. **Hazard**: SuddenSnow-IceMelting. **Threat**: ChemicalsIncreaseMicrobes/VirusResistanceToWaterTreatment-Measures. **System**: TreatedWaterTank. **Vulnerability**: LowImmuneSystemIn-Consumers. **Stakeholder**: Consumer. **Severity**: NumberOfInfectedConsumers.

4 Gamified Elicitation and Modelling of Water System Risks

4.1 Methodological Underpinnings

Our proposal is based on the assumption that experts participate in the process of collecting knowledge on water system risks. This is rarely the case as this process could be seen as a strenuous, time-consuming and annoying activity.

Hence our objective is to increase engagement of experts by means of a gamification approach supported by a software application where game elements [25] are introduced to support knowledge elicitation. We deem that a gamified application used in a non-entertainment context could unleash a broader participation of experts and an increased capacity in collecting knowledge of risks for water systems. This would lead to safety, security and economic benefits. To this aim we selected seven game elements and we adopted them in a knowledge elicitation workflow. These are: (1) *avatars*, (2) *points and leaderboards*, (3) *feedback*, (4) *rules*, (5) *teams*, (6) *parallel communication systems*, and (7) *time pressure*.

Avatars (1) are personalized characters representing and controlled by the participants. According to [19], anonymization of participants provides several advantages. In particular, with our proposal, we deem that, with avatars, participants would have lower barriers to new relationships. They would feel free to give fair opinions, avoid embarrassment and fear of being judged and criticized. Furthermore they would protect their privacy by having control over the professional information to be disclosed and increase their sense of security by avoiding the fear of legal repercussions in case of disclosing information about water system risks concerning specific companies. *Points* (2) are units of count in the score of a game. Together with leaderboards they show the level of competences of participants and determine their reputation by means of a hierarchy. The goal of the game is to increase their placement in the leaderboard. Participants are encouraged to participate and engage as interactions with the ICE app lead to an improvement of their score. *Feedback* (3) is the visual means provided by the game showing the participant performance, the leaderboard and the time left. *Rules* (4) are the laws for participants. They define what is possible and how to win points during the risk model harvesting phase. *Teams* (5) have to reach the common goal of defining risk mini-models. They offer interaction opportunities that increase engagement of participants. Each team is open and can be dynamically created by a proposer of the risk mini-model and some contributors. Every participant can take part in one or more teams. To increase collaboration, the number of points won by the team members is proportional to the number of participants of the team. *Parallel communication systems* (6), i.e. a text chat, allow to increase social engagement of participants working together on a risk model. *Time pressure* (7) is one of the factors providing uncertainty to achieving the goal of the collaborative activity. We deem that this game element would also stimulate participants to provide their input as soon as possible (for instance, by weighting more contributions provided at an early stage).

4.2   Game Mechanics

We describe the game mechanics supported by the ICE-CREAM system. A representation of the corresponding workflow as UML activity diagram is depicted in Fig. 2.

We envisage three different roles: the *coordinator*, the *risk mini-model proposer*, and the *risk mini-model contributor* (for the sake of concision we refer to them in the following as *contributor* and *proposer*). The *coordinator* is in charge of starting and ending the risk model harvesting activity, and/or may decide its duration. Indeed, the ICE-CREAM application provides flexibility to organize a game session lasting a few hours, as in the case of traditional participative risk assessment workshops, or days/weeks to give participants more time to define the models, of even an indefinite time, until the coordinator decides to close the activity. We remind the reader that a risk model consists of a set of risk mini-models characterizing the system or subsystem under analysis. The *coordinator* is also in charge of deciding whether a risk mini-model deserves to be part of the risk model or should be rejected. As this decision affects assignment of points to the participants, this role should be given to a participant trusted by the community of experts. All the participants can be both *proposer* and *contributor*.

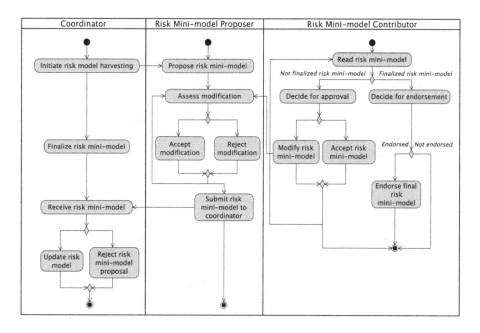

Fig. 2. ICE process flow

The *coordinator* starts the process by initiating risk model harvesting. Hence, *proposers* create risk mini-models by means of the ICE app. Other participants can read the proposed RMMs and decide to contribute by modifying one of them or, simply, accepting it. In case of modification, the corresponding *proposer* can decide to accept or reject the update. Once the *proposer* deems that the RMM is valuable or if the *coordinator* decides to finalize it, the *proposer* sends it to the *coordinator* who may decide to reject it or to use it to update the risk model. It should be noted that, to perform this decisional activity, the *coordinator* can be supported by a committee of experts (if available). Once the RMM is part of the risk model, contributors can still decide to endorse it.

Table 1. Points won by proposers and contributors for the performed activities. Harvey balls indicate the amount of points: ○ indicates no points and ● indicates 4 points. (For the activities marked with *, the points should be intended as the maximum amount of points assigned to a contributor for each risk mini-model.)

Player activity	Points	Points recipient
Proposer proposes risk mini-model	◕	Proposer
Contributor modifies risk mini-model*	◑	Contributor
Contributor accepts risk mini-model*	◑	Contributor
Contributor endorses risk mini-model*	◔	Contributor
Contributor decides to not endorse risk mini-model*	◔	Contributor
Proposer accepts or rejects modification	◔	Proposer
Coordinator updates risk model (with risk mini-model)	●	Proposer
Coordinator updates risk model (with risk mini-model)	◑	Contributor
Coordinator assigns extra points based on participation in risk mini-model definition (number of preliminary acceptances and final endorsements of risk mini-model)	from ○ to ●	Team

Both *proposers* and *contributors* of the risk model harvesting process win points by performing the above-mentioned activities. The idea is that participation is rewarded and that the larger the participation on defining a RMM the more points are collected by the team members. Table 1 shows a proposal of point assignments for each of the performed activity. This was conceived to reward collaborative participation. In case the *coordinator* wants to reward, for instance, more independent proposers, the point assignment profile should be defined accordingly (e.g., rewarding only proposals and modifications). However, this choice could result in a large amount of different RMMs that would be hard to manage.

5   Innovation Through a Collaborative Environment (ICE)

The main role of the ICE application is to manage the ICE game, that is, to share risk mini-model information among the clients participating in the game. The ICE application was developed on top of the WildFly application server [5] from JBoss technology that implements JEE (Java Enterprise Edition) specifications.

The clients of the ICE application can be: web clients, desktop clients (applications running on Windows, Mac OS or Linux platform), and mobile clients, i.e. applications developed for a mobile device, a smartphone or a tablet.

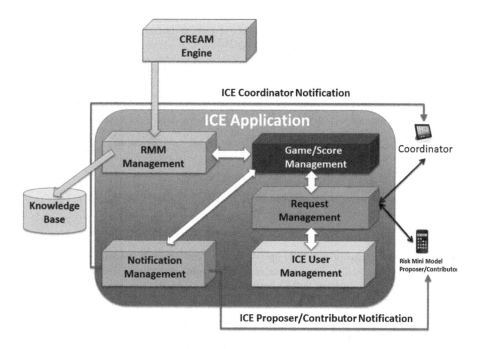

Fig. 3. ICE architecture

Figure 3 shows the detailed architecture of ICE including the modules developed and deployed in the ICE application server. The *ICE user management* module takes care of all users participating in a game session. The *request management* module manages all the requests coming from the registered users including coordinators of ICE sessions and game participants. The *RMM (Risk Mini Model) management* module manages all the RMMs proposed, accepted, modified, and finalized in a game session. Its main task is to interact with the *CREAM engine*, to retrieve concepts and RMM insights, and with the *knowledge base* to save new RMMs. The *game/score management* module is in charge of managing the game session and assigning the score to ICE users according to predefined rules (see Table 1). It may interact directly or indirectly with the other modules. It has also the task to activate the *notification management* module which is in charge of providing information to ICE game participants and to game coordinators in asynchronous mode. Indeed, this module enables a user (or an application) to receive information from a server without asking for it. A ICE user could be notified that some RMM (e.g., the one proposed) was modified by another user or that a RMM was accepted and evaluated.

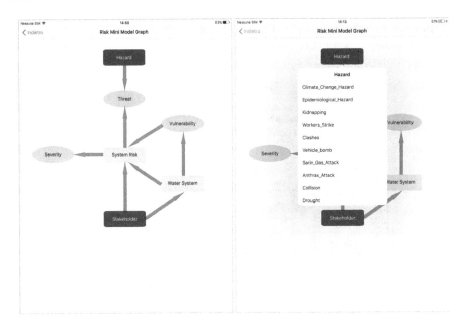

Fig. 4. Example usage of the ICE app. The left part shows a screenshot of the risk mini model pattern still to be instantiated. The right part shows a screenshot where hazard is selected by clicking on the corresponding diagram element.

The client developed in this first demonstration is an application for mobile devices, specifically, a iOS app for iPhone/iPad. This app will then be available in the App Store. The app allows the user to register and login to the ICE application. Furthermore, the user is able to propose a new risk mini-model (see Fig. 4 for an example of usage), to download and accept or modify the risk mini-model created by other users. The app is able to receive notifications from the ICE application server in asynchronous mode. For example, a user could login to the system and propose a new risk mini-model. At this point, for any reason, the user could logout from the ICE application. Subsequently, the risk mini-model proposed by that user could be modified by another user. At this point the ICE application server may notify the first user about this event.

6   Conclusions

As recently demonstrated by The Grenfell Action Group [3], whose members participated in collecting risks related to fire safety standards of the Grenfell Tower by means of an open collaboration approach, stakeholders of a system contribute in describing risks and providing useful information related to them when there is an urgent need. Meanwhile there is a need of tailored risk management systems that, with a lightweight and engaging approach, are suitable to collect risk information in a structured way so that this can be easily processed by a machine. To this purpose we propose a mobile app that allows collecting risks in a flexible way without organizing ad-hoc meetings and by means of a gamification approach that increases the engagement of risk knowledge contributors. The application is able to support the construction of a knowledge base collecting risks related to a critical infrastructure system (e.g. the water system) in both a semi-formal representation, as a conceptual model, and a formal one, as an ontology.

Acknowledgements. The work of Alex Coletti was conducted at SMRC, with partial funding from a NOAA-CPO research grant. The work of Antonio De Nicola, Giordano Vicoli, and Maria Luisa Villani was conducted at ENEA and was partially supported by the Italian Project ROMA (Resilience enhancement Of Metropolitan Area) (SCN_00064).

References

1. Apache Jena, version 2.11.1. http://jena.apache.org/. Accessed 22 June 2017
2. Badgeville. https://badgeville.com/. Accessed 13 June 2017
3. Grenfell Action Group. https://grenfellactiongroup.wordpress.com. Accessed 14 June 2017
4. MUMBA: Multi-faceted metrics for ICS Business Risk Analysis. https://ritics.org/mumba/. Accessed 31 July 2017
5. WildFly application server project. http://wildfly.org. Accessed 31 July 2017
6. World climate. http://www.climateinteractive.org/. Accessed 22 June 2017
7. Amorim, J.A., Hendrix, M., Andler, S.F., Gustavsson, P.M.: Gamified training for cyber defence: methods and automated tools for situation and threat assessment. In: NATO Modelling and Simulation Group (MSG) Annual Conference, vol. 2013 (2013)
8. Bajdor, P., Dragolea, L.: The gamification as a tool to improve risk management in the enterprise. Ann. Univ. Apulensis: Ser. Oecon. **13**(2), 574 (2011)
9. Coletti, A., De Nicola, A., Villani, M.L.: Building climate change into risk assessments. Nat. Hazards **84**(2), 1307–1325 (2016)
10. Coletti, A., De Nicola, A., Villani, M.L.: Enhancing creativity in risk assessment of complex sociotechnical systems. In: Gervasi, O. (ed.) ICCSA 2017. LNCS, vol. 10405, pp. 294–309. Springer, Cham (2017). https://doi.org/10.1007/978-3-319-62395-5_21
11. Coletti, A., Howe, P.D., Yarnal, B., Wood, N.J.: A support system for assessing local vulnerability to weather and climate. Nat. Hazards **65**(1), 999–1008 (2013)
12. Colton, S., Wiggins, G.A.: Computational creativity: the final frontier? In: Proceedings of the 20th European Conference on Artificial Intelligence, pp. 21–26. IOS Press (2012)
13. Cook, A., Smith, R., Maglaras, L., Janicke, H.: Using gamification to raise awareness of cyber threats to critical national infrastructure. In: Proceedings of the 4th International Symposium for ICS & SCADA Cyber Security Research 2016, ICS-CSR 2016, Swindon, UK, pp. 1–11. BCS Learning & Development Ltd. (2016)
14. Deltares. Circle. www.deltares.nl/circle. Accessed 14 June 2017
15. Deterding, S., Dixon, D., Khaled, R., Nacke, L.: From game design elements to gamefulness: defining gamification. In: Proceedings of the 15th International Academic MindTrek Conference: Envisioning Future Media Environments, pp. 9–15. ACM (2011)

16. Dow, A.K., Dow, E.M., Fitzsimmons, T.D., Materise, M.M.: Harnessing the environmental data flood: a comparative analysis of hydrologic, oceanographic, and meteorological informatics platforms. Bull. AMS **96**(5), 725–736 (2015)
17. Haase, D.: Participatory modelling of vulnerability and adaptive capacity in flood risk management. Nat. Hazards **67**(1), 77–97 (2013)
18. Hamari, J., Koivisto, J., Sarsa, H.: Does gamification work? A literature review of empirical studies on gamification. In: Proceedings of the 47th HICSS Conference, pp. 3025–3034 (2014)
19. Kang, R., Brown, S., Kiesler, S.: Why do people seek anonymity on the internet?: informing policy and design. In: Proceedings of the SIGCHI Conference on Human Factors in Computing Systems, CHI 2013, pp. 2657–2666. ACM, New York (2013)
20. Komendantova, N., Mrzyglocki, R., Mignan, A., Khazai, B., Wenzel, F., Patt, A., Fleming, K.: Multi-hazard and multi-risk decision-support tools as a part of participatory risk governance: feedback from civil protection stakeholders. Int. J. Disaster Risk Reduct. **8**, 50–67 (2014)
21. Lund, M.S., Solhaug, B., Stølen, K.: Model-Driven Risk Analysis: The CORAS Approach. Springer, Heidelberg (2010). https://doi.org/10.1007/978-3-642-12323-8
22. Maiden, N., Zachos, K., Lockerbie, J., Hoddy, S., Camargo, K.: Establishing digital creativity support in non-creative work environments. In: Proceedings of the 11th ACM Creativity and Cognition Conference. ACM (2017)
23. Meske, C., Brockmann, T., Wilms, K., Stieglitz, S.: Social collaboration and gamification. In: Stieglitz, S., Lattemann, C., Robra-Bissantz, S., Zarnekow, R., Brockmann, T. (eds.) Gamification. PI, pp. 93–109. Springer, Cham (2017). https://doi.org/10.1007/978-3-319-45557-0_7
24. Morschheuser, B., Werder, K., Hamari, J., Abe, J.: How to gamify? Development of a method for gamification. In: Proceedings of the 50th HICSS Conference, pp. 4–7 (2017)
25. Reeves, B., Read, J.L.: Total engagement: how games and virtual worlds are changing the way people work and businesses compete (2009)
26. Stanford: Protégé Ontology Management System. http://protege.stanford.edu. Accessed 24 Feb 2016

Managing Gas and Electric Power Network Dependencies to secure Energy Supply: Application to the UK System

Dominique Wassermann, Andrea Antenucci, and Giovanni Sansavini[✉]

Reliability and Risk Engineering, Institute of Energy Technology,
Department of Mechanical and Process Engineering, ETH, Zurich,
Leonhardstrasse 21, Zurich, Switzerland
sansavig@ethz.ch
http://www.rre.ethz.ch/

The availability of natural gas plays an important role in electricity network, which employs gas-turbine-driven power generation. It influences not only the generation unit commitment, but also the costs of operations and the reliability of the network [1,2]. In the event of power system faults, gas-operated units can be started up relatively fast in comparison to nuclear- and coal-fired plants, thus responding quickly to potential shortages or contingencies and preventing loss of stability and blackouts. For this reason, natural gas delivery must be reliable and adequate.

However, most gas-operated units have interruptible contracts, i.e. they are preferred candidates for curtailments when the gas network becomes congested or delivery reaches its maximum capacity. Moreover, modern gas turbines employed for electricity generation are operated under high-pressure conditions, which makes them more vulnerable to pressure drops in the system compared to other loads in the gas network [3].

To be able to fully satisfy the gas demand in the network, the operations of compressors and gas wells or terminals must be scheduled beforehand in order for the pressures to stay within safety margins [4]. In addition to that, the amount of gas stored in the pipelines owing to the gas pressure, referred to as linepack, must be taken into account and managed. In the past, several studies on the simulation and modelling of interdependent electricity and gas networks have been conducted [5–7]; however, most of them neglect the aspect of the transient behaviour of gas flows in high-pressure systems. However, considering steady-state operations may fail in acknowledging critical pressure conditions during transients, and therefore lead to gross underestimation of the risks to the operations. Liu et al. [8] presented a work in which a model for the analysis of interdependent electricity and gas networks including transient flows is derived.

This work aims to emphasize on the importance of a secure operation of gas networks in combined electrical and gas networks. A transient model for gas flows in gas networks is developed. The flow of natural gas through pipelines depends on several factors such as the temperature and composition of natural gas as well as properties of the pipelines, for instance diameter, length and roughness.

© Springer Nature Switzerland AG 2018
G. D'Agostino and A. Scala (Eds.): CRITIS 2017, LNCS 10707, pp. 181–184, 2018.
https://doi.org/10.1007/978-3-319-99843-5_16

In general, gas transportation is described by the mass and momentum conservation equations:

Mass conservation:

$$\frac{\partial \rho}{\partial t} + \frac{\partial (\rho \cdot v)}{\partial x} = 0 \tag{1}$$

Momentum conservation:

$$\frac{\partial (\rho v)}{\partial t} + \frac{\partial (\rho v^2)}{\partial x} + \frac{\partial p}{\partial x} = -\frac{2 f \rho v |v|}{D} - \rho g sin(\theta) \tag{2}$$

In this work, the assumptions of isothermal 1-D flow [9], constant gas compressibility, horizontal pipes are considered. Furthermore, the convective and the gravitational acceleration terms are neglected [10].

Equations 1 and 2 are discretized in space and time, and are solved via the Newton-Raphson iteration method. The solution of the transient equations is embedded in an optimization framework, which minimizes costs stemming from the operation of compressors, from the penalty of gas curtailments (c_{GSL}) and from gas supply. The objective function can be stated as follows:

$$Min \left\{ C(\boldsymbol{GSL}, \boldsymbol{H}, \boldsymbol{v}) = \sum^{NN} c_{GSL} \cdot \boldsymbol{GSL} + \sum^{NC} c_{gas} \cdot m_c(\boldsymbol{H}) + \sum^{NT} c_{term/stor} \cdot \boldsymbol{v} \right\} \tag{3}$$

where $\boldsymbol{GSL}$ is the amount of gas curtailment, c_{gas} is gas price, $\boldsymbol{H}$ is compressor power, $\boldsymbol{v}$ is gas delivery, $m_c(\boldsymbol{H})$ is the amount of gas used by compressors, and $c_{term/stor}$ is the cost of gas delivery. The optimization is carried out under maximum and minimum pressure constraints, compressor technical limits and supply constraints. By running the cost minimization, the minimum amount of gas demand not supplied can be determined. Then, the model can be integrated into an upper-level security-constrained unit commitment (SCUC) problem that ensures the stability of electrical power generation and considers gas curtailments to power plants.

The previously derived optimization framework is applied to a simplified version of the Great Britain gas pipeline network, which is based on the grid data of the UK gas operator National Grid. In total, there are 69 nodes, 81 branches and 21 compressors. Gas can be supplied by 9 terminals and 9 storage sites. During one day, a maximum of around $396 \cdot 10^6$ m^3 gas can be supplied [11]. On the demand side, there are 23 gas fired power plants and 51 non-electrical off-takes. The total non-electrical gas demand over the day was $340 \cdot 10^6$ m^3, which is the highest value of December 2005 [5]. The combined non-electrical and electrical demand was $467.64 \cdot 10^6$ m^3. This value is higher than the maximum amount of gas via the terminals that can be supplied; it represents a peak load condition.

In order to emphasize the importance of the network operations, i.e. linepack management, two test cases have been conducted. In case 1, a higher initial linepack of $350 \cdot 10^6$ m^3 and in case 2, a lower linepack of $320 \cdot 10^6$ m^3 is present at the beginning of the day.

Figure 1 shows results for case 1. The linepack in the system varies significantly over the course of one day. The maximum value is at around $380 \cdot 10^6 \, \text{m}^3$ in the 6th hour. During the first 6 h of the day, the total gas demand is lower than the total input, which is why the linepack in the system increases. After that, the linepack starts to decrease as the total load rises above the system input; this happens until the 22nd hour, when demand decreases again. Here linepack hits its lowest point at $240 \cdot 10^6 \, \text{m}^3$; at the end of the day, a significantly lower linepack is present than at the beginning of the day.

In hour 16 a load curtailment occurs. First, only a slight curtailment is present, but during the hours of peak demand, i.e. between hour 16 and hour 20, the total curtailment increases up to 500 kg/s. In total $4.37 \cdot 10^6 \, \text{m}^3$ of load is shed, which is about 1% of the daily consumption. This amount of gas is the equivalent of 2.25 GW of power missing in the scheduling of the electrical system. Therefore, the electricity generation fleet has to be re-dispatched to compensate for the loss of the 2.25 GW power production, e.g. by activating (I) further gas-fired plants located in more favourable sites of the gas transmission network or (II) generators exploiting other technologies.

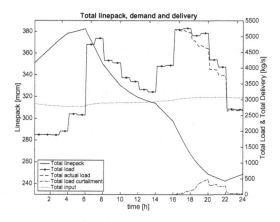

Fig. 1. Linepack, total demanded and actual load, total input, test case 1

In test case 2, the initial linepack was set at $320 \cdot 10^6 \, \text{m}^3$ at the start of day. As in test case 1, the linepack decreases drastically over the day. In this scenario, load curtailment already happens at an earlier time of the day, in hour 15. The total amount of curtailed gas is $24.12 \cdot 10^6 \, \text{m}^3$, or 12.4 GW - which is about 5.5 times higher than for the same total load, but with the higher initial linepack of test case 1.

As the two test cases show, the operation of the gas network has a significant impact on the generation planning and operations of the electrical network. When pressure levels, i.e. the linepack in the system, are not controlled properly, large generation power shortages can arise in the electrical network. As a consequence, security of supply cannot be guaranteed and worse, outages or total system failures can occur in the electrical system. Especially with the rise of fluctuating renewable energy sources such as wind and photovoltaic power, the gas network has to be operated robustly and must be prepared to compensate for rapid changes in demand and generation.

In order to increase security of supply in both systems, the results of the optimization could be used to reduce stress on the gas network during peak demand hours. As the amount of curtailed load is known accurately due to the non-heuristic nature of the optimization framework, electricity generation can be shifted from gas-fired power plants to different energy sources in order to decrease the natural gas demand and thereby preventing critically low pressure levels in the gas network. Alternatively, compressor set points may be varied, leading to higher costs.

Furthermore, recent developments in power-to-gas (PtG) technologies have opened up more uses for the gas transmission network - for instance the one as a large scale energy storage. This however poses new challenges for the gas network operator, which have to be accounted for in the scheduling of the gas network operations.

References

1. Fu, Y., Shahidehpour, M., Li, Z.: Security-constrained unit commitment with AC constraints. IEEE Trans. Power Syst. **20**(2), 1001–1013 (2005)
2. Shahidehpour, M., Fu, Y., Wiedman, T.: Impact of natural gas infrastructure on electric power systems. Proc. IEEE **93**(5), 1042–1056 (2005)
3. NAER Council: Reliability assessment 2001–2011: The the reliability of bulk electric systems in North America (2002)
4. Carter, R.G., Rachford Jr., H.H., et al.: Optimizing line-pack management to hedge against future load uncertainty. In: PSIG Annual Meeting, Pipeline Simulation Interest Group (2003)
5. Chaudry, M., Jenkins, N., Strbac, G.: Multi-time period combined gas and electricity network optimisation. Electr. Power Syst. Res. **78**, 1265–1279 (2008)
6. Liu, C., Shahidehpour, M., Fu, Y., Li, Z.: Security-constrained unit commitment with natural gas transmission constraints. IEEE Trans. Power Syst. **24**(3), 1523–1536 (2009)
7. Geidl, M., Andersson, G.: Optimal power flow of multiple energy carriers. IEEE Trans. Power Syst. **22**(1), 145–155 (2007)
8. Liu, C., Shahidehpour, M., Wang, J.: Coordinated scheduling of electricity and natural gas infrastructures with a transient model for natural gas flow. Chaos **21**(2), 1–12 (2011)
9. Osiadacz, A.: Simulation and Analysis of Gas Networks. Gulf Publishing Company, Houston (1987)
10. Herrán-González, A., De La Cruz, J., De Andrés-Toro, B., Risco-Martín, J.: Modeling and simulation of a gas distribution pipeline network. Appl. Math. Model. **33**(3), 1584–1600 (2009)
11. Qadrdan, M., Abeysekera, M., Chaudry, M., Wu, J., Jenkins, N.: Role of power-to-gas in an integrated gas and electricity system in Great Britain. Int. J. Hydrog. Energy **40**(17), 5763–5775 (2015)

What the Stack? On Memory Exploitation and Protection in Resource Constrained Automotive Systems

Aljoscha Lautenbach[✉], Magnus Almgren, and Tomas Olovsson

Chalmers University of Technology, Gothenburg, Sweden
{aljoscha,magnus.almgren,tomas.olovsson}@chalmers.se

Abstract. The increased connectivity of road vehicles poses significant challenges for transportation security, and automotive security has rapidly gained attention in recent years. One of the most dangerous kinds of security relevant software bugs are related to memory corruption, since their successful exploitation would grant the attacker a high degree of influence over the compromised system. Such vulnerabilities and the corresponding mitigation techniques have been widely studied for regular IT systems, but we identified a gap with respect to resource constrained automotive systems.

In this paper, we discuss how the hardware architecture of resource constrained automotive systems impacts memory exploitation techniques and their implications for memory protection. Currently deployed systems have little to no protection from memory exploitation. However, based on our analysis we find that the simple and well-known measures like stack canaries, non-executable RAM, and to a limited extent memory layout randomization can also be deployed in this domain to significantly raise the bar for successful exploitation.

Keywords: Embedded system security · Electronic control unit
Resource constraints · Memory exploitation · Memory protection

1 Introduction

In the automotive domain, considerations of safety have a long tradition in vehicle development. Security considerations on the other hand, often called "cybersecurity" to distinguish from physical security, are still relatively new.

Several recent developments necessitate the introduction of security measures. One such development is the gradual introduction of "Intelligent Transport Systems (ITS)" which aims to improve traffic flow and safety through real-time information exchange between traffic participants and traffic infrastructure. Incidentally, with the advent of self-driving cars, the correct functioning of these "Intelligent Transport Systems" will be crucial. Another factor is the emergence of the "Internet of Things" which opens the door to machine-to-machine communication and interoperability to facilitate completely new types of services,

© Springer Nature Switzerland AG 2018
G. D'Agostino and A. Scala (Eds.): CRITIS 2017, LNCS 10707, pp. 185–193, 2018.
https://doi.org/10.1007/978-3-319-99843-5_17

including automotive services such as remote diagnostics or smartphone apps to control vehicle functions. This offers a large attack surface to potential attackers.

Newly manufactured vehicles have around 50–100 electronic control units (ECUs), which are specialized microcontrollers of differing complexity, connected in smaller networks, forming one large internal network. The vulnerability of the in-vehicle network and their connected systems has consistently been highlighted and demonstrated by security researchers for several years [1–4]. The work by Miller and Valasek was particularly media-effective [5–9].

Meanwhile, in the world of desktop computers and servers, an arms race between memory exploit writers and memory protection developers has been going on for decades [10,11]. Ever more advanced defensive techniques inspire ever more creative and complicated attacks. Due to the limited hardware capabilities and limited connectivity, automotive systems and other embedded systems have not been primary targets for such exploits. But with increased connectivity and computing capabilities, this is slowly changing. Therefore it is important to understand how effective such exploits could be in the automotive domain, and what trade-offs are required to deploy known mitigation techniques.

2   Resource Constrained Microcontrollers

Due to cost, power and size constraints, microcontrollers have limited capabilities and very particular architectures. In the following we will sketch the most typical hardware and processor architecture [12–16]. The specifications of a typical resource constrained microcontroller used for safety-critical automotive applications are listed in Table 1.

Table 1. Highlights of typical ranges of resource constrained microcontroller configurations

Hardware	Specification	Most common
RAM	4 KB - 500 KB	40 KB
Flash memory	256 KB - 6 MB	1 MB
Processor speed	16–150 MHz	80 MHz

All modern microcontrollers (MCUs) support at least two different execution modes: privileged and unprivileged mode [16]. Applications generally execute in unprivileged mode, whereas the operating system executes in privileged mode.

There are several different types of memory: flash memory, for the boot loader, OS and other program code; data flash, for permanent data storage; RAM, for dynamic state information; and often there is memory-mapped I/O. The different kinds of memory are commonly mapped into a single, linear 32-bit address space. The concrete mapping is configurable. For instance, the flash memory could be mapped into 0x00000000 - 0x009FFFFF, and the RAM into 0x00A00000 - 0x00AFFFFF, as depicted in Fig. 1.

Flash Memory	RAM	Data Flash	Mem.-Mapped Input/Output
0x00000000	0x00A00000	0x00B00000	0x00C00000

Fig. 1. An example of a linear memory address space mapping

The amount of available RAM is very limited. Every task has a *statically assigned memory region* dedicated to it; there is *no virtual memory* [16]. For instance, the first OS task could have its dynamic memory in the address range 0x00AFFFFF–0x00AFFD01, while the second task would have range 0x00AFFD00–0x00AFFC01. This mapping is ordinarily *enforced by a memory protection unit (MPU)*, which is available on most microcontrollers. This unit keeps track which memory regions are readable, writable or executable. If, for instance, Task 2 tries to access the stack of Task 1, and they were configured to be in separate memory regions, the MPU will not allow the access. This is illustrated in Fig. 2. Note that the stack grows downwards, as usual.

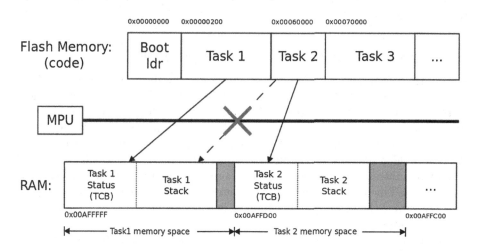

Fig. 2. Static task memory mapping into RAM

Two data structures are relevant for running tasks and thus kept in RAM: (1) the task control block (TCB), which keeps status information, and (2) the call stack. The common microcontroller architectures are link-register based, i.e., they keep track of the next return address in a special CPU register (the link-register lr) [16]. Before a function call, the return address (lr) is pushed on the stack, just like on x86. There are some minor differences in stack-handling among the architectures: on ARM, for instance, parameters are loaded from registers rather than from the stack. Regularly, RAM is executable; this can be necessary to reprogram the flash memory outside a workshop, e.g., for unsupervised firmware upgrades.

The flash memory contains all program code: the boot loader, the operating system and application code. Since the RAM is too small to contain the operating system code and the code of the programs, everything is executed directly from flash. A context switch from one task to another then simply requires that the registers are stored for later retrieval, that the task status is changed and that the current execution mode is updated. Finally the program counter (pc) is changed to point to the task to be executed next.

To summarize the main differences with x86 type architectures in desktops and servers: there is no heap, there are no dynamically loaded libraries or shared objects and there is no virtual memory. Furthermore, the code is executed directly from flash, and *RAM is statically mapped.*

3   Exploiting Memory-Related Software Bugs and Protection Mechanisms

Given the architecture outlined in the previous section, we will now look into possible memory corruption bugs, how they can be exploited, and possible protection mechanisms.

3.1   Stack-Based Buffer Overflows and Stack Canaries

During the design and development of automotive systems, great care is taken not to introduce memory corruption bugs due to their safety implications, for instance by enforcing the MISRA C guidelines which help to reduce software bugs. However, memory corruption bugs still occur occasionally, and when they do, they also pose a security risk. Using dynamic memory during run-time is generally forbidden in automotive software; all memory must be statically assigned. Therefore, most memory corruption bugs commonly found on regular PCs, such as heap-based memory corruption bugs or string-formatting errors, are not a priority. However, the most common type of memory corruption bug, stack-based buffer overflows [11], can occur.

An important observation is that *the principles of exploiting stack-based buffer overflows are the same for all common architectures.* As long as the return address is written to the stack, buffer overflows can be exploited by an attacker. Since the available RAM is rather limited, the attack code needs to be fairly compact, but this will not stop an attacker from finding useful exploits. Even an extremely short exploit which crashes the targeted task can be dangerous.

Stack canaries, also known as stack cookies or stack-guards [17], can be used to detect and prevent buffer overflow exploits. They write a random canary value before the return address on the stack, and before a function returns, the canary value is validated. If the value changed, program integrity can no longer be guaranteed, and a memory exception is triggered. Figure 3 depicts a simple stack using a canary: if the vulnerable buffer vuln_buf in func() overflows, the canary in front of the saved return address will be overwritten, and the program will be aborted before the potential attack code written to vuln_buf can be

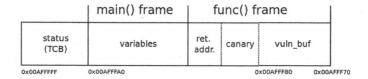

Fig. 3. Memory layout of a vulnerable task using a canary

executed. This comes at the expense of performance, but it is an effective safeguard. There are techniques to circumvent canaries [11], but they make successful exploitation of stack-based memory corruption bugs harder.

3.2 Non-executable RAM and Return Oriented Programming

The straight-forward exploitation of a buffer overflow only works if the RAM is executable [18]. As mentioned earlier, an executable RAM is often necessary during firmware upgrades, but since all code is stored in flash memory, most of the time RAM can, and should, be non-executable.

To prevent regular buffer overflow exploitation, it is common practice in desktop operating systems to make the data section non-executable; all major processor architectures have hardware support for this. In response, attackers have found ways to circumvent non-executable stacks with so called code-reuse attacks. One of the first attacks of this kind is called "return-into-libc" [19], and it was shown to be Turing complete: arbitrary computations can be achieved with this technique [20]. There is an even more fine-grained code-reuse technique called return oriented programming (ROP) [21]. Instead of using an entire function, the attacker uses *gadgets*, trailing function code snippets before a return instruction. The attack is then composed of a chain of fake stack frames pointing to gadgets. A key point for code-reuse attacks to work is that the gadget locations in memory are known.

Applying these techniques to the world of constrained automotive systems, one will find many similarities and a few differences. Since the microcontrollers we consider have no virtual memory, the entire memory space is addressable, within the confines of the MPU. Therefore, it should be possible to construct a working exploit using ROP, since all memory addresses are known a priori. Moreover, since everything is statically compiled, an exploit which works for a single ECU will work for all ECUs of the same type, implying that a resourceful attacker can study one vehicle to write an exploit which works across the fleet.

Successful construction of a ROP attack requires a substantial number of gadgets within the process or task address space. On regular PCs, these gadgets are relatively easy to find in shared libraries. Since there are no shared libraries in resource constrained automotive systems, and the code base of the executing tasks is typically small, it is not certain that a sufficient number of gadgets can be found. Furthermore, ROP attacks require more space than a regular attack since every gadget, each containing a small number of instructions, requires its own stack frame. When RAM is very limited, this additional space may be a problem for successful exploitation.

The practical construction of ROP exploits on resource constrained automotive systems should be thoroughly studied by the security community to explore their feasibility.

3.3   Compile-Time Memory Layout Randomization

On desktop systems, the answer to return oriented programming is memory layout randomization: the stack and the shared libraries are loaded at random locations in virtual memory, rather than in predictable ones. This makes successful exploitation much harder.

Due to the static memory in constrained automotive systems, this technique can not be applied directly. However, it can still be utilized by randomizing the program memory mappings at compile-time. This would make them different for every ECU, and consequently, writing consistent exploits would be harder. The downside is that it would require custom images for every ECU.

Another caveat, apart from the potential production difficulties, is that the entropy is very low. Layout randomization has been shown to be relatively ineffective on regular 32-bit systems, due to low entropy of the memory locations [22]. However, this is only true under certain conditions, and it should be investigated if the same conditions also hold in resource constrained automotive systems.

4   Discussion

In this paper, we have discussed several simple measures that could be implemented to improve security, but further investigations are necessary to judge the cost and effectiveness of these mitigation techniques.

The first measure would be to add stack canaries to detect and prevent the exploitation of buffer overflows. The main concern with this technique is the associated performance degradation since automotive systems have strict real-time requirements and any impact on performance must be carefully evaluated. Nevertheless, the simplicity of canaries and their long use in desktop operating systems make them a very good candidate for immediate adoption, and the costs should be manageable.

The second measure would be to ensure that RAM is generally non-executable. RAM should only be executable when necessary, e.g., during (authenticated) firmware upgrades. Since virtually all microcontrollers include a memory protection unit, this should be relatively straight-forward and cheap to implement. Non-executable RAM raises the bar for successful exploitation significantly, so this is another good candidate for immediate adoption.

The third measure, compile-time memory layout randomization, may help to combat attacks via return oriented programming. However, this technique has several practical difficulties. Changing the production process so that every ECU uses a slightly different image may be very costly. Given the cost, the added level of protection may be too small, and it aims to protect against complex attacks which currently are not likely to occur since simpler attacks will work. Therefore, this technique is unlikely to be adopted soon, but in anticipation of future ROP attacks on ECUs, it should be further investigated and improved.

There is also a new trend in the automotive industry to consolidate several smaller ECUs onto a single, more powerful ECU, as a result of efforts to reduce weight, costs, power and fuel consumption. The ECU architecture will resemble regular PCs, including virtual memory and complex operating systems. Nevertheless, it is unlikely that the light-weight ECUs as described in this paper will disappear quickly, and they still need to be secured.

5   Conclusion

With the advent of intelligent transport systems, the internet of things and self-driving cars, the protection of vehicles against malicious manipulation becomes ever more important. We have discussed three memory protection mechanisms to hinder successful exploitation of memory corruption bugs: stack canaries, non-executable RAM and compile-time memory layout randomization.

Since code typically executes directly from flash memory, and since memory protection units are in wide-spread use, we highly recommend to make RAM non-executable. When necessary, executing from RAM can be allowed for specific events such as firmware upgrades. Similarly, stack canaries have a proven track record, and their performance impact can be measured and accounted for, so we also highly recommend to adopt them in automotive systems. The idea of compile-time memory layout randomization on the other hand has serious flaws at this point, and it requires more work to be a viable protection mechanism. The analysis in this paper clearly shows that additional protection mechanisms are urgently needed, and that the techniques are readily available.

Finally, it should also be noted that the issues discussed in this paper are not necessarily unique to the automotive domain, and probably apply to a wide number of embedded systems.

Acknowledgments. We would like to thank all anonymous reviewers for their valuable feedback. The research leading to these results has been partially supported by the HoliSec project (2015-06894) funded by VINNOVA, the Swedish Governmental Agency for Innovation Systems, and by the Swedish Civil Contingencies Agency (MSB) through the project "RICS".

References

1. Wolf, M., Weimerskirch, A., Paar, C.: Security in automotive bus systems. In: Workshop on Embedded Security in Cars (2004)
2. Koscher, K., et al.: Experimental security analysis of a modern automobile. In: 2010 IEEE Symposium on Security and Privacy (SP), pp. 447–462. IEEE (2010)

3. Checkoway, S., et al.: Comprehensive experimental analyses of automotive attack surfaces. In: Proceedings of the 20th USENIX Security Symposium, San Francisco, CA, USA, vol. 7792, August 2011

4. Kleberger, P., Olovsson, T., Jonsson, E.: Security aspects of the in-vehicle network in the connected car. In: 2011 IEEE Intelligent Vehicles Symposium (IV), pp. 528–533, June 2011

5. Greenberg, A.: Hackers remotely kill a jeep on the highway with me in it. Wired.com (2015). https://www.wired.com/2015/07/hackers-remotely-kill-jeep-highway/. Accessed 01 June 2017

6. Greenberg, A.: Hackers remotely kill a jeep on the highway with me in it. Wired.com (2016). https://www.wired.com/2016/08/jeep-hackers-return-high-speed-steering-acceleration-hacks/. Accessed 01 June 2017

7. Valasek, C., Miller, C.: Adventures in automotive networks and control units. Technical report, Defcon 21, August 2013. http://www.ioactive.com/pdfs/IOActive_Adventures_in_Automotive_Networks_and_Control_Units.pdf

8. Miller, C., Valasek, C.: A survey of remote automotive attack surfaces. Technical report, Defcon 22, August 2014. http://blog.hackthecar.com/wp-content/uploads/2014/08/236073361-Survey-of-Remote-Attack-Surfaces.pdf

9. Miller, C., Valasek, C.: Remote exploitation of an unaltered passenger vehicle. Technical report, Defcon 23, August 2015. http://illmatics.com/Remote%20Car%20Hacking.pdf

10. Szekeres, L., Payer, M., Wei, T., Song, D.: SoK: eternal war in memory. In: 2013 IEEE Symposium on Security and Privacy (SP), pp. 48–62, May 2013

11. van der Veen, V., dutt-Sharma, N., Cavallaro, L., Bos, H.: Memory errors: the past, the present, and the future. In: Balzarotti, D., Stolfo, S.J., Cova, M. (eds.) RAID 2012. LNCS, vol. 7462, pp. 86–106. Springer, Heidelberg (2012). https://doi.org/10.1007/978-3-642-33338-5_5

12. Quigley, C.P., McMurran, R., Jones, R.P., Faithfull, P.T.: An investigation into cost modelling for design of distributed automotive electrical architectures. In: 2007 3rd Institution of Engineering and Technology Conference on Automotive Electronics, pp. 1–9, June 2007

13. Mayer, A., Hellwig, F.: System performance optimization methodology for Infineon's 32-bit automotive microcontroller architecture. In: Proceedings of the Conference on Design, Automation and Test in Europe, DATE 2008, pp. 962–966. ACM, New York (2008)

14. Erjavec, J., Thompson, R.: Automotive technology: a systems approach. Cengage Learning (2014)

15. Gai, P., Violante, M.: Automotive embedded software architecture in the multi-core age. In: 2016 21st IEEE European Test Symposium (ETS), pp. 1–8, May 2016

16. ARM: ARMv7-M architecture reference manual. Technical report, December 2014

17. Cowan, C., et al.: Stackguard: automatic adaptive detection and prevention of buffer-overflow attacks. USENIX Secur. **98**, 63–78 (1998)

18. Aleph One: Smashing the stack for fun and profit. Phrack Mag. **7**(49), 14–16 (1996)

19. Solar Designer: Getting around non-executable stack (and fix), August 1997. http://seclists.org/bugtraq/1997/Aug/63

20. Tran, M., Etheridge, M., Bletsch, T., Jiang, X., Freeh, V., Ning, P.: On the expressiveness of return-into-libc attacks. In: Sommer, R., Balzarotti, D., Maier, G. (eds.) RAID 2011. LNCS, vol. 6961, pp. 121–141. Springer, Heidelberg (2011). https://doi.org/10.1007/978-3-642-23644-0_7

21. Shacham, H.: The geometry of innocent flesh on the bone: return-into-libc without function calls (on the x86). In: Proceedings of the 14th ACM Conference on Computer and Communications Security, pp. 552–561. ACM (2007)
22. Shacham, H., Page, M., Pfaff, B., Goh, E.J., Modadugu, N., Boneh, D.: On the effectiveness of address-space randomization. In: Proceedings of the 11th ACM Conference on Computer and Communications Security, CCS 2004, pp. 298–307. ACM, New York (2004)

Dealing with Functional Safety Requirements for Automotive Systems: A Cyber-Physical-Social Approach

Mohamad Gharib$^{(\boxtimes)}$, Paolo Lollini, Andrea Ceccarelli, and Andrea Bondavalli

University of Florence - DiMaI, Viale Morgagni 65, Florence, Italy
{mohamad.gharib,paolo.lollini,andrea.ceccarelli,
andrea.bondavalli}@unifi.it

Abstract. Road transport system is one of the essential infrastructures in the world, where the majority of the population use its facilities on a daily basis. That is why ensuring their safety has been always a growing concern for most authorities. The automotive industry is already aware of that, and the ISO 26262, a standard for developing functional safety systems for vehicles, has been developed. Although current studies have shown that the root cause for most of the accidents has shifted from vehicle-centric to driver-centric, the main objective of ISO 26262 is covering electronic and electric (E/E) systems of vehicles with almost no emphasis on the driver itself. To this end, we propose a holistic approach based on the ISO 26262 standard that not only considers the E/E systems of the vehicle but also the driver's behaviour. We illustrate the utility of the approach with an example from the automotive domain.

Keywords: Transport · Automotive systems
Functional safety requirements · ISO 26262
Cyber-Physical-Social Systems

1 Introduction

Automotive systems can be described as safety-critical systems, which have to fulfil safety requirements in addition to functional requirements [1]. More specifically, safety requirements describe the characteristics that a system must have in order to be safe [1], and it is a crucial property that must be ensured to avoid or mitigate any potentially unacceptable hazards events [2]. Failing to comply with safety requirements leave the system open to various kinds of vulnerabilities that might endanger the safety of its users. Therefore, it is very important to consider safety requirements during the design and development of automotive systems to reduce the risk of hazards events occurrence [3].

The automotive industry is already using safety analysis, validation and verification techniques to increase vehicle safety. Moreover, the ISO 26262 [4], a functional safety standard has been developed, which provides appropriate development processes, requirements and safety integrity levels specific for the automotive manufacturer. However, ISO 26262 has been mainly developed to cover E/E

G. D'Agostino and A. Scala (Eds.): CRITIS 2017, LNCS 10707, pp. 194–206, 2018.
https://doi.org/10.1007/978-3-319-99843-5_18

systems of vehicles and it assumes that vehicle drivers can perform the necessary actions to stay safe. But this is not always the case, since several studies have shown that drivers are the main reason for many accidents [5,6], i.e., the challenges of vehicle safety are more than purely technical. In this context, the focus should be on mitigating the root cause of these accidents (i.e., drivers) [5]. Therefore, to design an effective safety automotive system, the driver behaviour should be better understood, modeled and considered during the system design.

Driving is a situation awareness process, and more than half of the crashes that require the driver awareness were caused by driver inattention and/or distraction [7,8]. Although modeling the driver behaviour is not new, it has not been considered in well-adopted standards such as ISO 26262. We advocate that integrating the social (driver behaviour) and technical (E/E systems) components of automotive systems during the system design is essential for the development of safer systems. More specifically, an approach that addresses the driver behaviour along with the E/E systems of the vehicle can significantly improve the safety of road transport system [6]. To this end, we propose a holistic approach based on the ISO 26262 standard that not only considers the E/E systems of the vehicle but also the driver and his behaviour as an integral of the system.

The rest of the paper is organized as follows; (Sect. 2) presents the research background, and we describe an illustrative example in (Sect. 3). In (Sect. 4), we present our approach for dealing with functional safety requirements, and we apply it to the illustrative example in (Sect. 5). Related work is presented in (Sect. 6), and we conclude and discuss future work in (Sect. 7).

2   Background

1. ISO 26262 [4] is a functional safety standard that has been developed with a main objective to provide guidelines and best practices to increase the safety of E/E systems in vehicles. It covers the overall automotive safety life cycle including specification, design, implementation, integration, verification and validation. ISO 26262 focuses on the hazards of the E/E systems and their associated risks. The associated risks are then assigned an Automotive Safety Integrity Level (ASIL). The ASILs can be classified under, Quality Management (QM[1]), ASIL A, ASIL B, ASIL C, and ASIL D, where ASIL D requires the highest risk reduction effort. Table 1 shows the clauses of ISO 26262 relevant to this paper.

2. Cyber-Physical-Social Systems (CPSSs) can be described as systems consisting of cyber components (e.g., computer system), controlled components (e.g., physical objects) and interacting social components (e.g., humans). For example, a vehicle is seen as a combination of cyber components (e.g., software, sensors, actuators), controlled components (e.g., other vehicles, road objects) and interacting social components (e.g., drivers, passengers, pedestrian). Ensuring the safety of a CPSS requires considering the three main components along with their interactions. For instance, we cannot guarantee the safety of such system

---

[1] QM is assigned to hazards with very low probability or causing only slight injuries.

Table 1. Clauses of ISO 26262 we consider in this paper

Clause	Description
3–5	**Item definition,** aims to develop a description of the item with regard to its functionality, interfaces, known hazards, etc
3–6	**Hazard Analysis and Risk Assessment (HARA),** aims to estimate the probability of exposure, controllability and severity of hazardous events with regard to the item. Based on these parameters, the ASILs of the hazardous events are determined and then assigned to corresponding safety goals
3–7	**Functional safety concept** is developed by deriving functional safety requirements from safety goals and allocating them to the elements of the item
4–6	**Technical safety concept,** aims to specify the technical implementation of the functional safety concept, and to verify that the technical safety requirements comply with the functional safety requirements
5–6	**Specification of Hardware Safety Requirements (HWSRs),** aims to provide specifications on how to elicit and manage the HWSRs
6–6	**Specification of Software Safety Requirements (SWSRs),** aims to provide specifications on how to elicit and manage the SWSRs
4–9	**Safety validation,** aims to provide evidence that the safety goals are adequate, can be achieved at the vehicle level, and the safety concepts are appropriate for the functional safety of the item

by considering only its cyber and/or controlled components since many safety related hazards might be due to its social components, and vice versa.

3   Illustrative Example: Maneuver Assistance System

Although most Advanced Driver Assistance Systems (ADAS) are developed to meet specific functional safety requirement provided by ISO 26262, they are developed with the implicit assumption that driver's actions are intended. Therefore, the focus of this example is on driver's unintended actions that may result due to its lack of awareness (inattention or distraction). Our example concerns the Maneuver Assistance System (MAS), which is expected to increase the driver's safety by monitoring its behaviour, detecting unintended maneuvers, and respond in a way that guarantees the highest possible level of driver safety.

In [9], three different types of maneuvers have been identified: 1- *strategically-planned* are associated with long-term time scale (minutes or hours), and they are motivated by destination goal of the driver; 2- *tactical-planned* are associated with a short-term timescale (few tens of seconds), and they are motivated by a recently modified desire of the driver (e.g., lane changes, turns, upcoming exit); 3- *operational* are associated with a very short time scale (hundreds of milliseconds), and they are generally a result of a driver's desire to remain safe.

We will focus on the last two types of maneuvers since the first one does not involve safety-critical situation. In both of them, the MAS is expected to collect information about the vehicle, vehicle surroundings, as well as driver behaviour. Then, it analyzes such information to determine whether the driver's maneuver (action) is intended or unintended. More specifically, when the analysis determines that there is a need, desire and/or a motivation for the maneuver, it is considered as an *intended* maneuver. Otherwise, it is considered as an *unintended* one. Consequently, MAS should either allow or halt the maneuver.

4   A Holistic Approach to Deal with Functional Safety Requirements for Automotive Systems

Our approach adopts and extends the ISO 26262 standard to consider both the E/E systems of the vehicles along with the driver's behaviour. The process underlying our approach (depicted in Fig. 1[2]) consists of eight main activities. Activities 1, 2, 3, 4, and 8 are based on ISO 26262 clauses C.3–5, C.3–6, C.3–7, C.4–6, and C.4–9 respectively, and they have been extended to consider the driver behaviour. Activities 5 & 6 are based on clauses C.5–6 and C.6–6 respectively, and activity 7 is a new activity that focuses mainly on the specification of social safety requirements. In what follows, we discuss each of these activities.

1- Item definition is the first activity of the process, and it aims to define the item in terms of its main functionalities, interfaces, known hazards, its dependencies and interactions with the environment [4]. In our approach, this activity is extended to consider the driver as an integral part of the item, i.e., dependencies and interactions between the driver (social component) and the cyber and physical components of the item are considered as well during the definition of the item. The outcome of this activity is the item definition.

2- Hazard Analysis and Risk Assessment (HARA), which can be started when the item definition is considered complete. HARA activity can be divided into two related sub-activities, 1- hazard analysis, in which the item definition is used to identify possible hazards events. Since the driver is considered as an integral part of the item, this activity should consider the hazards that may result from their behaviour and interactions/dependencies with other components of the item. 2- risk assessment, in which the identified hazards events are categorized based on three variables. 1- *Severity,* measures the potential harm for each hazardous event, and it can range from S0 to S3, where S0 means no injuries and S3 means life-threatening injuries. 2- *Exposure,* measures the probability of the item being in an operational situation that is described in the hazardous event, and it can range from E0 to E4, where E0 means the lowest occurrence probability and E4 means high probability. 3- *Controllability,* measures the ability to avoid a specified *harm/damage* through the timely reactions of the persons involved, and it ranges from C0 to C3, where C0 means controllable in general and C3 means difficult to control or uncontrollable.

Based on these three parameters, an ASIL is assigned for each hazard. ASIL is a measure of necessary risk reduction, and its level range from QM, ASIL A, ASIL B, ASIL C, and ASIL D, where ASIL D is the highest. Then, at least one Safety Goal (SG)[3] is assigned to each hazard rated as ASIL A, B, C or D as it is

---

[2] P. and C. represent the Parts and Clauses of ISO 26262 respectively.
[3] A SG may cover multiple hazardous events.

required by ISO 26262. These SGs can be used to derive the Functional Safety Requirements (FSRs), which specify the functionality required to mitigate their corresponding hazard. The outcome of this activity is SGs.

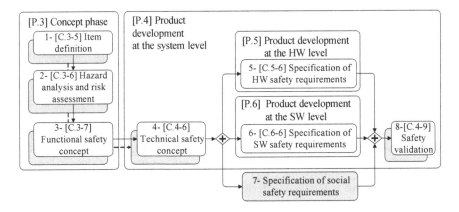

Fig. 1. A process compliant with ISO 26262 for dealing with FSR

3- Functional safety concept, the main objective of this activity is developing the functional safety concept by deriving FSRs from the SGs, and then allocating FSRs to the elements of the item. According to ISO 26262, FSRs are specification(s) of implementation-independent safety behaviour/safety measure(s), including their safety-related attributes. Therefore, FSRs are used for defining the safety functionalities of the item without specifying how such functionalities can be implemented. Unlike ISO 26262, this activity should specify the FSRs taking into consideration the behaviour of driver with a special emphasis on its interaction/dependencies with other components of the item, which facilitates the allocation of the FSRs to the elements of the item in later activities.

4- Technical safety concept aims to derive the Technical Safety Requirements (TSRs) from the FSRs. In particular, FSRs might be at a high level of abstraction, and they need to be refined into more detailed technical requirements. Similar to activity 4, this activity should specify the TSRs in a way that provides more detailed information about the driver behaviour along with its interaction/dependencies with other components of the item. Note that fulfilling the complete set of TSRs is considered sufficient to ensure that the item is compliant with its functional safety concept.

5- Specification of Hardware Safety Requirements (HWSRs) aims to derive HWSRs from TSRs that can be allocated to hardware. The HWSRs are safety requirements related to the physical hardware of the item. According to ISO 26262, HWSRs shall include information about each hardware requirement that relates to functional safety, including relevant attributes of safety mechanisms to (a) control internal failures of the hardware of the element; (b) control or tolerate failures external to the element; (c) comply with the safety requirements of other elements; and (d) detect and signal internal or external failures. In addition, criteria for design specification & verification of the hardware elements of the item shall be specified at this activity.

6- Specification of Software Safety Requirements (SWSRs) aims to derive SWSRs from TSRs that can be allocated to software. The SWSRs are safety requirements related to the software functionality of the item. According to ISO 26262, SWSRs shall be derived from TSRs considering the required safety-related functionalities and properties of the software, whose failures could lead to violations of a technical safety requirement allocated to software. Then, SWSRs can be used to define software design specification.

7- Specification of SoCial Safety Requirements (SCSRs) aims to derive SCSRs from TSRs that can be allocated to the driver's social behaviour. The SCSRs are safety requirements related to the social aspects of the item. Unlike the previous two activities, this activity is not based on any of the ISO 26262 clauses. Yet it follows the same pattern of activity 5 & 6, i.e., SCSRs also use TSRs to define clear design specification concerning the driver's behaviour and its interactions and dependencies with other components of the item.

8- Safety validation aims to 1- provide evidence that the safety goals are adequate, 2- provide evidence that the safety goals are achieved at the vehicle level, and 3- provide evidence that the safety concepts are appropriate for the functional safety of the item.

5   The Application of the Approach to the MAS Example

In this section, we apply our approach to the MAS example.

1- Item Definition. The main function of MAS is to allow/prevent intended/unintended drivers' tactical and operational maneuvers when the vehicle is moving faster than 50 km/h. MAS depends on sensors to collect informational cues about the driver: 1- head pose and motion, which can be used to identify the driver's visual orientation, and predict some driver's maneuvers, e.g., head motion may precede a maneuver; 2- hands/foot location and motions, which can be used to predict some driver's actions. Moreover, MAS depends on LIDAR and Radar, which can provide information about surrounding vehicles/objects. In addition, MAS will include software system that enables for analyzing all cue information in an appropriate time to determine whether a driver's maneuver is intended, i.e., it is a result of a need, desire and/or a motivation, or it is unintended, i.e., there is no need, desire and/or a motivation to perform such maneuver. Finally, MAS depends on lock actuator to prevent a driver's unintended maneuvers.

2- Hazard Analysis and Risk Assessment. This activity has two sub-activities:

1- Hazard Identification. It analyzes the item definition focusing mainly on hazard events that may result due to the behaviour of the item components along with their interaction and dependencies. Two main hazards[4] related to MAS have been identified:

H1: categorizing an intended maneuver as an unintended one when the vehicle is moving faster than 50 km/h, which prevents the driver from performing an intended maneuver.

H2: categorizing an unintended maneuver as an intended one when the vehicle is moving faster than 50 km/h, which allows an unintended maneuver to be performed.

2- Risk Assessment. Each identified hazard is categorized based on its severity, exposure and controllability.

The occurrence of **H1** prevents a driver from performing an intended maneuver, which may lead to life-threatening injuries or even death. Therefore, the highest severity level (S3) is chosen. The exposure level E3 (medium probability) is chosen because several reasons could result in categorizing an intended maneuver as an unintended one (e.g., wrong informational cues about the head pose and motion, hands/foot location). Finally, the highest controllability level C3 is chosen since the driver will not have the required time to perform any corrective action to avoid a potential harm. Based on the severity (S3), exposure (E3) and controllability (C3) of **H1**, ASIL C is determined for this hazard.

Similarly, the occurrence of **H2** is of highest severity level (S3) because allowing an unintended maneuver to be performed may lead to life-threatening injuries or even death. The exposure level is of a medium probability (E3) since identifying the unintended might be mistaken due to wrong informational cues. Moreover, the highest controllability level C3 is chosen since the driver might not be aware of such maneuver to perform any corrective action to avoid a potential harm/ damage. Hence, ASIL C is determined for this hazard. Following our approach, at least one Safety Goal (SG) should be assigned to each hazard rated as ASIL A, B, C or D. To this end, we assign the following two SGs (SG1 and SG2) to hazards **H1** and **H2** respectively:

SG1: a driver intended maneuver shall not be prevented when the vehicle is moving faster than 50 km/h.

SG2: a driver unintended maneuver shall be prevented when the vehicle is moving faster than 50 km/h.

3- Functional Safety Concept. Based on the **SGs** identified in the previous activity we derive the related Functional Safety Requirements (FSRs). In particular, we derive the following FSRs from **SG1**:

– **FSR1.1:** MAS shall be activated when the vehicle is moving faster than 50 km/h.

---

[4] The identified hazards are not complete nor exclusive due to space limitation.

- **FSR1.2:** MAS shall be able to collect all related cue information to determine whether there is a need for a maneuver.
- **FSR1.3:** MAS shall be able to collect all related cue information to determine whether the driver has a desire or a motivation to make a maneuver.
- **FSR1.4:** MAS shall be able to verify whether the driver's maneuver is intended within an appropriate time.
- **FSR1.5:** MAS shall not prevent intended maneuvers.

From **SG2**, we derive the following FSRs[5]:

- **FSR2.1:** MAS shall be able to identify drivers unintended maneuvers within an appropriate time.
- **FSR2.2:** MAS shall prevent unintended maneuver.

4- Technical Safety Requirements. The main purpose of this activity is refining the FSRs identified in the previous activity into more detailed technical requirements. The process of deriving the TSRs is similar to the process of deriving the FSRs from SGs, yet ISO 26262 does not require that for each FSR at least one TSR should be defined. It only requires that TSRs should be specified in accordance with FSRs. Based on the FSRs identified in the previous activity, we derive the following TSRs:

- **TSR1.1.1:** MAS shall depend on reliable sensor(s) to identify vehicle speed and activate/deactivate MAS when the vehicle is moving faster/slower than 50 km/h.
- **TSR1.1.2:** MAS shall depend on reliable technique(s) (e.g., sensors, LIDAR, Radar) that allows to predict needed operational maneuvers.
- **TSR1.1.3:** MAS shall depend on reliable technique(s) (e.g., head pose and motion, hands and foot location and motions) that allows predicting desired and/or motivated tactical maneuvers.
- **TSR1.1.4:** MAS shall be able to verify whether the driver's operation maneuvers are needed within an appropriate time.
- **TSR1.1.5:** MAS shall be able to verify whether the driver's tactical maneuvers are desired and/or motivated within an appropriate time.
- **TSR1.1.6:** MAS shall not prevent needed operational maneuvers.
- **TSR1.1.7:** MAS shall not prevent desired and/or motivated tactical maneuvers.
- **TSR1.2.1:** MAS shall depend on reliable technique(s) that allows identifying unneeded operational maneuvers.
- **TSR1.2.2:** MAS shall depend on reliable technique(s) that allows identifying undesired and/or unmotivated tactical maneuvers.
- **TSR1.2.3:** MAS shall prevent unneeded operational maneuvers.
- **TSR1.2.4:** MAS shall prevent undesired and/or unmotivated tactical maneuvers.

---

[5] **FSR1.1, FSR1.2, FSR1.3** can also be derived from SG2, but since ISO 26262 requires to keep the FSRs list atomic, they are not derived again from **SG2**.

5- Specification of Hardware Safety Requirements (HWSRs). After identifying the TSRs list, TSRs that can be allocated to the physical hardware of the item are used to derive the specification of HWSRs. Based on the TSRs identified in the previous activity, we derive the following HWSRs:

- **HWSR.001:** Each hardware component of/related to MAS (e.g., sensors, actuators, radars, etc.) shall be described by its hardware safety requirements and relevant attributes of safety mechanisms to control internal failures.
- **HWSR.002:** Each hardware component of/related to MAS shall be described by its hardware safety requirements and relevant attributes of safety mechanisms to control or tolerate failures external to the element.
- **HWSR.003:** Each hardware component of/related to MAS shall be described by its hardware safety requirements and relevant attributes of safety mechanisms to comply with the safety requirements of other elements.
- **HWSR.004:** Each hardware component of/related to MAS shall be able to deal with any disturbances/noise on their inputs.
- **HWSR.005:** Each hardware component of/related to MAS shall not allow any unintended signal on their outputs.
- **HWSR.006:** Each hardware component of/related to MAS shall be described by its hardware safety requirements and relevant attributes of safety mechanisms to detect and signal internal or external failures.
- **HWSR.007:** Any communication errors/lost between hardware components of/related to MAS shall be identified.
- **HWSR.008:** Any unusual behaviour of each hardware component of/related to MAS that may result due to error, fault or a failure shall be identified by diagnosing their inputs/outputs signals.
- **HWSR.009:** Each hardware component of/related to MAS should be tested in an environment complying with the same real environmental it might function in.
- **HWSR.010:** Communications and dependencies among hardware components of/related to MAS should be tested in an environment complying with the same real environmental it might function in.

6- Specification of Software Safety Requirements (SWSRs). After identifying the TSRs list, TSRs that can be allocated to the software functionality of the item are used to derive the specification of SWSRs. Based on the TSRs identified in the previous activity, we derive the following SWSRs:

- **SWSR.001:** MAS shall be able to detect and appropriately communicate any error in signals received from its related component (e.g., sensors, actuators, radars, etc.).
- **SWSR.002:** MAS shall be able to detect any delay, loss, corruption in signals received from its related components.
- **SWSR.003:** MAS shall be able to detect if any of its related components is not responding and/or is not responding in an appropriate time.
- **SWSR.004:** MAS shall implement a mitigation plan to deal appropriately with any error, delay, loss, corruption in signals received from its related component.

- **SWSR.005:** MAS shall be able to detect errors, faults, malfunctions in its related components that might lead to failures.
- **SWSR.006:** MAS shall implement a mitigation plan to deal appropriately with errors, faults, malfunctions in its related components in order to avoid potential failures.
- **SWSR.007:** MAS shall assign a special code for each error, faults, malfunctions, etc., which enables to easily identify them and differentiate them from one another.
- **SWSR.008:** MAS safety-related software functionalities and properties concerning timely response should be tested in an environment complying with the same real environmental it might function in.
- **SWSR.009:** MAS safety-related software functionalities and properties (e.g., robustness against erroneous inputs, fault tolerance capabilities of the software, etc.) should be tested in an environment complying with the same real environmental it might function in.

7- Specification of SoCial Safety Requirements (SCSRs). After identifying the TSRs list, TSRs that can be allocated to the driver's social behaviour of the item are used to derive the SCSRs.

- **SCSR.001:** MAS shall be able to identify available information concerning the driver state (e.g., head pose and motion, hands and foot location and motions) at any point in time.
- **SCSR.002:** MAS shall be able to collect all possible information concerning the driver state at any point in time.
- **SCSR.003:** MAS shall be able to evaluate the correctness of collect cues information concerning the driver state.
- **SCSR.004:** MAS shall be able to fuse all available cues information to determine the driver awareness state (e.g., attention, inattention) within an appropriate time.
- **SCSR.005:** MAS shall be able to fuse all available cues information to predict whether a driver tactical maneuver is desired and/or motivated with respect to cue information collected from driver state, vehicle (e.g., speed) and vehicle environment (e.g., LIDAR and Radar information) within an appropriate time.
- **SCSR.006:** MAS shall be able to determine whether a driver's tactical maneuver is intended within an appropriate time.
- **SCSR.007:** MAS shall be able to fuse all available cues information to determine whether a driver's operational maneuver is needed with respect to cue information collected from driver state, vehicle and vehicle environment within an appropriate time.
- **SCSR.008:** MAS shall be able to implement the lock actuator to prevent a driver's unintended (operational/tactical) maneuver within an appropriate time.
- **SCSR.009:** Each technique/mechanism that is used for determining the driver awareness state, predicting driver tactical maneuver, evaluating whether a driver's tactical maneuver is intended, determining whether a

driver's operational maneuver is needed should be tested in an environment complying with the same real environmental it might function in.

- **SCSR.010:** The implementation of the actuator mechanism to prevent a driver's unintended operational/tactical maneuver should be tested in an environment complying with the same real environmental it might function in.

8- Safety Validation. The main purpose of this activity is assuring that the safety goals are sufficient and have been achieved, based on examination and tests, providing reliable evidence that the identified safety goals have been realized at the vehicle level. Such validation can only be performed on a complete implementation of the proposed system, which is outside of the scope of this paper. In our approach, we validated the results by manually reviewing the derived HWSRs, SWSRs, and SCSRs lists, which if realized appropriately can fulfil the TSRs. In turn, fulfiling the complete set of TSRs is considered sufficient to ensure that the item is compliant with its functional safety concept.

6   Related Work

Several works for dealing with functional safety requirements for automotive systems have been proposed. For example, Jesty et al. [10] propose guidelines for hazard identification and analysis, and identifying the safety integrity levels. Giese et al. [11] develop an approach for systematically identifying which hazards/failures are most critical, which components require a more detailed safety analysis, and which restrictions to the failure propagation should be considered. Zhang et al. [3] introduce a comprehensive hazard analysis method based on functional models. Li and Zhang [12] present a software hazard analysis method for automotive control systems that extends the traditional software development process to incorporate safety procedures as a fundamental part of the process.

While Basir et al. [13] propose an approach that adopts the Goal Structuring Notation (GSN) to construct safety cases. In which, the defined safety cases reflect the results of the system analysis and provide a high-level argument that traces the requirements on the model via inferred model structure to code. Palin et al. [14] provide guidelines, patterns, and a number of reusable safety arguments covering all parts of ISO 26262 for creating safety cases. Habli et al. [15] examine how model-driven development and assessment can provide a basis for the systematic generation of functional safety requirements. Finally, Mehrpouyan et al. [16] introduce a model-based hazard analysis methodology that maps hazard and vulnerability models to specific components in the system and analyzes the hazard propagation paths for risk control and protection strategies.

To the best of our knowledge, no existing work extends the ISO 26262 standard by integrating the driver and his behaviour as an integral part of the item.

7 Conclusions and Future Work

We discussed the limitation in the current standard (ISO 26262) for developing functional safety systems for vehicles, which mainly cover E/E systems of vehicles. Therefore, we proposed a holistic approach built based on the ISO 26262 standard and considers both the E/E systems and the driver's behaviour. We described the approach in terms of its main activities, and we have illustrated its utility by applying it to an example from the automotive domain.

For future work, we intend to formalize all the previously introduced concepts and develop SysML profile based on them, which allows for modeling FSRs, derive the TSRs, and then derive the HWSRs, SWSRs, and SCSRs from TSRs. Moreover, we are planning to propose a set of Object Constraint Language (OCL) constraints for specifying rigorous rules for the derivation of HWSRs, SWSRs, and SCSRs from TSRs, and the derivation of TSRs from FSRs.

Acknowledgment. This work has been partially supported by the "Ente Cassa Di Risparmio di Firenze", Bando per progetti 2016, and by the FAR-FAS 2014 TOSCA-FI project funded by the Tuscany Region.

References

1. Ridderhof, W., Gross, H.-G., Doerr, H.: Establishing evidence for safety cases in automotive systems – a case study. In: Saglietti, F., Oster, N. (eds.) SAFECOMP 2007. LNCS, vol. 4680, pp. 1–13. Springer, Heidelberg (2007). https://doi.org/10.1007/978-3-540-75101-4_1
2. Törner, F., Öhman, P.: Automotive safety case a qualitative case study of drivers, usages, and issues. In: 11th HASE, pp. 313–322. IEEE (2008)
3. Zhang, H., Li, W., Chen, W.: Model-based hazard analysis method on automotive programmable electronic system. In: International Conference on Biomedical Engineering and Informatics (BMEI), pp. 2658–2661. IEEE (2010)
4. ISO: 26262: Road Vehicles-Functional safety. IS ISO/FDIS 26262 (2011)
5. McCall, J.C., Trivedi, M.M.: Driver behavior and situation aware brake assistance for intelligent vehicles. Proc.-IEEE **95**(2), 374 (2007)
6. Taib, R., Yu, K., Jung, J., Hess, A., Maier, A.: Human-centric analysis of driver inattention. In: Intelligent Vehicles Symposium Workshops, pp. 7–12. IEEE (2013)
7. Dong, Y., Hu, Z., Uchimura, K., Murayama, N.: Driver inattention monitoring system for intelligent vehicles: a review. IEEE Trans. Intell. Transp. Syst. **12**(2, SI), 596–614 (2011)
8. Lee, J.D., Young, K.L., Regan, M.A.: Defining driver distraction. Driv. Distraction: Theor. Eff. Mitig. **13**(4), 31–40 (2008)
9. Tawari, A., Sivaraman, S., Trivedi, M.M., Shannon, T., Tippelhofer, M.: Looking-in and looking-out vision for urban intelligent assistance: estimation of driver attentive state and dynamic surround for safe merging and braking. In: Intelligent Vehicles Symposium Proceedings, pp. 115–120. IEEE (2014)
10. Jesty, P.H., Hobley, K.M., Evans, R., Kendall, I.: Safety analysis of vehicle-based systems. In: Proceedings of the Safety-Critical Systems Symposium, pp. 90–110 (2000)

11. Giese, H., Tichy, M., Schilling, D.: Compositional hazard analysis of UML component and deployment models. In: Heisel, M., Liggesmeyer, P., Wittmann, S. (eds.) SAFECOMP 2004. LNCS, vol. 3219, pp. 166–179. Springer, Heidelberg (2004). https://doi.org/10.1007/978-3-540-30138-7_15
12. Li, W., Zhang, H.: A software hazard analysis method for automotive control system. In: International Conference on Computer Science and Automation Engineering (CSAE), vol. 3, pp. 744–748. IEEE (2011)
13. Basir, N., Denney, E., Fischer, B.: Deriving safety cases for hierarchical structure in model-based development. In: Schoitsch, E. (ed.) SAFECOMP 2010. LNCS, vol. 6351, pp. 68–81. Springer, Heidelberg (2010). https://doi.org/10.1007/978-3-642-15651-9_6
14. Palin, R., Ward, D., Habli, I., Rivett, R.: ISO 26262 safety cases: compliance and assurance. In: International Conference on System Safety, pp. 1–6 (2011)
15. Habli, I., Ibarra, I., Rivett, R.S., Kelly, T.: Model-based assurance for justifying automotive functional safety. Technical report, SAE Technical Paper (2010)
16. Mehrpouyan, H., Bunus, P., Kurtoglu, T.: Model-based hazard analysis of undesirable environmental and components interaction. In: Aerospace Conference, pp. 1–8. IEEE (2012)

Side-Channel Based Intrusion Detection
for Industrial Control Systems

Pol Van Aubel[1]([⊠]), Kostas Papagiannopoulos[1], Łukasz Chmielewski[2],
and Christian Doerr[3]

[1] Digital Security Group, Radboud University, Nijmegen, The Netherlands
{pol.vanaubel,k.papagiannopoulos}@cs.ru.nl
[2] Riscure BV, Delft, The Netherlands
Chmielewski@riscure.com
[3] Department of Intelligent Systems, Delft University of Technology,
Delft, The Netherlands
c.doerr@tudelft.nl

Abstract. Industrial Control Systems are under increased scrutiny. Their security is historically sub-par, and although measures are being taken by the manufacturers to remedy this, the large installed base of legacy systems cannot easily be updated with state-of-the-art security measures. We propose a system that uses electromagnetic side-channel measurements to detect behavioural changes of the software running on industrial control systems. To demonstrate the feasibility of this method, we show it is possible to profile and distinguish between even small changes in programs on Siemens S7-317 PLCs, using methods from cryptographic side-channel analysis.

Keywords: EM · Side-channel · Intrusion detection · ICS
Industrial control system · PLC · Programmable logic controller

1 Introduction

Industrial control systems (ICS) are used to manage most of our critical infrastructures. With the move toward more centralized control using IP-based networks, these systems, which historically have not needed advanced protection mechanisms, are opened to a wider range of attack scenarios. One such scenario is an attacker modifying the software running on the system, e.g. to perform a long-running attack on the industrial process being controlled, as happened with Stuxnet in the uranium enrichment facilities in Natanz; or in preparation for a later, sudden attack that takes down a significant part of the electricity grid, as happened in Ukraine in 2015 and 2016.

This work was supported by the Dutch electricity transmission system operator TenneT TSO B.V. Permanent ID of this document: **b7751e7466fc1c298da31a8 40c902cbc**. Date: 2017-12-14.

© Springer Nature Switzerland AG 2018
G. D'Agostino and A. Scala (Eds.): CRITIS 2017, LNCS 10707, pp. 207–224, 2018.
https://doi.org/10.1007/978-3-319-99843-5_19

In general, an operator of ICSs would like to prevent compromised software from being installed. Solutions for this can be found in software integrity verification, and software inspection. Software integrity can be determined by e.g. taking a signed software image and verifying the signature with a trusted platform module.

Prevention of system compromise through software inspection is a technique widely used, with varying success, in the IT landscape. There exists a variety of intrusion detection & prevention systems that are capable of monitoring the network or the host systems themselves [17,21,28]. To actively prevent ICS compromise during an attack, these systems can e.g. stop communication between the attacker and the ICS, or stop execution of the software under attack. However, this requires software integration in the monitored ICS, which is not always a feasible option for existing legacy systems, and comes with other drawbacks such as influencing the characteristics of the system being monitored.

Even if these solutions are available and effective in preventing compromised software from running, uncompromised software may still be made to misbehave. Bugs in the software or compromise of the underlying system can allow an attacker to circumvent prevention mechanisms. Detecting this situation is an important part of any system intended to defend ICSs against attackers. In this paper, we will focus on this *detection*, rather than prevention. Specifically, we attempt to detect changes in the behaviour of software.

Detecting the anomalous behaviour that compromised software exhibits becomes harder when the system running that software behaves unpredictably to begin with. This is often the case for systems with a lot of human interaction. However, ICSs are inherently more stable and predictable, making our task easier. Nonetheless, detecting software compromise on ICSs is not straightforward.

Proposed methods for detecting software compromise often rely on non-existent hardware support, instruction set modifications, operating system modifications, etc. [6,33,34] These are all unavailable for the huge number and wide range of control systems currently deployed in the world's heavy industry and critical infrastructure. Symbiotes, proposed by Cui and Stolfo [11], try to remedy this by offering a general solution that allows retrofitting defensive software in existing firmware images. The exact functionality of the original firmware does not need to be known for this, which means the technique can be applied to a wide range of embedded systems. However, it does require changing the original manufacturer-provided firmware image, and might therefore not be an acceptable solution for many operators of ICSs.

Detection systems running on the ICS itself may not be able to detect all targeted attacks. For instance, Abbasi and Hashemi have shown that it is possible to circumvent existing host-based intrusion detection with an attack that reconfigures a Programmable Logic Controller's (PLC) processor pin configuration on-the-fly [1]. Another attack that may not be detected is the complete replacement of a device's firmware [3,10,23], since the detection system is part of that. Indeed, the threat model of Symbiotes explicitly excludes the replacement of the entire firmware image [11].

Our Contribution. In this work, we propose an alternative approach to detecting software compromise which uses side-channel measurements of the underlying hardware. Side-channel analysis is a common technique in security evaluations, since it can be used to distinguish system behaviour that differs slightly based on some secret information such as a cryptographic key. We posit that similarly, it is possible to use side-channels to verify that software is still behaving as intended, based on some baseline of behaviour. Our approach using side-channels has the advantage that there is no need for monitoring support in the device firmware, and, by extension, that it will continue to function if the device is compromised. Our contributions are as follows:

1. We verify the applicability of a side-channel-based intrusion detection system (IDS) in a real-world scenario, using measurements of the electromagnetic (EM) emissions from the processor on a Siemens Simatic S7-317 Programmable Logic Controller (PLC).
2. We describe in detail how to deploy such an IDS, highlighting its modus operandi, the adversarial model considered and the necessary modifications to the existing ICS hardware.
3. We suggest a two-layer intrusion detection strategy that can effectively detect the illegitimate behaviour of a user program (part of the software running on a PLC), even when only minor malicious alterations have been performed. We describe the statistical models that profile the user program and demonstrate how side-channel emission templating is directly applicable in the IDS context.

Related Work. Side-channel-based techniques are becoming an increasingly popular tool to verify software, as suggested by Msgna et al. [20] and Yoon et al. [32]. Similarly, Liu et al. [18] managed to perform code execution tracking and detect malicious injections via the power side-channel and a hidden Markov model. In a hardware-oriented scenario, Dupuis et al. [12] have used side-channel approaches in order to detect malicious alterations of integrated circuits, such as hardware trojan horses. In the field of reverse engineering, work by Goldack [15], Eisenbarth et al. [13], Quisquater et al. [25] and Vermoen et al. [31] has shown the feasibility of using power traces to reverse-engineer software, reaching instruction-level granularity. More recently, Strobel et al. have shown that EM emissions can similarly be used for reverse engineering purposes [30].

Previous works attempt detection at various levels of granularity ranging from recognizing single instructions to detecting larger blocks. In our work, we demonstrate that using EM emissions as a mechanism to detect software compromise is possible without mapping the observed measurements to specific instructions, or indeed even knowing the instruction set of the chip being monitored. Our analysis is carried out on a processor that is part of a larger PLC, deployed in many systems around the world. In particular, we do not control the clock speed, cannot program the processor directly with its low-level instruction set, and cannot predict its behaviour with regards to EM emissions beforehand.

2   Software Behaviour Verification on Programmable Logic Controllers

In Sect. 2.1, we briefly describe the general architecture of PLCs, and explain why they are particularly suited for the approach we propose. Next, we introduce the EM side-channel in Sect. 2.2. Then, in Sects. 2.3 and 2.4, we describe our attacker model and propose a two-layer IDS strategy that employs the EM leakage to perform behavioural verification. We also describe the required PLC modifications to apply the IDS to legacy systems. Finally, in Sect. 2.5 we highlight the operation of our system.

2.1   Programmable Logic Controllers

A Programmable Logic Controller (PLC) is an industrial computer designed for highly reliable real-time measurement and control of industrial processes. PLCs are designed to be easy to program, and in their most basic function simply emulate a logic network that reads inputs and drives outputs based on the values of those inputs. The operator of a PLC creates a program, which we will call *"user program"*, to perform this control. A modern PLC runs some version of a real-time operating system (OS), which provides functionality such as network connectivity to other machines, communication bus control, reading inputs into memory, driving outputs from memory, and running the user program. The latter three form the Read-Execute-Write (REW) cycle.

During the run of the user program, most low-priority tasks such as network communication are postponed. This is to guarantee a maximum execution time on the program, offering real-time guarantees to the operator. This means that in theory, the execution of a user program is not often preempted by other code, and it should therefore be relatively easy to observe the behaviour of the user program and determine whether it is, in fact, still behaving the way it should be.

Doing this observation from within the PLC itself is not trivial and requires extensive modifications to their OS. Even though support of the PLC vendor is not always required for this [11], it is unclear whether it would be wise to modify the OS on existing PLCs, because it introduces concerns such as the possibility of breaking real-time guarantees.

2.2   EM Side-Channel Analysis

To enable us to still observe the user program in a less intrusive manner, we consider a concept used in cryptanalysis to observe and break cryptographic implementations, namely side-channel leakage. A side-channel can be thought of as a non-functional transmission of information about the state of a system. E.g., the temperature of a processor is not a functional aspect of it, but its level of activity can easily be derived from it[1]. Silicon chips emit electromagnetic (EM)

---
[1] TEMPEST is an NSA program dealing with spying on information systems through the use of these side-channels.

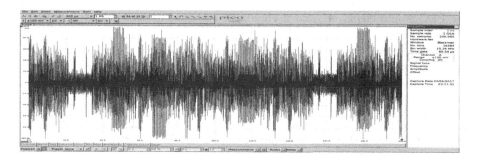

Fig. 1. EM radiation captured from a running Siemens S7-317 PLC

radiation caused by the electrical characteristics of the operations they perform. This radiation can be captured using an EM-probe, basically a looped wire responding to changes in the EM field it resides in, connected to a high-speed oscilloscope. Figure 1 shows a capture of EM radiation from the control chip of a PLC, revealing when the OS, user program, and specific blocks of operations in the user program are executed, and showing clear regularity.

Side-channel leakages are most commonly used in the analysis of cryptographic hardware such as smart cards; a large body of research exists that shows how to extract cryptographic keys from otherwise protected devices, using sophisticated EM techniques [16,19,24]. More interestingly, the side-channel literature has established a wide spectrum of *templating* techniques, i.e. statistical models that, once sufficiently trained, can help us distinguish between different states of a system [5,8,29]. Our work employs such templating techniques to provide intrusion detection capabilities.

2.3   Attacker Model

Our system is intended to defend against an attacker who can upload new software to the PLC to replace or modify the existing user program. The attacker does not control the PLC operating system. Although this is not a very strong attacker model, it is a realistic one. Public analysis of Stuxnet has revealed that it functioned by replacing the user program on the PLCs it targeted [14], which means it falls within our attacker model. However, the more recently revealed Industroyer malware [7,9] does not modify software on a PLC, and therefore does not fall within our attacker model.

2.4   User Program Intrusion Detection System

We propose a two-layer intrusion detection system (IDS) that uses this EM side-channel to verify that a PLC's user program is still behaving the way it was programmed to behave. For this, it is not necessary to know which exact operations a chip is performing; only that they are still the same based on some baseline profile established in the past. The IDS would record this profile when the PLC is first deployed, and it should be updated whenever legitimate code changes are performed.

To verify that the user program behaves as expected, the system uses the following two layers of verification, alerting the operator as soon as one layer shows compromise.

1. The first layer checks user program runtime. If the user program deviates in runtime, this is a clear indicator that it is not behaving as intended. If the runtime is deemed to be close enough to potentially be legitimate, the system checks the second layer.
2. For the second layer, the user program's EM trace is compared to a baseline profile that has been crafted by templating the emitted side-channel leakage. If it matches sufficiently, the software is behaving legitimately.

Extensive malicious alterations by an adversary unaware of this system are easy to detect via layer 1. If an adversary is aware of the functioning of the system, or by coincidence happens to craft a user program that runs in the same amount of time, they will be detected by layer 2.

Layer 1: Timing Side-Channel. Program runtime can be determined either by the PLC informing the IDS when it hands over execution to the user program, and when it regains control (we call this a trigger signal); or by analysing the EM waveform to spot when the control handover happens.

1. Trigger signals can be used by the monitoring oscilloscope to know when to capture the EM waveform. The PLC's operating system could send such a signal every time it hands over execution to the user program, and drive the signal low again once it regains control. The advantage of this is that the oscilloscope always captures the exact waveform that we are interested in, without any need for the post-processing described in Sect. 4.1. This does require a modification to the PLC operating system, however, which may not always be possible. Obviously, the emission of this signal should not be blockable from the user program logic, and so could also require the addition of a hardware output that cannot be driven from the user program.
2. Waveform analysis uses the same EM side-channel as layer 2, described below, for matching the user program: an oscilloscope can simply capture long runs of the complete EM waveform, both OS and user program emissions. These waveforms can then be searched for some profiled parts of the operating system known to be right before the start and right after the end of the user program.

Layer 2: EM Side-Channel. It is not straightforward to distinguish user program compromise from other deviations from the norm: there is the case where the controlled industrial process goes outside of its target values, and needs to be corrected; or the case where a very infrequent but legitimate action is taken, such as opening a breaker in a power distribution grid. At that point, the user program's behaviour will deviate from the norm, but we should not alert when it happens. This shows that it is not sufficient to profile only the common case; the user program must be profiled under each combination of inputs that leads to a different path through the program.

When the user program actually behaves differently than intended, either through misconfiguration, bugs, or malicious intervention, these unintended deviations from the norm should all be detected. This means our problem is to reliably distinguish between:

- when the user program is running in one of its usual paths;
- when the same user program is taking a legitimate, yet unusual path;
- when something other than a legitimate path is taken, or another user program is running.

Distinguishing between the first two cases is not strictly necessary for our IDS, but may be useful for checking if the legitimate but unusual path is taken under the correct conditions. We split this problem into four distinguishing cases:

1. Can we reliably distinguish user program A from user program B?
2. Can we reliably distinguish between different paths in the same user program?
3. Can we reliably distinguish paths in user program A from paths in user program B?
4. Can we reliably recognize whether a user program is user program A or not?

Question 4 is not strictly a distinguishing case. Instead, we need a threshold beyond which we no longer accept a program as being program A. We determine this threshold experimentally using a few programs with minor modifications. Different user programs might require a different threshold, and determining such a threshold would be part of any profile building effort.

PLC Modifications. Our system does require one modification to existing hardware: the processor needs to be fitted with an *EM sensor*. Although this might imply that our technique is, in fact, not applicable to existing legacy systems, we believe that this is a modification that can realistically be performed on existing systems, without support from the vendor. The exact location of the sensor depends on the location of the processor executing the user program; in general, the sensor would be a loop situated right on top of the processor. Stable orientation of the sensor would require it to either be fixed in place using e.g. hot glue, or use of a bracket mounted on the external housing of the PLC, with the sensor inserted through ventilation grating.

2.5 Operation

There are two ways to use our IDS: first, constant operation, where the EM side-channel is constantly monitored and checked for anomalies; and second, spot-checks, where an engineer manually attaches monitoring equipment every so often which then checks whether the PLC is behaving satisfactory. Considering the potential cost of the monitoring equipment, in particular the high-speed oscilloscopes, spot-checks seem the more likely way to use our system.

A smart attacker could try to hide in the periods between spot-checks. However, consider that for an attacker to hide their presence, they would need logic to determine whether a check is happening. The execution of this logic is detectable by our IDS. The same is true for a dormant backdoor, since it must contain logic to check whether it should start executing.

3   Experimental Setup

We experimentally verify the feasibility of our proposed system.

Our main experiment setup consists of a Siemens S7-317 PLC, modified to enable it to run outside of its casing. We use a PCBGRIP [22] kit to hold both the main PLC board and the probe, so that any disturbances do not move the probe relative to the chip under test.

3.1   Measurement Setup

We measure EM radiation of the PLC's main processor, an Infineon Tricore SAFTC11IA64D96E[2], using a Langer RF-R 50-1 10 mm loop probe, which has a frequency range of 30 MHz–3 GHz. The probe is connected to a DC-powered Riscure amplifier with a frequency range of 100 kHz–2.5 GHz, with a gain of 25 dB at 500 MHz and noise figure of 2.4 dB at 500 MHz. Finally, the output of the amplifier is passed through a 48 MHz hardware low-pass filter. Our setup is situated in a normal office environment, not in an EM-clean room. Capturing is done with a PicoScope 3207B set to a 100 mV range and 1 GS/s capture rate at an 8-bit resolution.

3.2   Locating the User Program

Our PLC OS is not equipped to emit a trigger as described in Sect. 2.4. When faced with this issue, we first verified that the alternative of waveform matching works. However, we also concluded that our analysis for layer 2 would be easier if we could indeed trigger the oscilloscope instead of searching the entire waveform.

One solution we have tried to achieve this is waveform triggering. This uses the waveform matching approach, but with a dedicated, relatively inexpensive low-speed oscilloscope that constantly scans the waveform for a pattern and generates a trigger signal when it finds a match. Two devices that implement this are Riscure's icWaves [27] and KU Leuven's waveform matching trigger [4]. We had access to an icWaves, and we managed to produce a reliable and stable trigger signal based on the transition from the operating system to the user

---

[2] No data sheet for this particular chip is available. However, data sheets for the TC11IB do exist, and the period of manufacture for this chip indicates it may be related to the TC11IA.

program. One issue we encountered was that having two oscilloscopes on the same signal line with a T-splitter causes artefacts in the measurements, causing us to abandon this approach. We have not explored this further, but it could be remedied by using a second probe.

We decided next on trying to emulate an OS trigger, by sending it from the user program. As mentioned in Sect. 2.1, the software on the PLC performs a read-execute-write-cycle. Since we are not interested in analysing either the read or the write cycle, we can consider only part of the user program as interesting, and treat other parts around it as though they were part of the OS. We introduce empty operations around the interesting part, and after these empty operations we add a toggle that toggles one of the output LEDs of an I/O simulator module. We have soldered a pin to the back of this LED, and hook up a normal current measuring probe to the EXT port of the oscilloscope. We now have a rising/falling edge trigger for the oscilloscope, and a clear demarcation of the part of the user program intended for analysis. For real-world operation, such an invasive measure is clearly not an option, but it does not detract from our analysis. The resulting trigger is not perfect, and requires us to preprocess the measurements before analysis, as described in Sect. 4.1.

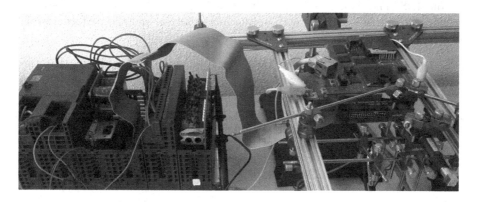

Fig. 2. PLC with extruded mainboard and probe in place

3.3   Code Under Test

The Siemens S7-317 can be programmed in four different languages. Our analysis focuses on one of these, SCL.

We initially attempted to make our analysis easier by eliminating branching in the user program entirely, so that it would a single path through the program that would take a constant amount of time and only deviate if different instructions were executed. However, this proved to be impossible: first, because experimental results show that there are timing variations even when the same instructions are executed on the same inputs; and second, because even simple programs like the one in Listing 1.1 have multiple paths through the program depending on their inputs.

The legitimate user program we want to recognize is given in Listing 1.1. We will refer to this as program A, or PrA. It is a very simple representation of a control system used to keep a water level between two acceptable values, e.g. in a canal. Based on whether the water level, simulated as a 4-bit input, is too low, too high, or in-between, three different simulated outputs are driven. These outputs could also be outputs to water pumps, warning lights, etc. Lines 1 and 2 read the water level input byte, compare it to the acceptable levels, and set internal variables to indicate high or low water. Next, line 3 uses these internal variables to determine whether this is or is not an acceptable water level. This could obviously be done with a different construction; the current logic of inverting the XOR of the existing variables is a result of the aforementioned attempt to achieve constant-time operation. We have kept it since it lowers the number of comparisons and introduces additional operations (NOT and XOR). Finally, on lines 4–6, the three outputs are driven.

Next, we define two programs, PrB and PrC, that we want to distinguish from PrA. These simulate slight changes that an adversary might make to the program to influence its execution without influencing its runtime, thereby evading layer 1 of our IDS. The changes are shown in Listings 1.2 and 1.3. We have tested our method with other programs with only minor changes, and the performance is similar. The changes are:

- In PrB, the attacker flips the logic of the water_low variable, so that the system indicates low water when in fact, it is okay, or even high, and indicates okay when the water level is low. This simulates the attack where an attacker changes an instruction in the program code.
- In PrC, the attacker changes the constant in the comparison for water_high to 12, so that the system potentially overflows without ever indicating anything other than an okay water level. This simulates the attack where an attacker changes only a comparison constant in the program code.

Listing 1.1. Program A

```
1  #water_low := "DIGITAL_IN_CHAR" < CHAR#5;
2  #water_high := "DIGITAL_IN_CHAR" > CHAR#10;
3  #water_good := NOT (#water_low XOR #water_high);
4  "WATER_ADD_PUMP" := #water_low;
5  "WATER_OK" := #water_good;
6  "WATER_REMOVE_PUMP" := #water_high;
```

Listing 1.2. Changes in Program B

```
1  #water_low := "DIGITAL_IN_CHAR" > CHAR#5;
```

Listing 1.3. Changes in Program C

```
2  #water_high := "DIGITAL_IN_CHAR" > CHAR#12;
```

4 Intrusion Detection Results

We have described how an adversary can alter the code with minimal impact on the program timing in Sect. 3.3. Since this evades layer 1 of our IDS, in the next sections we will discuss the techniques applied for layer 2. We explain the steps we took to prepare the captured dataset for analysis, the different analysis techniques used, and the accuracy we achieved with these techniques.

4.1 Template Construction

The dataset captured from the Siemens S7-317 contains small interrupts, variability in instruction execution time and clock jitter. These all cause trace misalignment. To correct for this, we align the traces at the beginning of the user program and filter out those traces where the user program has been severely altered by interrupts. This filters out roughly 10% of traces. As mentioned in Sect. 3.2, for the purpose of our analysis we can treat the start and end of the user program as though they are part of the OS. We ensure that these parts are areas of low EM emissions, and use a peak finding algorithm to align on the first high peak after a valley: the part of the user program being analysed.

We build profiles, or templates, for user programs in several different ways, using progressively more complex and more informative statistical models. Our aim is to test the accuracy of such models in the intrusion detection context and identify the best model for layer 2. For every chosen model we answer questions 1–4 posed in Sect. 2.4, and show their performance for question 4, the recognition problem, via the Receiver Operator Characteristic (ROC), False Accept Rate/False Reject Rate (FAR/FRR), and Kernel Density Estimation curves[3].

We commence our analysis creating templates based on average and median traces, i.e. we partition our experimental data in training and test sets and compute the mean and median trace vectors using the training set. Template matching with the test sets is performed using Sum of Absolute Differences (SAD) and cross-correlation (XCORR) as distinguishing metrics.

Continuing, we also construct full side-channel templates [5]. We assume that the EM leakage $\mathbf{L}$ can be described by a multivariate normal distribution, i.e. $\mathbf{L} \sim \mathcal{N}(\mathbf{m}, \mathbf{\Sigma})$ with mean vector $\mathbf{m}$ and covariance matrix $\mathbf{\Sigma}$, that are estimated using the training set. Specifically, for every program PrI, $\mathrm{I} \in \{\mathrm{A,B,C}\}$, we estimate the parameters of the distribution $(\mathbf{L}|\,\mathrm{PrI})$, and template matching is performed using a maximum likelihood approach. The EM leakage $\mathbf{L}$ contains a large number of samples (in the range of several thousands), requiring a high data complexity for the sufficient training of the multivariate model. Thus, we rely on dimensionality reduction techniques such as linear discriminant analysis (LDA) [2] in order to compress the traceset and select the most informative samples, often referred to as Points of Interest (POIs).

---

[3] The ROC curve shows how, as the rate of genuine accepts (GAR) increases, the rate of false accepts (FAR) increases as well. An ideal system has a 100% GAR with a 0% FAR, and a perfect ROC curve looks like the one in Fig. 6. The FAR/FRR curve shows the balance between the two error counts, and the intersection in the graph denotes the Equal Error Rate (EER): it indicates the threshold where the FAR is equal to the FRR, and is a good indication of the accuracy of the system. An EER of 50% is bad performance, an EER of 0% is perfect. For illustration purposes, we also include the kernel density estimation plots of the scores for the genuine user program and the manipulated user program. The more overlap these kernels have, the harder it is to recognize one as genuine and the other as compromised.

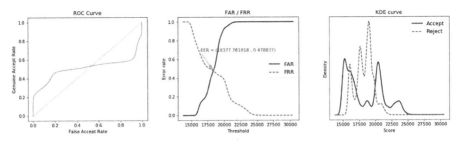

Fig. 3. SAD results for a combined average trace of PrA compared to PrB

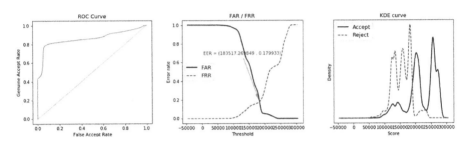

Fig. 4. XCORR results for a combined average trace of PrA compared to PrB

4.2 Averages and Medians with SAD and XCORR

To answer question 1, "can we distinguish PrA from PrB, and PrA from PrC?",
we have built an average of all paths taken for every input of the entire program
for PrA, PrB, and PrC. For distinguishing PrA and PrB, this works unexpectedly
well; both Sum of Absolute Differences (SAD) and cross-correlation (XCORR)
manage to reach an 85% recognition rate, i.e. for both programs, 85% of their
traces are correctly identified as belonging to that program. For distinguishing
PrA and PrC, however, PrA is only matched for 60% of its traces, and PrC
is only matched for 50% of its traces, with XCORR performing slightly worse
than SAD.

For question 2, "can we distinguish between different paths in the *same*
program?", we have built averages of every input for PrA. When only accepting
a match if the exact input for each trace is matched, both SAD and XCORR
perform very badly, with a match rate lower than 20%. Since multiple inputs lead
to the same path, we change our analysis to accept a match if any of the inputs
for that path match a certain trace. This improves the accuracy significantly,
with SAD reaching 93%, and XCORR reaching 87%.

For question 3, "can we distinguish paths in user PrA from paths in PrB", this
shows a combined behaviour from questions 1 and 2: distinguishing rates increase
as we accept paths, rather than specific inputs; and distinguishing between PrA
and PrB performs better than between PrA and PrC.

For question 4, "recognizing PrA", SAD with an averaged trace for all inputs
on PrA performs very badly. Figure 3 shows the performance of this method

when using it for the changed instruction in PrB. Important to note is the overlap between the estimated kernels in the results. The dotted graph is the set that should be rejected, the unbroken one is the set that should be accepted. The overlap in SAD scores shows that this algorithm simply is not good enough to distinguish between variation from changing instructions and variation inherent in a single program with multiple execution paths. Using a combined median trace does not significantly change the performance of the SAD method. However, XCORR does perform rather well for recognizing PrB as not being PrA on a combined average traceset, as can be seen in Fig. 4. The equal error rate is 18%, significantly better than the 48% that SAD achieves here. For the case of recognizing PrC as not being PrA, however, both XCORR and SAD perform badly, achieving an EER of 50%. Figure 5 shows the graphs for SAD.

Thus, we conclude that SAD is useless for the recognition problem, and although XCORR can be used to recognize instruction changes, it cannot be used to recognize comparison constant changes.

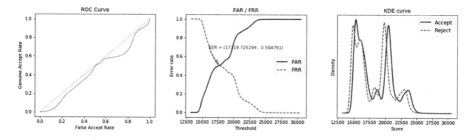

Fig. 5. SAD results for a combined average trace of PrA compared to PrC

4.3   Multivariate Templates

The results of multivariate templating show significant improvements upon the simpler models. For question 1, using LDA and only 10 POIs we get a perfect distinguishing rate between both PrA and PrB, and PrA and PrC, when combining all the inputs in a single dataset to train on.

However, for question 2, when taking every input as a separate template, the performance degrades significantly. Using an increased amount of POIs, attack traces and the improved performance formulas of Choudary et al. [8], the correct distinguishing rate for many inputs does not exceed 25%, indicating the need for a more detailed training phase. If we combine the different inputs for the same path into a single template, however, the distinguishing rate improves again.

For question 3, we see that distinguishing between paths for the same program functions well if only a single path for each program is considered. When multiple paths for each program are templated, the same effect we saw in question 2 degrades the results.

However, for an IDS, question 4 is the most important one, and multivariate templates do perform very well for this. The best method we have found is to combine all the traces for a single program into a single template, which relates to question 1. For recognizing PrA with the attack of PrB, the changed instruction, we get a perfect acceptance and rejection rate, with a very broad margin to set the threshold. This can be seen in Fig. 6. The broad margin indicates that changing an instruction is easily detected by multivariate templating. However, recognizing PrA with the attack of PrC shows that the scores when changing only a comparison constant are very close together. Still, where both SAD and XCORR were unable to recognize PrA in the presence of PrC, full templates are able to perform with a 13% equal error rate, as shown in Fig. 7.

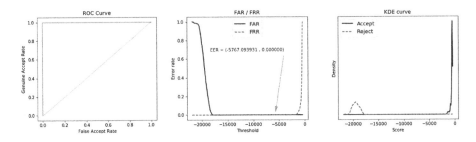

Fig. 6. Template results for PrA compared to PrB

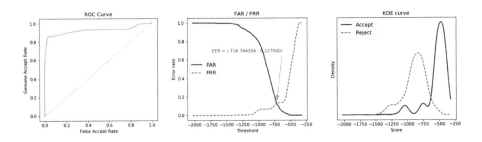

Fig. 7. Template results for PrA compared to PrC

5   Discussion and Future Work

Our results indicate that our IDS is capable of detecting very minor program alterations through the use of full templating of EM emissions. We stress that simple models such as sum of absolute differences and cross-correlation are incapable of detecting the same alterations, so multivariate techniques are a de facto requirement against detection-aware attackers. However, even with multivariate templating, we note that the recognition threshold has a much narrower margin for the most subtle attack of changing a comparison constant; as can be seen by comparing the distance between kernels in the KDE plots of Figs. 6 and 7.

Future work could expand to other classification techniques, including unsupervised machine learning, to improve these recognition rates.

Our proposed IDS focuses on the user program, because it is rather stable and can be treated as a grey box. We do have access to the source code, if not to the specific hardware designs and machine code. The operating system, however, remains a black box to us, introducing interrupts, unpredictability of network communications, etc. Thus, future work could look into profiling the normal behaviour of these PLCs, including operating system operation, interrupts, and timing variations. Similarly, more complex user programs could be considered. As the numbers of possible inputs and control flows increase, potential program behaviours become prohibitively numerous. For more complex user programs, then, our technique could be applied to smaller units, like functions, with another method to verify that these are executing in an expected order.

Our analysis is performed on programs written in SCL. However, as mentioned in Sect. 3.3, the Siemens S7-317 can also be programmed in three other languages. These three languages provide the same functionality to the programmer, and all three are converted into STL before being uploaded to the device. STL, short for Statement List, is Siemens' implementation of the IEC 61131-3 language Instruction List, a low-level language resembling assembly. However, when executing user programs based on STL on the PLC, a just-in-time (JIT) compilation seems to occur. The first execution of an STL-block in a user program run produces a longer and different waveform from subsequent executions in the same user program run. Future work can look into dealing with this JIT compilation and STL.

We stress that the actual deployment of our side-channel IDS is not trivial. The main hindrance is template transferability [26], i.e. the fact that we can only train our statistical models on a limited amount of devices, yet the model needs to be representative of a larger population of devices. Even devices of the exact same model exhibit electrical variations due to ageing and different manufacturing techniques, thus limiting the effectiveness of our detection process. On top of that, PLCs are often deployed in environments rich in EM-noise, which may negatively impact our analysis. We did not have access to such an environment, but it should be noted that our setup was in an office building, not an EM-clean room. Also, the particular sensor we used seemed more sensitive to noise coming from the chip than from the environment.

Another important consideration for deployment is whether the system being tested can be disconnected from its controlled process for the duration of the test. Since the user program behaviour should depend on its inputs, this way the operator can verify all expected paths are still present. The concern here is that a potential attacker may simply remove the fail-safe code path, but leave the conditional check on whether it should be taken in place. Since no additional code is executed, nor any code normally executed is removed, the behaviour of the program stays the same. Unfortunately, for most applications of PLCs, it is not feasible to stop the industrial process being controlled or disconnect the PLC, to check for this attack.

The final hindrance we wish to highlight here is cost: fitting a large amount of legacy systems with EM probes would require a significant investment of engineering time and money.

These issues combined may make it infeasible to deploy our system for anything but the most critical systems. Future work can aim towards effective deployment of high-accuracy side-channel IDSs, and analyse the effect of environmental noise in detail.

6   Conclusion

In our work, we have shown that through time- and EM-monitoring techniques it is possible to distinguish between user programs on programmable logic controllers. This severely limits attackers and forces them to apply more advanced techniques than naively replacing the user program. In addition, we have demonstrated that even a detection-aware adversary making very small modifications to an existing user program can be effectively detected through the use of full templating of EM emissions. We have proposed an IDS for industrial control systems based on these techniques, and demonstrated its feasibility for systems where only limited knowledge of the platform and exact software instructions running on it is required.

To the best of our knowledge, we are the first to propose and demonstrate the possibility of using the EM side-channel for this type of IDS on industrial control systems.

All software created in the course of this research is made freely available to the extent possible under applicable law at https://polvanaubel.com/research/em-ics/code/.

References

1. Abbasi, A., Hashemi, M.: Ghost in the PLC: designing an undetectable programmable logic controller rootkit via pin control attack. In: Black Hat Europe, pp. 1–35, November 2016
2. Archambeau, C., Peeters, E., Standaert, F.-X., Quisquater, J.-J.: Template attacks in principal subspaces. In: Goubin, L., Matsui, M. (eds.) CHES 2006. LNCS, vol. 4249, pp. 1–14. Springer, Heidelberg (2006). https://doi.org/10.1007/11894063_1
3. Basnight, Z., Butts, J., Lopez, J., Dube, T.: Firmware modification attacks on programmable logic controllers. Int. J. Crit. Infrastruct. Prot. 6(2), 76–84 (2013). https://doi.org/10.1016/j.ijcip.2013.04.004
4. Beckers, A., Balasch, J., Gierlichs, B., Verbauwhede, I.: Design and implementation of a waveform-matching based triggering system. In: Standaert, F.-X., Oswald, E. (eds.) COSADE 2016. LNCS, vol. 9689, pp. 184–198. Springer, Cham (2016). https://doi.org/10.1007/978-3-319-43283-0_11
5. Chari, S., Rao, J.R., Rohatgi, P.: Template attacks. In: Kaliski, B.S., Koç, K., Paar, C. (eds.) CHES 2002. LNCS, vol. 2523, pp. 13–28. Springer, Heidelberg (2003). https://doi.org/10.1007/3-540-36400-5_3

6. Chaudhari, A., Abraham, J.: Stream cipher hash based execution monitoring (SCHEM) framework for intrusion detection on embedded processors. In: International On-Line Testing Symposium - IOLTS, pp. 162–167 (2012). https://doi.org/10.1109/IOLTS.2012.6313864

7. Cherepanov, A.: Win32/industroyer - a new threat for industrial control systems. White paper. ESET, June 2017. https://www.welivesecurity.com/2017/06/12/industroyer-biggest-threat-industrial-control-systems-since-stuxnet/

8. Choudary, O., Kuhn, M.G.: Efficient template attacks. In: Francillon, A., Rohatgi, P. (eds.) CARDIS 2013. LNCS, vol. 8419, pp. 253–270. Springer, Cham (2014). https://doi.org/10.1007/978-3-319-08302-5_17

9. CRASHOVERRIDE - analysis of the threat to electric grid operations. White paper. Dragos Inc., June 2017. https://www.dragos.com/blog/crashoverride/

10. Cui, A., Costello, M., Stolfo, S.J.: When firmware modifications attack: a case study of embedded exploitation. In: NDSS (2013). https://www.ndss-symposium.org/ndss2013/ndss-2013-programme/when-firmware-modifications-attack-case-study-embedded-exploitation/

11. Cui, A., Stolfo, S.J.: Defending embedded systems with software symbiotes. In: Sommer, R., Balzarotti, D., Maier, G. (eds.) RAID 2011. LNCS, vol. 6961, pp. 358–377. Springer, Heidelberg (2011). https://doi.org/10.1007/978-3-642-23644-0_19

12. Dupuis, S., Natale, G.D., Flottes, M., Rouzeyre, B.: On the effectiveness of hardware trojan horse detection via side-channel analysis. Inf. Secur. J.: Glob. Perspect. **22**(5–6), 226–236 (2013). https://doi.org/10.1080/19393555.2014.891277

13. Eisenbarth, T., Paar, C., Weghenkel, B.: Building a side channel based disassembler. In: Gavrilova, M.L., Tan, C.J.K., Moreno, E.D. (eds.) Transactions on Computational Science X. LNCS, vol. 6340, pp. 78–99. Springer, Heidelberg (2010). https://doi.org/10.1007/978-3-642-17499-5_4

14. Falliere, N., Murchu, L.O., Chien, E.: W32. stuxnet dossier. White paper, Symantec Corporation, Security Response 5.6 (2011). https://www.symantec.com/connect/blogs/w32stuxnet-dossier

15. Goldack, M.: Side-channel based reverse engineering for microcontrollers. Master's thesis, Ruhr-Universität Bochum, Germany (2008). https://www.emsec.rub.de/research/theses/

16. Heyszl, J., Mangard, S., Heinz, B., Stumpf, F., Sigl, G.: Localized electromagnetic analysis of cryptographic implementations. In: Dunkelman, O. (ed.) CT-RSA 2012. LNCS, vol. 7178, pp. 231–244. Springer, Heidelberg (2012). https://doi.org/10.1007/978-3-642-27954-6_15

17. Lin, H., Slagell, A., Di Martino, C., Kalbarczyk, Z., Iyer, R.K.: Adapting Bro into SCADA: building a specification-based intrusion detection system for the DNP3 protocol. In: Cyber Security and Information Intelligence Research Workshop - CSIIRW 2013, pp. 1–4 (2013). https://doi.org/10.1145/2459976.2459982. Article no. 5

18. Liu, Y., Wei, L., Zhou, Z., Zhang, K., Xu, W., Xu, Q.: On code execution tracking via power side-channel. In: ACM SIGSAC Conference on Computer and Communications Security, pp. 1019–1031 (2016). https://doi.org/10.1145/2976749.2978299

19. Longo, J., De Mulder, E., Page, D., Tunstall, M.: SoC It to EM: electromagnetic side-channel attacks on a complex system-on-chip. In: Güneysu, T., Handschuh, H. (eds.) CHES 2015. LNCS, vol. 9293, pp. 620–640. Springer, Heidelberg (2015). https://doi.org/10.1007/978-3-662-48324-4_31

20. Msgna, M., Markantonakis, K., Naccache, D., Mayes, K.: Verifying software integrity in embedded systems: a side channel approach. In: Prouff, E. (ed.) COSADE 2014. LNCS, vol. 8622, pp. 261–280. Springer, Cham (2014). https://doi.org/10.1007/978-3-319-10175-0_18

21. Open Source SECurity. https://ossec.github.io/

22. PCBGRIP. https://pcbgrip.com/

23. Peck, D., Peterson, D.: Leveraging ethernet card vulnerabilities in field devices. In: SCADA Security Scientific Symposium, pp. 1–19 (2009)

24. Peeters, E., Standaert, F.-X., Quisquater, J.-J.: Power and electromagnetic analysis: improved model, consequences and comparisons. Integration **40**(1), 52–60 (2007). https://doi.org/10.1016/j.vlsi.2005.12.013

25. Quisquater, J.-J., Samyde, D.: Automatic code recognition for smart cards using a Kohonen neural network. In: CARDIS 2002, vol. 5, pp. 51–58. USENIX Association, Berkeley (2002). https://dial.uclouvain.be/pr/boreal/object/boreal:68059

26. Renauld, M., Standaert, F.-X., Veyrat-Charvillon, N., Kamel, D., Flandre, D.: A formal study of power variability issues and side-channel attacks for nanoscale devices. In: Paterson, K.G. (ed.) EUROCRYPT 2011. LNCS, vol. 6632, pp. 109–128. Springer, Heidelberg (2011). https://doi.org/10.1007/978-3-642-20465-4_8

27. Riscure: icWaves. https://www.riscure.com/security-tools/hardware/icwaves

28. Roesch, M.: Snort - lightweight intrusion detection for networks. In: Proceedings of the 13th USENIX Conference on System Administration, LISA 1999, pp. 229–238. USENIX Association, Berkeley (1999)

29. Schindler, W., Lemke, K., Paar, C.: A stochastic model for differential side channel cryptanalysis. In: Rao, J.R., Sunar, B. (eds.) CHES 2005. LNCS, vol. 3659, pp. 30–46. Springer, Heidelberg (2005). https://doi.org/10.1007/11545262_3

30. Strobel, D., Bache, F., Oswald, D., Schellenberg, F., Paar, C.: SCANDALee: A side-ChANnel-based DisAssembLer using local electromagnetic emanations. In: Design, Automation and Test in Europe - DATE, pp. 139–144, March 2015. https://doi.org/10.7873/DATE.2015.0639

31. Vermoen, D., Witteman, M., Gaydadjiev, G.N.: Reverse engineering Java Card applets using power analysis. In: Smart Cards, Mobile and Ubiquitous Computing Systems: First IFIP TC6/WG 8.8/WG 11.2 International Workshop - WISTP, pp. 138–149 (2007). https://doi.org/10.1007/978-3-540-72354-7_12

32. Yoon, M.-K., Mohan, S., Choi, J., Sha, L.: Memory Heat Map: anomaly detection in real-time embedded systems using memory behavior. In: Design Automation Conference - DAC, vol. 35, no. 1–35, p. 6 (2015). https://doi.org/10.1145/2744769.2744869

33. Zhang, T., Zhuang, X., Pande, S., Lee, W.: Anomalous path detection with hardware support. In: Compilers, architectures and synthesis for embedded systems - CASES, pp. 43–54 (2005). https://doi.org/10.1145/1086297.1086305

34. Zhang, T., Zhuang, X., Pande, S., Lee, W.: Hardware supported anomaly detection: down to the control flow level. Technical report, March 2004. http://hdl.handle.net/1853/96

Security Evaluation of Cyber-Physical Systems Using Automatically Generated Attack Trees

Laurens Lemaire[1(✉)], Jan Vossaert[1], Bart De Decker[2], and Vincent Naessens[1]

[1] MSEC, iMinds-DistriNet, Department of Computer Science, KU Leuven,
Gebroeders Desmetstraat 1, 9000 Ghent, Belgium
{laurens.lemaire,jan.vossaert,vincent.naessens}@cs.kuleuven.be
[2] iMinds-DistriNet, Department of Computer Science, KU Leuven,
Celestijnenlaan 200A, 3001 Heverlee, Belgium
bart.decker@cs.kuleuven.be

Abstract. The security of cyber-physical systems (CPS) is often lacking. This abstract presents a methodology that performs a security evaluation of these systems by automatically generating attack trees based on the system model. The assessor can define different kinds of attackers and see how the attack tree is evaluated with respect to a specific type of attacker. Optimal attacker strategies are calculated and from here the most vulnerable elements of the system can be derived.

Keywords: Cyber-physical systems · Attack trees
Security assessment

1 Introduction

Cyber-physical systems (CPS) are networks of interacting elements with physical input and output, usually containing various remote field sites where a certain process is taking place [4]. Each field site consists of sensors and actuators, controlled locally by a programmable logic controller (PLC) or similar device. These remote sites are connected to a centralized control network where operators can remotely monitor and control the processes. In the past decades, these systems have evolved from proprietary, isolated systems to complex interconnected systems that are remotely accessible and often use commercial off-the-shelf (COTS) components. This has made them easier to use, but also easier to attack [2].

Various research initiatives have been undertaken in previous years to improve the security of cyber-physical systems, both in the academic world and by industry. One of the areas in which a lot of research is situated is risk assessment. A risk assessment process evaluates the likelihood and impact of identified threats to the CPS. A recent review of risk assessment methodologies for CPS lists various remaining research challenges [1], among which are better tool support, the necessity of proper methodology validation, more attention towards

© Springer Nature Switzerland AG 2018
G. D'Agostino and A. Scala (Eds.): CRITIS 2017, LNCS 10707, pp. 225–228, 2018.
https://doi.org/10.1007/978-3-319-99843-5_20

the system architecture when performing a risk assessment, and the need for reliable sources of probabilities. In this abstract, a methodology for the security evaluation of CPS is presented which can be used in a risk assessment process and which tackles the aforementioned challenges.

2   Methodology

Figure 1 shows a general overview of the methodology. The process is divided in two parts: a *tree generation algorithm* and a *tree evaluation algorithm*. The tree generation algorithm takes as input a *system*, a list of extracted system *vulnerabilities* and an *attacker goal*. The *system* is a model of the CPS which will be subject to the security evaluation. The *vulnerabilities* themselves are automatically derived from the system model by the FAST-CPS framework [5]. The *attacker goal* is the global objective of the attacker with regards to the CPS. For each attacker goal for a system, a separate attack tree will be built. *Templates* are used by the tree generation algorithm, they generate parts of the tree. The templates are part of the methodology and do not require human interaction. Once the attack tree is generated, the assessor can provide an *attacker* as input for the tree evaluation algorithm. The *attacker* is an entity that attempts to reach the attacker goal by following a path of attack steps through the attack tree. An attacker is defined in terms of his capabilities, the credentials he possesses and the parts of the system he has physical access to. Different kinds of attackers can be modelled, each with their own capabilities. The tree evaluation algorithm results in an *optimal attacker strategy* and the *difficulty* of the attack.

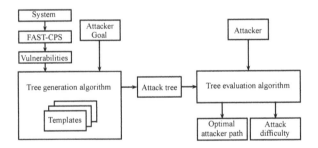

Fig. 1. The flow of the methodology.

2.1   Input Model

The assessor must provide three input elements: the system model, the attacker goal, and the type of attacker.

System Model. The attack trees are based on the system architecture, hence the assessor must provide a *system model*. An existing framework can be used for this task: FAST-CPS. This framework allows the assessor to model his system architecture in SysML, a modelling language derived from UML used for model-based systems engineering [3].

Attacker Goal. The *attacker goal* will become the root node of the attack tree. The assessor chooses this goal, the rest of the tree is then automatically generated. If an assessor wants to reason about multiple attacker goals, a separate tree is built for each goal. Three main types of attacker goals were identified based on the NIST guide to ICS security [6]:

- *Modify(Parameter)*: Changing the process behaviour of the CPS. The assessor must provide which process parameter the attacker wants to modify.
- *DenialOfService(SystemPart)*: Halting the workings of a component or module in the CPS.
- *Obtain(Asset)*: Obtaining a data asset stored in the CPS.

Attacker. An Attacker $\mathcal{A} = (C, M, A)$ is defined by the set of credentials "C" the attacker owns, a mapping of *attacker capabilities* to integer values "M", and a set of components in the system "A" which the attacker has physical access to.

2.2 Output

The output of the methodology is an optimal attacker strategy. An *Optimal Attacker Strategy S* is a sub-tree of the attack tree T. This sub-tree represents the optimal way for a modelled attacker to reach the attacker goal. What is optimal depends on the chosen heuristic in the tree evaluation stage. Once the optimal attacker strategy is returned, the assessor can identify the most vulnerable parts of the system by looking at the leaves of S. Once the system model has been changed accordingly, the assessor can see if the optimal attacker strategy has changed and which other system parts require attention.

2.3 Tree Generation

The tree generation algorithm takes the attacker goal and a CPS model and generates an attack tree. The algorithm uses templates that represent attacks on the system or assess the impact of vulnerable components on possible threats. The algorithm is shown below:

```
GenerateTree(AttackerGoal, SystemModel, Templates):

tree.root = AttackerGoal
goals = { AttackerGoal }
while goals ≠ ∅ do
    goal = goals.pop()
```

```
foreach Template t ∈ Templates do
    if t.goal = goal then
        Tree s = t.execute(goal, SystemModel)
        goals.push(s.leaves)
        tree.replace(goal, s)
```

Initially there is only one goal in the set of goals, which is the attacker goal chosen by the assessor. Each template has a unique goal associated with it, once the template that matches the attacker goal is found, this template is executed and a tree is generated. This tree is then added to the main tree where the goal used to be. Each template has a specific execute method. The leaves of an executed template are then added to the set of goals so they can be matched with other templates. If a goal finds no match, it is a leaf of the final tree.

2.4   Tree Evaluation

Once a possible attack on a system has been modelled in an attack tree, the tree can be used to analyse security properties of the system, for instance the difficulty of attacks. The analysis proceeds in three steps: First the difficulty of each leaf is determined, then the difficulty of parent nodes is synthesized from the difficulty of their children. Once all nodes are annotated, the optimal attacker strategy is calculated.

3   Conclusions

This abstract presents a methodology that automatically builds system-dependent attack trees for the security evaluation of cyber-physical systems. The assessor can model different types of attackers and evaluate the attack tree with respect to a specific type of attacker. Optimal attacker strategies are calculated during this evaluation phase.

References

1. Cherdantseva, Y., et al.: A review of cyber security risk assessment methods for scada systems. Comput. Secur. **56**, 1–27 (2016)
2. ENISA. Protecting industrial control systems: Recommendations for Europe and member states (2011)
3. Friedenthal, S., Moore, A., Steiner, R.: A Practical Guide to SysML: The Systems Modeling Language. Morgan Kaufmann, Burlington (2014)
4. Lee, E.A.: Cyber physical systems: design challenges. In: 2008 11th IEEE International Symposium on Object Oriented Real-Time Distributed Computing (ISORC), pp. 363–369. IEEE (2008)
5. Lemaire, L., Lapon, J., De Decker, B., Naessens, V.: A SysML extension for security analysis of industrial control systems. In: Proceedings of the 2nd International Symposium for ICS & SCADA Cyber Security Research, p. 1 (2014)
6. Stouffer, K., Lightman, S., Pillitteri, V., Abrams, M., Hahn, A.: Guide to industrial control systems (ICS) security (2015)

Faulty or Malicious Anchor Detection Criteria for Distance-Based Localization

Federica Inderst[1], Gabriele Oliva[2], Stefano Panzieri[1], Federica Pascucci[1(✉)], and Roberto Setola[2]

[1] Department of Engineering, University Rome Tre,
Via della Vasca Navale 79, 00146 Rome, Italy
{federica.inderst,stefano.panzieri,federica.pascucci}@uniroma3.it
[2] Complex Systems and Security Laboratory,
University Campus Bio-Medico of Rome, Via A. del Portillo 21, 00128 Rome, Italy
{g.oliva,r.setola}@unicampus.it

Abstract. The reliability of the localization of Wireless Sensor Networks in presence of errors or malicious data alteration is a challenging research topic: recently, several studies have been carried out to identify, remove or neglect the faulted/malicious nodes. This paper addresses the capability of a network, composed of range-capable nodes and anchor nodes (i.e., nodes that know their position), to detect a faulty or malicious alteration of the information provided by the anchor nodes. Specifically, we consider biases for the position of anchor nodes that alter the localization of the network, and we provide conditions under which the nodes are able to detect the event, with particular reference to two distance-based localization algorithms, namely trilateration and Shadow Edge Localization Algorithm.

1 Introduction

Nowadays, Wireless Sensor Networks (WSN) are regarded as key technology for several applications in several fields, ranging from surveillance and data acquisition to Cyber Physical Systems and Internet of Things.

Although it cannot be considered as the main goal of a network, localization is one of the fundamental bricks for any autonomous functionality demanded to the network. Localization, in fact, contributes to increase situation awareness [21] and, in particular, spatial awareness that is mandatory for processing large data streams. Moreover, it plays a significant role in several applications such as routing, surveillance and monitoring, and military application. For instance sensors deployed to monitor the environment may need to spatially correlate data, while in military applications sensors play an important role, e.g., to drive robots deactivating land-mines. The taxonomy for WSN localization approaches is large, due to the different hardware and software settings that have been proposed in the literature.

In this paper we focus on *range-based* approaches, that rely on relative distance measurements and anchor nodes, i.e., few nodes that know their position [1–7].

© Springer Nature Switzerland AG 2018
G. D'Agostino and A. Scala (Eds.): CRITIS 2017, LNCS 10707, pp. 229–240, 2018.
https://doi.org/10.1007/978-3-319-99843-5_21

Most of range-based approaches in literature show a strong dependency on the anchors, and may fail when the anchors provide a faulty or maliciously altered position. In the literature several methodologies have been proposed to detect malicious node in range-based localization algorithms, in order to provide a trusted location for nodes. To this end, some strategies to eliminate or contain the impact of malicious nodes are also considered.

A detection strategy is proposed in [8], where the position of a node is computed combining noisy localization by trilateration: a test based on Mahalanobis distance is performed to certify the location computed or detect the infected node. In [9] a methodology to detect wormhole attacks of different kind is developed in a range-free localization setting. In [10] a methodology is provided to detect and counteract attacks that create a wormhole to try to deceive an isolated remote WSN node into believing that it is a neighbor of a set of local nodes. The *Verifiable Multilateration* is introduced in [11,12], as a methodology to validate the claimed position for a node by resorting to a central authority. In [13] the complexity of the nodes is increased by considering also the transmission power and the angle of rotation of the antennas. A metodology that applies convex constraints in the space in order to match hops and distances is given in [14]. In [15] a robust trilateration approach is given, as well as a condition for having bounded error.

In this paper we focus on the ability of a set of range-capable sensors to detect the presence of faulty or malicious alterations of the information provided by some anchor nodes, which may result in incorrect absolute or relative localization for the nodes.

Specifically, we assume some biases are added to the information provided by the anchor nodes on their position, and show the conditions that guarantee the existence of distinct biases for the anchor that alter the result of the relative localization which is obtained by executing a Trilateration algorithm [1–3] or a Shadow Edge Localization Algorithm (SELA) [4–7]. The results are Faulty or Malicious Anchor Detection Criteria for Trilateration and SELA that are quite challenging to check, as they involve several global rigidity tests [16] on subsets of the nodes and edges of the network.

The remainder of the paper is as follows: Sect. 2 reviews the WSN localization problem and the trilateration algorithm; In Sect. 3 the SELA algorithm is discussed. In Sects. 4 and 5, in the case of Trilateration and SELA, we develop the conditions for the existence of biases that affect the position of the anchor nodes and are able to alter the localization of the nodes without the possibility for the nodes to detect the event. Some conclusions and future work directions are drawn in Sect. 5.

2   WSN Localization Problem

The goal of localization in a WSN is to determine the position of the nodes in the network. In the literature, several solutions are provided. The taxonomy for WSNs localization problem is based on the available type of measurements, the mathematical framework adopted for representing both network and measurement, the environment, the techniques exploited for computing the position, the implemented algorithms, and the presence of anchors (i.e., nodes aware of their position).

Let us consider a WSN Σ, composed by n fixed sensors σ_j. The network is deployed in a planar environment, so that the position of the sensor σ_j can be written as $p_j = [x_j, y_j]^T \in \mathbb{R}^2$ with respect to a global reference frame. Each sensor σ_j is equipped with an isotropic communication antenna characterized by a maximum communication range ρ. Given two nodes σ_j, σ_i, the antenna is also used as a rangefinder for computing the Euclidean distance $d_{j,i} = ||p_j - p_i||$.

From a theoretical perspective, the WSN can be described using the disk model: a node is capable of sensing those sensors that fall within its communication range ρ. According to this approach, a WSN can be represented by a unit disk graph $G = \{V, E\}$, where the set V denotes the nodes $v_1, \ldots, v_N$ (i.e., the sensors $\sigma_1, \ldots, \sigma_n$) and E is the set of edges (v_j, v_i) (i.e., the presence of a communication link between sensors σ_j and σ_i). The localization problem can be set as finding a coordinate assignment P for the non-anchor nodes, i.e., to choose the location p_j for each sensor $\sigma_j \in \Sigma \setminus \Sigma_s$ in a way such that d_{ij} holds for all sensor pairs σ_j, σ_i such that $(v_j, v_i) \in E$. In Graph Theory, this problem is the same as finding a framework (G, P) such that the coordinate assignment P does not violate the distance constraints, where a framework is a graph $G = \{V, E\}$ together with a coordinate assignment $P : V \to \mathbb{R}^2$ for the vertices of the graph. A unique solution for the theoretical problem is proved to exist if the framework is globally rigid, i.e., the position of the nodes cannot be continuously deformed nor flipped without breaking the distance constraints [2,17]. However, the computational load of the global rigidity test is high [16].

A classical approach for solving the localization problem is to find a trilateration graph $G_T = \{V, E_T\}$ with $E_T \subseteq E$, as shown in [1,3]. Trilateration is the process of determining the location of a sensor σ_j by measurement of distances d_{ji}, d_{jh} and d_{jk} from three localized sensors σ_i, σ_h and σ_k, using the geometry of circles [1,18]. A way to localize a sensor network (composed of all distance-based sensors) is thus to let each sensor check for the existence of 3 localized neighbors, while localized sensors broadcast their position to their neighbors. When a sensor to be localized finds such 3 neighbors, it calculates its own location by means of trilateration and broadcasts its location to its neighbors; then, it contributes to the localization of the other sensors and so on, until no other sensor can be localized. If the graph G contains a trilateration graph, all the nodes will eventually be localized; when $G_T = \{V_T, E_T\}$ with $V_T \subset V$, a localizable component of the WSN is retrieved using the given seeds.

In [7], it is shown that this localized subgraph does not represent the maximum localizable component, i.e., the maximum globally rigid sub framework. To improve the localization in the case of unit disk graphs, the Shadow Edge Localization Algorithm (SELA), introduced in [4–7] can be applied. SELA exploits the *negative information* of *not being connected*, which is available if we assume the network is a *unit disk graph* with radius ρ, i.e., all pair of sensors with $d_{ij} \leq \rho$

will have distance information. The details of the algorithm are reported next for sake of clarity.

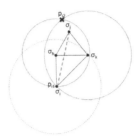

Fig. 1. Shadow Edges Localization: sensors σ_j, σ_h and σ_k are localized, sensor σ_i is localizable by means of the *negative information* of not been connected to sensor σ_j, as represented by the shadow edge (blue dotted line) (Color figure online)

3   Shadow Edges Localization Algorithm

SELA is an extension of the standard trilateration for range-based networks over unit disk graphs. The algorithm, although improving the localization with respect to trilateration, results in a slightly increased communication load, since few 2-hop information is used. Considering the example shown in Fig. 1, the sensor σ_i is able to localize itself knowing that it is out of the range of sensor σ_j. This knowledge is not provided directly from the sensor σ_j, but forwarded from nodes σ_h and σ_k. This indirect knowledge can be formally described by *virtual edges*, i.e., the shadow edges. In other terms, supposing that σ_i has two localized neighbors $\mathcal{L}(\sigma_i) = \{\sigma_h, \sigma_k\}$ and that d_{ih}, d_{ik} are known, two alternatives p_{i_1} and p_{i_2} exist for the location of σ_i; a shadow edge is an edge $(v_i, v_j) \notin E$ such that either $||p_{i_1} - p_j|| < \rho$ or $||p_{i_2} - p_j|| < \rho$. It is worth noticing that SELA algorithm can be implemented in a distributed fashion: the localization propagates from the localization seeds across the network. The protocol to be implemented on each node σ_i is provided in Algorithm 1.

In [5] it is shown that if the *extended shadow graph* $G = \{V, E \cup E_s\}$, i.e., the graph obtained including also the shadow edges E_s, found by SELA algorithm, contains a trilateration graph over all the nodes, then all sensors can be localized. Notice further that a shadow edge does not always exist, since the conditions that define it may not be verified for particular frameworks. In [7] some localizability conditions for SELA are given, based on the concept of *shadow localizable framework*. Specifically, a subframework (G', P) of (G, P) over all the nodes is a shadow localizable framework if G' is connected and perfectly chordal (i.e., the nodes have all at least two neighbors and every cycle with more than 3 nodes has at least a chord, i.e., link that joins two non consecutive nodes in the cycle) and for each perfectly chordal sub-framework (G_{sub}, P_{sub}) of (G, P) with 4 nodes which is not complete, the corresponding sub-framework (G'_{sub}, P_{sub}) of (G', P) is

Algorithm 1. Shadow Edge Localization Protocol

```
while CheckStatus(σᵢ) == UnLoc & loop do
    C=|L(σᵢ)|
    switch (C)
    case 0,1:
        SetStatus(σᵢ, UnLoc)
    case 2:
        L₂ₕ(σᵢ) = L(σₕ) ∩ L(σₖ)
        if !IsEmpty(L)₂ₕ(σᵢ) then
            p = FindIntersect(pₕ, pₖ, dᵢₕ, dᵢₖ)
            pᵢ = CheckListen(p, L₂ₕ(σᵢ))
            if !IsEmpty(pᵢ) then
                SetPosition(σᵢ, pᵢ)
                SetStatus(σᵢ, Loc)
            end if
        end if
    default:
        pⱼ = Trilaterate(σᵢ, L(σᵢ))
        SetPosition(σᵢ, pⱼ)
        SetStatus(σᵢ, Loc)
    end switch
end while
```

Delaunay (a framework (G, P) is a *Delaunay framework* if G is perfectly chordal and for each 3 vertices v_i, v_j and v_k of G the circumference passing through the points p_i, p_j and p_k does not contain any other point in (G, P), e.g., Fig. 2(a)) and Gabriel [19,20] (a framework (G, P) is a *Gabriel framework* [19,20] if for each edge (v_i, v_j) of G the circle whose diameter coincides with the edge does not contain any other point of P–an example is given in Fig. 2(b)).

Remark 1. Although not directly available, the length d_{ij} of a shadow edge (v_i, v_j) can be estimated using the Carnot's Theorem (see Fig. 3). Specifically, by some algebra it is immediate to verify that

$$d_{ij} = \sqrt{d_{ih}^2 + d_{jh}^2 - 2d_{ih}d_{jh} \cos\left(\alpha_{khj} - \alpha_{khi}\right)} \tag{1}$$

where the generic angle α_{abc} is given by:

$$\alpha_{abc} = \cos^{-1}\left(\frac{d_{ab}^2 + d_{ac}^2 - d_{bc}^2}{2d_{ab}d_{ac}}\right) \tag{2}$$

4   Malicious Anchors in Trilateration

In this section we provide some results on the effect of incorrect or malicious information provided by the anchors. Specifically we assume that each anchor

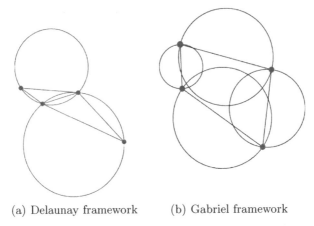

(a) Delaunay framework   (b) Gabriel framework

Fig. 2. Delaunay framework and Gabriel framework: a framework (G, P) is a *Delaunay framework* if G is composed of triangles (i.e., G is perfectly chordal) and for each 3 vertices v_i, v_j and v_k of G the circumference passing through the points p_i, p_j and p_k does not contain any other point in (G, P); a framework (G, P) is a *Gabriel framework* if for each edge (v_i, v_j) of G the corresponding Gabriel circle does not contain any other point of P

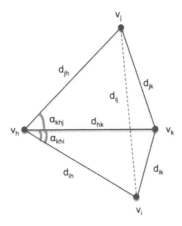

Fig. 3. Information required to compute the length d_{ij} of the shadow edge (v_i, v_j).

$\sigma_i \in \Sigma_a$ broadcasts an incorrect position $p_i^* = p_i + p_i^b$, where p_i^b is a bias. We say that the localization for a sensor $\sigma_j \in \Sigma \setminus \Sigma_a$, with respect to a specific algorithm, is *altered* by the above biases if the sensor selects an incorrect location without noticing the violation of some distance constraints due to the presences of the biases. If the node is not localized in the case of zero bias, we say its localization is not altered, meaning that it poses no constraint on the alteration of the localization. We can further specify this concept in terms of alteration of the absolute or relative localization. We say the localization of the whole network

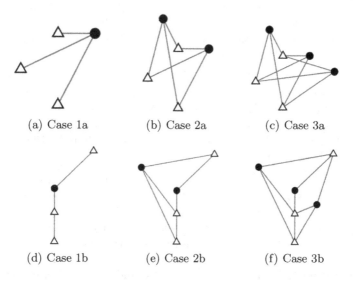

(a) Case 1a   (b) Case 2a   (c) Case 3a

(d) Case 1b   (e) Case 2b   (f) Case 3b

Fig. 4. Visual explanation of Theorem 2: Anchor nodes are white triangles, unlocalized nodes are black circles, regular links are blue lines, and links added to detect malicious nodes are red lines. (Color figure online)

Σ, with respect to a specific localization algorithm, is altered if the localization of each sensor in $\Sigma \setminus \Sigma_a$ is altered. In the following we will assume Σ_a contains $m \geq 3$ anchors which are in distinct positions, and at least 3 of them are fully connected and not collinear.

In the case of the absolute localization, we can provide the following remark for trilateration.

Remark 2. It is always possible alter the absolute localization of any network by selecting $p_i^b = p^b$ for all $\sigma_i \in \Sigma_a$ and for any $p^b \in \mathbb{R}^2$. In this way, in fact, the position of all localized sensors $\sigma_j \in \Sigma \setminus \Sigma_a$ is equal to $p_j + p^b$.

We wonder if a similar result exists for trilateration in the relative localization case. We can provide the following result.

Theorem 1. *Let a sensor network Σ represented by a graph $G = \{V, E\}$ with n nodes and by a set of positions P. Suppose that the nodes in $\Sigma' \subseteq \Sigma \setminus \Sigma_a$ are localized via trilateration. Let $G' = \{V', E'\}$ be the subgraph induced by the set of localized nodes and by the anchors and let $P' \subseteq P$ the set of their positions. Let further G'' be the subgraph of G' where the links among anchor nodes are removed, i.e.,*

$$G'' = \{V', E' \setminus E_a\},$$

where

$$E_a = \{(v_i, v_j) \in E \text{ s.t. } \sigma_i, \sigma_j \in \Sigma_a\}.$$

It is possible to select biases p_i^b, not all equal, for the anchor nodes $\sigma_i \in \Sigma_a$ such that the relative localization of the network is altered iff the framework (G'', P') does not contain any globally rigid sub-framework which contains at least 3 anchors.

Proof. It is well known that, for a globally rigid framework there is a unique realization. This implies that a globally rigid sub-framework of (G'', P') containing at least 3 anchors satisfies the distance constraints *iff* the biases are all coincident, hence the relative localization can not be altered without violating some distance constraints.

Figure 4 provides a visual explanation of Theorem 1 in 3 different cases. The upper plots (Cases 1.a–3.a) show the true position of some anchor nodes and nodes to be localized, as well as the links that represent the distance constraints between them (the links between anchors are not plotted). The lower plot show the incorrect relative localization obtained when the anchor nodes select three distinct biases. According to Theorem 1, in Case 1 and Case 2 there is no rigid subframework involving all the anchor nodes, and possible biases are selected as shown in the lower plots. It the case of Case 3, instead, the graph obtained by removing the links between anchors is globally rigid, hence any 3 distinct biases generate the violation of at least a distance constraint (in Example 3.b, a constraint is violated, and the corresponding link is shown in red).

Notice that, in the case of trilateration, it is well known that a framework containing a trilateration graph is globally rigid. In the above figure, however, the graph of Case 3.b (see Fig. 4(e)) is globally rigid but is not a trilateration graph. It follows, therefore, that the effort required to verify the condition of Theorem 1 can be non trivial as the size of the network grows.

Notice further that, in the case of trilateration, if the condition of Theorem 1 is verified, then some nodes are able to detect autonomously the alteration by comparing the measured distances for its neighbors with the distances calculated after the localization algorithm has terminated.

5   Malicious Anchors in SELA

In this section we extend our analysis to SELA algorithm. First of all, notice that the argument of Remark 1 applies also in this case, hence it is always possible to alter the absolute localization. Let us now discuss the case of the relative localization. We can provide the following result.

Theorem 2. *Let a sensor network Σ represented by a unit disk graph $G = \{V, E\}$ with n nodes and by a set of positions P. Suppose that the nodes in $\Sigma' \subseteq \Sigma \setminus \Sigma_a$ are localized via SELA algorithm. Let $G' = \{V', E'\}$ be the subgraph induced by the set of localized nodes and by the anchors and let $P' \subseteq P$ the set of their positions, and let $G'_e = \{V', E' \cup E_s\}$ be the extended shadow graph that includes also the shadow edges E_s found by SELA algorithm. Let further G'' be the subgraph of G'_e where the links among anchor nodes are removed, i.e.,*

$$G'' = \{V', E' \setminus E_a\},$$

where

$$E_a = \{(v_i, v_j) \in E \text{ s.t. } \sigma_i, \sigma_j \in \Sigma_a\}.$$

It is possible to select biases p_i^b, not all equal, for the anchor nodes $\sigma_i \in \Sigma_a$ such that the relative localization of the network is altered iff the framework (G'', P') does not contain any globally rigid sub-framework $(\hat{G}, \hat{P})$, with $\hat{G} = \{\hat{V}, \hat{E}\}$, that contains at least 3 anchors and is such that either:

1. *$(\hat{G}, \hat{P})$ is globally rigid;*
2. *The complement framework $(\hat{G}^c, P)$, where*

$$\hat{G}^c = \{\hat{V}, \hat{V} \times \hat{V} \setminus \hat{E}\}$$

has some link (v_i, v_j) such that $||p_i - p_j|| > \rho$.

Proof. The proof is similar to the one of Theorem 1, except for the fact that, if the distance between the altered positions of two nodes that are not able to sense each other over the unit disk graph is less than ρ, then it is possible to detect the alteration because of the unit disk graph structure.

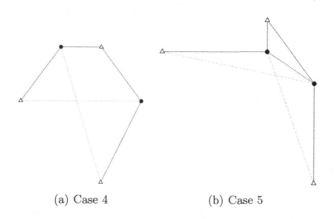

(a) Case 4   (b) Case 5

Fig. 5. Visual explanation of Theorem 2: Anchor nodes are white triangles, unlocalized nodes are black circles, regular links are blue lines, shadow edges are magenta dotted lines, and links added to detect malicious nodes are red lines. (Color figure online)

Figure 5 provides a visual explanation of Theorem 2. Besides the cases covered by Theorem 1 (which applies also to SELA), in the case of a unit disk graph we have to check not only that the existing distance constraints are not violated, but also that no new edges are created. In the example of Fig. 5(a) two nodes are localized by means of regular links and shadow edges. Although the extended shadow graph obtained by removing the links between anchor nodes is not globally rigid, in Case 4 (see Fig. 5(b)) the anchors are able to select some

---

Algorithm 2. Malicious Anchor Detection

---

   while $CheckStatus(\sigma_i) == UnLoc$ & *loop* **do**
     $SetStatus(\sigma_i, UnLoc)$
     $C = |\mathcal{L}(\sigma_i)|$
     switch (C)
     case 3:
       % Nodes Localization using Trilateration
       $p_i = Trilateration(\sigma_i)$
       $SetPosition(\sigma_i, p_i)$
       $SetStatus(\sigma_i, Loc)$
       % Malicious Anchor Detection using Trilateration
       $SetNewPosition(\sigma_i, p_i^*), p_i^* = p_i + p_i^*$
       if $\sigma \in \Sigma_a$ **&&** $(G'', P') \not\supset (\hat{G}, \hat{P}) == TRUE$ **then**
         $Select(p_i^b)$
       end if
     case 2:
       %Nodes Localization using Shadow Edge
       $p_i = SELA(\sigma_i)$
       $SetPosition(\sigma_i, p_i)$
       $SetStatus(\sigma_i, Loc)$
       % Malicious Anchor Detection using Shadow Edge
       $SetNewPosition(\sigma_i, p_i^*), p_i^* = p_i + p_i^*$
       if $\sigma \in \Sigma_a$ **&&** $(G'', P') \not\supset (\hat{G}, \hat{P}) == TRUE, \hat{G} = \{\hat{V}, \hat{E}\}$ **then**
         if $|\hat{G}| = 2|V| - 3$ **&&** $\exists (V_i, V_j) \in \hat{G}^c = \{\hat{V}, \hat{V} \times V \setminus \hat{E}\}$ **then**
           $Select(p_i^b)$
         end if
       end if
     default:
       $p_j = Trilaterate(\sigma_i, \mathcal{L}(\sigma_i))$
       $SetPosition(\sigma_i, p_j)$
       $SetStatus(\sigma_i, Loc)$
     end switch
   end while

---

biases and the relative position of the nodes is modified. However, since the distance of the two nodes to be localized becomes smaller than ρ, a link between them is eventually created which allows to detect the alteration.

Notice that, in order to detect this kind of alteration, we need a centralized perspective (or a non-trival amount of information exchange among the sensors). This happens because the condition on the complement framework can only be checked in a centralized way, as a node does not know, in principle, the position of the nodes which are not in its neighborhood. This implies that SELA algorithm is vulnerable to this kind of alteration. However, since shadow edges are virtual links of length between ρ and 2ρ, it is still possible to spot those alterations that result in shadow edges with length outside this range.

The overall algorithm for joint localization and malicious nodes detection is sketched in Algorithm 2. Each node in the graph tries to localizes according to the information provided by the localized nodes in the graph. Moreover the nodes check for the reliability of the information provided by the nodes in the graph, so to identify malicious nodes.

6   Conclusions and Future Work

In this paper we provide conditions for the detectability of faulty or malicious information provided by the anchor nodes in trilateration and SELA localization algorithms. Specifically, we consider biases for the position of anchor nodes that alter the localization of the network, and we provide conditions under which the nodes are able to detect the event, with particular reference to two distance-based localization algorithms, namely trilateration and Shadow Edge Localization Algorithm.

Future work will be devoted to provide distributed algorithms to detect and isolate the malicious anchors, as well as robust localization approaches able to grant a bounded error even when some anchors are faulty or malicious.

References

1. Eren, T., et al.: Rigidity, computation, and randomization in network localization. In: INFOCOM, : Twenty-Third AnnualJoint Conference of the IEEE Computer and Communications Societies 2004, vol. 4, pp. 2673–2684. IEEE (2004)
2. Connelly, R.: Generic global rigidity. Discret. Comput. Geom. **33**(4), 549–563 (2005)
3. Aspnes, J., Eren, T., Goldenberg, D.K., Morse, A.S., Whiteley, W., Yang, Y.R., Anderson, B.D., Belhumeur, P.N.: A theory of network localization. IEEE Trans. Mob. Comput. **5**(12), 1663–1678 (2006)
4. Oliva, G., et al.: Network localization by shadow edges. In: 2013 European Control Conference (ECC), pp. 2263–2268. IEEE (2013)
5. Oliva, G., et al.: Exploiting routing information in wireless sensor networks localization. In: IEEE 2nd 2013 Network Science Workshop (NSW), pp. 66–73. IEEE (2013)
6. Pascucci, F., Panzieri, S., Oliva, G., Setola, R.: Simultaneous localization and routing in sensor networks using shadow edges. Intell. Auton. Veh. **8**(1), 199–204 (2013)
7. Oliva, G., Panzieri, S., Pascucci, F., Setola, R.: Sensor network localization: extending trilateration via shadow edges. IEEE Trans. Autom. Control. **60**(10), 2752–2755 (2015)
8. Kuriakose, J., Amruth, V., Nandhini, S., Abhilash, V.: Sequestration of malevolent anchor nodes in wireless sensor networks using mahalanobis distance, CoRR (2014)
9. Kashani, M.A.A., Mahriyar, H.: A new method for preventing wormhole attacks in wireless sensor networks. Adv. Environ. Biol. **8**(10), 1339–1346 (2014)
10. García-Otero, M., Población-Hernández, A.: Secure neighbor discovery in wireless sensor networks using range-free localization techniques. Int. J. Distrib. Sens. Netw. **8**(11), 763182 (2012)

11. Lazos, L., Poovendran, R., Čapkun, S.: Rope: robust position estimation in wireless sensor networks. In: Proceedings of the 4th International Symposium on Information Processing in Sensor Networks, p. 43 IEEE Press (2005)

12. Capkun, S., Hubaux, J.-P.: Secure positioning in wireless networks. IEEE J. Sel. Areas Commun. **24**(2), 221–232 (2006)

13. Lazos, L., Poovendran, R.: Hirloc: high-resolution robust localization for wireless sensor networks. IEEE J. Sel. Areas Commun. **24**(2), 233–246 (2006)

14. Niu, Y., Gao, D., Gao, S., Chen, P.: A robust localization in wireless sensor networks against wormhole attack. J. Netw. **7**(1), 187–194 (2012)

15. Prakruthi, M., Varalatchoumy, M.: Detecting malicious beacon nodes for secure localization in distributed wireless networks (2011)

16. Jacobs, D.J., Hendrickson, B.: An algorithm for two-dimensional rigidity percolation: the pebble game. J. Comput. Phys. **137**(2), 346–365 (1997)

17. Laman, G.: On graphs and rigidity of plane skeletal structures. J. Eng. Math. **4**, 331–340 (1970)

18. Saxe, J.B.: Embeddability of weighted graphs in k-space is strongly NP-hard. Carnegie-Mellon University, Department of Computer Science, Pittsburgh (1980)

19. Gabriel, K.R., Sokal, R.R.: A new statistical approach to geographic variation analysis. Syst. Biol. **18**(3), 259–278 (1969)

20. Matula, D.W., Sokal, R.R.: Properties of gabriel graphs relevant to geographic variation research and the clustering of points in the plane. Geogr. Anal. **12**(3), 205–222 (1980)

21. Abate, V., Adacher, L., Pascucci, F.: Situation awareness in critical infrastructures. Int. J. Simul. Process Model. **9**(1–2), 92–103 (2014)

One Step More: Automatic ICS Protocol Field Analysis

Yeop Chang[✉], Seungoh Choi, Jeong-Han Yun, and SinKyu Kim

National Security Research Institute, Jeonmin-dong, Yuseong-gu, Daejeon, Korea
{ranivris,sochoi,dolgam,skkim}@nsr.re.kr

Abstract. Industrial control system (ICS) protocols have been developed to obtain the values measured using sensors, control the field devices, and share the collected information. It is necessary to monitor the ICS network continuously based on the ICS protocol knowledge (protocol field's meaning and protocol's behavior) for detecting ICS attackers' suspicious activities. However, the ICS protocols are often proprietary, making it difficult to obtain their exact specifications. Hence, we need an automatic ICS protocol analysis because the tasks involved in the manual reverse engineering are tedious. After analyzing the network traffic obtained from a real ICS, we found that the variable structures were common and packet fragmentation frequently occurred during the operation. We recognized the need for an automated process wherein the packet fragmentation and variable structures are considered. In this paper, we describe our ongoing research to resolve the intricate structures of the ICS protocols in addition to the existing statistical analysis approach and present the implementation results.

Keywords: ICS protocol · Binary protocol · Protocol reversing

1 Introduction

A proprietary protocol is mostly used in industrial control systems (ICSs), which is kept private from the public by vendor or stakeholder. The exact specification of protocol is not open; hence the protocols must be reverse engineered to identify any vulnerability or to develop security devices related to the protocol. The reverse engineering of a protocol can be broadly divided into dynamic binary analysis (e.g., taint analysis) and trace (network)-based analysis. If a target protocol is used in critical infrastructures or in other industrial systems, it is difficult to set up identical environment for the dynamic binary analysis. Hence, the trace-based analysis is an appropriate approach for ICS protocol analysis.

Most studies on protocol reversing have focused on public (known) protocols based on a plain text [1,5]. With the increase in the number of cyber threats, such as DDoS due to botnet, several researches particularly dealt with a customized protocol, which is used in the communication between the botnet and the command-and-control (C&C) server, to mitigate and respond to potential

© Springer Nature Switzerland AG 2018
G. D'Agostino and A. Scala (Eds.): CRITIS 2017, LNCS 10707, pp. 241–252, 2018.
https://doi.org/10.1007/978-3-319-99843-5_22

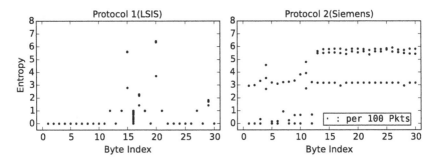

Fig. 1. Byte entropy analysis example of ICS protocols

threats [3,4,6,8]. The target protocol has recently been extended to a binary protocol [11].

Most ICS protocols use binary format and are not text based. However, few protocol reversing studies have been conducted on binary protocols [2,7,10]. [9] focused on ICS protocol reversing based on a byte analysis using statistical method such as Shannon entropy and variance to dissect fields and infer a role of fields. [12] conducted reversing using a byte-level analysis including CRC (Cyclic Redundancy Check), entropy, and etc. for wireless customized protocol over IEEE 802.15.4 in an IoT environment. These researches ignored multi-layer or fragmented packets even though those packets may lead to confusion.

Figure 1 shows the results of the byte entropy analysis performed on ICS protocols without considering the multi-layered protocol structure and fragmentation. In Fig. 1, the packets that conform to the communication protocol structure used by LSIS[1] and Siemens are targeted, and the entropy value of each byte is represented by dots in the first 30 bytes per 100 packets. As shown in the figure, the entropy value of each byte is remarkably stable in the left but not in the right. The gap between the dots in the right graph resulted from the packet fragmentation due to by a low computing/networking power of the ICS devices. The fragmentation packets must be preprocessed before performing a byte-level analysis to obtain an accurate and reliable analysis result. The multi-layered protocol structure is another obstacle to the automatic analysis because the starting position of the subsequent layer varies.

In this paper, we propose a process to infer the fields of the binary ICS protocol from the network traffic. First, we identified the characteristics of the fields that are mainly used in the ICS protocols. Based on the characteristics, we employed a filtering strategy wherein only those packets appropriate for each step of the analysis were selected. After filtering the packets, we repeatedly obtained the protocol fields from not only the characteristics of the byte at each position (such as entropy, number of unique values, and increasing tendency) but also from the structural patterns of the ICS protocol.

---

[1] LS Industrial Systems, http://www.lsis.com/.

Table 1. Typical ICS protocol field

Category	Related field
Protocol/session	Protocol identifier, Protocol version, Session ID, Transaction ID
Packet assemble	Total block, Current block, Start/End flag
Length	Length of total packet, Length of current packet, Length of current layer
Command	Command, Sub-command, Request-Response(flag)
Network address	Sender address, Receiver address, Master ID, Slave ID
Memory address	Memory address value, Memory name
Data size	Item count, Item size, Request size
CRC	CRC
Time	Time, Date

The rest of this paper is organized as follows. Section 2 addresses background of the ICS protocol. In Sect. 3, we explain the strategies designed to distinguish each field in ICS protocol. In Sect. 4, we present the proposed process for reversing the protocol. Finally, in Sect. 5, the conclusions of this study are given.

2   Background : ICS Protocol

The conventional ICS protocol was designed to obtain the values measured from the sensors and to control the actuators. The protocol behavior generally comprises 'connection initialization', 'data read/write' and 'connection termination'. Nowadays, the ICS protocols are specialized for each requirement in various areas such as industrial automation, process control system, and vehicle automation systems.

2.1   Difficulties of ICS Protocol Analysis

Although the structures of ICS Protocols are considered as simple, they are more complicated than expected. The relatively new protocols, such as EtherNet/IP or S7Comm, provide diverse functions such as 'memory read/write', 'configuration of devices', 'file transfer', 'control logic upload/download', 'firmware update', and 'user authentication'. Moreover, latest protocols comprise multi-layers and variable-length fields.

It is difficult to obtain an *exact specification* of the ICS protocols. Many vendors use their own private protocols, which they do not share with the public. Although some systems use a public protocol, it often does not exactly follow the protocol standard. Fragmentation or repeated re-transmission caused by deficient computing power of ICS devices is another obstacle to the analysis.

2.2 Common Fields of ICS Protocols

Based on the analyses of several ICS protocols, typical fields such as protocol identifier, protocol version, packet length, and command are commonly used in many ICS protocols, though different names are given in their specifications. We categorized the frequently used fields of the ICS protocols into nine groups. Thereafter, we extracted the characteristics of each field based on the entropy, number of unique values, and increasing tendency. Table 1 lists the fields of each category. We use these characteristics as decision criteria to infer the field of the ICS protocol.

3   Proposed Approach

We analyzed several control system protocols, such as S7Comm (Siemens S7-1500), EtherNet/IP, and DNP 3.0, and LSIS protocols. The accuracy of inferring the field depends on the type of packets analyzed. This section describes a method of selecting the packets among the entire network traffic for each field inference analysis based on the field-specific characteristics.

3.1   Fixed Position Field Inference

Some fields in most packets are fixed at the same position, but not in all packets. To obtain such fixed-position fields, we filter the exceptional packets.

- **Maximum size packets** may appear along with fragmentation. Fragmentation can randomize field positions at each packet.
- **Minimum size packets** can be considered simple acknowledgement packets with no specific field values.
- **Packets during session initiation or termination** usually have different structures particularly when the protocol is multi-layered.

After filtering the packets, we focus on a field wherein only fixed values are used. When the same value is continuously found at the same byte position from several packets in the same session, we infer that the position is either a protocol header or a session identifier. When continuous '0x00's remain the same in the sessions, the fields may be reserved. If the byte values in one session are the same and are different in other sessions, the field may represent a session identifier. We are convinced of the session identifier if the values are set at an early stage of the session. The command fields have few unique values and only some command values, such as *read*, are mainly used. This tendency is more prominent after filtering packets pertaining to initialization and termination.

We also investigate fields where the values vary widely. When the packets are sorted in the order received, a field wherein the value sequentially increased is considered as a sequence number. Figure 2 shows the characteristics of the sequence field described above. In the figure, we show the first 30 bytes of the

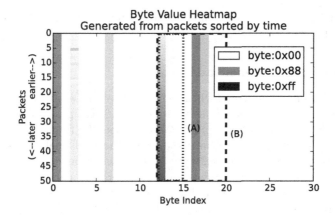

Fig. 2. Sequence field characteristic

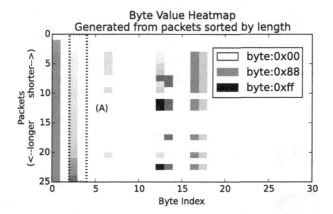

Fig. 3. Length field characteristic

packets sorted in chronological order as black from white, which implies hexadecimal '0x00' to hexadecimal '0xFF'. As shown in the figure, the region corresponding to 'A' indicates the automatically deduced sequence field. However, in practice, the byte range corresponding to the region 'B' is a sequence field. If the packets were fully analyzed, the range of the bytes corresponding to the region B can be identified as a sequence field because the byte value changes beyond the '0xFF' to the next byte.

The other characteristics of the fields are evident when the sorting criteria changes. Figure 3 shows the value of each byte in the form of a heatmap by arranging the packet length order. The gradations of color of 'A' in the figure shows strong relationship with the length of packets. Therefore, we infer the byte position of 'A' as a length field. Similar to the characteristics of the sequence and the length fields in the ICS protocols, the fixed-position fields were extracted

using the entropy, uniqueness, and increasing tendency with the help of the
sorting and filtering strategies.

3.2 Assembling of Fragmented Packets

The packets become fragmented when a client repeatedly sends the packets prior
to receiving the response from the server-side or when the protocol was originally
designed with fragmentation in mind. We excluded the fragmented packets at
the early stage of the analysis because they make the statistical analysis difficult.
However, after the fixed-positioned byte analysis, we obtained clues to assemble
the packets. Figure 4 shows the common fragmentation pattern of ICS Protocols. The first and second cases could be neglected because the protocol header
was easily identified. In the third case, it is possible to easily analyze when the
packets having the maximum length are filtered. To deal with the last case, we
need to determine the beginning of each fragmented packet. In the worst case, it
may be assumed that all the packets are fragmented, and thus, we cannot find
any characteristics of the position of each byte. We need to obtain the packet
header through some speculations. The most reasonable assumption is that frequently used bytes can be a candidate as protocol identifiers. Each assumption
is validated by testing other packets. As we obtain more well-organized packets
via defragmentation, the statistical analysis becomes easier.

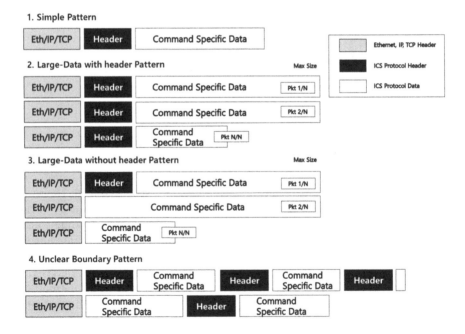

Fig. 4. Common fragmentation patterns in ICS protocols

3.3   Variable-Length Field Inference

After identifying the fixed-position fields, we need to infer a length-variable field and command-related optional fields in the ICS protocols. Typical ICS protocols were used for long durations only with minor changes over various physical layers, from serial communication to TCP/IP. To maximize the productivity of the ICS protocol knowledge, the developers encapsulated a legacy protocol structure into the TCP/IP. That is the reason why current many ICS Protocols have multiple application layer (OSI 7) like DNP 3.0 and EtherNet/IP. The length of the first or mid-layer of the ICS protocol can be changed during the communication. The length of the variable layer must be known for the ICS protocol parser to properly parse the incoming packets. Hence, the packets must contain the length information in the variable-length layer or in the previous layer.

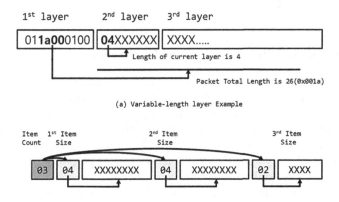

Fig. 5. Variable-length field example

One of the challenges is finding the end of the variable-length layer such as that in fragmentation analysis. We considered statistically meaningful byte values at the beginning of the following layer because frequently used byte values may be a protocol identifier (fixed value) or a command-like value (frequently used value). This assumption was acceptable for the inspected ICS protocols, and hence, we extended our approach to other ICS protocols. The strategy for searching the command-related optional fields involves clustering the packets using the same command. One of the candidate field is 'sub-command', which can be found as command field inference. 'Item count' and 'item length' pattern used in read-like or write-like command packets are common. We believe that these patterns are used when the client or server sends several sub-items at once, as shown in Fig. 5(b). To distinguish these item description field from the item data, we need to focus on smaller values (between 0x01–0x10) which can be used mostly item count and item length. First, we choose small-value bytes in front part of packets as a candidate of the item length. In the case shown in Fig. 5(b), first byte (0x03) and second byte (0x04) are chosen as candidates. Next, we examined the byte value after the small value(3 or 4) to check whether our assumption is valid. After repeated inspection, We could tentatively assume that the first byte represented the item count and the second, seventh and twelfth bytes represented the item length. Finally, we checked the other packets to confirm whether the assumption is correct.

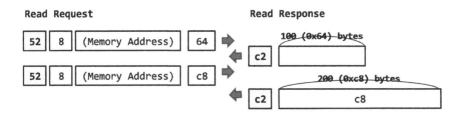

Fig. 6. Client-server relationship example

3.4   Client-Server Relationship Field Inference

When examining the relationship between the packets from a client and a server, we obtain more information about the protocol fields. One of the typical fields related to the clientserver relationship is a *request/response field*. The type of the request/response field varies based on the protocol format. In some protocols, the entire byte is used to determine whether the packet is a request or a response. In other protocols, only a single bit flag is used as the response flag. Sometimes, the field is discovered only on one side.

Further, we can infer a *request size field* through a client-server pair size analysis. For example, the command, such as 'read', specifies the size to be read. The request size field becomes clear after grouping the client-server pairs into the same read-like command. Figure 6 shows a common pattern of the ICS protocols. After the client sends a read request (0x52) packet with a start address and the size to be read, the server replies with response flag (0x52 | 0x80) along with the requested data. In this example, we could extract more meaningful fields through the clientserver relationship analysis.

4   Field Inference Process

In this section, we explain the proposed field inference process described in Fig. 7. and explain the detailed operation of the length-field inference.

4.1   Proposed Process

The first step in the process of inferring the field is splitting the sessions. During the preprocessing, we select appropriate filters and packets assemblers. In the first cycle it is desirable to perform analysis except for the small size of packets, which probably indicate simple acknowledgement, and large size of packets,

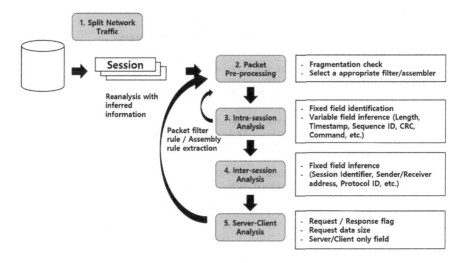

Fig. 7. Packet field inference process

which probably indicate fragmentation. As the analysis proceeds, more reliable filter and assemble rules may be found. During the intra-session analysis, we check whether the fixed position byte in the session has a variable value such as CRC, time stamp, and sequences. In the following step, the inter-session analysis is performed. In this stage, as the characteristic of the fixed-value bytes becomes more concrete, we can extract the protocol ID, session ID, network address, and other fields. Finally, server-client analysis is carried out to check and compare the value where the field is related to response flag or found in the response packet only. At the end of one cycle, the analysis is started again using the calculated information to obtain more precise results.

Figure 8 shows the proposed length-field inference algorithm in detail. First, the packets with the same length are divided into each same-length packet group. As the length field should not change among the same-length packets, the *changing bytes* in the packet group are discarded. Every candidate byte was calculated from each packet group. Second, we compared candidate bytes with the ones computed from the packet groups with different lengths. We obtained the second-stage candidate bytes after discarding the *non-changing bytes* because length field should change among the different-length packets. However, the non-changing '0x00's adjacent to the second stage candidate bytes are not discarded at this time. The '0x00's adjacent to the changing bytes could possibly belong to length field. Finally, We could determine a length field after checking direct proportional relationship between candidate bytes and the length of packets. The third and fourth bytes of the application layer, shown in Fig. 8, were inferred as the length field by following the described procedures.

```
Step 1. Discard 'changing bytes' among same-length
        packets

len(46)-1: 6f00160001000b0000000000001400....
len(46)-2: 6f00160001000b0000000000001600....
len(46)-3: 6f00160001000b0000000000001800....

Step 2. Select 'changing bytes' and
        '0x00' adjacent to the 'changing bytes'
        among different-length packets

len(46)  : 6f00160001000b0000000000--00....
len(50)  : --001a0001000b0000000000--00....
len(51)  : 70001b0001000b00000000000000....
len(52)  : --001c0001000b0000000000--00....
....
....
Len(349) : 700045010001000b000000000000000000....

Step 3. Find length-candidate bytes and
        calculate length formula

Final
Results  : --00++++----------------------....
```

Fig. 8. Length field inference process

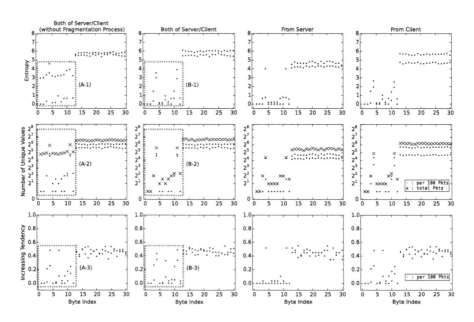

Fig. 9. Fragmented protocol analysis results

4.2   Prototype Result

We applied the proposed method to the fragmented protocol (e.g. S7Comm) and obtained the results. Figure 9 shows the three types of characteristics at each byte position: the entropy, number of unique values, and increasing tendency. For each characteristic per 100 packets marked with dots, the total unique values during the session are represented with the symbol 'X'. Each analysis was conducted on a client, a server, and both. To demonstrate the efficiency of our approach, we show the analysis result obtained without assembling the fragmentation packets in the leftmost column. The areas 'A-1', 'A-2', and 'A-3' in the figure show that the characteristic of each byte position is not uniform, making it difficult for automatic inference. However, the areas 'B-1', 'B-2', and 'B-3' in the figure are representative of uniform characteristics. This is very helpful for reverse engineering the automated ICS protocol. We could easily infer a protocol identifier, a packet length field, and other fields.

5   Conclusion

The ICS protocol analysis is essential in protecting the ICS from the increasing number of cyber threats. Because the ICS protocols are not as simple as expected and their exact specifications are difficult to acquire, an automated analysis tool is necessary for reverse engineering the ICS protocol. In this paper, we presented a reverse engineering process to deal with the variable structures and fragmentation of the ICS binary protocols. We implemented a prototype tool based on the proposed process and demonstrated how it can be used in the ICS protocol reversing analysis. In the near future, we will analyze and present more ICS protocol fields and its characteristics. Further, we will apply our prototype to other known and unknown ICS protocols and enhance the accuracy of the prototype.

References

1. Caballero, J., Song, D.: Polyglot: automatic extraction of protocol message format using dynamic binary analysis. In: Proceedings of the 14th ACM Conference on Computer and Communications Security, pp. 317–329 (2007)
2. Cui, W., Kannan, J., Wang, H.J.: Discoverer: automatic protocol reverse engineering from network traces. In: USENIX Security, pp. 199–212 (2007)
3. Caballero, J., Poosankam, P., Kreibich, C., Song, D.: Dispatcher: enabling active botnet infiltration using automatic protocol reverse-engineering. In: ACM Conference on Computer and Communications Security, pp. 621–634 (2009)
4. Wang, Z., Jiang, X., Cui, W., Wang, X., Grace, M.: ReFormat: automatic reverse engineering of encrypted messages. In: Backes, M., Ning, P. (eds.) ESORICS 2009. LNCS, vol. 5789, pp. 200–215. Springer, Heidelberg (2009). https://doi.org/10. 1007/978-3-642-04444-1_13
5. Li, H., Shuai, B., Wang, J., Tang, C.: Protocol feature word construction based on machine learning n-gram generation, pp. 93–97 (2011)

6. Caballero, J., Song, D.: Automatic protocol reverse-engineering: message format extraction and field semantics inference. Comput. Netw. **57**, 451–474 (2013)
7. Luo, J.Z., Yu, S.Z.: Position-based automatic reverse engineering of network protocols. J. Netw. Comput. Appl. **36**, 1070–1077 (2013)
8. Sood, A.K., Enbody, R.J., Bansal, R.: Dissecting SpyEye-Understanding the design of third generation botnets. Comput. Netw. **57**, 436–450 (2013)
9. Choi, S., Chang, Y., Yun, J.-H., Kim, W.: Multivariate statistic approach to field specifications of binary protocols in SCADA system. In: Rhee, K.-H., Yi, J.H. (eds.) WISA 2014. LNCS, vol. 8909, pp. 345–357. Springer, Cham (2015). https://doi.org/10.1007/978-3-319-15087-1_27
10. Tao, S., Yu, H., Li, Q.: Bit-oriented format extraction approach for automatic binary protocol reverse engineering, pp. 709–716 (2015)
11. Bermudez, I., Tongaonkar, A., Iliofotou, M., Mellia, M., Munaf, M.M.: Towards automatic protocol field inference. Comput. Commun. **84**, 40–51 (2016)
12. Choi, K., Son, Y., Noh, J., Shin, H., Choi, J., Kim, Y.: Dissecting customized protocols: automatic analysis for customized protocols based on IEEE 802.15.4. In: ACM Conference on Security and Privacy in Wireless and Mobile Networks, pp. 183–193 (2016)

Motion Magnification for Urban Buildings

Vincenzo Fioriti[(✉)], Ivan Roselli, Angelo Tati, Roberto Romano,
and Gerardo De Canio

ENEA, Casaccia R. C., S. Maria Di Galeria 301, 00123 Rome, Italy
vincenzo.fioriti@enea.it

Abstract. Vibration monitoring of buildings in the urban environment is a relevant issue for health survey and early damaging detection in sustainable and enhanced resilient cities. To this end, we explore the potentialities of vibration monitoring by motion magnification analysis that acts like a microscope for motion in video sequences, but affecting only some groups of pixels. The magnified motion is a new discipline in the field of the analysis of mechanical structures and buildings. It was developed from the analysis of small motions in videos. The motion magnification uses the spatial resolution of the video camera to extract physical properties from images to make inferences about the dynamical behavior of the observed object. The methodology does not rely on optics, but on algorithms capable to amplify only the tiny changes in the video frames, while the large ones remain. Recently, a number of experiments conducted on simple geometries like rods and other small objects, as well as on bridges, showed the reliability of this methodology compared to accelerometers and laser vibrometers. The extension of magnified motion to monitoring of buildings would provide many advantages: a clear, simple, immediate and intuitive diagnosis of the structure, flexibility, predictive potentialities, ease of use, low costs. But also some difficulties still do exist and are discussed. Here we give an introduction to the methodology and some case-studies, both in laboratory and in the real-world (see videos from the link): applications to the short-term urban resilience is straightforward.

Keywords: Resilience · Video · Magnified motion

1 Introduction

Evaluating the health of a large urban structure or of a building in a short time span and possibly by simple devices that do not require expert operators may be a pivotal issue of the urban resilience, especially after natural disasters or an explosion. Thus, the availability of simple and intuitive methodologies such as those based on a digital acquisition of images could result in a major breakthrough for the evaluation of the buildings resilience, especially for the short-term [1]. However, the analysis of image sequences in the field of civil engineering is not new. For many years attempts to produce qualitative (visual) and even quantitative analysis using high quality videos of large structures have been conducted, but with poor results. This was because of the resolution in terms of pixels, of the noise, of the camera frame rate, computer time and finally because of the lack of appropriate algorithms able to deal with the extremely

© Springer Nature Switzerland AG 2018
G. D'Agostino and A. Scala (Eds.): CRITIS 2017, LNCS 10707, pp. 253–260, 2018.
https://doi.org/10.1007/978-3-319-99843-5_23

small motions related to a building displacement. These and others limitations have restricted the applications of digital vision methodologies to just a few cases. Nevertheless, recently important advances have been obtained by Freeman and collaborators of the Massachusetts Institute of Technology (MIT) [2]. Their algorithms, named motion magnification (MM), seems able to act like a microscope for motion and, more importantly, in a reasonably short computer time. The latter point is crucial, as it is well known that video processing takes a lot of time and resources. Therefore, any viable approach must consider the reduction of the calculation time as an absolute priority. The basic MM version looks at intensity variations of each pixel and amplifies them, revealing small motions which are linearly related to intensity changes through a first order Taylor series for small pixel motions. Since our intention is only to give a general idea of the potentiality of the motion magnification in the protection of critical infrastructures, with particular regard to applications for urban resilience, we will not enter into the full formal description of the algorithms, rather we will propose some practical implementation examples.

2 The Magnified Motion

Videos are made up of a temporal sequence of 2D images, whose pixel intensity is $I(x, t)$. The 2D array of color intensity is the spatial domain, while the time domain corresponds to the temporal sequence. Here, in order to describe the Eulerian version of the magnification algorithm [2], we consider only a 1-D translating image with displacement $\delta(t)$. $I(x, 0) = f(x)$ at the image-position x and video-time $t = 0$ (for the treatment of the general problem, see [2–4]). We have:

$$I(x, t) = f(x - \delta(t)) \tag{1}$$

The final expression of its motion magnified by constant α is defined as:

$$\Delta I = f(x - (1 + \alpha)\delta(t)) \tag{2}$$

Now, if the displacement $\delta(t)$ is small enough, it is possible to expand the relation (1) as Taylor's first order series around x, at time t:

$$I(x, t) = f(x) - \delta(t)(\partial f/\partial x) + \varepsilon \tag{3}$$

where ε is the error due to the Taylor's approximation and to δ being non-zero. The intensity change at each pixel can be expressed as:

$$\Delta(x, t) = I(x, t) - I(x, 0) \tag{4}$$

Which, taking into account Eq. (3), becomes:

$$\Delta(x, t) = f(x) - \delta(t) \, (\partial f / \partial x) + \varepsilon - f(x) \tag{5}$$

and finally:

$$\Delta(x, t) \approx -\delta(t) \, (\partial f / \partial x) \tag{6}$$

disregarding the error ε, meaning that the absolute pixel intensity variation Δ is proportional to the displacement and to the spatial gradient. Therefore, pixel intensity can be written as follows:

$$I(x, t) \approx I(x, 0) + \Delta(x, t) \tag{7}$$

Magnifying motion by a given constant α, using Eqs. (3) and (4), simply means that pixel intensity $I(x, t)$ is replaced by magnified pixel intensity $I_{magn}(x, t)$ according to the following:

$$I_{magn}(x, t) \approx I(x, 0) + \alpha \, \Delta(x, t) \approx f(x) - \delta(t) \, (\partial f / \partial x) - \alpha \, \delta(t) \, (\partial f / \partial x) + O(\varepsilon, \delta) \tag{8}$$

where $O(\varepsilon, \delta)$ is the remainder of the Taylor series. Finally, magnified intensity can be calculated as:

$$I_{magn}(x, t) \approx f(x) - (1 + \alpha)\delta(t) \, (\partial f / \partial x) \tag{9}$$

but Eq. (9) is immediately derived from the first order Taylor's expansion of the magnified motion of the following:

$$\Delta I = f(x - (1 + \alpha) \, \delta(t)) \tag{10}$$

It is important to observe that (6) is obtained by a band-pass derivation, thus the process can be basically summarized as in Fig. 1. Therefore, we can say that to magnify the motion displacement it suffices to add $\alpha \Delta(x, t)$ to $I(x, t)$, as long as the Taylor's expansion (9) is valid, that is until its remainder $O(\varepsilon, \alpha)$ is small. This limitation depends on the linear approach entailed in the Taylor's expansion, either if the initial expansion (3) or the amplification α are too large. In practice, to remain into the linearity bound, we need slowly changing images and small amplifications.

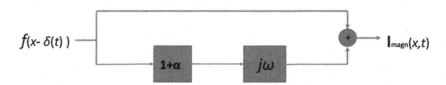

Fig. 1. Temporal filtering applied to each pixel time history. Cut-off frequencies have to be chosen carefully in order to enclose the band of the phenomenon to be analyzed and exclude other frequencies.

Moreover, here we do not consider the noise of variance σ^2 to be added to the intensity, that is amplified too, resulting in an amplified noise variance $2\sigma^2\alpha^2$, thus the error to be evaluated should be $O(\varepsilon, \alpha, 2\sigma^2\alpha^2)$. Also, it should be noted that the calculation of $\Delta(x, t)$ implies the whole time span needed from frame 0 to the current frame at the time t.

If the video is a long-lasting one, the calculation time may be a major problem.

Other physical limitations, such as the ones regarding illumination, shadows, camera unwanted vibrations, poor pixel resolution, low frame rate, presence of large motion, distance from the object, decrease severely the quality of the motion magnification, should also be taken into account in order to achieve good-quality results. In particular, the scene illumination should remain constant, as changing the background light could produce apparent motions.

3 Case Studies

Some videos have been recorded by means of low resolution, low frame-rate video cameras, in laboratory and outdoor in an urban environment. The laboratory tests have been carried out at the ENEA shaking tables facility of the Casaccia research center, located near Rome, Italy, on a scaled model of an ancient church and on a full-scale model of a two-story reinforced concrete structure. The experimentation in urban environment concerned a public building situated in Rome, very close to a tramway. Vibrations induced by the shaking table and by the trams produced small displacements on the specimens and on the building, hardly or not visible to the eye, but clearly evident after the magnification (see or download ppt Video 1_11 and Videos 2, 22, 3, 33 [9]).

During the laboratory tests, a 1:10 scaled mockup of the ancient church of Hagia Irene, located in the ancient Constantinople, was perturbed by base vibrations simulating the effect of an earthquake (Figs. 2 and 3).

Such excitation reproduced by the shaking table (were based on real ground motion recordings [5]. The quality of Hagia Irene ppt Video 1_11 is poor, due to the low illumination, shadows and to the recording device.

Thus, a skeletonization has been applied to the magnified video to reduce noise and to facilitate the understanding of the displacements. Note also that even if the displacement in the original source were not easily distinguishable to the naked eye, nevertheless they were large enough to disturb the algorithm, confirming what was stated before in the previous section. As a consequence, large distortions of the images are generated.

Analogously, in the Videos 2, 22 the reinforced concrete structure is also perturbed by a reproduced seismic motion [6]. In the original version it is possible to observe the table and a wire on the left moving, but the structure appears still, while after the processing of the video the displacements are evident, making clear the dynamic behavior of the structure. In fact, in such seismic tests the dynamic behavior of specimens is usually studied by analyzing the data acquired by numerous sensors able to record the motion parameters (acceleration, displacements, etc.) in a series of measurement points. In this context, MM can give a valuable contribution to

Fig. 2. The mockup of Hagia Irene, tested on shaking table at ENEA Casaccia Research Center (from the original ppt Video 1_11 [9]).

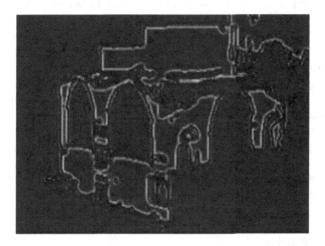

Fig. 3. The magnified skeletonization of Hagia Irene (from magnified ppt Video 1_11 [9]).

comprehend the overall dynamic behavior of structures, as if they were monitored by an amount of "virtual sensors" as numerous as the frame pixels, without installing any physical instrument. In this sense, the MM technique enables a predictive, non-contact capability of enormous potentiality.

All recordings last no more than one minute, requiring about 30 min of computer elaboration, once the algorithm parameters have been set (Fig. 4).

Having demonstrated the viability of MM for large structures in a laboratory, we turn to the application to buildings in the real urban environment. We recorded Videos 3, 33 (30 fps, pixel resolution 720 × 1280) at 12:30 (Rome local time) during a sunny day, air temperature of 20 °C, moderately windy. Such videos show a public building,

Fig. 4. The reinforced concrete structure (from the original Video 2 [9]).

dated back to the 1930s, located close to an urban road. Besides road traffic, also heavy trams pass by on tramways at a distance of less than 8 m from the building. The building is depicted in Fig. 5: an antenna at the top left, two poles and two flags at the bottom right are present in the image. The flags waving in the wind and the larger pole on the road surface supporting the tramway electric supply system are moving too much, affecting the MM algorithms with noise. The presence of large motions is the most significant disadvantage of MM, requiring the experimenter to isolate part of the image, but usually this is not a feasible option. The issue is still open.

In the magnified Video 33, in addition to the antenna and the pole, it is possible to observe the edges of the building oscillating. However, these motions are affected by noise because of shadows, camera unwanted vibrations, poor pixel resolution, low frame rate, presence of large motion, such as the waving flags. Many of these drawbacks could be fixed easily increasing the pixel resolution and the frame rate of the video camera. Anyway, the displacements at the edges are well defined, mitigating the noise problem and allowing more accurate measurements with respect to non-textured surfaces of the buildings.

The antenna and the smaller pole are built-in to the building, thus their vibrations depend directly on the building, but are more evident respect to the vibrations of the walls (see the MM of Video 33).

This circumstance makes possible to devise these elements as some sort of virtual sensors that are particularly sensitive to vibrations. Pixels locations of the antenna and pole at each frame may be considered (though not directly) as the time series of the displacements.

Spectral analysis of videos may be also performed to detect resonances and modal identification, since MM alters the amplitude of objects motion, but retains objects natural frequencies and modal shapes. Experiments on this issue have been conducted at the ENEA Casaccia SITEC Laboratory on a masonry wall [7]. It is worth noting that the modal parameters, especially the first natural frequency, typically has a fundamental

Fig. 5. The analyzed public building (from the original Video 3 [9]). In the red dotted circle an antenna is highlighted. The red arrow indicates a built-in flagpole. Near it also two flags and another pole supporting the tramway electric supply system are visible. (Color figure online)

role in the diagnosis of the health of the building, as their substantial variation might indicate the arising of possible structural damage [8]. Download videos at the link [9].

4 Conclusions

The estimation of the structural health of urban buildings *ex-post* or *ex-ante* a natural or artificial disaster is a key issue for the urban resilience of infrastructures, but it is mandatory to have quickly available, appropriate, easy-to-use tools. In such context, the continuous developments in digital vision technologies are very promising. Even if till a few years ago such kind of methodologies were not viable, recent advances in the digital image and video processing have opened the door to applications to the analysis of vibrations, in particular by motion magnification strategies. Actually, MM was quite effective in amplifying subtle motions in videos, making distinguishable the tiny displacements of structures exposed to mechanical disturbances and facilitating the evaluation of the building stability within a reasonable time. Advantages are many: a large number of "virtual sensors" available, no wires, no data storage, no physical contact, simplicity, low costs. Unfortunately, for a number of reasons, noise is a pervasive obstacle to MM, especially outdoor. Nevertheless, we obtained satisfactory results also in the urban environment, even using low frame-rate video cameras.

References

1. Bozza, A., Asprone, D., Fabbrocino, F.: Urban resilience: a civil engineering perspective. Sustainability **9**, 103 (2017)
2. Yu-Wu, H. et al.: Eulerian video magnification for revealing subtle changes in the world (2012)
3. https://people.csail.mit.edu/mrub/papers/vidmag.pdf. Accessed 2 Mar 2017
4. Wadhwa, N., et al.: Eulerian video magnification and analysis. Commun. ACM **60**(1), 87–95 (2017)
5. Roselli, I., Mongelli, M., Tati, A., De Canio, G.: Analysis of 3D motion data from shaking table tests on a scaled model of Hagia Irene, Istanbul. Key Eng. Mater. **624**, 66–73 (2015)
6. Mongelli, M., et al.: Experimental tests of reinforced concrete buildings and ENEA DySCo virtual laboratory. In: 5th International Conference on Structural Health Monitoring of Intelligent Infrastructure (SHMII-5), Cancùn, Mexico (2011)
7. Fioriti, V., Roselli, I., Tatì, A., De Canio, G.: Applicazione della vibrometria visuale alla sperimentazione sismica su tavola vibrante. In: 17th Conferenza Nazionale sulle Prove non Distruttive, Milan (2017, accepted)
8. Sinou, J.: A review of damage detection and health monitoring of mechanical systems from changes in the measurement of linear and non-linear vibrations. In: Sapri, R.C. (ed.) Mechanical Vibrations: Measurement, Effects and Control, pp. 643–702. Nova Science Publishers, Inc., New York (2009)
9. https://drive.google.com/drive/folders/0Bz540aXsdKTnVUFHdWxwRHRHazQ?usp=sharing

Reputation Systems to Mitigate DoS Attack in Vehicular Network

Gianpiero Costantino, Fabio Martinelli, and Ilaria Matteucci$^{(\boxtimes)}$

Istituto di Informatica e Telematica, CNR,Via G. Moruzzi, 1, Pisa, Italy
{gianpiero.costantino,fabio.martinelli,ilaria.matteucci}@iit.cnr.it

Abstract. The introduction of ICT systems into vehicles impacts on safety requirements in the automotive domain. We provide a defence mechanism based on two reputation systems: *Rational* and *History-Based* to identify insider attackers and isolate them to preserve the functionalities of the whole system. We focus on the *Denial of Service* attack. Finally, we experimentally evaluate our systems on a real dataset of mobility traces of taxis in Rome.

1 Overview

We propose two reputation systems to detect and prevent the DoS attack [5], aiming at reducing the availability of the network, perpetrated by an insider attacker, within an automotive scenario. The reputation of a vehicle is calculated according to the *principle of collaboration*: a vehicle that sends generated messages more than forwarded ones is *suspected* to be an attacker, while a *collaborative* vehicle behaves in such a way that the functionalities of the network are maintained [2]. Hence, according to the BUG threat model [1], a vehicle can assume three different behaviour: **Bad behaviour** when the vehicle is essentially malicious, neglecting or limiting communications. **Ugly behaviour** when the vehicle assumes an opportunistic behaviour. **Good behaviour** when the vehicle uses its resources to provide V2V communication nodes without any direct interest.

Based on the number of forwarded and generated messages, we calculate the reputation of a vehicle and characterize its behaviour according two possible reputation systems: the *Rational Reputation* (*Rational*) that takes into account the quotient between number of forwarded and generated messages, and a *History Based Trend Reputation* system (*HBT*) that establishes the reputation of each vehicle according to history of forwarded and generated messages during the whole activity period of the vehicle. Then, we experimentally evaluate the two reputation systems on a real dataset of mobility traces of taxis in Rome. As a result, we note that *HBT* system presents some advantages with respect to *Rational*.

This work has been partially supported by the GAUSS (MIUR, PRIN 2015, Contract 2015KWREMX) and by the H2020 EU funded NeCS (GA 675320).

© Springer Nature Switzerland AG 2018
G. D'Agostino and A. Scala (Eds.): CRITIS 2017, LNCS 10707, pp. 261–265, 2018.
https://doi.org/10.1007/978-3-319-99843-5_24

2 The Proposed Reputation-Based Approach

We assume that: (i) the roadside infrastructure acts as a trusted third party, (ii) vehicles are able to observe the behaviour of the other that they meet during the journey and to communicate with the infrastructure, and (iii) all communications preserve the integrity of transmitted data (both messages and local observations). Our approach is composed of four steps: **Local Observation.** Each vehicle performs a *direct observation* of *close* vehicles and evaluates their behaviour by comparing the number of *generated* and *forwarded* messages. When a vehicle receives a message, it checks if it has been generated or forwarded by a close vehicle. This information is stored into a local table, *Vehicles Local Observation* (VLO). **Uploading Local Observation on Central Server.** At fixed time, each vehicle securely[1] transmits the collected values to a central server belonging to the roadside infrastructure by using V2X communications. The roadside infrastructure central server acts as a collector of all local observations done by vehicles. **Global Reputation.** When, the server receives VLOs, it populates its table named *Vehicles Global Observation* (VGO) with aggregated values of generated (G) and forwarded (F) messages sent by each vehicle circulating on the network and calculates a single value of reputation for each vehicle according to different reputation systems. Below, we propose two of them: *Rational Reputation* System and *History-based Trend Reputation* System. **Broadcasting Global Observations.** All vehicles will receive updated reputation values of other vehicles they are able to communicate with.

Rational Reputation System. Rational System is based on the percentage of the forwarded messages w.r.t. the totality of the sent messages [3]. Each vehicle directly observes the behaviour of close vehicles and locally saves how many forwarded and generated messages received from its neighbours in its VLO. Starting from the collection of VLOs of all vehicles, the central server populates its VGO: if the server receives a VLO that contains a new vehicle identity, the server creates a new entry in the table and appends its values of G and F. If the server has already values of G and F, then it updates those values: $G^j_{new} = G^j_{old} + G^j_{rcv}$ and $F^j_{new} = F^j_{old} + F^j_{rcv}$, where G^j_{old} and F^j_{old} represent the number of messages generated and forwarded stored in the VGO for the vehicle j, G^j_{rcv} and F^j_{rcv} represent the number of messages generated and forwarded messages calculated locally for the vehicle j, and G^j_{new} and F^j_{new} are the new values for messages generated by j and the aggregation of the previous two values, respectively. The central server calculates the *global reputation* of each vehicle j as $Rep^j = \frac{F^j}{F^j + G^j}$.

History-Based Trend Reputation System. It is based on the history of the behaviour of a vehicle. The HBT function starts from a neutral value, *i.e.*, 0.5

---

[1] Using a protocol like the Transport Security Layer (TLS) we protect tables integrity from unexpected manipulations.

in the range $[0, 1]$. The reputation of a vehicle increases or decreases according to:

$$HBT(x) = \begin{cases} g(x) & \text{if } x \leq 0.4 \\ z(x) = (f(x) + g(x))/2 & \text{if } 0.4 < x < 0.6 \\ f(x) & \text{if } x \geq 0.6 \end{cases} \tag{1}$$

The server collects all the local observations and for each couple of vehicles T_i and T_W calculates the value $LO_j^{T_i, T_W} = \frac{F_j^{T_i}}{F_j^{T_i} + G_j^{T_i}}$ that represents the local reputation of T_i w.r.t. T_W at the time j. The global reputation at time j is as follows:

$$GO_j^A = \frac{\sum\limits_{i=1}^{n_1} g(LO_j^{A,i}) + \sum\limits_{w=1}^{n_2} f(LO_j^{A,w}) + \sum\limits_{v=1}^{n_3} z(LO_j^{A,v})}{n_1 + n_2 + n_3}$$

where $n_1 + n_2 + n_3$ is the total number of vehicles that met A. Vehicles that send local values greater than 0.6 contribute to the summation of $f(x)$, the ones that send local values lower than 0.4 contribute to the summation of $g(x)$, and local values between 0.4 and 0.6 are summed with $z(x)$.

The History Based Global reputation is calculated as the average between the old value of the global reputation and the new one at time j.

Identification and Isolation of the DoS Attacker. According to the Rational Reputation system, we statically fix the reputation thresholds: $Rep^j \leq 0.3$ is an indication of an anomalous and Bad behaviour; $0.3 < Rep^j < 0.7$ is an Ugly vehicle; a reputation $Rep^j \geq 0.7$ indicates a Good behaviour.

The HBT Reputation system, in addition to reputation, we also calculate a global value denoting if a vehicle in a certain instant in time t_i, according to the current observations should be considered collaborative or not. It is a flag: value 1 if the vehicles is not collaborative and 0 if it is collaborative. A vehicle is not collaborative if: (i) the ratio between the number of forwarded messages and generated one at time t_i is less than 1 and (ii) considering the history of forwarded and generated messages, the sum of the differences between the number of forwarded messages at two consecutive observation instants is lower than or equal to the sum of the difference between the number of generated messages in the same interval of time: $\sum_{i=0}(F_{i+1} - F_i) \leq \sum_{i=0}(G_{i+1} - G_i)$. Hence, a vehicle has a Bad behaviour when the boolean value is set to 1 and the global reputation is less than or equal to 0.4. If one of this two conditions does not hold, we have an Ugly vehicle. If the flag is set to "0" and the reputation is greater than 0.6, then the vehicle is Good.

Once the DoS attackers have been identified as the ones having a Bad behaviour, the other vehicles act as firewall by dropping messages generated by it.

3 Experimental Evaluation

We developed a simulator using Java 8 and we applied on it a dataset of taxis mobility traces, generated in Rome during February 2014, that were stored into a MySQL database. The original mobility trace was downloaded at the *crawdad* web-site (http://crawdad.org/roma/taxi/20140717). and it is composed by 320 taxi mobility traces collected for 30 days. We used a subsets of 199 taxis observed in a period of 48 h, from *2014-02-01 00:00:01* to *2014-02-03 00:00:00*. Taxis are connected to the road infrastructure via the nearest access point, which is connected with the network infrastructure. The entire dataset is stored into a MySQL table to allow our simulator to seamlessly work with the mobility traces. We start from the first time-stamp, and we verify if there are two close taxis (the distance between the two taxies is minor than *200* m, calculated using the latitude and longitude available for both taxis considering the earth radius equal to *6.371.000* m). Each time that two taxis are close, they forward all messages they have in their messages-buffer identified on two different ways: *forwarded* or *generated*. The upload of VLO tables to the central server is triggered every 30 min, moment in which each taxi offloads its VLO table to the server that calculates the global reputation of any taxi. As final step, the server broadcasts every 30 min the VGO table to all taxis. We adopted the *push*-model according to a vehicle sends its VLO table to the server and, then, it pushes the VGO to the same vehicle exploiting the same active-connection. To validate and compare our reputation systems we run several simulations that lasted 48 h of time-trace and lower than 10 min of real time. We selected 4 taxis as packet generators (they generates more than *6000* message transmissions overloading the V2V infrastructure). In addition, we set the Time-To Live (TTL) for each message equal to one day from the moment when the message is generated. Also, a message is not forwarded any-more when the Hop Counter is equal to 2. Figure 1 shows the reputation of a taxi that starts as Good and then becomes Bad.

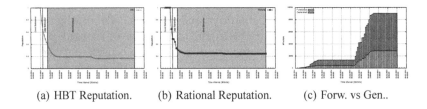

(a) HBT Reputation.   (b) Rational Reputation.   (c) Forw. vs Gen..

Fig. 1. Reputation observed of a taxi that switches its behaviour from good-to-bad.

4   Related Work and Conclusion

Most of the existing works are survey on reputation systems in Vehicular Networks or applications of solution to asses security in such networks. [6] presented a systematic review of existing papers about trust models in VANETs from 2005 and 2014. All reviewed reputation systems has not a central entities able to collect local observations and acts as a trusted third parties. [4] proposed a novel reputation management framework in an automotive VANETS that integrates entity-centric and event-centric mechanism. They consider the roadside infrastructure as a central point to collect vehicles observations but they know the mobility trace in advance. Here, we presented two *Rational* and *History-Based* reputation systems as a mechanism to detect and mitigate the DoS attack on a vehicular network. We developed a simulator to experimental evaluated and compare the two reputation systems on a real dataset of mobility traces of taxis in Rome.

References

1. Bella, G., Bistarelli, S., Massacci, F.: Retaliation: can we live with flaws? In: Workshop on Information Security Assurance and Security (2005)
2. Bella, G., Costantino, G., Riccobene, S.: Managing reputation over MANETs. In: Proceedings of the 4th International Conference on IAS 2008, pp. 255–260, September 2008
3. Costantino, G., Martinelli, F., Matteucci, I.: Exploiting vehicles' reputation to mitigate dos attack. In: Proceedings of the AMARETTO@MODELSWARD, pp. 75–82
4. Ding, Q., Li, X., Jiang, M., Zhou, X.: A novel reputation management framework for vehicular ad hoc networks. Int. J. of Mult. Tech. **3**(2), 62–66 (2013)
5. Razzaque, M., Salehi, A., Cheraghi, S.M.: Security and privacy in vehicular ad-hoc networks: survey and the road ahead. In: Khan, S., Khan Pathan, A.S. (eds.) Wireless Networks and Security. SCT, pp. 107–132. Springer, Heidelberg (2013). https://doi.org/10.1007/978-3-642-36169-2_4
6. Soleymani, S.A., et al.: Trust management in vehicular ad hoc network: a systematic review. EURASIP J. Wirel. Commun. Netw. **2015**(1), 146 (2015)

On the Security of Aircraft Communication Networks

Paul Berthier[✉], Corentin Bresteau, and José Fernandez

Polytechnique Montreal, 2900 Edouard Montpetit Blvd, Montreal, QC H3T 1J4,
Canada
{paul.berthier,corentin.bresteau,jose.fernandez}@polymtl.ca

Abstract. Modern aircraft now rely on complex navigation systems and communication networks which must be highly reliable in order to allow air travel to remain one of the safest modes of transportation. This article presents a high level description of those systems and introduces the different security threats which could affect them.

Keywords: Aviation networks · ATM · Secure communications

1 Introduction

The increasing complexity of commercial aircraft has triggered a massive use of computers and networks inside them. The safety of any flight is now highly relying on autonomous systems. These same systems depend on the normal operation of communication networks to ensure flight safety. Even though the increased use of networks on aircraft can improve flight performances and safety on many levels, they also represent a new attack surface for deliberate threats, making aircraft prime targets for cyber-attacks.

This situation creates the need for a security review of commercial aircraft communication networks. In this article, we present a high-level analysis of potential security threats caused by the extensive use of communication networks. Each subnetwork of an aircraft and a basic explanation of their operation will be conducted. Furthermore, we will identify potential threats related to both internal and external communications.

2 Description of Aviation Networks

2.1 Classification of Inner Networks

As commercial aircraft exchange more and more data, we need to identify which protocols and which networks are critical for the flight safety. Multiple studies identify three distinct networks inside most modern commercial airliners [8]: passenger network, crew network and command network.

© Springer Nature Switzerland AG 2018
G. D'Agostino and A. Scala (Eds.): CRITIS 2017, LNCS 10707, pp. 266–269, 2018.
https://doi.org/10.1007/978-3-319-99843-5_25

The **passenger network** allows travelers to enjoy different in-flight enter-tainment and provides non-critical information about the flight (position, speed, altitude). Moreover, some airlines now supply Internet access to their passenger for the whole duration of the flight. This network is the only one that allows connection of private devices, such as smart phones, laptops, etc.

The **crew network** is used by the flight crew for monitoring purposes and allows them to communicate with the cabin and the cockpit.

Finally, as its name suggests, the **command network** is the most criti-cal system. All avionics information - e.g. the pilot and autopilot instructions, navigation information, etc. - transit via this network. If it were to become unavailable, the safety of the flight would be highly endangered.

It is also important to consider that these networks communicate between themselves. For instance, the In-Flight Entertainment system (IFE) has access to the plane's position, velocity and altitude supplied by avionics components.

2.2   Communication Network Standards

Commercial aircraft communication networks used to be mainly based on the ARINC 429 standard. It allows unidirectional communication between the dif-ferent components of the same network. Some components are only capable of writing information, and others have only read access. In aircraft using ARINC 429, the networks are segregated at the physical layer and are completely inde-pendent. This results in high security since it is impossible for an attacker to access the command network from the passenger network.

However, the amount of information exchanged between avionics elements in recent airliners has become so important that a new protocol was needed. Airbus developed an Ethernet-based protocol called Avionics Full Duplex - AFDX. It was later adopted as the ARINC 664 Standard [5]. AFDX offers much improve-ment over its predecessor. It allows full duplex communication, thus reducing the number of cables needed and therefore the weight of the plane. However, the subnetworks (passenger, command and crew) now share the same physical layer. The separation between them is based on virtual networks and relies entirely on switches [8]. The exact impact of the shared physical layer on the potential attack surface is still to be determined.

2.3   Wireless Communication

Besides local communications, aircraft also need to be able to communicate with the ground and other aircraft at any time for various reasons - e.g. Air Traffic Control (ATC), airline company communication, etc.

Aircraft have always relied on radio signals, first for voice communication and navigation and more recently for performance and safety monitoring. In the 70s, a system of datalink was implemented allowing aircraft to exchange data over VHF, HF or SATCOM, called Aircraft Communication Addressing and Report-ing System (ACARS). Datalink does not actually represent a protocol, but rather a set of protocols and equipment deployed in order to enable data communication over radio links. It offers numerous services and allows the exchange of various types of information, both from ground to aircraft and between aircraft. Among all the proposed services, it is important to underline Automatic Dependent Surveillance Broadcast (ADS-B) used by aircraft to report their position and speed regularly to the controllers and other surrounding aircraft. Other services such as Controller-Pilot Data Link (CPDLC) are used to operate air traffic control operations, thus potentially replacing voice communication in that role.

3   Potential Threats

Over the last decades, much effort has been carried out in order to make aviation safe. High reliability standards are achieved through extensive testing and certification processes, and through redundancy in critical systems. This has resulted in one of the lowest accident rates amongst transportation modes, with only one major accident for every 3.1 million flights [7].

However, security has received much less consideration until the 9/11 attack, when security measures were taken to prevent dangerous items from being brought inside aircraft and to restrict cockpit access. Nevertheless, attacks on the communication systems of an aircraft have not been extensively studied. When talking about information systems security, three main topics are usually discussed: availability, confidentiality and authentication/integrity. Those concepts remain valid in the context of aviation:

Availability is essential for critical systems and their data sources. The control network of the aircraft and data coming from its different sensors (altitude, speed, compass, etc.) has to be protected from Denial of Service (DoS) attacks. A single failure on those systems could cause the loss of the aircraft. Communication with the Air Traffic Controllers are also critical to prevent collisions. If a critical system becomes unavailable, the pilot should start a forced emergency landing procedure. A temporary failure of the crew network prevents a commercial plane from being operated normally, because the crew is no longer able to monitor the cabin. The plane should start a precautionary emergency landing in order to abide by ICAO security procedures [3], but the security of the aircraft is not compromised as the pilots remain in control. The unavailability of the passengers networks may lower the company's prestige as the flight would not deliver the expected services, even though the safety is not affected. Availability is very difficult to be guaranteed for wireless communication protocols, like ADS-B as it would be very easy for an attacker to jam the frequency used.

Confidentiality is generally not considered as a security objective in aviation. It is even sometimes the opposite. For example, ADS-B data is used by some websites to display aircraft position in real time [4]. However, in some situations, confidentiality may remain necessary. It is the case of some communication between an airline and the aircraft it operates, or between a plane and control towers.

Even if they are not critical for a flight safety, some of them can harm the airline's reputation, give personal information about passengers or even violate pilot privacy. As an example, we intercepted a CPDLC message near the Montreal airport: *Good day Greg... Summer is coming up... Gas pricing rising... If you're interested in picking up some draft tomorrow let me know ! Got a lov.*

Authentication and integrity are also very important. Pilots, air traffic controllers and airlines must always have access to accurate information. This means an attacker should not be able to create or modify messages exchanged either between aircraft or with the ground. All data has to be trusted for an aircraft to operate safely. For example, with ADS-B, an attacker could easily create "ghost" planes, i.e, aircraft which are not actually flying, by sending false ADS-B messages. This only necessitates a few hundred dollars worth of equipment - an ADS-B antenna and a software-defined radio - and basic signal processing knowledge [2]. Datalink communication are not authenticated either and a pirate could easily impersonate a controller to misguide a plane [1,6].

4   Conclusion

We have given a description of aircraft communication networks and explained the different kinds of threats they could be subject to. Future work will take into consideration datalink communication and further analyze the threats we exposed. Once a potential threat has been found, the next step is to assess its scope, i.e evaluate what would be the impact of each threat on both pilots and air traffic controllers. A protocol should be elaborated with the help of a professional instructor in order to evaluate the reaction of pilots and controllers when they receive forged data from an attacker.

References

1. ARINC 618–8 Air/Ground Character-Oriented Protocol Specification. Standard, ARINC, August 2016
2. Berthier, P., Fernandez, J.M., Robert, J.M.: SAT: security in the air using TESLA. In: 2017 IEEE/AIAA 36th Digital Avionics Systems Conference (DASC) (IEEE-AIAA DASC 2017), St. Petersburg, USA, September 2017
3. FAA: Emergency procedures. In: Airplane Flying Handbook. FAA (2016). http://www.us-ppl.de/pdf/faa/hb/afh/faa-h-8083-3a-7of7.pdf
4. FlightRadar: Flightradar24.com - Live flight tracker! (2016). https://www.flightradar24.com/46.69,-76.41/5
5. Fuchs, C.M., et al.: The evolution of avionics networks from ARINC 429 to AFDX. Network Architectures and Services (2012)
6. ICAO: Global operational data link document, April 2013. https://www.icao.int/APAC/Documents/edocs/GOLD_2Edition.pdf
7. Insurance Information Institute: Aviation Accidents (2015). http://www.iii.org/fact-statistic/aviation
8. Thanthry, N., Pendse, R.: Aviation data networks: security issues and network architecture. In: 38th Annual 2004 International Carnahan Conference on Security Technology, pp. 77–81. IEEE (2004)

Author Index

Printed in the United States
By Bookmasters